D0169323

Labor Visions and State Power

PRINCETON STUDIES IN AMERICAN POLITICS: HISTORICAL, INTERNATIONAL, AND COMPARATIVE PERSPECTIVES

SERIES EDITORS

IRA KATZNELSON, MARTIN SHEFTER, THEDA SKOCPOL

Labor Visions and State Power

THE ORIGINS OF BUSINESS UNIONISM IN THE UNITED STATES

Victoria C. Hattam

PRINCETON UNIVERSITY PRESS

PRINCETON, NEW JERSEY

Library of Congress Cataloging-in-Publication Data

Hattam, Victoria Charlotte.
Labor visions and state power : the origins of business unionism
in the United States / Victoria C. Hattam.
p.   cm. — (Princeton studies in American politics)
Includes bibliographical references and index.
ISBN 0-691-07870-X
1. Trade-unions—United States—History—19th century.   2. Trade-
unions—United States—Political activity—History—19th century.
3. Labor—United States—History—19th century.   I. Title.
II. Series.
HD6508.H34   1993
322′.2′0973—dc20   92-22180

To my parents,
Kate and Harold Hattam

Contents

Preface and Acknowledgments

THIS BOOK defends the claim that a strong judiciary created a politically weak labor movement in the United States. Judicial regulation of industrial conflict was antithetical to labor politics, I argue, because even successful political campaigns could not ensure a corresponding change in government policy toward labor. Powers of judicial interpretation and review enabled the courts to eviscerate many postbellum labor laws, which left the American Federation of Labor (AFL) disillusioned with the payoffs of political reform. Given these conditions, I make the case that the AFL's strategy of business unionism (in which economic interests were privileged over political reform) was the product of the distinctive institutional structure of the American state rather than the consequence of the party system, workers' aspirations, or the composition of the work force. American workers were no more content with their declining social status and economic dislocation than were their West European counterparts; both vigorously protested the reorganization of work throughout the nineteenth century. How the AFL voiced this discontent at the turn of the century, however, did distinguish the development of the American labor movement from that of its West European counterparts. The AFL's strategy of business unionism was forged during its prolonged struggle with the courts over workers' industrial rights, particularly during the unsuccessful anticonspiracy campaign waged during the three decades following the Civil War.

Although state structure was decisive in the AFL's turn to business unionism at the end of the century, this pattern of state-labor relations is not transhistorical. The AFL's postwar struggle with the courts, and the resulting change in strategy, were predicated on a *particular* conception of workers' interests—a conception that had been hotly contested for much of the nineteenth century. In the antebellum decades and even lingering into the post–Civil War era, a different conception of class alliances and interests prevailed. The principal social division was said to fall between the producing and nonproducing classes rather than between labor and capital. Moreover, producer organizations, such as the National Labor Union and the Knights of Labor, did not find their antimonopoly programs thwarted by the courts. Indeed, producers were able to establish comparatively cooperative relations with the state and remained enamored with political reform throughout the nineteenth century.

Different visions of economic development, I have found, undergirded these competing conceptions of class. How workers understood the economic changes they experienced, how they conceived of their interests during industrialization, did not follow automatically from the changes in production but were shaped by different narratives of industrialization. By reconstructing the competing economic visions through the writings, platforms, and proceedings of labor elites and their organizations, I show how state-labor relations were mediated through changing conceptions of class during the nineteenth century. Focusing on labor leaders and formal organizations was critical because they self-consciously elaborated different interpretations of economic growth in the hopes of mobilizing workers into their ranks.

Historicizing the concept of class by attending more closely to the transition from producer to wage earner allows us to explain the indigenous tradition of antimonopoly protest in the United States as well as the subsequent turn to business unionism at the end of the century. The key lies in seeing how different conceptions of class intersected the surrounding political institutions, especially the courts, in dramatically different ways. Competing economic visions, and their differing interactions with state institutions, set the broad contours of American labor movement development over the course of the nineteenth century.

Finally, the story told here has implications beyond America: it underscores the importance of rethinking the concept of class more generally. Prevailing divisions between objective and subjective notions of class obscure the cultural and political construction of workers' economic interests during industrialization. Class interests cannot be unambiguously deduced from the reorganization of work and production, thereby providing a benchmark against which actual patterns of working-class formation can be evaluated. Instead, interests themselves must become the object of analysis. When, how, and why workers viewed their experiences through producers' versus wage earners' concepts of class largely determined their response to industrialization and their relations to the state. Only by setting aside objective definitions of class and accepting the participants' construction of class alliances and interests on their own terms can we make sense of the changing role of the state and thereby understand the origins of business unionism in the United States.

THIS BOOK has been a long time in the making, and many people and institutions have helped me along the way. I began the book for my Ph.D. dissertation in the Political Science Department at the Massachusetts Institute of Technology. My work there was made considerably easier by support from the following sources: a Fulbright Travel Grant, a Freda Bage Fellowship from the Australian Association of University Women, Queensland Branch, and an International Fellowship from the American Association of University Women. I was fortunate in being able to write my dissertation at the Center for European Studies at Harvard University. While at MIT, I was greatly influenced by Walter Dean Burnham, Joshua Cohen, Morton Horwitz, Charles Sabel, and Deborah Stone, all of whom shaped my intellectual development in unexpected ways. I completely revised the dissertation while at Yale University, where I have taught since 1987. At Yale, I have benefited greatly from extensive comments, prodding, and encouragement from Bruce Ackerman, Shelley Burtt, David Cameron, Joseph LaPalombara, David Mayhew, Douglas Rae, James Scott, Ian Shapiro, and David Weiman. I also had considerable help in research and production from William Munro, Shoon Murray, Pamela O'Donnell, Jonathan Stein, and Keith Whittington. The primary source research would not have been possible without the repeated help of Tom Kiely at the Inter-Library Borrowing Office at MIT and of Martha Hodges and Richard Strassberg at the Martin P. Catherwood Library of the New York State School of Industrial and Labor Relations at Cornell University.

My intellectual world is by no means delimited by the two institutions of MIT and Yale; many friends and colleagues have commented on earlier drafts of the book. I would like to thank Steven Amberg, Douglas Ashford, Amy Bridges, David Brody, Cecelia Bucki, James Coppess, Carlos Forment, the late J. David Greenstone, Gary Herrigel, Haggai Hurvitz, Ellen Immergut, Pamela Walker Laird, Christopher Lasch, Steve Lewis, Terrence McDonald, Uday Metha, Anne Norton, Richard Oestreicher, Karen Orren, John Padgett, Lee Perlman, Charles Perrow, Gretchen Ritter, Elizabeth Sanders, Ron Schatz, Philip Scranton, Serenella Sferza, Theda Skocpol, Katherine Stone, Kathy Thelen, Christopher Tomlins, and Margaret Weir.

With any project, there are always those who continue to listen and talk through ideas when everyone else is tired, who are willing to read yet another draft of Chapter 4. . . . I owe a particular debt to Suzanne Berger, Gerald Berk, Colleen Dunlavy, Richard Locke, George Shulman, Stephen Skowronek, and Rogers Smith.

Finally, I would like to thank Tom and Emily Graham for providing endless distractions and for helping me to keep my cool when the animals were out of the cage. If it weren't for the two of you, the book would probably have been finished at least a year or two earlier.

Abbreviations

AFL	American Federation of Labor
CAT	Conference of Amalgamated Trades
FOTLU	Federation of Organized Trades and Labor Unions
GTU	General Trades' Union
KOL	Knights of Labor
NLU	National Labor Union
TUC	Trades Union Congress

Labor Visions and State Power

CHAPTER ONE

Labor, Ideology, and the State: Working-Class Formation in the United States

THE PARTICULAR PATH of working-class formation in the United States has set the broad contours of American politics. While labor movements in many West European nations have provided the core constituents for progressive organizations and social movements, American labor has played a more limited role in national politics. Ever since the turn of the century, the American Federation of Labor (AFL) has advocated a distinctive strategy of business unionism that privileged economic interests over political reform. Where labor unions in Western Europe advocated workers' interests in the political arena, and advanced an extensive program of state-sponsored social reform, American unions focused instead on workplace concerns, achieved through collective bargaining and industrial action on the shop floor.[1] The high water mark of voluntarism was reached in the early decades of the twentieth century, under Samuel Gompers' leadership of the AFL. In this period, American labor adhered to a policy of nonpartisanship and political independence and at times even *opposed* government-sponsored social reforms, such as old-age pensions, minimum wage and maximum hours laws, and compulsory health and unemployment insurance.[2]

To be sure, even in the golden era of business unionism, or voluntarism, as it was known, American labor never withdrew from politics entirely. The AFL always maintained some contact with the Democratic party, and continued to participate in electoral politics. However, the AFL's political

---

[1] For two excellent accounts of AFL voluntarism in the early twentieth century, see Ruth L. Horowitz, *Political Ideologies of Organized Labor* (New Brunswick, N.J.: Transaction Books, 1978), chap. 1; and Michael Rogin, "Voluntarism: The Political Functions of an Antipolitical Doctrine," *Industrial and Labor Relations Review* 15, 4 (July 1962): 521–35.

[2] For classic assertion of voluntarist principles, see the following editorials by Samuel Gompers in the AFL magazine, the *American Federationist*: "Compulsory Arbitration's Latest Evangelist," *American Federationist* 21, 9 (September 1914): 731–33; "Economic Organization and the Eight-Hour Day," *American Federationist* 22, 1 (January 1915): 43–46; "Trade Union Health Insurance," *American Federationist* 23, 11 (November 1916): 1072–74. For more extended discussion of the AFL's legislative program, see Horowitz, *Political Ideologies of Organized Labor*, chap. 1; and the text and notes following.

activity was more circumscribed than that of its West European counterparts in three important respects: institutionally, strategically, and programmatically. Elaborating these three aspects of AFL strategy and contrasting them with English union activity at the turn of the century will help to identify the defining features of AFL voluntarism.

When the AFL entered electoral politics after the turn of the century, it did not sustain an institutional base from one election to the next. Instead, the AFL deliberately avoided creating a permanent political organization and even refused to establish formal ties with either of the major political parties. Nonpartisanship was needed, the AFL argued, to ensure labor's independence within the political system. If political action was pursued, it was carried out through ad hoc committees and temporary campaign organizations rather than through creation of more enduring political institutions.[3] Second, since the 1890s political action has remained an auxiliary strategy for the AFL, used to supplement the primary tasks of organizing, bargaining, and protesting in the economic arena. Political action rarely received the AFL's unqualified support and was prohibited explicitly in many trade union constitutions. On those occasions when political reform was pursued, its advocates were quick to stress both the nonpartisan and auxiliary nature of their action.[4] Finally, and most important, the limits of AFL politics can be seen in the program they supported in the political arena. After the turn of the century, the AFL both accepted and promoted a quite marked separation of work and politics: workplace concerns were to be addressed through collective bargaining and industrial conflict, leaving politics for citizens' concerns. The hallmark of AFL voluntarism was not complete abstention from electoral politics, but rather political participation with little or no regard for work-based concerns.[5] In

[3] For discussion of the intermittent presence of labor in electoral politics, see Irwin Yellowitz, *Labor and the Progressive Movement in New York State, 1897–1916* (Ithaca, N.Y.: Cornell University Press, 1965), 180–81. For examples of the nonpartisan nature of AFL politics at the turn of the century, see Horowitz, *Political Ideologies of Organized Labor*, 36–37; Yellowitz, *Labor and the Progressive Movement in New York State*, 161–69; and Mary Ann Mason Burki, "The California Progressives: Labor's Point of View," *Labor History* 17, 1 (Winter 1976): 28–29.

[4] For prohibition of political action within American unions, see Gary M. Fink, ed., *State Labor Proceedings: A Bibliography of the AFL, CIO, and AFL-CIO Proceedings, 1885–1974, Held in the AFL-CIO Library* (Westport, Conn.: Greenwood Press, 1975), Introduction. For the auxiliary nature of AFL politics, see Horowitz, *Political Ideologies of Organized Labor*, 36–37; and Yellowitz, *Labor and the Progressive Movement in New York State*, 18, 39, 133–37, 180–81.

[5] Ira Katznelson points to a similar separation of work and politics. See Ira Katznelson, *City Trenches: Urban Politics and the Patterning of Class in the United States* (Chicago: University of Chicago Press, 1981). However, Katznelson argues that this separation was established in the United States early in the nineteenth century with the rise of capitalism. In contrast, I believe the division was not created until the last decade of the nineteenth century

the early twentieth century, for example, whenever labor joined forces with middle-class reformers, they generally did so as Progressives rather than as workers, in an effort to advance the classless interests of democratic reform. Organized labor willingly joined in progressive cries for more efficient, competitive, and honest government through the introduction of referendum, initiative, and recall. But the AFL did not try to redress their workplace concerns through political reform.[6]

Social legislation in the Progressive Era that regulated hours and wages and introduced arbitration and workmen's compensation schemes might seem to belie AFL voluntarism, as these laws clearly were aimed at regulating and improving the terms of employment. However, when examined more closely we see that the AFL's role in the campaign for social reform had all the markings of American voluntarism. The AFL rarely led the fight for labor legislation and usually played a supporting role to middle-class initiatives. More importantly, the AFL did not endorse all progressive labor laws, but selected bills carefully so as not to compromise its voluntarist principles. The AFL only supported laws targeted at especially vulnerable segments of the population—women, children, government employees, and members of especially dangerous occupations—as these groups could not organize easily to protect themselves. In contrast, it consistently opposed regulation of its core constituents—white adult males—for fear of weakening their organizational base. Improving working conditions and wages for adult males was central to the AFL's mission, but this was to be secured through organization and protest on the shop floor.[7] Although the

---

and was a product of the AFL's unsuccessful fight for legal reform. I do not see the separation of work and politics in the early nineteenth century that Katznelson describes. Katznelson's nineteenth-century "city trenches" are largely a product of his concept of class in which twentieth-century social divisions and issues are imposed on the antebellum era.

[6] For discussion of organized labor's entry into politics as Progressives rather than as workers, see Michael Rogin, "Progressivism and the California Electorate," *Journal of American History* 55 (September 1968): 305–34; Burki, "The California Progressives," 25, 32; Yellowitz, *Labor and the Progressive Movement in New York State*, 49–50; and Frederick M. Heath, "Labor and the Progressive Movement in Connecticut," *Labor History* 12, 1 (Winter 1971): 61–62. For discussion of labor following middle-class initiatives, see Yellowitz, *Labor and the Progressives in New York State*, 89–93; Heath, "Labor and the Progressive Movement in Connecticut," 57; Robert F. Wesser, "Conflict and Compromise: The Workmen's Compensation Movement in New York, 1890s–1913," *Labor History* 11, 3 (Summer 1971): 346–51; and Thomas J. Kerr, "The New York Factory Investigating Commission and the Minimum Wage Movement," *Labor History* 11, 3 (Summer 1971): 374. For a more optimistic account of AFL politics in the Progressive Era, see Julia Greene, " 'The Strike at the Ballot Box': The American Federation of Labor's Entrance into Electoral Politics, 1906–1909," *Labor History* 32, 2 (Spring 1991): 165–92.

[7] See Horowitz, *Political Ideologies of Organized Labor*, chap. 1. For AFL leaders' opposition to protective labor legislation in the late nineteenth and early twentieth centuries, see Frank Foster's criticism of eight-hours legislation at the 1884 convention of the Federation of

AFL voluntarism was modified during the Depression and New Deal re-alignment, it was not transformed entirely. To this day, the AFL-CIO is still considered unusual in its pursuit of economic issues over larger questions of social transformation.[8]

The defining features of AFL voluntarism can be seen more clearly through a comparison of American labor politics with English trade union activity at the turn of the century. On all three dimensions—institutionalization, strategy, and program—the Trades Union Congress (TUC) adopted a very different approach from that of the AFL. In the last three decades of the nineteenth century, for example, English unions maintained a more continuous institutional presence in electoral politics. The Labour Representation League, the TUC's Parliamentary Committee, the Labour Electoral Association, and the Labour Representation Committee constituted a series of organizations through which workers could express their views in national politics. Moreover, creation of the Labour party in 1906 provided English unions with a permanent institutional base in electoral politics that has enabled labor to maintain close ties with parliamentary politics ever since. English unions also differed from their American counterparts in the priority they awarded political action. Political reform was not relegated to a minor role, but rather held coequal status with union organizing. To be sure, politics was at times a divisive issue within the English labor movement as individuals and organizations disagreed over

---

Organized Trades and Labor Unions in 1884, in *Report of the Fourth Annual Session of the Federation of Organized Trades and Labor Unions of the United States and Canada, Chicago, Illinois, October 7, 8, 9, and 10, 1884* (Bloomington, Ill.: Pantagraph Printing and Stationery Co., 1906), 11; and discussion of the political program at the AFL's Denver convention in 1894, reprinted in *A Verbatum [sic] Report of the Discussion on the Political Programme at the Denver Convention of the American Federation of Labor, December 14, 15, 1894* (New York: The Freytag Press, 1895), 19–21. See also Samuel Gompers' discussion of Legislative reform in the following editorials: Gompers, "The American Labor Movement: Its Makeup, Achievements and Aspirations," *American Federationist* 21, 7 (July 1914): 537–48; Gompers, "Labor vs. Its Barnacles," *American Federationist*, 23, 4 (April 1916): 268–74. For a useful discussion of the AFL's debate over political reform at the Denver convention in 1894, see J. F. Finn, "AF of L Leaders and the Question of Politics in the Early 1890s," *Journal of American Studies* 7, 3 (December 1973): 243–65.

[8] See David J. Greenstone, *Labor in American Politics* (New York: Knopf, 1969). For Greenstone the relationship between the AFL-CIO and the Democratic party established during the New Deal was a "functional equivalent" of European social democratic alliances. Although labor did become an important member of the New Deal coalition, the limits of this relationship in the United States have been documented by a number of scholars. For example, see Mike Davis, "The Barren Marriage of American Labour and the Democratic Party," *New Left Review* 124 (November–December 1980): 43–84; Karl E. Klare, "Judicial Deradicalization of the Wagner Act and the Origins of Modern Legal Consciousness, 1937–1941," 62 *Minnesota Law Review* 265 (1977–1978); and Christopher L. Tomlins, *The State and the Unions: Labor Relations, Law, and the Organized Labor Movement in America, 1880–1960* (New York: Cambridge University Press, 1985).

the specific program of reform. However, the central cleavage in England was not between advocates of politics and those of business unionism, but rather centered around disagreements between socialists and more moderate reformers over how radical their political platform ought to be. No significant faction within the English labor movement called for an antistatist strategy akin to AFL voluntarism. Finally, English labor did not promote a sharp division between work and politics. On the contrary, almost all factions within the English labor movement considered government legislation a legitimate and necessary weapon in their struggle to improve the terms and conditions of employment.[9]

The English campaign for social legislation in the early decades of the twentieth century provides a useful counterpoint to AFL voluntarism. Unlike the AFL, the TUC campaigned extensively for legislation introducing old-age pensions, unemployment and health insurance, the eight-hour day, and workmen's compensation. Moreover, passage of the National Insurance Act in 1911 underscores the different relationship that had developed between labor and politics on the two sides of the Atlantic. Although English workers criticized the new insurance act, their opposition was very different from the AFL's attacks on social legislation. The TUC did not want to restrict government intervention in the workplace, but rather objected to the proposed financing mechanism for the new government policy. If anything, the TUC wanted the government to make a greater commitment to social insurance by funding the new policies on a noncontributory basis. To diminish labor opposition to the legislation, the Liberal government established trade unions and friendly societies as the administrative agencies for the unemployment and health insurance schemes. By providing financial rewards to unions and incentives to potential members, the government not only secured labor's cooperation but also further integrated English unions into the political system.[10]

The puzzle to be explained, then, is why the English and American labor movements developed along divergent paths. Why, by the outbreak of the First World War, had the English and American labor movements begun to advocate workers' interests in such different realms? What led the AFL to adopt voluntarism as its principal strategy while across the Atlantic the TUC increasingly was incorporated into national party politics?

The divergent development of the English and American labor movements is all the more perplexing when we realize that the American labor

---

[9] See G.D.H. Cole, *British Working Class Politics, 1832–1914* (London: Routledge and Kegan Paul, 1941), esp. chaps. 8, 11, 12, 14, 19; Sidney Webb and Beatrice Webb, *The History of Trade Unionism* (New York: Augustus M. Kelley, 1965), chaps. 10, 11. For an extensive list of legislation supported by the English TUC at the end of the nineteenth century, see George Howell, *Labour Legislation, Labour Movements, and Labour Leaders* (London: T. Fisher Unwin, 1902), 469–72.

[10] See Cole, *British Working Class Politics*, chap. 17.

movement was not always so different from its West European counterparts. The "new labor history" of the last two decades has uncovered a rich heritage of workers' protest in the United States and has shown that, contrary to earlier claims, American workers were not always staunch advocates of business unionism.[11] Indeed, when one steps back to the 1820s and 1830s, it is difficult to distinguish American workers' protest from their West European counterparts. Displaced artisans on both continents protested the reorganization of work and production that accompanied industrialization, and looked to the government for assistance in their struggle.[12] Moreover, for most of the nineteenth century American workers were quite successful at harnessing state power to address their concerns. Before the Civil War, for example, several states enacted laws that abolished imprisonment for debt, introduced mechanics' liens, reformed the militia service, mandated the ten-hour workday, established a system of public education, and introduced a number of important currency reforms. All of these issues had been advocated by either the Working Men's political parties or the General Trades' Unions (GTUs) of the 1820s and 1830s, whose efforts were rewarded with new legislation at the state level.[13]

American labor, then, was not voluntarist from the beginning, but rather was quite actively engaged in party politics. It was not until the last decade

[11] The "new labor history" is extensive and is discussed at length in Chapters 3 and 4. For a useful, if somewhat dated, overview of this research, see David Brody, "The Old Labor History and the New: In Search of an American Working Class," *Labor History* 20, 1 (Winter 1979): 111–26.

[12] Interesting parallels among English, French, and American workers' protest can be seen by comparing the following works: Gareth Stedman Jones, "Rethinking Chartism," in his *Languages of Class: Studies in English Working Class History, 1832–1982* (London: Cambridge University Press, 1983); Iorwerth J. Prothero, *Artisans and Politics in Early Nineteenth Century London: John Gast and His Times* (Folkestone, Kent, Engl.: William Dawson and Son, 1979); William H. Sewell, Jr., *Work and Revolution in France: The Language of Labor from the Old Regime to 1848* (New York: Cambridge University Press, 1980); Sean Wilentz, *Chants Democratic: New York City and the Rise of the American Working Class, 1788–1850* (New York: Oxford University Press, 1984). For a similar discussion of the parallels between the United States and Europe, see Sean Wilentz, "Against Exceptionalism: Class Consciousness and the American Labor Movement," *International Labor and Working Class History* 26 (Fall 1984): 1–24.

[13] Labor achieved a number of important policy gains through state legislatures before the Civil War. For example, by 1842, imprisonment for debt had been abolished in Connecticut, New Jersey, Pennsylvania, New Hampshire, Massachusetts, and Ohio. Between 1834 and 1849, compulsory public education was established in New York, New Jersey, New Hampshire, Connecticut, and Massachusetts. The ten-hour workday was established, at least in theory if not in practice, in the following years: Philadelphia public employees in 1835, all federal employees in 1840, and all Pennsylvania workers in 1848. Finally, President Jackson's veto of the National Bank in 1832, the New York Free Banking Act of 1838, and Van Buren's Independent Treasury Act of 1840 all were considered important victories for the producers' program of financial reform. See Chapter 3 for elaboration.

of the nineteenth century that American labor turned away from the state and adopted instead a strategy of business unionism. To understand the particular pattern of working-class formation in the United States, we must set aside sweeping claims of American exceptionalism and focus more closely on this *shift* in labor strategy at the end of the century.[14] Exactly which aspects of labor strategy changed with the adoption of voluntarism at the end of the nineteenth century?

It is a common misperception to assume that American labor was generally "reformist" simply because the AFL operated principally in the economic realm.[15] Alongside the AFL's partial retreat from politics at the turn of the century has been a strong tradition of labor militance on the shop floor. In fact, strike rates have remained high in the United States even after the AFL's turn to voluntarism. As Table 1 indicates, the number of strikes per 100,000 employees often was higher in the United States than in the United Kingdom, and in many years was comparable to strike rates in France and Germany. American labor was easily as "radical" as its English counterpart on this score. As strike rates vary greatly from year to year, it is also useful to compare the mean strike rates in the United States and United Kingdom for the years 1900 to 1935. Despite the enormous standard deviations, the mean strike rates 8.2 and 4.7, respectively, again suggest that blanket claims of American exceptionalism need to be revised.

Neither notions of exceptionalism nor labor reformism adequately captures the unusual mixture of political moderation and industrial militance that constitutes American labor strategy. What is unusual about the American labor movement is not the absence of socialism, or the pervasive reformism, but rather the unusual bifurcation of labor strategies in the economic and political realms. Since the turn of the century, political moderation and industrial militance have existed side by side. What needs explaining in the American case is not the absence of a radical tradition per se, but rather its failure to take a political form. Why, we might ask, has the long heritage of workers' protest not been readily institutionalized within the political realm?[16]

---

[14] For the classic statement of American exceptionalism, see Werner Sombart, *Why Is There No Socialism in the United States?* (1906; New York: M. E. Sharpe, 1976).

[15] For a recent characterization of the American labor movement as reformist, see Seymour Martin Lipset, "Radicalism or Reformism: The Sources of Working-Class Politics," *American Political Science Review* 77, 1 (March 1983): 1–19. Earlier works that adhered to a similar characterization are John R. Commons, David J. Saposs, Helen L. Sumner, E. B. Mittleman, H. E. Hoagland, John B. Andrews, and Selig Perlman, *History of Labor in the United States*, 4 vols. (New York: Macmillan, 1936); Walter Galenson, ed., *Comparative Labor Movements* (New York: Russell and Russell, 1968); and Everett M. Kassalow, *Trade Unions and Industrial Relations: An International Comparison* (New York: Random House, 1969).

[16] For a similar characterization of the problem, see Eric Foner, "Why Is There No Socialism in the United States?" *History Workshop* 17 (Spring 1984): 57–80.

TABLE 1
Number of Strikes per 100,000 Nonagricultural Employees[17]

	U.S.	U.K.	France	Germany
1900	11.6	5.3	12.8	11.9
1905	11.1	7.3	11.4	18.8
1910	NA	3.8	20.0	20.1
1915	6.3	5.0	NA	0.8
1920	11.9	12.2	22.3	47.4
1925	3.9	4.2	9.8	9.5
1930	1.9	2.7	10.9	1.9
1935	6.4	3.4	4.2	NA
Mean	8.2	4.7	11.3	11.9
SD	5.4	2.5	5.7	10.0

Note: The mean strike rates were calculated from annual strike data for the years 1900 through 1935.
NA, not available; SD, standard deviation.

17 I would like to thank William Munro and Ton Notermans for helping to construct Table 1. Data were compiled from the following sources: Florence Peterson, *Strikes in the United States, 1880–1936* (Bureau of Labor Statistics, Bulletin 651, August 1937); U.S. Bureau of the Census, *Historical Statistics of the United States, Colonial Times to 1957* (Washington, D.C.: Government Printing Office, 1960), 99, 126; Peter Flora, Franz Kraus, and Winfried Pfenning, *State, Economy and Society in Western Europe, 1815–1975: A Data Handbook in Two Volumes* (Chicago: St. James Press, 1987), 2:708–53. Collecting comparative strike data from the turn of the century was no easy task. Data were not always available and comparability was difficult to maintain. In the United States, no official labor statistics were collected at the national level from 1906 through 1913, and reporting practices in other years varied as to the criteria used to define an official strike. Prior to 1905, strikes lasting less than one day were excluded, but there was no minimum number of workers required. Between 1914 and 1926, an effort was made to count all stoppages. Since 1927, only strikes involving at least six employees and lasting a full day or shift have been included. Despite these changes in reporting procedures, scholars generally consider the data to be reasonably reliable. At any rate, it is all that we have. See Peterson, *Strikes in the United States*, 2, 36; and P. K. Edwards, *Strikes in the United States, 1881–1974* (Oxford: Basil Blackwell, 1981), 301–10. Unfortunately, 1981 is the last year for which comparative strike rates can be obtained, because during the Reagan administration the Bureau of Labor Statistics changed the method of reporting work stoppages. In 1982, the definition of a stoppage as involving six or more workers was changed to 1,000 or more workers. This new criteria makes U.S. data no longer comparable with data collected in other advanced industrial societies and greatly *under*-reports the current American strike rate. For example, under the old method, there were 3,885 work stoppages in the United States in 1980, while under the new method the number of recorded stoppages for the very same year was to 187. A complete table of comparative strike data for all years from 1900 through 1935 was used to calculate the mean strike rates in the United States and the United Kingdom.

STATE STRUCTURE, IDEOLOGY, AND LABOR STRATEGY

The central argument of this book has two interrelated components—one institutional, the other interpretative. The institutional argument claims that the unusual structure of the American state played a decisive role in shaping American labor strategy. The division of power between branches and across levels of government, combined with the dominance of the courts within the divided American state, provided a distinctive set of incentives and constraints that shaped working-class formation along its peculiar American path. While no government welcomed the increase in workers' power in the early nineteenth century, different state structures left different institutions in charge of regulating workers' collective action. In France and Germany, for example, legislatures were the primary institutions responsible for curbing working-class organization through Le Chapelier and Socialist laws. In the United States, however, courts were the principal institution for containing workers' collective action under the common law doctrine of criminal conspiracy. England provides a hybrid case in which both Parliament and the courts were used to prevent workers from organizing.[18] The unusual power of judicial interpretation and review in the United States repeatedly undermined the rewards of political organization as hard-won legislative victories were continually eroded by the courts. Even successful political mobilization seemed to provide little or no leverage over government policy toward labor in the United States.[19]

[18] For discussion of government regulation of working-class organization in France and Germany, see Julio Samuel Valenzuela, "Labor Movement Formation and Politics: The Chilean and French Cases in Comparative Perspective, 1850–1950" (Ph.D. diss., Columbia University, 1979); Chris Howell, *Regulating Labor: The State and Industrial Relations Reform in Postwar France* (Princeton: Princeton University Press, 1992), chap. 2; and Mary Nolan, "Economic Crisis, State Policy, and Working-Class Formation in Germany, 1870–1900," in Ira Katznelson and Aristide Zolberg, eds., *Working-Class Formation: Nineteenth-Century Patterns in Western Europe and the United States* (Princeton: Princeton University Press, 1986). For an innovative comparison of Britain, Germany, and the United States, see Gary Marks, *Unions in Politics: Britain, Germany, and the United States in the Nineteenth and Early Twentieth Centuries* (Princeton: Princeton University Press, 1989). For judicial regulation of labor in the United States during the nineteenth century, see Alpheus T. Mason, *Organized Labor and the Law: With Special Reference to the Sherman and Clayton Acts* (Durham, N.C.: Duke University Press, 1925); and Chapter 2. For discussion of labor regulation in England, see M. Dorothy George, "The Combination Laws," *Economic History Review* 6, 2 (April 1936): 172–78; and John Victor Orth, "Combination and Conspiracy: The Legal Status of English Trade Unions, 1799–1871" (Ph.D. diss., Harvard University, 1977). Orth quite rightly stresses that in England the government relied on both legislative regulation through the combination laws and judicial regulation via the common law doctrine of criminal conspiracy. Even granting the dual nature of English labor regulation, the courts played a less prominent role in regulating working-class organization than their counterparts in the United States. For elaboration, see Chapter 5.

[19] My argument highlighting the autonomy and influence of institutional interests draws on earlier work of several scholars within the burgeoning field of the "new institutionalism."

The institutional argument, however, takes us only partway toward explaining the divergent patterns of labor movement development in England and the United States. After all, differences in English and American state structure existed throughout the nineteenth century but came to play a decisive role in the AFL's turn to voluntarism only in the last decade of the century. The interpretative leg of the argument considers the ways in which state-labor relations varied over the course of the nineteenth century. In order to explain the changing role of the state, we must attend to the ways in which ideology and culture mediated workers' relation to the courts. Only by considering the meaning or significance that workers brought to their particular institutional environments can we begin to decipher the distinctive pattern of working-class formation in the United States.[20]

To explore the impact of state structure on labor strategy, I focused my research explicitly on labor's relation to the state, paying particular attention to workers' perceptions of, and responses to, judicial regulation of working-class organization and conflict. Two states, New York and Pennsylvania, formed the core of my research. Analysis at the state level was essential, as throughout much of the nineteenth century, especially in the

---

For useful discussions of this literature and for more general arguments concerning the underlying assumptions of this perspective, see Suzanne Berger, ed., *Organizing Interests in Western Europe: Pluralism, Corporatism and the Transformation of Politics* (New York: Cambridge University Press, 1981); Colleen A. Dunlavy, *Political Structure and Industrial Change: Early Railroads in the United States and Prussia* (Princeton: Princeton University Press, 1993); Peter A. Hall, *Governing the Economy: The Politics of State Intervention in Britain and France* (New York: Cambridge University Press, 1986); James G. March and Johan P. Olsen, "The New Institutionalism: Organizational Factors in Political Life," *American Political Science Review* 78, 3 (September 1984): 734–49; Karen Orren and Stephen Skowronek, "Beyond the Iconography of Order: Notes for a 'New' Institutionalism" (Paper presented at the annual meeting of the American Political Science Association, Washington, D.C., 30 August 1991); Theda Skocpol, "Bringing the State Back In: Strategies of Analysis in Current Research," in Peter Evans, Dietrich Rueschemeyer, and Theda Skocpol, eds., *Bringing the State Back In* (New York: Cambridge University Press, 1985), chap. 1; Stephen Skowronek, *Building a New American State: The Expansion of National Administrative Capacities, 1877–1920* (New York: Cambridge University Press, 1982); and Rogers M. Smith, "The New Non-Science of Politics: On Turns to History in Political Science" (Working Paper 59, Comparative Studies of Social Transformation, Ann Arbor, Mich., 1990).

[20] The interpretative dimension of my work has been influenced by discussions of language, meaning, and interpretation in the following works: Clifford Geertz, *The Interpretaion of Cultures* (New York: Basic Books, 1973); J.G.A. Pocock, *Politics, Language and Time: Essays on Political Thought and History* (New York: Atheneum, 1973); Marshall Sahlins, *Culture and Practical Reason* (Chicago: University of Chicago Press, 1976); Sewell, *Work and Revolution in France*; Jones, "Rethinking Chartism"; Anne Norton, *Alternative Americas: A Reading of Antebellum Political Culture* (Chicago: University of Chicago Press, 1986); Roberto Mangabeira Unger, *Politics, A Work in Constitutive Social Theory* (New York: Cambridge University Press, 1987); Joan Wallach Scott, *Gender and the Politics of History* (New York: Columbia University Press, 1988).

antebellum decades, there was no national labor movement to speak of. Instead, almost all workers' organization and protest was carried out at the state level, with only tentative and short-lived forays into the national arena.

More specifically, the research was organized around three distinct comparisons: a comparison over time, a comparison across organizations, and a comparison across nations. For the comparison over time, workers' relation to the New York and Pennsylvania governments was tracked for almost a century, from the first criminal conspiracy cases in the early 1800s through the turn to voluntarism at the end of the century. In practice, this component of the research involved a "before-and-after" comparison of workers' response to the two waves of conspiracy convictions before and after the Civil War. This first wave of conspiracy cases lasted from 1806 through 1842 and the second wave from 1865 through 1896. For the second comparison, I examined different labor organizations' responses to the same conspiracy trials in the 1870s and 1880s. Contrasting the responses of the Knights of Labor (KOL) and the New York Workingmen's Assembly to the postwar trials enabled me to hold economic conditions and social relations reasonably constant, thereby highlighting the importance of ideology and culture in shaping different labor organizations' relation to the state. Finally, in order to test further my argument for the American case, I examined English state-labor relations as well. The English comparison makes clear the importance of different configurations of institutional power for shaping working-class formation in the two nations.

One last feature of the research design should be noted, namely, the periodization of the study. Examining state-labor relations across the nineteenth century in the years 1806 through 1896 had two advantages. First, these decades provide virtually complete coverage of judicial regulation under the common law doctrine of criminal conspiracy. Tracking cases under the *same* legal doctrine helps hold state structure and policy constant, thereby enabling us to identify more clearly the impact of the state on labor strategy. To be sure, the turn to voluntarism was by no means complete at the end of the century: in fact, the struggle between organized labor and the courts continued into the twentieth century with the AFL's campaign against the labor injunction. However, if the research were extended into the Progressive Era, the causal relationship between labor and the state would be obscured by the shift in legal remedy from conspiracy to the labor injunction. In Chapter 4 I sketch briefly the succeeding struggle over the labor injunction and show how the same pattern of judicial obstruction continued in the Progressive Era, only this time the contest was carried out at the national level between the AFL, Congress, and the federal courts.

Second, the long time span of the study, in which labor's reaction to conspiracy convictions was followed for almost a century, highlights the variable nature of state-labor relations. Unfortunately, most studies break the nineteenth century at the Civil War and focus almost exclusively on either the prewar or the postwar era.[21] This convention of dividing the nineteenth century in two has obscured the larger patterns of continuity and change in the century. Covering workers' relation to the state from 1806 to 1896 brings into sharper focus the changing conceptions of class from producer to worker, which, in turn, make sense of the variable nature of judicial power in shaping working-class formation in the United States.

In the last two decades, other scholars in a variety of disciplines also have begun to explore the impact of judicial regulation on American labor.[22] While I have profited immensely from this research, I find most of these accounts to present too narrow and deterministic a view of state-labor relations. By confining their studies primarily to the AFL, many scholars have misunderstood the nature and significance of judicial power. Once the field of research was extended, I found that a variety of state-labor relations prevailed. Courts indeed were important for American labor, but in a more varied and indirect way than previous scholars have claimed. The common law doctrine of conspiracy proved to be an excellent vehicle for broadening the field of analysis, as conspiracy prosecutions remained the principal legal remedy for regulating industrial conflict for most of the nineteenth century.[23]

[21] For recent works that do not divide the nineteenth century at the Civil War, see Nick Salvatore, *Eugene V. Debs: Citizen and Socialist* (Urbana: University of Illinois Press, 1982); Stephen Hahn, *The Roots of Southern Populism: Yeoman Farmers and the Transformation of the Georgia Upcountry, 1850–1890* (New York: Oxford University Press, 1983); and Steven J. Ross, *Workers on the Edge: Work, Leisure, and Politics in Industrializing Cincinnati, 1788–1890* (New York: Columbia University Press, 1985).

[22] Most of this work has focused on judicial regulation in the twentieth century. Despite their different substantive focus, I have found the following works to be useful precursors to my own study: Klare, "Judicial Deradicalization of the Wagner Act"; Katherine Van Wezel Stone, "The Post War Paradigm in American Labor Law," 90 *Yale Law Journal* 7 (June 1981); Peter H. Irons, *The New Deal Lawyers* (Princeton: Princeton University Press, 1982); Joel Rogers, "Divide and Conquer: The Legal Foundations of Postwar U.S. Labor Policy" (Ph.D. diss., Princeton University, 1984); Tomlins, *The State and the Unions*; Leon Fink, "Labor, Liberty, and the Law: Trade Unionism and the Problem of the American Constitutional Order," *Journal of American History* 74, 3 (December 1987): 904–25; William E. Forbath, "The Shaping of the American Labor Movement," 102 *Harvard Law Review* 1109 (1989); Karen Orren, *Belated Feudalism: Labor, the Law, and Liberal Development in the United States* (New York: Cambridge University Press, 1991); Daniel R. Ernst, "The Danbury Hatters' Case," in Christopher L. Tomlins and Andrew J. King, eds., *Labor Law in America: Historical and Critical Essays* (Baltimore: Johns Hopkins University Press, 1992); Robert J. Steinfeld, "The Philadelphia Cordwainers' Case of 1806: The Struggle Over Alternative Legal Constructions of a Free market in Labor," in Tomlins and King, *Labor Law in America*.

[23] Many accounts of American labor law limit the conspiracy doctrine to the period from 1806 to 1842. The landmark case of Commonwealth v. Hunt, 4 Metc. 111 (Mass. 1842), is said to have ended the use of conspiracy, and to have established the right to organize and strike for American workers. However, limiting conspiracy to the antebellum era is incorrect.

Before the impact of state structure over labor strategy could be explored, the legal basis of labor regulation in the United States had to be established and elaborated. Chapter 2 both lays out the legal reasoning behind the conspiracy doctrine and presents new evidence of a revival of the doctrine after the Civil War, thereby establishing conspiracy as the principal form of government regulation of labor for most of the nineteenth century. Chapters 3 and 4 turn away from the state and focus instead on workers' reaction to judicial regulation of industrial conflict before and after the Civil War. I show that state structure indeed played an important role in shaping labor strategy, but in rather different ways than I had anticipated. When beginning my research, I expected workers to have challenged the conspiracy prosecutions, denounced the courts, and demanded a change in government policy toward labor. However, antebellum workers did not behave as I had expected. After several abortive efforts to identify working-class opposition to the conspiracy convictions before the Civil War, I eventually set aside my assumptions about what workers ought to have done and began looking more carefully at what workers in fact organized and protested for. I discovered that workers' relation to the state was by no means a fixed phenomenon, but rather changed considerably over the course of the nineteenth century.

Much to my surprise, when workers organized their own political parties and labor unions in the 1820s and 1830s, they generally did not make repeal of the conspiracy law one of their demands. In fact, neither the Working Men's parties nor the GTUs paid much attention to the antebellum conspiracy convictions and showed little interest in legal reform. To be sure, the Loco-foco or Equal Rights party of the mid-1830s did protest the *Fisher* and *Faulkner* trials and made legal reform an important plank in their platform. Although the Loco-foco protest certainly marked a change from the Working Men's parties and GTUs, this change should not be overdrawn. Significant continuities remained between the Loco-focos and earlier workingmen's organizations—continuities that the Loco-focos themselves ultimately placed ahead of their objections to the conspiracy law. In 1837, the Loco-focos set aside their newfound interest in legal reform in order to reunite with the Democratic party and support Martin Van Buren in the long-standing campaign to establish a more decentralized system of currency and credit.[24] It was only after the Civil War that *some*

There is considerable evidence of a revival of the doctrine from the 1860s through the 1890s. For example, see Herbert Hovenkamp, "Labor Conspiracies in American Law, 1880–1930," 66 *Texas Law Review* 919 (1988); Hyman Kuritz, "Criminal Conspiracy Cases in Postbellum Pennsylvania," *Pennsylvania History* 18 (October 1950): 292–301; Edwin Emil Witte, "Early American Labor Cases," 35 *Yale Law Journal* 825 (1926); and Chapter 2.

[24] Neither the New York Working Men's parties in Philadelphia and New York nor the GTUs in Philadelphia, New York, and New England called for repeal of the conspiracy

labor organizations, such as the New York Workingmen's Assembly, the Federation of Organized Trades and Labor Unions (FOTLU), and the AFL, made repeal of the conspiracy law their central objective and pushed relentlessly for state protection of the right to organize and strike. Even in the postwar decades, however, other organizations, such as the National Labor Union (NLU) and the KOL, were not preoccupied with legal reform, but rather continued to advocate a very different political program. When considering the nineteenth century as a whole, it was clear that no one set of state-labor relations prevailed. Workers' response to the courts varied considerably both over time and across organizations.

To evaluate the impact of state structure on labor strategy, it was essential to understand how and why workers' relation to the courts changed in the middle decades of the nineteenth century. Why was it that workers initially assented to the conspiracy convictions, and only later considered the very same legal doctrine to be unjust and in need of immediate reform? Why, in short, was judicial regulation of working-class organization politicized after the Civil War? Answering these questions took me well beyond my initial interest in state structure and labor strategy into the changing ideology and social relations of the nineteenth century.

CHANGING CONCEPTIONS OF CLASS AND THE POLITICIZATION OF JUDICIAL REGULATION

Workers' initial assent and subsequent protest against the conspiracy convictions cannot be accounted for by state structure and capacity alone, as both the principal institutions and legal doctrine for regulating workers' collective action remained essentially unchanged between 1806 and

---

doctrine. This is not to say that workers never objected to antebellum conspiracy convictions, but rather to draw attention to the limits and particular form of their protest against the courts. The largest protest against antebellum conspiracy convictions occurred in response to People v. Fisher, 14 Wendell 2 (N.Y. 1835), and People v. Faulkner, 4 Doc. Hist. 315 (N.Y. 1836). A "meeting in the park" was called to denounce Judges Savage and Edwards' rulings, and was attended by almost 30,000 citizens. However, even at the height of this protest, we see that workingmen continued to analyze their plight in light of eighteenth-century assumptions about politics and society in which antimonopoly reforms remained their central demand. The Loco-focos, I argue, were unwilling to abandon their antimonopoly commitments when faced with a choice between advocating a decentralized system of finance and credit and calling for legal reform. See the Correspondence Committee's address written after the "meeting in the park" in the *New York Evening Post*, 23 July 1836, p. 2, cols. 4, 5; and F. Byrdsall, *The History of the Loco-Foco or Equal Rights Party, its Movements, Conventions and Proceedings, with Short Characteristic Sketches of Its Prominent Men* (New York: Clement and Packard, 1842), 174–89. The argument for continuity in the antebellum decades is developed at length in Chapter 3.

1896.[25] Instead, I argue that a more relational approach must be adopted in which we attend to both the institutional form of government regulation *and* the changing social context within which the conspiracy convictions were embedded. Specifically, changes in labor ideology and culture in the middle decades of the nineteenth century had an enormous impact on workers' perceptions of, and responses to, judicial regulation. Only by historicizing the concept of class, and attending more closely to the different social divisions and ideology that prevailed before the Civil War, can we begin to unravel the varied and changing relationship between labor and the courts.

Analyzing the quite distinct language of antebellum labor protest provided the key to historicizing the concept of class. Labor newspapers, workingmen's manuals, and the platforms and proceedings of workingmen's political parties and labor unions were filled with very different idioms and ideology from our twentieth-century language of class. Taking these earlier self-identifications and linguistic categories seriously provided a means of reconstructing antebellum conceptions of class. Moreover, identifying the republican influence in antebellum workingmen's discourse not only provided a larger intellectual context within which to situate the workingmen's claims, but also helped to highlight the distinctiveness of antebellum social relations. All too often, workingmen's protest of the 1820s and 1830s has been read through twentieth century conceptions of class, and the earlier linguistic categories collapsed into our more familiar twentieth-century terms. Once antebellum conceptions of class are identified and maintained, we can begin to understand how and why different state-labor relations prevailed beyond the bounds of the AFL.[26]

[25] Many aspects of state structure and capacity certainly changed over the course of the nineteenth century, but not the institutions and policy that are central to this study, namely, the separation of powers, the dominance of the courts over other branches of government, and the persistence of the conspiracy doctrine for regulating industrial conflict during the nineteenth century. To be sure, state courts eventually were eclipsed by federal courts after the Civil War, but this nationalization of judicial power did not occur in labor law until the 1890s with the shift in legal remedy from conspiracy to the labor injunction. See Mason, *Organized Labor and the Law*; Harry N. Scheiber, "Federalism and the American Economic Order, 1789–1910," *Law and Society Review* 10, 1 (Fall 1975): 57–118; and Chapters 2 and 4. For a different argument from my own, but one that also highlights the continuities of nineteenth-century labor law, see Orren, *Belated Feudalism*. It is also important to note that penalties did increase between the antebellum and postbellum conspiracy trials. In Chapter 4, however, I contrast the KOL and New York Workingmen's Assembly response to the same postbellum trials, and document that the increased penalties were not the source of labor's hostility toward the courts. Finally, for discussion of the limited impact of the introduction of an elective judiciary at midcentury, see Chapter 4, note 112.

[26] My approach here has been strongly influenced by the work of William Sewell, Gareth Stedman Jones, and Joan Scott, all of whom have made language or discourse central to their analyses of class. See Sewell, *Work and Revolution in France*, and, more recently, "A Post-

Before the Civil War, many skilled workers did not view the world in terms of twentieth-century, or industrial, notions of class, in which workers identified as wage earners and members of a distinct working class. Instead, in the early decades of the nineteenth century, skilled workers considered themselves to be producers rather than wage earners. The primary social cleavage for many workers, even into the 1870s and 1880s, was not between labor and capital, or workers and employers, but rather between the producing and nonproducing classes. Under the producers' alliance, skilled workers united with small manufacturers in opposition to bankers, lawyers, and land speculators—the quintessential nonproducers—who were supposedly endangering the nation through their abuse of political and economic power.[27] Producers generally did not welcome women,

---

Materialist Rhetoric for Labor History," in Lenard Berlanstein, ed., *Rethinking Labor History* (Urbana: University of Illinois Press, in press); Stedman Jones, "Rethinking Chartism"; and Scott, *Gender and the Politics of History*, esp. chap. 3. For accounts of antebellum workers' protest that rely on twentieth-century notions of class, see Philip Taft, "On the Origins of Business Unionism," *Industrial and Labor Relations Review* 17, 1 (October 1963): 20–38; and Selig Perlman, *A Theory of the Labor Movement* (Philadelphia: Porcupine Press, 1928). Although the new labor history has gone a considerable distance toward revising these earlier accounts, even the best of this new work continues to emphasize the newly emerging working-class consciousness in the 1820s and 1830s at the expense of continuity with the past. For example, see Wilentz, *Chants Democratic*, chap. 5, for an interpretation of the New York Working Men's party in which Thomas Skidmore is said to be the authentic voice of the working class while contending party leaders are dismissed as middle-class infiltrators who divert workingmen from their true course. These criticisms are elaborated in Chapter 3.

[27] The existence of a "producers' alliance" between skilled workers and small manufacturers permeates most of the primary source material. For example, most "labor organizations" before the Civil War readily allowed small businessmen or employers to join their organizations, since they too were members of the producing classes. After the war, organizations such as the KOL still allowed small manufacturers to join, but limited them to a quarter of the membership in any particular assembly. By the end of the century, most trade unions excluded employers altogether, and placed considerable emphasis on establishing "bona fide" labor organizations for workers only.

For a fascinating discussion of these different class alliances within the KOL, see the testimony of Robert D. Layton and George Blair before the Senate Committee upon the Relations between Labor and Capital, *Report of the Committee of the Senate upon the Relations between Labor and Capital* (Washington, D.C.: Government Printing Office, 1885), 1:5, 2:44. See also a very pertinent quotation from the same Senate hearings in Leon Fink, *Workingmen's Democracy: The Knights of Labor and American Politics* (Urbana: University of Illinois Press, 1983), 10.

See the following sources for discussion of nineteenth-century class divisions: William H. Sylvis, "What Is Money?" in James C. Sylvis, ed., *The Life, Speeches, Labors and Essays of William H. Sylvis* (Philadelphia: Claxton, Remsem Y. Haffelfinger, 1872), 365, 367; Terence Vincent Powderly, *Thirty Years of Labor, 1859–1889* (Columbus, Ohio: Excelsior, 1889), 101, 102, 150, 162, 503; Industrial Brotherhood Platform, plank 12, quoted in Powderly, *Thirty Years of Labor*, 119; Knights of Labor Platform, *Proceedings of the General Assembly of the Knights of Labor*, Reading, Pa., 1–4 January 1878, plank 10, quoted in Papers of

blacks, day laborers, and the very poor into their ranks, all of whom were thought to be too dependent to qualify as citizens in the new republic.

Like many other groups in American society, the producers' worldview was strongly influenced by eighteenth-century republican, or Country party, ideology.[28] To be sure, the actual content of the republican legacy was by no means certain, as different individuals and organizations fashioned this common heritage to their own ends. The enormous variation within the republican tradition, however, does not diminish its importance for understanding the producers' worldview. Workingmen's writing, protest, and organization before the Civil War clearly reflected their commitment to several assumptions with long-standing republican antecedents. Civic virtue, independence, monopoly, and corruption were the central concepts workingmen used to interpret the economic changes they were witnessing. Moreover, the producers' alliance did not break down quickly or in a uniform fashion, but rather disintegrated slowly and unevenly in the middle decades of the nineteenth century. Between 1840 and 1880, the producers' vision began to unravel as dissenting individuals and groups began to question the republican assumptions and to construct a new interpretation of industrialization. Even as the alliance broke down, the producers' vision continued to hold sway in particular labor organizations, such as the NLU and the KOL, until it was finally displaced in the last quarter of the nineteenth century. Exploring the producers' vision in the chapters that follow enables us to capture the very different conception of class that prevailed before the Civil War. Attending more closely to the social relations and ideology of the producing classes, in turn, allows us to make sense of labor's changing relationship to the state, and ultimately provides the basis for a more satisfying account of working-class formation in the United States.

In Chapters 3 and 4, I show that initially workers accepted the conspiracy convictions as part of their larger vision of republican political

---

Terence Vincent Powderly, 1864–1924, and John William Hayes, 1880–1921, microfilm edition. The original papers are held in the Catholic University Archives, Washington, D.C. (Hereafter cited as Powderly Papers.)

28 The literature on republicanism is extensive, but the major works in the field are Bernard Bailyn, *The Ideological Origins of the American Revolution* (Cambridge, Mass.: Harvard University Press, 1967); Gordon S. Wood, *The Creation of the American Republic, 1776–1787* (Chapel Hill: University of North Carolina Press, 1969); J.G.A. Pocock, *The Machiavellian Moment: Florentine Political Thought and the Atlantic Republican Tradition* (Princeton: Princeton University Press, 1975). For extension of republican assumptions to labor history, see Wilentz, *Chants Democratic*; Salvatore, *Eugene V. Debs*; and Fink, *Workingmen's Democracy*. For a useful review of the literature, see Robert E. Shalhope, "Republicanism and Early American Historiography," *William and Mary Quarterly*, 3d series, 39, 2 (April 1982): 334–456.

economy. Government regulation was needed, the producers argued, to limit a wide range of monopolies that were endangering the republic.[29] As long as both labor and capital were prevented from organizing, there was no need for workers to contest government regulation. Producers were willing to accept regulation of their own collective action as long as non-producers also were prevented from organizing. Hence the producers' principal demand was for more effective antimonopoly legislation to foster a healthy republican political economy. By the 1870s and 1880s, however, the social context of judicial regulation had changed considerably. Several labor organizations, especially trade union federations such as the New York Workingmen's Assembly and the FOTLU, began to break with the producers' alliance, and to question the appropriateness of republican assumptions for understanding workers' place in a modern industrial economy. As several trade union leaders began to construct a very different analysis of the postwar economic and social order, judicial regulation of labor, even under the very same legal doctrine, took on an entirely different significance. Conspiracy convictions were no longer accepted as legitimate government policy. Instead, convictions were viewed increasingly as unjust and became one of the main targets of labor reform.[30]

Only after having set for themselves the task of changing legal doctrine did postwar trade unions have to contend with the unusual structure of the American state. The division of political power, and the dominance of the courts over other branches of government, we will see, provided few rewards for political mobilization. Trade unions' principal lesson from their thirty-year struggle to repeal the conspiracy doctrine between 1865 and 1896 was the enormous limits to political reform. Chapter 4, in particular, examines the trade unions' struggle for state protection of the right to organize and strike between 1865 and 1896. In order to secure state recognition, labor either had to change the legal doctrine under which workers were being prosecuted for organizing, or remove the courts as the primary regulatory institution in the field of industrial relations. The history of the

---

[29] For republican fear of concentrated power, see Bailyn, *Ideological Origins*, esp. chap. 3; and J.G.A. Pocock, "Machiavelli, Harrington and English Political Ideologies in the Eighteenth Century," in his, *Politics, Language and Time*.

The conspiracy doctrine was not restricted to workingmen's associations, but was applied to a wide range of offenses, including conspiracies to cheat and defraud, conspiracies in restraint of trade, and conspiracies to obstruct the administration of justice. Moreover, employers' combinations also were subject to government regulation, especially in the antebellum era. Legislative charters and the common law doctrine of ultra vires were the principal mechanisms for regulating employers' associations. For more extended discussion and sources, see Chapter 2.

[30] The New York State Workingmen's Assembly, for example, declared repeal of the conspiracy doctrine to be one of its highest priorities, and worked to change government policy for over thirty years (1865–1897). The Workingmen's Assembly's campaign against the conspiracy doctrine is described at length in Chapter 4.

struggle for state recognition of working-class organization reveals the limits of electoral and party politics for changing labor law. After a series of electoral victories followed by judicial defeats, workers became disillusioned with political reform and began to bypass the state to negotiate with and protest against their employers directly. The unusual structure of the American state thus played an important role in the AFL's turn to voluntarism at the end of the century.

However, the trade unions' encounter with the courts was not universal. Most labor organizations in the antebellum era and some of the postwar associations as well were not engaged in prolonged struggles with the courts. The conspiracy doctrine was politicized for those organizations that broke with the producers' alliance and advocated a very different program of labor reform—a program that brought them face to face with the power of the courts.

Thus, we will see that the American state played a dual role in the process of working-class formation. On the one hand, the courts and workers' relation to them are best understood as a window through which we can glimpse the changing social relations and ideology of the nineteenth century. Here workers' different response to the two waves of conspiracy prosecutions signaled the changing conception of class from producer to wage earner; a change that, to a considerable extent, lay beyond the influence of the courts. On the other hand, within a specific historical context, namely, the last three decades of the nineteenth century, the courts also played an explicitly causal role in shaping American labor strategy. Chapter 4 lays out the relevant historical conditions and shows why some trade unions, as opposed to other labor reform associations, found their efforts at political mobilization thwarted by the courts. In short, I argue that the AFL's turn to voluntarism was produced by the intersection of particular labor ideologies with the unusual configuration of political institutions in the United States. Neither ideology nor structure alone can explain the decisive change in labor strategy at the turn of the century. But taken together, they enable us to decipher the origins of business unionism in the United States.

ALTERNATIVE EXPLANATIONS

Before beginning my analysis in detail, I will comment briefly on two alternative explanations of the origins of business unionism. The literature on American exceptionalism is enormous and has already been reviewed carefully by other scholars; it need not be repeated here.[31] I have found the two most compelling alternative explanations to date to be those that focus

[31] For extensive reviews of the literature, see Foner, "Why Is There No Socialism in the United States?"; and Gwendolyn Mink, *Old Labor and New Immigrants in American Political Development: Union, Party, and State, 1875–1920* (Ithaca, N.Y.: Cornell University Press, 1986), chap. 1.

on the unusual nineteenth-century labor market conditions and party system in the United States.

Many scholars have argued that the heterogeneity of the American labor force made it more difficult for American workers to unite as a class. The successive waves of immigration in 1843–1857, 1878–1893, 1898–1914, and 1919–1921, and the more constant division of race, undermined working-class consciousness in several ways. Not only have workers of different ethnic and racial backgrounds had multiple and competing identities that often cut across class lines, but employers, too, have been able to exploit these differences by pitting one ethnic group against another in order to foster a sense of distrust. Finally, ethnic and racial divisions, regardless of employers' intent, often have intersected labor market competition so as to intensify cultural differences at the expense of a common sense of class.[32]

Although the American labor movement indeed was fragmented both by ethnicity and race, the evidence linking these factors to voluntarism remains inconclusive. Much recent research on ethnicity, for example, has invoked labor's diverse immigrant heritage as *both* a source of labor radicalism and a factor in its demise. When the labor movement is strong, as in the May Day protests of 1886, immigrant traditions often have been viewed as important sources of working-class solidarity and left-wing ideals. Yet when the movement subsides, the decline also is attributed to the presence of ethnic divides. How and why ethnicity is a resource one mo-

[32] For works linking labor market heterogeneity to American labor reformism, see John R. Commons, "Immigration and Labor Problems," in Robert M. La Follette, ed., *The Making of America* (Chicago: The Making of America Co., 1906), 8:236–61; Melvyn Dubofsky, *We Shall Be All: A History of the I.W.W.* (Chicago: Quadrangle Books, 1969); Alexander Saxton, *The Indispensable Enemy: Labor and the Anti-Chinese Movement in California* (Berkeley: University of California Press, 1971); Gerald Rosenblum, *Immigrant Workers: Their Impact on Labor Radicalism* (New York: Basic Books, 1973); Robert Asher, "Union Nativism and the Immigrant Response," *Labor History* 23, 3 (Summer 1982): 325–48; Richard J. Oestreicher, *Solidarity and Fragmentation: Working People and Class Consciousness in Detroit, 1875–1900* (Urbana: University of Illinois Press, 1986); Mink, *Old Labor and New Immigrants*; Martin Brown and Peter Philips, "Competition and Racism in Hiring Practices Among California Manufacturers, 1860–1882," *Industrial and Labor Relations Review* 40, 1 (October 1986): 61–74; Elliot J. Gorn, " 'Good-Bye Boys, I Die a True American': Homicide, Nativism, and Working-Class Culture in Antebellum New York City," *Journal of American History* 74, 2 (September 1987): 388–410; and Stanley Nadel, *Little Germany: Ethnicity, Religion, and Class in New York City, 1845–80* (Urbana: University of Illinois Press, 1990).

Issues of race and immigration should by no means be kept separate. Indeed, Alexander Saxton, Gwendolyn Mink, and Richard Slotkin all have shown how racism and immigration often were intimately linked in the last quarter of the nineteenth century. See Saxton, *The Indispensable Enemy*; Richard Slotkin, *The Fatal Environment: The Myth of the Frontier in the Age of Industrialization* (New York: Atheneum, 1985); and Mink, *Old Labor and New Immigrants*.

ment and a liability the next is not sufficiently explored. Nor is there adequate attention to the changing impact of immigration over time. Given the successive waves of immigration, labor market theorists need to provide a more effective explanation of why business unionism only emerged at the end of the century and not before. Finally, arguments from ethnicity to labor strategy break down at the individual level as well. Even the classic immigrant labor leaders such as Joseph Labadie, Adolph Strasser, and Samuel Gompers himself initially advocated socialist principles, only to reject them in the 1880s and 1890s and join the ranks of the AFL. It is difficult to account for this change in political orientation on the basis of ethnicity alone. Put simply, the impact of immigrant heritage on labor strategy has been indeterminate and thus is insufficient, in and of itself, to explain the AFL's turn to business unionism at the end of the nineteenth century.[33]

Preliminary evidence on the interplay of race and class is more promising, as the primary sources are filled with references to slavery as a counterpoint to workers' experience of wage labor. Here, too, however, as with ethnic divisions, racial differences did not always prove to be an insurmountable obstacle to labor unity; we can well imagine ways in which emancipation might have provided a positive model for working-class political action in the northern states. Exactly how racial divisions and images shaped labor strategy remains unclear and needs further study.[34]

Recently, Gary Marks has offered an innovative labor market analysis that breaks with dominant research practice in the field in which he con-

[33] For a classic argument invoking ethnicity as both a source of and an obstacle to labor radicalism, see Oestreicher, *Solidarity and Fragmentation*, chaps. 5–7. Mink provides perhaps the best argument as to the timing of labor's change in strategy and immigrant diversity by attending to the tensions between old labor and new immigrants. Mink's argument, however, is not sustained with sufficient clarity in the critical decades at the turn of the century. Mink's analysis of the system of 1896 is convoluted and ultimately unconvincing as to the relevant causal dynamic behind union, class, and party alliances at the turn of the century. See Mink, *Old Labor and New Immigrants*, chap. 4.

For recent work that acknowledges and explores the indeterminacy of ethnic diversity, see John Bodner, *The Transplanted: A History of Immigrants in Urban America* (Bloomington: Indiana University Press, 1987); David Emmons, *The Butte Irish: Class and Ethnicity in an American Mining Town, 1875–1925* (Urbana: University of Illinois Press, 1989); and Gunther Peck, "Crisis in the Family: Padrones and Radicals in Utah, 1908–1912," in Dan Georgakas and Charles C. Moskos, eds., *New Directions in Greek-American Studies* (New York: Pella Press, 1991), 73–94.

[34] For a useful review of the literature on race and class, see David Roediger, "'Labor in White Skin': Race and Working-Class History," in Mike Davis and Michael Sprinker, eds., *Reshaping the US Left: Popular Struggles in the 1980s* (New York: Verso, 1988), 287–308. See also Peter Rachleff, *Black Labor in Richmond, 1865–1890* (Urbana: University of Illinois Press, 1989); and Michael Goldfield, "Class, Race, and Politics in the United States: White Supremacy as the Main Explanation for the Peculiarities of American Politics from Colonial Times to the Present," *Research in Political Economy* 12 (1990): 83–127

siders industrial sectors rather than national labor movements to be the appropriate unit of comparison. Coal miners' *or* printers' unions in different nations, Marks argues, have more in common with each other than they do with unions from other sectors in the same country. Thus Marks concludes that labor strategies, too, vary from sector to sector as unions adapt to the particular incentives and constraints that they face in a particular industry.[35] Although Marks's approach is intriguing, his explanation falters in two important respects. First, Marks's assumption that workers' initial line of recourse was to industrial rather than political action cannot be sustained. My own research, and that of many others as well, has shown that for most of the nineteenth century New York and Pennsylvania workers did not view political reform as a subordinate strategy to be pursued only when all else failed. In fact, quite the opposite was true: New York and Pennsylvania workers remained firmly committed to political reform throughout the nineteenth century and only turned to business unionism when their repeated efforts at political reform were undermined by the courts. Second, ultimately Marks, too, is unwilling to abandon national models entirely and is much less convincing when he shifts from his sectoral analysis back to explanations of national labor strategies. The different composition of national trade union federations, Marks argues, led to the pursuit of different labor strategies in Britain, Germany, and the United States. However, Marks does not present any systematic data comparing the composition of all three national federations and the limited evidence that is provided on Britain and the United States is insufficient to sustain his argument from sectors back to national models.[36]

The second major explanation of American labor strategy has looked to the party system as the critical factor in the AFL's turn to business unionism. Both electoral laws and machine politics have been identified as the principal obstacles to working-class political action in the United States. Many scholars have lamented the single member–simple plurality system

[35] See Marks, *Unions in Politics*, Introduction and chap. 1.

[36] Although much of the book is taken up with distinguishing the labor strategies of different sectors in Britain, Germany, and the United States, Marks nevertheless returns to the question of national variation in chap. 6. The American labor movement eschewed political reform, Marks claims, because, unlike Britain, craft unions were able to dominate the AFL. Although Marks presents some evidence comparing the British and American federations, what is presented is insufficient to sustain his claim. No data for Germany are provided, and the British and American figures are quite vague and need to be broken down by year. See Marks, *Unions in Politics*, pp. 210–11. Even granting the difference in federation composition, which I remain unconvinced of, Marks's underlying assumption that successful craft unions were inherently opposed to political reform does not sit easily with the extensive AFL political activity in the 1870s and 1880s. The AFL's political campaigns in New York and Pennsylvania are elaborated in chap. 4.

of electoral laws in the United States, which has made it more difficult for third parties to compete effectively with the two parties in power. As a consequence, so the argument runs, American workers have been unable to establish a foothold in the political system from which they might have accumulated political power.[37] Another group of scholars have taken a slightly different tack and argued that the emergence of the political machine and the absence of programmatic political parties have been responsible for the separation of work and politics in the United States. By mobilizing workers into politics through patronage relations rather than on the basis of ideological or substantive grounds, these scholars claim, American workers were provided with few opportunities to mobilize as a class.[38]

Comparative studies of electoral laws indeed can help distinguish the American party system from many of its West European counterparts, in which proportional representation has enabled small parties to prevail. However, the electoral variable cannot discriminate sufficiently for my purposes, as both England and the United States have similar electoral laws and yet quite different labor strategies have taken hold. The argument for machine politics also has been overdrawn. Although patronage was an important feature of late-nineteenth-century politics, I have found the argument from political machines to put the cart before the horse. My criticism here rests on the very different view of nineteenth-century party politics that has emerged from my research. We will see in the story that follows that the party system and workers' political actions, at least in New York and Pennsylvania, were not always of a nonprogrammatic sort. Indeed, I would claim that throughout much of the nineteenth century, New York and Pennsylvania parties advanced quite distinct platforms of a pro-

[37] The classic argument concerning electoral laws was made by Duverger. See Maurice Duverger, *Political Parties: Their Organization and Activity in the Modern State* (New York: John Wiley and Sons, 1959). Douglas Rae has subsequently confirmed many of Duverger's insights with quantitative analysis. See Douglas W. Rae, *The Political Consequences of Electoral Laws* (New Haven: Yale University Press, 1967). For more specific arguments linking electoral laws to labor strategy, see Richard J. Oestreicher, "Urban Working-Class Political Behavior and Theories of American Electoral Politics, 1870–1940," *Journal of American History* 74, 4 (March 1988): 1257–86; Lipset, "Radicalism or Reformism"; and Peter Bruce, "Political Parties and the Evolution of Labor Law in Canada and the United States" (Ph.D. diss., Massachusetts Institute of Technology, 1988).

[38] See Amy Beth Bridges, *A City in the Republic: Antebellum New York and the Origins of Machine Politics* (Ithaca, N.Y.: Cornell University Press, 1987); Amy Beth Bridges, "Becoming American: The Working Classes in the United States Before the Civil War," in Katznelson and Zolberg, *Working-Class Formation,* 157–96; Katznelson, *City Trenches;* Martin Shefter, "Trade Unions and Political Machines: The Organization and Disorganization of the American Working Class in the Late Nineteenth Century," in Katznelson and Zolberg, *Working-Class Formation,* 197–276; and Steven P. Erie, *Rainbow's End: Irish America and the Dilemmas of Urban Machine Politics, 1840–1895* (Berkeley: University of California Press, 1988).

grammatic kind. However, in order to grasp the ideological and class cleavages that prevailed, we must set aside our presentist notions of class and read the platforms and proceedings in light of the division between the producing and nonproducing classes. To the extent that machine politics dominated American elections in the 1890s and the early twentieth century, they are best understood, I believe, as a further manifestation rather than the cause of AFL voluntarism.[39]

In sum, while theories of American labor movement development that focus on labor market conditions and party politics have captured some important aspects of American labor politics, they remain inadequate for explaining the origins of business unionism. Neither theory provides a convincing account of the nature and timing of the shift in AFL strategy at the turn of the century. Focusing instead on the interaction of state structure and labor ideology leads to a better explanation for the two defining features of AFL voluntarism, namely, antistatism and militance on the shop floor. After all, it was only legislative politics that was discredited by judi-

---

[39] Neither England nor the United States had systems of proportional representation that generally have been seen as fostering a multiparty system. For comparison of English and American electoral laws, see Rae, *Political Consequences of Electoral Laws*, 42–44. For critical readings of the literature on political machines, see M. Craig Brown and Charles N. Halaby, "Bosses, Reform, and the Socioeconomic Bases of Urban Expenditure, 1890–1940," in Terrence J. McDonald and Sally K. Ward, eds., *The Politics of Urban Fiscal Policy* (Beverly Hills: Sage Publications, 1984), 69–99; and Terrence J. McDonald, "The Burdens of Urban History: The Theory of the State in Recent American Social History," *Studies in American Political Development* 3 (1989): 3–29. For a rebuttal, see Ira Katznelson's response in the same volume.

Several scholars have begun to revise earlier accounts of nineteenth-century party politics and have found that there were, in fact, important substantive and class differences in partisan divisions for much of the nineteenth century. See Marvin Meyers, *The Jacksonian Persuasion: Politics and Belief* (Stanford: Stanford University Press, 1957); Daniel Walker Howe, *The Political Culture of the American Whigs* (Chicago: University of Chicago Press, 1979); Bridges, *A City in the Republic*, chap. 4; John Ashworth, *'Agrarians' and 'Aristocrats': Party Political Ideology in the United States, 1837–1846* (New York: Cambridge University Press, 1987); and Eric Foner, *Free Soil, Free Labor, Free Men: The Ideology of the Republican Party Before the Civil War* (New York: Oxford University Press, 1970). Political divisions in the late nineteenth century are considerably more complicated, as the Civil War made it difficult for northern workers to continue to support the Democratic party. It is a mistake, however, to assume that just because workers backed away from the Democratic party, they retreated from substantive politics completely. Instead, third parties took up many workers' concerns in the three decades after the Civil War, and the AFL did not begin its turn to voluntarism until the last decade of the century. For an interesting reinterpretation of party politics after the Civil War, see Gretchen Ritter, "The People Versus the Money Power: Anti-Monopolism and the Politics of Finance, 1865–1896" (Ph.D. diss., Massachusetts Institute of Technology, 1992). This revised view of nineteenth-century party politics, however, can be reconciled with some aspects of the literature on political machines. Patronage politics would have to be limited to the late 1880s and beyond and would be seen, at least in part, as a manifestation of AFL voluntarism.

cial obstruction, not working-class protest as a whole. The AFL recognized the double-jointedness of the American state and directed its energy and resources into strategies that would not leave its members trapped in between legislatures and the courts.[40] Moreover, attending to the intersection of ideology and the courts also helps to explain the timing of the AFL's change in strategy at the turn of the century.

IMPLICATIONS OF THE RESEARCH

Historicizing the concept of class by distinguishing more carefully between producer and industrial notions of class has important implications for two additional areas of research, namely, comparative labor movement development and nineteenth-century electoral politics in the United States. The producers' concept of class that proved so central to my account of American labor history raises interesting questions about working-class formation in other nations as well. Chapter 5 examines the English case and shows that the producers' alliance and ideology were by no means restricted to the United States. Historicizing the concept of class in the English context requires that traditional accounts of both the Chartist movement and the mid-Victorian era be recast.[41] Once this is completed, the English experience provides a useful contrast with the American case. The producers' alliance, and the transformation from producer to worker, were remarkably similar in the two countries. Yet the two labor movements followed quite different strategies, throwing into sharp relief the impact of different state structures on labor movement development. Specifically, the division of power within the English state, which left Parliament supreme, provided greater rewards for working-class politics at the end of the century. The political victories of English workers in the 1870s through the

[40] Many scholars, especially the new labor historians, have been calling for an end to debates on American exceptionalism for some time. For example, see Wilentz, "Against Exceptionalism." Moreover, the new labor historians have done a wonderful job of recovering the rich heritage of labor radicalism in the United States. However, the debate on exceptionalism refuses to die away precisely because there is something distinctive about labor strategy in the twentieth century. The pressing task, then, is to reconcile the old and the new labor history by explaining what happened to the long tradition of workers' protest with the turn to voluntarism at the end of the century. The literature encompassing the old and new labor history is too extensive to be identified here. For two useful, if somewhat outdated, overviews of the field, see Brody, "The Old Labor History and the New"; and Sean Wilentz, "Artisan Origins of the American Working Class," *International Labor and Working Class History* 19 (Spring 1981): 1–22.

[41] Several scholars already have begun work along these lines. For example see Stedman Jones, "Rethinking Chartism"; Dorothy Thompson, *The Chartists: Popular Politics in the Industrial Revolution* (New York: Pantheon, 1984); and John Smail, "New Languages for Labour and Capital: The Transformation of Discourse in the Early Years of the Industrial Revolution," *Social History* 12, 1 (January 1987): 49–71.

1890s were *not* undermined repeatedly by the courts, but rather resulted in important changes in government policy toward labor. As a consequence, English workers remained committed to political reform, which had proved an effective means of protecting and advancing workers' interests.

Whether or not this revised view of working-class formation holds true for the Continent as well remains an open question. Some recent research on France and Italy suggests that a similar recasting of the concept of class may be appropriate for these nations as well.[42] William Sewell, for example, has shown how the 1848 revolution in France not only was an early manifestation of working-class consciousness, but also contained an extensive eighteenth century legacy more typical of the producers' notions of class. In Italy, too, recent work has begun to rethink the basic social divisions and political alliances that accompanied industrialization in ways that provide intriguing parallels with the producers' concept of class developed here. My own research makes clear the need to revise traditional accounts of American working-class formation in two important respects. First, we see that in the United States and England, the process of working-class formation was more gradual than previously assumed, as eighteenth-century assumptions continued to shape workers' understanding of economic change well into the nineteenth century. Second, the social changes under way were channeled along different national paths in important and complex ways by the structure of their respective states.

In the conclusion I reconsider the relevance of class for electoral and party politics during the nineteenth century and lay out a research agenda based on my revised view of nineteenth-century class relations. Existing accounts of electoral politics generally have concluded that class was *not* a salient factor in shaping electoral outcomes, and have emphasized instead the importance of ethnocultural factors as the cornerstone of party politics.[43] Ethnic identities and religious affiliations, in particular, are thought to have played a more important role than class in shaping political al-

---

[42] For recent work on France that emphasizes the eighteenth-century legacy in nineteenth-century artisan protest, see Sewell, *Work and Revolution in France*. For new research on Italy raises similar notions of a producers' alliance, see Giuseppe Berta, "La formazione del movimento operaio regionale: il caso dei tessili (1860–1900)," in Aldo Agosti e Gian Maria Bravo, eds., *Storia del movimento operaio, del socialismo, e delle lotte in piedmonte* (Bari: De Donato, 1979), vol. 1; and Giulio Sapelli, "La cultura della produzione: 'autorita tecnica' e 'autonomia morale,'" in Bruno Bottiglieri and Paolo Ceri, eds., *Le Culture de lavoro: L'esperienza di Torino nel guardo europeo* (Bologna: Il Mulino, 1987).

[43] Ethnocultural explanations are developed as an alternative to class in the following works: Lee Benson, *The Concept of Jacksonian Democracy: New York as a Test Case* (Princeton: Princeton University Press, 1961); Paul Kleppner, *The Cross of Culture: A Social Analysis of Midwestern Politics, 1850–1900* (New York: The Free Press, 1970); Sam Bass Warner, Jr., *The Private City: Philadelphia in Three Stages of Its Growth* (Philadelphia: University of Pennsylvania Press, 1968).

liances. My analysis of labor's relation to the state, however, has led me to question the basic assumptions behind the ethnocultural theories. Their central defect has been the way in which they have operationalized the concept of class. By taking wealth, income, and occupation as surrogates for class, the ethnocultural historians have relied on twentieth-century notions of class to explore nineteenth-century politics. Their conclusion, that there was little or no correspondence between class and party during the nineteenth century, is incorrect and is largely a product of their presentist conception of class. Once we set aside industrial notions of class, and take seriously the division between the producing and nonproducing classes, we see that class was indeed central to nineteenth-century electoral and party politics.

A note of warning before beginning my analysis. This study of labor's relationship to the state is based primarily on an examination of the *organized* labor movement. There are obvious limitations to this approach in that we are hearing disproportionately from labor leaders rather than the rank and file. However, studying formal organizations has some advantages as well. Most labor organizatons, even in the antebellum era, kept records of their platforms and proceedings that constitute an invaluable source of working-class deliberation and debate. We should not assume that labor leaders spoke directly for all workers, but nor should we assume they were hopelessly out of touch. Instead, we should view these elite debates as efforts to mobilize the rank and file behind particular, and at times competing, interpretations of economic change. The rank-and-file response to particular economic visions can be discerned, at least in part, by following the fate of particular leaders and their platforms. This perspective helps transcend the division between the old labor history and the new by linking leaders to the rank and file through their narratives of industrialization: narratives that the elite played a central role in constructing. It is nevertheless important to remember that the story that follows is an account of organized labor, rather than of the working class as a whole.[44]

[44] For characterization of the old labor history and the new, see Brody, "The Old Labor History and the New." I do not want to claim complete harmony between the elite and the rank and file. Further research might well uncover some important differences between leaders and their followers. But I do want to contest characterizations of formal labor organizations and their leaders as necessarily removed from, and largely irrelevant to, the concerns of the rank and file.

CHAPTER TWO

Judicial Regulation of Labor: The Common Law Doctrine of Criminal Conspiracy, 1806–1896

IN THE LATE eighteenth and early nineteenth centuries, workingmen began to organize in both Western Europe and the United States in order to protest the economic and social changes that accompanied industrialization. No government welcomed this increase in workers' power, and all tried to contain workers' protest by regulating trade unions, friendly societies, and strike actions. Not all governments, however, relied on the same institutions to implement their policy. While other nations looked to legislatures to prevent workers from organizing, the United States relied primarily on the judiciary to accomplish this task.[1] The primary mechanism through which American courts regulated working-class organization during the nineteenth century was the common law doctrine of criminal conspiracy. The conspiracy doctrine determined whether or not workers were allowed to organize, and specified which tactics could and could not be used by workers during industrial disputes. This particular form of government regulation, via the courts, created a unique set of incentives and constraints that shaped labor strategy in the United States. In order to unravel the impact of judicial regulation on American labor, we must first identify the central features of the doctrine and trace its application to working-class organization and protest.[2]

THE COMMON LAW DOCTRINE OF CRIMINAL CONSPIRACY

The conspiracy doctrine was a notoriously vague and amorphous doctrine that is not easily captured in a single definition. Despite conflicting interpretations, some defining features of the doctrine can be identified. At bottom the conspiracy doctrine tried to regulate the increased harm that often accompanied collective action. Eighteenth- and nineteenth-century

---

[1] For discussion of government regulation of working-class organization in England and France, see Valenzuela, "Labor Movement Formation and Politics"; George, "The Combination Laws"; Orth, "Combination and Conspiracy"; and Marks, *Unions in Politics*.

[2] For an excellent discussion of conspiracy as the primary regulatory mechanism during the nineteenth century, see Mason, *Organized Labor and the Law*.

legal scholars and practitioners alike considered confederation to be so menacing a practice that it could transform otherwise unlawful acts into criminal offenses. Unlike most crimes, execution of the confederacy was not required to sustain the indictment; rather, combination alone was considered "the gist of the offense, though nothing be done in pursuance of it."[3] Execution of the conspiracy merely aggravated rather than constituted the crime. The conspiracy doctrine did not originate with labor disputes, but rather was used first in England during the fifteenth century for crimes against the administration of justice. In the seventeenth century, the doctrine was extended beyond the obstruction of justice and applied to a wider range of offenses, such as conspiracies to cheat and defraud, conspiracies against the government, and conspiracies in restraint of trade. The doctrine was not applied to labor disputes in England until the eighteenth century. In America, too, the doctrine was never confined to labor combinations alone, but was used to remedy a similar range of offenses; workingmen's associations were only one example of a larger group of combinations covered by the conspiracy doctrine.[4]

[3] Quoted from Hampton L. Carson, *The Law of Criminal Conspiracies and Agreements: As Found in the American Cases* (Philadelphia: Blackstone, 1887), 92. The notion of confederacy providing the gist of the offense was first established in 1611 in Poulterers' Case, 9 Coke, 55 (1611).

[4] In the United States, the conspiracy doctrine also included conspiracies to cheat and defraud, conspiracies against the administration of justice, against government, against public policy, and against individual rights and property.

The literature on the conspiracy doctrine is extensive, but the following sources have been especially useful in discerning the competing interpretations of the doctrine: Arthur M. Allen, "Criminal Conspiracies in Restraint of Trade at Common Law," 23 *Harvard Law Review* 531 (1910); Clifford Brigham, "Strikes and Boycotts as Indictable Conspiracies at Common Law," 22 *American Law Review* 41 (1887); Francis M. Burdick, "Conspiracy as a Crime, and as a Tort," 7 *Columbia Law Review* 229 (1907); Wythe Holt, "Labour Conspiracy Cases in the United States, 1805–1842: Bias and Legitimation in Common Law Adjudication," 22 *Osgoode Hall Law Journal* 591 (Winter 1984); Hovenkamp, "Labor Conspiracies in American Law"; Kuritz, "Criminal Conspiracy Cases"; Leonard W. Levy, *The Law of the Commonwealth and Chief Justice Shaw* (Cambridge, Mass.: Harvard University Press, 1957); Mason, *Organized Labor and the Law*; Walter Nelles, "Commonwealth v. Hunt," 32 *Columbia Law Review* 1128 (1932); Walter Nelles, "The First American Labor Case," 41 *Yale Law Journal* 165 (1931); Sylvester Petro, "Unions and the Southern Courts: Part III—The Conspiracy and Tort Foundations of the Labor Injunction," 60 *North Carolina Law Review* 544 (March 1982); Francis B. Sayre, "Criminal Conspiracy," 35 *Harvard Law Review* 393 (1922); Arthur James Selfridge, "American Law of Strikes and Boycotts as Crimes," 22 *American Law Review* 233 (1888); Christopher Tomlins, *Law, Labor, and Ideology in the Early American Republic* (New York: Cambridge University Press, 1993); Marjorie S. Turner, *The Early American Labor Conspiracy Cases: Their Place in Labor Law* (San Diego: San Diego State College Press, 1967); Witte, "Early American Labor Cases"; and Anthony Woodiwiss, *Rights v. Conspiracy: A Sociological Essay on the History of Labour Law in the United States* (New York: Berg, 1990).

For legal treatises on conspiracy, see Joseph Chitty, *A Practical Treatise on the Criminal*

It is misleading, however, to present too consensual a view of the conspiracy doctrine. In fact, during the seventeenth, eighteenth, and nineteenth centuries there was considerable disagreement within the legal profession over the definition and boundaries of the doctrine. Exactly which confederacies were vulnerable to criminal prosecution was not at all clear as treatise writers, attorneys, and judges advanced different and at times conflicting interpretations of conspiracy law. Three distinct views of conspiracy can be identified, each advocated by a distinguished set of scholars and practitioners. Put simply, the central point of contention among the three views was in specifying the limits of the doctrine.

The narrowest view of conspiracy claimed that the doctrine ought to be limited to offenses in which the action was itself an indictable offense regardless of the confederacy. Murder, theft, and rape, for example, were all subject to criminal prosecution when committed by an individual; when contemplated by two or more persons, whether or not they actually executed the crime, these actions could be prosecuted for criminal conspiracy. Almost all lawyers agreed that such confederacies clearly fell within the bounds of the doctrine, but only a few wanted to restrict conspiracy exclusively to such offenses. Perhaps the strongest advocate of this position in the United States was Judge Gabriel Ford of New Jersey. In his charge to the jury in *State v. Rickey* in 1827, Judge Ford distinguished indictable (criminal) from actionable (civil) offenses and claimed that "[c]onspiracy is limited, *at least*, to combinations to commit *an act*, which, if committed, would be an *indictable offence. . . .* It is this extension of conspiracy to private injuries not otherwise of an indictable nature, and in which the public have no concern, to which I object, and insist that it cannot be maintained, neither on the principles of the common law, nor by

---

Law (Philadelphia: Edward Earle, 1819), vol. 3; R. S. Wright, *The Law of Criminal Conspiracies and Agreements* (Philadelphia: Blackstone, 1887); Carson, *Criminal Conspiracies and Agreements*; Albert Stickney, *State Control of Trade and Commerce by the National or State Authority* (New York: Baker, Voorhis and Co., 1897); Arthur J. Eddy, *The Law of Combinations: Embracing Monopolies, Trusts, and Combinations of Labor and Capital; Conspiracy, and Contracts in Restraint of Trade, Together with Federal and State Anti-Trust Legislation* (Chicago: Callaghan and Co., 1901), vol. 2; and Joel Prentiss Bishop, *Bishop on Criminal Law* (Chicago: T. H. Flood and Co., 1923), vol. 2.

For additional discussion of labor and conspiracy, see Barry F. Helfand, "Labor and the Courts: The Common-Law Doctrine of Criminal Conspiracy and Its Application in the Buck's Stove Case," *Labor History* 18, 1 (Winter 1977): 91–114; Stephen Mayer, "People v. Fisher: The Shoemakers' Strike of 1833," *New York Historical Society Quarterly* 62 (1978): 6–21; Richard B. Morris, "Criminal Conspiracy and Early Labor Combinations in New York," *Political Science Quarterly* 52, 1 (March 1937): 51–85; Ian M. G. Quimby, "The Cordwainers' Protest: A Crisis in Labor Relations," *Winterthur Portfolio* 3 (1967): 83–101; Francis B. Sayre, "Labor and the Courts," 39 *Yale Law Journal* 682 (1929–1930); and Steinfeld, "The Philadelphia Cordwainers' Case of 1806."

adjudged cases."[5] Conspiracies could only be sustained, Ford argued, against contemplated actions that were themselves indictable offenses independent of the conspiracy. The Ricky decision, however, was not the dominant position of the American legal profession and was overruled at mid-century by Chief Justice Henry Green in *State v. Norton*.[6]

The second view of conspiracy was more inclusive and did not require that the contemplated action itself be criminal. Instead, all unlawful—as opposed to criminal—acts might become criminal when agreed to collectively. Both cheats and defrauds and trespasses, for example, were actionable offenses when committed by individuals. When contemplated or carried out collectively, these same activities could be subject to criminal prosecution under the conspiracy doctrine and as such were subject to harsher penalties and jail terms. Lord Denman's celebrated antithesis captured this position nicely: "An indictment for conspiracy ought to show, either that it was for an unlawful purpose, or to effect a lawful purpose by unlawful means."[7] In 1842, Chief Justice Lemuel Shaw of Massachusetts established a similar position in American law by reiterating the importance of either the means' or ends' of the confederacy being unlawful in the landmark case of *Commonwealth v. Hunt*.[8]

The legal consensus broke down, however, when it came to specifying whether the unlawfulness fell under statute or common law. Distinguishing the two was a highly contentious task and ultimately separated the second and third interpretations of conspiracy. Those who remained in the second camp claimed that conspiracy convictions should be limited to statutory offenses. Combinations to commit acts that did not violate statute law when committed by an individual ought not be subject to criminal prosecution when contemplated collectively. This middle position, which required the prospect of a statutory offence before the confederacy was vulnerable to criminal prosecution, was the most commonly advocated definition of conspiracy in both England and the United States. Distinguished treatise writers such as R. S. Wright and Sir William Erle endorsed this interpretation, as did Justices Denman, Green, and Shaw from the bench.[9]

---

[5] State v. Rickey, 4 Halsted 364, 379 (N.J. 1827). In addition to Judge Ford, the early Massachusetts cases also adhered to a strict interpretation of conspiracy. For example, see Commonwealth v. Eastman, 1 Cush. 189 (Mass. 1848); and Commonwealth v. Shedd 7 Cush. 514 (Mass. 1851).

[6] State v. Norton, 3 Zabriskie 33 (N.J. 1850).

[7] Quoted from Carson, *Criminal Conspiracies and Agreements*, 110.

[8] Commonwealth v. Hunt (Mass. 1842). The case is discussed at length later in the chapter.

[9] See Wright, *The Law of Criminal Conspiracies and Agreements*; and Sir William Erle, *On the Law Relating to Trade Unions* (London: Macmillan, 1869). Interestingly, Erle also headed the 1869 Trade Union Commission on the status of English labor law. The commission's report helped shape the 1871 Trade Union Act, which attempted to limit the conspiracy

Cases in which the unlawfulness lay at common law were quite a different matter and were the most controversial of all the conspiracy decisions. Advocates of this third position, such as Chief Justice John Bannister Gibson in Pennsylvania and Justice John Buchanan in Maryland, argued that a combination could be subject to criminal conviction if it violated principles established by common law precedent rather than by statute.[10] For example, common law prohibitions against restraint of trade, prejudice to the public, and infringement of individual liberty often were cited as the basis of unlawfulness when convicting a wide range of combinations of conspiracy. Even actions that would have been legal when committed by an individual could at times become criminal when contemplated collectively. For example, although hissing in a theater was not usually an actionable offence, doing so collectively had been considered grounds for conviction owing to the increased power of collective action. Similarly, one person whistling late at night was inconsequential, but a combination of whistlers might disturb the peace and result in a conspiracy trial.[11] Not all cases in this third category were as extreme as these examples, but even with cases involving the long-standing common law principles prohibiting restraint of trade and infringement of individual liberty, the precise grounds of the offence were extremely vague.

What united advocates of this third definition of conspiracy was the belief that the confederacy itself rather than the contemplated action provided the grounds for prosecution. Hence this view of conspiracy at common law sometimes was referred to as conspiracy per se or as the substantive crime of conspiracy.[12] This third view of conspiracy was clearly the

---

doctrine to unlawful actions. For further discussion of the 1871 act, see Chapter 5. For discussion of Lord Denman's judicial decisions articulating this middle position, see Carson, *Criminal Conspiracies and Agreements*, 110. For Green and Shaw's views, see State v. Norton and Commonwealth v. Hunt (Mass. 1842).

[10] For Gibson's decisions, see Commonwealth *ex rel.* Chew v. Carlisle, Brightly Nisi Prius 36 (Pa. 1821). This case was actually a combination of master ladies cordwainers and thus provides a useful glimpse of the courts' treatment of employers' conspracies. The case is discussed at greater length later in the chapter. Gibson's views of conspiracy can also be seen in Commonwealth v. Mifflin, 5 Watts and Serg. 461 (Pa. 1843); and Hood v. Palm, 8 Pa. St. 237 (Pa. 1848). For Buchanan, see State v. Buchanan, 5 Harris and Jhn. 317 (Md. 1821). For additional cases advancing this view of conspiracy, see State v. Younger, 1 Devereux 357 (N.C. 1827); and Smith v. The People, 25 Ill. 9 (Ill. 1860). For an interesting biographical sketch of Gibson, see Samuel Dreher Matlack, "John Bannister Gibson, 1780–1853," in William Draper Lewis, ed., *Great American Lawyers: A History of the Legal Profession in America* (Philadelphia: John C. Winston, 1908), 3:353–404.

[11] For a case involving hissing in the theater, see Gregory v. Duke of Brunswick, 134 Eng Rep. 866, 1178 (1843–44). For whistling at night, see Sayre, "Criminal Conspiracy," 410. For a more extensive discussion of these controversial cases, see Petro, "Unions and the Southern Courts."

[12] For useful discussions of conspiracy at common law, see Carson, *Criminal Conspiracies and Agreements*, chap. 3; Hans B. Thorelli, *The Federal Antitrust Policy: Origination of an*

most sweeping of the three and left considerable room for judicial discretion when applied to actual disputes.

Perhaps the two most frequently cited authorities used to sustain conspiracy convictions at common law were Serjeant William Hawkins' *Pleas of the Common Crown*, first published in 1716, and the English labor conspiracy of *Rex v. Journeymen Tailors* decided in 1721. In a frequently quoted passage, Hawkins wrote, "there can be no doubt, but that all confederacies whatsoever, wrongfully to prejudice a third person, are highly criminal at common law."[13] The word "wrongfully" was sufficiently ambiguous so as to extend the doctrine beyond statutory offenses to include common law offenses and even immoral acts as well. Similarly, when convicting the twenty Cambridge tailors for conspiring to raise their wages, the court of King's Bench established an equally sweeping definition of the crime. Although the indictment had charged the defendants with violating a statute passed the preceding year that explicitly prohibited tailors from entering an agreement to raise their wages or reduce their hours of work, the court waived the statute and sustained the conviction at common law. In so doing the court declared: "A conspiracy of any kind is illegal, although the matter about which they conspired might have been lawful for them, or any of them, to do, if they had not conspired to do it."[14] Even though the English law reports of the period are considered unreliable and may well provide an inaccurate account of the judgment, the journeymen tailors' case was reaffirmed in several subsequent English decisions and has had a considerable influence on the evolution of the conspiracy doctrine. By establishing conspiracy as a common law crime, the court made way for some of the most expansive and controversial interpretations of the doctrine on both sides of the Atlantic.[15]

American Tradition (London: Allen and Unwin, 1954), chap. 1; Brigham, "Strikes and Boycotts as Indictable Conspiracies at Common Law"; Selfridge, "American Law of Strikes and Boycotts as Crimes"; and Burdick, "Conspiracy as a Crime, and as a Tort."

[13] Quoted from Serjeant William Hawkins, *A Treatise of the Pleas of the Crown; or, a System of the Principal Matters Relating to that Subject, Digested Under Proper Heads* (1716; London: His Majesty's Law-Printers, 1787), vol. 2, chap. 72, sec. 3, 348.

[14] Quoted from Commonwealth v. Pullis, 3 Doc. Hist. 59, 193 (Pa. 1806). ("Doc. Hist." is an abbreviation for John R. Commons, Elrich B. Philips, Eugene A. Gilmore, Helen L. Sumner, and John B. Andrews, eds., *A Documentary History of American Industrial Society* [Cleveland, Ohio: Arthur H. Clark, 1910].)

[15] Hawkins is quoted in a number of antebellum conspiracy trials. For example, see Commonwealth v. Pullis, 196; People v. Melvin, 3 Doc. Hist. 251, 280 (N.Y. 1809). Finally, for a similar expansion of the doctrine to Hawkins, see Bishop's discussion of conspiracy in his *Criminal Law*. Bishop's definitions are quoted in Carson, *Criminal Conspiracies and Agreements*, 120.

The Journeymen Tailors' decision was reaffirmed in the following cases: Rex v. Eccles, 1 Leach C.C. 274 (1783); Rex v. Mawbey, 6 T.R. 619 (1796); and Rex v. Turner, 13 East 227 (1811) all of which declared conspiracy itself to be a substantive crime.

This third definition of conspiracy as a common law crime is especially relevant for studies of labor regulation, as most labor cases fell into this category. In fact, both the English and American labor cases played an important role in expanding the doctrine along these lines in the eighteenth and nineteenth centuries when courts on both sides of the Atlantic began to convict workingmen's combinations for violating common law principles. Restraint of trade, injury to the public, and infringement of individual liberty frequently were identified as the bases for convicting both English and American workingmen for combining. Moreover, labor combinations were especially interesting because the workingmen's actions often would have been lawful when committed by an individual. Demanding higher wages and quitting work generally were considered perfectly legal actions when pursued by individual workers, but when agreed to collectively, both English and American courts often determined that trade had been restrained or liberty infringed and thus found the defendants guilty of criminal conspiracy.[16] Recorder Moses Levy and Chief Justice John Savage are perhaps the best advocates of this broad definition of conspiracy in the Pennsylvania and New York courts. Given the contested nature of the conspiracy doctrine, the early labor trials became an important forum for debating the precise grounds and limits of the common law.[17]

One of the earliest applications of criminal conspiracy to workingmen's combinations in the United States was the case of *Commonwealth v. Pullis*, generally known as the Philadelphia cordwainers' case of 1806.[18] Other state courts soon followed the Pennsylvania example; by 1842, courts in New York, Maryland, Connecticut, and Massachusetts all had tried striking workingmen for criminal conspiracy. In most instances, the defendants were convicted, strikes broken up, and the journeymen's associations at least temporarily disbanded.[19] Unfortunately, it is difficult to identify a complete list of conspiracy trials, as many lower court decisions were not officially reported, especially in the early decades of the nineteenth century. Nevertheless, a number of important trials have been identified documenting that the conspiracy doctrine was the primary legal remedy for regulating industrial conflict between 1806 and 1896.[20]

---

[16] After *Commonwealth v. Pullis* in 1806, American courts no longer considered combination to raise wages in and of itself unlawful. Additional evidence of unlawful means or ends generally was needed to sustain convictions in the subsequent conspiracy trials. For example, see Judge Roberts' charge to the jury in Commonwealth v. Morrow, 4 Doc. Hist. 15, 81 (Pa. 1815).

[17] For Levy's view of conspiracy, see the Pennsylvania case of Commonwealth v. Pullis, 233. For Savage's views, see the New York case of People v. Fisher, 15–16.

[18] See Commonwealth v. Pullis, 58–248. For reference to this being one of the first American labor conspiracy cases, see p. 163.

[19] See Turner, *The Early American Labor Conspiracy Cases*.

[20] Extensive lists of cases have been compiled by Nelles, Turner, and Tomlins. See Nelles, "Commonwealth v. Hunt," 1166–69; Turner, *The Early American Labor Conspiracy Cases*,

The social origins of the labor conspiracy trials lay in early rifts that emerged between master craftsmen and their journeymen in the initial stages of industrialization. Conflict was particularly high in the consumer finishing trades such as shoemaking, tailoring, and carpentry, where traditional methods of production were being reorganized in the late eighteenth and early nineteenth centuries. When displaced journeymen organized to defend their position in the changing economy, district attorneys frequently charged striking journeymen with conspiracy.[21] These changes in antebellum work relations are discussed at greater length in Chapter 3. What is important to note here is that the labor cases reflected, at least in part, the increased tension between masters and their journeymen in the early stages of industrialization. To be sure, the underlying class cleavages and level of class conflict were different before and after the Civil War, at times resulting in important changes in workers' response to judicial intervention over the course of the century.[22] Despite these shifts in labor's reaction, the basic contours of judicial regulation of industrial conflict remained largely unchanged; for almost a hundred years, state courts opposed working-class organization and protest by convicting workers of criminal conspiracy.

Most studies of the labor conspiracy cases to date have linked the changing class relations and the conspiracy convictions of the antebellum decades. The emergence of the American working class in the 1820s and 1830s generally has been considered the most relevant historical context for interpreting the judicial decisions at hand. Although increased conflict between master craftsmen and their journeymen clearly played an important role in bringing these disputes to court, I will argue that class antagonism was not the judiciary's primary motivating concern when convicting workingmen during the antebellum trials. Social context and judicial doctrine were intimately related, but in a different way than previous scholars have claimed.[23] After examining both the legal cases and workingmen's protest in the antebellum decades, I found state courts to be

2–3; and especially Tomlins, *Law, Labor, and Ideology*, chap. 5. However, each of these lists includes only the antebellum cases. For a record of both the ante- and postbellum conspiracy cases in New York and Pennsylvania, see Appendix A. For useful discussion of conspiracy as the principal doctrine in nineteenth-century labor law, see Mason, *Organized Labor and the Law.*

[21] For one of the best discussions linking changes in the organization of work to the conspiracy trials, see Quimby, "The Cordwainers' Protest."

[22] Before the Civil War, workers generally did not contest the conspiracy convictions, while after the war the doctrine was quite politicized. This shift in workers' perceptions of, and response to, judicial intervention in industrial conflicts is discussed at length in Chapters 3 and 4.

[23] Both the legal realists and critical legal scholars have insisted for some time on the importance of linking legal doctrine to the larger social context. Legal doctrine, in and of itself, these scholars have shown, is indeterminate; particular legal decisions can be under-

equally if not more concerned with maintaining judicial authority and a healthy economy in the new republic than they were with containing the increased power of the nascent working class. The preceding revolution and eighteenth-century conceptions of economic growth rather than the subsequent process of industrialization had the greatest impact, I believe, on the antebellum conspiracy trials. Before considering the American cases in detail, a brief review of the prevailing views of early American labor law is needed to highlight the distinctive features of my own interpretation.

TRADITIONAL INTERPRETATIONS OF NINETEENTH-CENTURY LABOR LAW

Existing accounts of nineteenth-century labor law have obscured the courts crucial role in shaping working-class organization and politics in the United States. Two aspects of the standard approach have been particularly misleading. First, the conspiracy doctrine generally has been relegated to the antebellum era, and the critical struggle to repeal the conspiracy doctrine after the Civil War has been ignored. Second, discussions of American labor law have centered around questions of judicial bias and hostility toward labor, leading most scholars to overlook the more subtle impact of judicial regulation on working-class formation and politics.

Typically, scholars divide nineteenth-century American labor law into two eras. The conspiracy doctrine is said to have dominated in the early period from 1806 until 1842, when the doctrine was suspended in the landmark case of *Commonwealth v. Hunt*.[24] The second era is thought to

---

stood only by analyzing the interrelationship between law and society. I am in complete agreement with this general line of argument. My disagreement here is over *which* social relations provided the relevant context for interpreting the antebellum conspiracy trials. For the legal realists' position, see Morton J. Horwitz, *The Transformation of American Law, 1870–1960: The Crisis of Legal Orthodoxy* (New York: Oxford University Press 1992), chaps. 6, 7. For discussion of critical legal studies, see Robert W. Gordon, "Critical Legal Histories," 36 *Stanford Law Review* 57 (1984); Morton J. Horwitz, "The Changing Common Law," 9 *Dalhousie Law Journal* 55 (1984); Roberto Mangabeira Unger, *The Critical Legal Studies Movement* (Cambridge, Mass.: Harvard University Press, 1986); Duncan Kennedy, "The Structure of Blackstone's Commentaries," 28 *Buffalo Law Review* 205 (1979); and articles in Allan C. Hutchinson, ed., *Critical Legal Studies* (Totowa, N.J.: Rowman and Littlefield, 1989).

[24] Commonwealth v. Hunt (Mass. 1842). Even the best accounts of criminal conspiracy in the United States still limit their discussion to the antebellum cases. For example, see the following works: Morris, "Criminal Conspiracy and Early Labor Combinations in New York"; Sayre, "Criminal Conspiracy"; Quimby, "The Cordwainers' Protest"; Holt, "Labour Conspiracy Cases in the United States"; Turner, *Early American Labor Conspiracy Cases*; Levy, *The Law of the Commonwealth and Chief Justice Shaw*; and Nelles, "Commonwealth v. Hunt." Important exceptions have been Witte, "Early American Labor Cases," which despite the title does discuss some of the postwar trials; Kuritz, "Criminal Conspiracy Cases"; and Hovenkamp, "Labor Conspiracies in American Law."

have begun with adoption of the labor injunction in the 1880s and to run through to the Norris–La Guardia Act of 1932. Thus, the standard periodization of nineteenth-century labor law generally confines conspiracy convictions to the antebellum decades. Some scholars have noted that workers continued to be convicted of conspiracy after the *Hunt* victory, but have not attempted a more extensive reevaluation of labor law in light of the postwar convictions.[25]

The conspiracy doctrine, however, did not die with *Hunt*, but was revived with considerable vigor for three decades after the Civil War. Recognizing the *two* waves of conspiracy convictions suggests that we distinguish at least three eras of nineteenth-century labor law. The first era continues to encompass the early conspiracy trials in the years between 1806 and 1842. A new second era of conspiracy convictions must be recognized based on the resurgence of conspiracy prosecutions between 1865 and 1896. The shift in legal remedy from conspiracy to the labor injunction in the mid-1880s marks the third era of nineteenth-century labor law, which continues through the passage of the Norris–La Guardia Act in 1932. Attending to the second wave of conspiracy convictions in the postwar decades not only helps to fill in the neglected middle decades of judicial regulation but also provides essential data for examining labor's changing relationship to the state during the nineteenth century. Chapters 3 and 4 take up labor's response in detail and show how the postwar conspiracy convictions played a decisive role in shaping working-class formation in the United States. The task here is to lay out the broad contours of the doctrine and to identify more carefully the legal arguments used to sustain judicial regulation of labor under the two waves of conspiracy prosecutions—what, in short, motivated courts to convict workers during the nineteenth-century conspiracy trials.

The central concern for many previous scholars has been to explore the underlying class allegiance of the judiciary in its role as mediator of industrial conflict in the United States. The persistent conclusion of both old and new research has been that the conspiracy convictions clearly reflected the long-standing hostility of American courts to organized labor. For example, in one of the most recent analyses of the antebellum conspiracy cases, Wythe Holt sums up his discussion of conspiracy as follows: "It is important to recognize that the law rarely recognizes the point of view of the worker. Class bias does exist in the law." In a similar vein, Christopher Tomlins concludes his review of nineteenth-century labor law as follows: "What the courts objected to, seemingly, was not the spread of organization per se, but the spread of labor organization in particular." For most

---

[25] Witte, "Early American Labor Cases"; and James McCauley Landis and Marcus Manoff, *Cases on Labor Law* (Chicago: The Foundation Press, 1942), chap. 1.

scholars of nineteenth-century labor law, the antebellum conspiracy convictions provide important evidence of the pervasive class bias of the American legal system.[26]

Three aspects of the antebellum conspiracy trials generally have been identified to substantiate claims of judicial bias. First, several scholars argue that antebellum judges revealed their class allegiance when they accepted the language and arguments of prosecution attorneys over those of the defense counsel. In so doing, judges supposedly legitimated the entrepreneurial vision of employers while denying the conflicting claims and economic interests of the working class.[27] Second, the class bias of the courts is further reinforced, many scholars claim, through a comparison of nineteenth-century labor and corporation law; while the courts prohibited workers from joining unions, employers were permitted to act collectively. The Pennsylvania case of *Commonwealth v. Carlisle* is said to provide a telling comparison with the antebellum labor trials because it involved one of the few prosecutions of *master* craftsmen for criminal conspiracy. Judge Gibson's remarks make clear, so the argument runs, the courts' inequitable treatment of workers' and employers' collective action. The Pennsylvania court accepted both business competition and the defensive nature of the master shoemakers' combination as ameliorating factors on their criminal intent even though similar arguments had been rejected by state courts in earlier labor trials.[28]

Finally, some theorists look to antebellum workers' protest as further confirmation of judicial hostility toward labor. The extensive demonstrations against the New York convictions in *People v. Fisher* and *People v. Faulkner* dominate these interpretations. By calling mass meetings in the park to protest the unjust rulings, burning effigies of Judges Savage and Ogden Edwards for their part in the trials, and calling for creation of an independent political party, workingmen made clear their opposition to

[26] For the Holt quotation, see Holt, "Labour Conspiracy Cases in the United States," 656. For Tomlins' remark, see Tomlins, *The State and the Unions*, 31. I should note that the central focus of Tomlins' book is the period from 1880 through 1960, in which he develops a more subtle account of the interaction of labor and the law. Tomlins also has qualified his claims concerning judicial bias in his more recent study of the labor conspiracy cases where he argues that containing working-class conflict only came to dominate the conspiracy trials in the 1830s. See Tomlins, *Law, Labor, and Ideology*, chaps. 5, 6. Class-based arguments also can be found in the following sources: Turner, *The Early American Labor Conspiracy Cases*, 31–57; Sayre, "Criminal Conspiracy," 415, 427; and Steinfeld, "The Philadelphia Cordwainers' Case of 1806."

[27] See Holt, "Labour Conspiracy Cases in the United States," 619–25; and Turner, *The Early American Labor Conspiracy Cases*, 31–57.

[28] See discussion of *Commonwealth v. Carlisle* in Sayre, "Criminal Conspiracy," 414–16, 420; and Holt, "Labour Conspiracy Cases in the United States," 627–29. For more general claims about the unequal treatment of labor organizations by the courts, see Tomlins, *The State and the Unions*, pt. 1, esp. pp. 30–31, 33, 43.

the *Fisher* and *Faulkner* rulings. Workers were well aware, many scholars claim, of the class bias of the courts and mobilized to contest this unjust use of judicial power.[29]

Existing accounts of the antebellum conspiracy trials have gone a considerable distance toward explaining the origins of the conspiracy trials and have enabled us to see how increased conflict between masters and journeymen that accompanied industrialization also fueled the first wave of conspiracy prosecutions. Despite these insights, however, I have found the traditional accounts of the early labor cases to be too narrow. By focusing almost exclusively on the increased conflict between masters and journeymen, they have overlooked other, more important, influences on judicial behavior in the antebellum conspiracy trials. Indeed, when I looked more closely at the evidence used to sustain the class analysis, I found all three claims concerning judicial language, corporate regulation, and workers' protest to be inadequate and in need of review. Briefly outlining the limits of the prevailing view opens the way for an alternative explanation of judicial behavior during the antebellum conspiracy trials.

It is certainly true that prosecution attorneys explicitly raised the specter of diminished manufacturing and trade as grounds for restricting workers' collective action. Moreover, several judges did adopt the prosecution arguments and instructed juries to take questions of economic growth into consideration when deciding the defendants' fate. However, in the section that follows we will see that attention to questions of economic growth did not simply reflect the courts' pro-employer bias. Instead, I argue that the economic language and categories used in the antebellum trials were shaped primarily by eighteenth-century assumptions which viewed economic growth as a public good rather than a private interest of the employing class. Maintaining a healthy pattern of economic growth was important, but the significance of the courts' economic arguments needs to be reexamined.

Similarly, arguments about the courts' inequitable treatment of unions and corporations have oversimplified the pattern of state regulation in the antebellum decades; even though employers' combinations were rarely indicted for conspiracy and thus were not subject to exactly the same form of judicial regulation as workingmen's associations, nor were corporations simply left to their own devices. Legislative charters and the associated doctrine of ultra vires rather than conspiracy were used to regulate employers' collective action.[30] To be sure, in the last decade and a half of the

[29] See Tomlins, *Law, Labor, and Ideology*, chap. 5; and Holt, "Labour Conspiracy Cases in the United States," 593–94, 634–36.

[30] Before the Civil War, the act of incorporation was considered a special privilege to be granted to particular associations through individual legislative charters that specified the limits of their corporate authority. Should the corporation abuse this public trust, its charter

nineteenth century, when the Supreme Court recognized the corporation as a person and began to expand the legal definitions of property rights, scholars' claims about the unequal treatment of labor and capital have more force. Employers' combinations increasingly were exempt from judicial regulation while labor unions only secured similar protection a half-century later during the New Deal.[31] In the antebellum decades, however, both employers' and workingmen's associations were regarded with equal suspicion and were subject to different but nevertheless similarly restrictive regulation by the state.

Finally, arguments that look to workers' protest as confirmation of judicial bias also miss the mark. Although workers indeed mobilized to protest some of the antebellum convictions and by the mid-1830s identified Judges Savage and Edwards as hostile to their interests, it is important to acknowledge the limits of workers' attack on the courts. For example, when workers established labor unions and political parties in the 1820s and 1830s, they did not make repeal of the conspiracy doctrine a part of their platform. In fact, the programs and proceedings of these organizations contain very little discussion of the conspiracy trials. Instead, as we will see in Chapter 3, workingmen's associations were more interested in questions of education and financial reform and in securing the position of skilled craftsmen during the reorganization of their trades. In short, workingmen were primarily concerned with issues other than judicial regulation; protest against the conspiracy trials simply did not translate into an organized campaign for legal reform.

Even at the height of workers' protest over the *Fisher* and *Faulkner* trials, when conspiracy convictions clearly were the object of workers' ire, it is important to look more closely at the terms workers used to voice

---

could be revoked or the corporation sued under the doctrine of ultra vires. For discussion of nineteenth-century corporation law, see Morton J. Horwitz, "Santa Clara Revisited: The Development of Corporate Theory," 88 *West Virginia Law Review* 173 (1985–1986); Herbert Hovenkamp, "The Classical Corporation in American Legal Thought," 76 *Georgetown Law Journal* 1593 (1988); Willard Hurst, *The Legitimacy of the Business Corporation in the Law of the United States, 1780–1970* (Charlottesville: University Press of Virginia, 1970); Morton J. Horwitz, *The Transformation of American Law, 1780–1860* (Cambridge, Mass.: Harvard University Press, 1977), chap. 4; Lawrence M. Friedman, *A History of American Law* (New York: Simon and Schuster, 1973), chap. 8; Michael Barzelay and Rogers M. Smith, "The One Best System? A Political Analysis of Neoclassical Institutionalist Perspectives on the Modern Corporation," in Warren J. Samuels and Arthur S. Miller, eds., *Corporations and Society: Power and Responsibility* (New York: Greenwood Press, 1987); and Haggai Hurvitz, "American Labor Law and the Doctrine of Entrepreneurial Property Rights: Boycotts, Courts, and the Juridical Reorientation of 1886–1895," *Industrial Relations Law Journal* 8, 3 (1986): 307–61.

[31] See Horwitz, "Santa Clara Revisited"; and Hurvitz, "American Labor Law and the Doctrine of Entrepreneurial Property Rights."

their discontent. Interestingly, workingmen continued to view the courts through modified eighteenth-century assumptions about how to maintain a healthy republic. Thus, rather than assailing Judges Savage and Edwards as pawns of the ruling class, antebellum protesters frequently railed against unhealthy monopolies and corrupt systems of finance that were undermining the republic at its core. Workingmen clearly objected to the current state of affairs, but the worldview they used to explain the nature and source of their problems continued to be shaped, to a considerable extent, by established assumptions about economic and social relations rather than by explanations centered on class struggle.[32]

Many limitations to traditional views of conspiracy stem from the common practice of removing labor cases from their original historical and legal context. Labor conspiracies, for the most part, have *not* been considered alongside other offenses also covered by the common law doctrine of criminal conspiracy, such as conspiracies to cheat and defraud, or in restraint of trade, or to slander. Instead, the labor cases have been extracted from their historical context and examined in light of subsequent developments in American labor law. The implicit context for most discussions of the early labor conspiracies has been the evolution of workers' industrial rights from conspiracy through the labor injunction to the Wagner Act, rather than as one example of a larger class of conspiracy cases. Evidence of the isolation of labor cases from the broader legal context of conspiracy can be seen in the classic collection of antebellum conspiracy trials compiled by John R. Commons and his associates.[33] The collection is invaluable and yet quite misleading. The problem stems from the fact that only labor disputes are included in the collection. No other conspiracy cases are presented, even though many *non*labor disputes centered on the same legal issues and were decided under the same common law doctrine of criminal conspiracy. This isolation of labor conspiracies from similar cases, I believe, has distorted interpretations of the first phase of American labor law.

Antebellum labor conspiracies take on quite a different appearance when considered in light of the broader conspiracy doctrine. Shifting the field of comparison, from labor cases to conspiracy cases more generally, changed my conception of the early labor convictions in two ways. First,

[32] For example, see the description of the New York parade protesting the *Fisher* trial of Geneva tailors quoted in Wilentz, *Chants Democratic*, 290. Rather than targeting the courts directly, workingmen attacked banks, party politicians, and chartered corporations, and denounced the master tailors' combination as unrepublican. See also the protest against the *Faulkner* trial in the Loco-focos' Correspondence Committee's address in the summer of 1836. Again, the persistence of modified eighteenth-century assumptions can be seen in this response to the *Faulkner* conviction. The address is reprinted in full in the *New York Evening Post*, 23 July 1836, p. 2, cols. 4, 5. For further discussion of these issues, see Chapter 3.

[33] Commons et al., *Documentary History*, vols. 3, 4.

when placed in their original legal context, labor convictions no longer appeared so inequitable, as conspiracy cases as a whole were treated with remarkable comparability by state courts. To be sure, workingmen were convicted by the courts, but most forms of combination were considered dangerous and were thought to need special government regulation. Judicial opposition was not reserved exclusively for workingmen's associations, nor did state courts punish labor combinations more harshly than other forms of conspiracy before the Civil War. Second, setting aside notions of judicial bias and reconsidering the labor cases in the context of the early national period allowed alternative explanations of judicial behavior to come to the fore. Specifically, I have found that the antebellum conspiracy trials were filled with references to two of the most pressing issues in early national politics, namely, how to maintain the continuity of common law after political independence and how to promote a republican pattern of economic growth in the new nation. A more satisfying account of the labor convictions must pay greater attention to these neglected issues and explain why they came to a head during the antebellum conspiracy trials.

THE ANTEBELLUM CONSPIRACY TRIALS RECONSIDERED: RETHINKING QUESTIONS OF JUDICIAL AUTHORITY AND ECONOMIC GROWTH

Although all branches of government were reorganized with political independence, the Revolution raised especially difficult issues for traditional conceptions of judicial authority. In the eighteenth century, judicial authority had been derived from a conception of common law doctrine as the embodiment of natural law, independent of political will. Within this conception of the common law, judges were neutral arbiters applying legal principles to particular cases. Partisan policymaking was a task for the legislature rather than the judiciary, leaving the courts to find and not make law.[34] After the Revolution, natural law conceptions of common law came under attack. The Revolution cast a shadow over American courts and legal doctrine, which were no longer seen as neutral institutions applying timeless legal principles, but rather were viewed by many as undesirable remnants of British authority.

In short, the central legal problem after the Revolution was to determine the role the courts were to play in the new republic. At the end of the eighteenth century, a number of questions remained unanswered: How were the courts to reconcile political independence and the common law? If legal doctrine was not founded on natural law, what was the basis of judicial authority? Finally, if the legal system was to be reorganized, how might this be done along republican lines? These questions were debated

[34] See Edward S. Corwin, *The 'Higher Law' Background of American Constitutional Law* (Ithaca, N.Y.: Cornell University Press, 1959).

both inside and outside the legal profession and framed the legal issues for the antebellum conspiracy trials. Debates over convictions at common law, which occupied much of the testimony during the conspiracy trials, were by no means abstract arguments over legal doctrine. On the contrary, convictions and acquittals carried with them very different implications for the nature and extent of judicial power.[35]

Questions of judicial authority came to a head in the conspiracy trials precisely because convictions often were sustained at common law. Thus, conspiracy cases in general, and labor conspiracies in particular, provided a perfect opportunity for critics to question natural law arguments, and to pose alternative views of judicial authority. Throughout the antebellum cases, judges and attorneys alike presented juries with the choice of accepting or rejecting the common law. If striking journeymen were convicted of conspiracy, American courts would be upholding the legitimacy of common law crimes and thereby reaffirming natural law conceptions of common law. Sustaining the authority of English convictions in American courts carried with it an implicit confirmation of expansive conceptions of judicial authority in the new republic. On the other hand, should the courts acquit the journeymen, the viability of common law principles would be undermined, and traditional conceptions of an independent legal system would be called into question.[36]

[35] For an interesting account of the contested nature of judicial authority in the early national period, see Richard E. Ellis, *The Jeffersonian Crisis: Courts and Politics in the Young Republic* (New York: Norton, 1971). Conflicting views of the appropriate role of the courts in the late eighteenth and early nineteenth centuries also can be seen in the repeated attacks on the judiciary, such as Shays' Rebellion in Massachusetts in 1786, the Pennsylvania Whiskey Insurrection of 1794, the Kentucky Judicial Insurrection of 1823–1824, and the New York Anti-Rent Strikes in 1839–1846. For discussion of these events, see the following: Francis R. Aumann, *The Changing American Legal System: Some Selected Phases* (Columbus: Ohio State University Press, 1940), chap. 8; Lawrence M. Friedman, "Law Reform in Historical Perspective," 13 *St. Louis University Law Journal* 351 (1969); Maxwell Bloomfield, "Lawyers and Public Criticism: Challenge and Response in Nineteenth-Century America," *American Journal of Legal History* 15, 4 (October 1971); 269–77; Elizabeth K. Henderson, "The Attack on the Judiciary in Pennsylvania, 1800–1810," *Pennsylvania Magazine of History and Biography* 61, 2 (April 1937): 113–36; Gerard W. Gawalt, "Sources of Anti-Lawyer Sentiment in Massachusetts, 1740–1840," *American Journal of Legal History* 14, 4 (October 1970); 283–307; and Edward P. Cheyney, "The Anti-Rent Movement and the Constitution of 1846," in Alexander C. Flick, ed., *History of the State of New York*, (New York: Columbia University Press, 1934), vol. 6. For the legal profession's perspective, see Charles M. Cook, *The American Codification Movement: A Study of Antebellum Legal Reform* (Westport, Conn.: Greenwood Press, 1981).

[36] Juries, rather than courts, actually convicted workingmen of conspiracy. However, when charging the jury, judges usually left little doubt as to the court's opinion on the outcome of the case. For the most part, juries followed the judges' directives in the antebellum conspiracy trials. One exception in which the jury acquitted workers despite a very clear directive from the judge to convict was *People v. Cooper* (N.Y. 1836), reprinted in Commons et al., *Documentary History* 4:277–312.

It is possible to imagine other ways in which state courts might have resolved the tension between common law doctrine and political independence. There is no a priori reason why the courts had to frame the issue so starkly as an either/or choice between accepting and rejecting the common law. For example, when instructing juries, American judges might have rejected English labor conspiracy convictions as controlling precedents owing to their unreliable origins and acquitted American workingmen of conspiracy charges without rejecting the common law in toto. Although an alternative response was possible, it was not the path followed by American courts. Instead, state courts seemed unwilling to concede even a partial retreat from English law.

The courts' extreme position, in which common law principles and dubious precedents were sustained, can be understood more easily when we consider how questions of judicial authority intersected questions of economic growth. Although judicial authority and the continuity of common law might have been maintained through a more moderate policy in which some aspects of English law were rejected, opting for the stronger position and convicting workingmen of conspiracy enabled state courts to address questions of economic growth at the same time. Specifically, we will see that although the conspiracy cases originated in conflicts between master craftsmen and their protesting journeymen, when these disputes came before state courts they were embedded in a larger set of political debates over how best to sustain trade and prosperity in the new republic.

To be sure, defense and prosecution arguments in the conspiracy trials clearly represented opposing sides on the question of workers' right to organize, and there is some evidence that judges too were aware of, and sought to limit, the increased industrial conflict in the antebellum decades.[37] Questions of class conflict, however, have been overdrawn. In

---

[37] An awareness of the increased working-class organization can be seen at moments in several of the antebellum trials. For example, see defense counsel arguments in *Commonwealth v. Morrow* where Mr. Forward asked the jury "whence comes this recent dread of associations among the laboring classes! do the master manufacturers in our cities and large towns, begin to feel that spirit which pervades the same class of men in Great Britain?" Forward also bemoaned the "perpetual conflict" that now exists between employers and their journeymen. See Commonwealth v. Morrow, 64, 65. Similarly, in *People v. Faulkner*, Judge Edwards remarked that "[t]he combination had been of so extensive a character and created so great an excitement that it might possibly have involved some persons for whom the jury might directly or indirectly feel some interest—but the court and jury must raise themselves above all feelings of friendship or sympathy and be true to their oaths, and the well being of the public at large; and it was impossible that the acts of the defendants could escape with impunity unless the court and jury violate their duty in order to take them out of the operation of the law." Quoted from, People v. Faulkner, 324. See also 323, 330. Finally, perhaps the most explicit references to class conflict can be seen in the initial ruling in *Commonwealth v. Hunt*, where Judge Thacher argued that the new workingmen's associations "would tend directly to array them [laborer and employer] against each other, and to convulse the social

fact, they remained a minor refrain throughout the antebellum trials. Only after the Civil War were questions of judicial authority and economic growth eclipsed by the desire to contain the newfound power of the working class.

The Philadelphia Cordwainers' Case and Antebellum Legal Arguments

The Philadelphia Cordwainers' case of 1806 provides an excellent point of departure for rethinking the antebellum labor cases, as many additional themes can be seen in this well-reported trial. George Pullis and seven other cordwainers (shoemakers) appeared before the Philadelphia Mayor's Court under indictment for combining and conspiring to raise their wages. Recorder Moses Levy presided at the trial.[38] By examining the legal arguments advanced in court we will see, first, that disagreements over the origins of the conspiracy law were, at bottom, struggles over whether to maintain the continuity of common law in the new republic. Second, looking more closely at the language and categories used to describe the economic consequences of the cordwainers' combination sheds new light on the relationship between antebellum judicial behavior and the emerging question of class.

Joseph Hopkinson and Jared Ingersoll presented the prosecution's case, which rested on the twin concerns of legal continuity and economic growth. First, they asserted the continuing authority of the common law by declaring the conspiracy doctrine, as stated in Hawkins' *Pleas of the Crown*, to be in force in Pennsylvania courts. "It will be seen," Hopkinson argued, "that the mere combination to raise wages is considered an offence at common law: . . . All combinations to regulate the price of commodities is against the law."[39] Moreover, Hopkinson continued, English courts had extended the conspiracy doctrine to workingmen's combinations in two important cases, *Rex v. Journeymen Tailors of Cambridge* and *Tubwomen v. The Brewers of London*. Thus, the Pennsylvania cordwainers' combination clearly fell within the bounds of the conspiracy law.[40] Hopkinson justified obedience to the common law by appealing to arguments of con-

---

system to its core." Quoted from Commonwealth v. Hunt, Thacher's Crim. Cases 609, 654 (Mass. 1890). Although there was some awareness of the emerging working class, these remarks are infrequent and are not representative of the prevailing view of workingmen's associations in the first three decades of the nineteenth century.

[38] A complete transcript of the trial can be found in Commons et al., *Documentary History*, 3:58–248. For a summary of the indictment as a conspiracy to raise their wages, see the title page of the trial report.

[39] Commonwealth v. Pullis, 140.

[40] Commonwealth v. Pullis, 140–43, 223–24.

stitutional authority. "Why a combination in such a case is criminal, will not be difficult to explain: We live under a government composed of a constitution and laws . . . and every man is obliged to obey the constitution, and the laws made under it." The American constitution entailed, prosecution attorneys argued, wider claims as to the authority of law.[41]

In addition, Ingersoll, in particular, tried to underscore the illegality of the cordwainers' combination by drawing attention to the compulsion that accompanied such undesirable collective action: "We charge a combination, by means of rewards and punishments, threats, insults, starvings and beatings, to compel the employers to accede to terms, they the journeymen present and dictate. If the journeymen cordwainers may do this, so may the employers; the journeymen carpenters, brick-layers, butchers, farmers, and the whole community will be formed into hostile confederacies, the prelude and certain forerunner of bloodshed and civil war."[42] Voluntary association might well be lawful, but as soon as compulsion was used to gain their end, the confederates clearly fell within the bounds of the conspiracy law.

At times, when characterizing the ominous nature of the cordwainers' association, prosecution attorneys argued that the court ought to protect the "rights" and "liberty" of other journeymen. For the most part, however, these more individualistic categories were not yet the principal terms of debate at the *Pullis* trial. Instead, the primary legal arguments continued to be framed in terms of the public welfare and authority of law. In fact, Hopkinson explicitly asserted the importance of community interest over individual liberty when introducing his argument to the jury as follows: "The cause is an important one. . . . It is said on the one side to involve an important principle of civil liberty, that men in their transactions with others, have a right to judge in their own behalf, and value their labour as they please: on the contrary, we shall shew [sic] that the claims and conduct of the defendants are contrary to just government, equal laws, and that due subordination to which every member of the community is bound to submit . . . all these are essentially connected with the present prosecution."[43] The defendants' rights and duties, according to Hopkinson, did not inhere in them as individual citizens but rather were derived, at least in part, from the social norms and practices of the community they inhabited.

Finally, when making the last argument of the case, Ingersoll explicitly rebutted the defense counsel's claims that the authority of the common law had been broken with the revolutionary war. "The counsel are right in their

[41] Quoted from Commonwealth v. Pullis, 135. See also 142 and Ingersoll's argument at 223–24.

[42] Commonwealth v. Pullis, 221.

[43] For reference to liberty and individual rights, see Commonwealth v. Pullis, 142, 208, 212. For Hopkinson's remark, see 132.

plan of defence; there is a direct collision between the law and the conduct of the defendants . . . which . . . is to controul? is the question."[44] The answer for Ingersoll was perfectly clear; he completed his argument by reaffirming his "love" for the common law and by pondering the recent attacks on this most important element of the American heritage: "Whence comes this enmity to the common law? It is of mushroom growth. Look through the journals of congress during the revolutionary war; you will find it claimed as the great charter of liberty; as the best birthright and noblest of inheritance. Caesar A. Rodney, the revolutionary patriot [and defense counsel at the trial], hazarded his life to secure and perpetuate the blessing."[45] Ingersoll, it seems, was quite perplexed by the recent attacks on the common law. Surely those who fought for independence should understand that the security of the new community could not be maintained if the common law was abandoned and "clubs and self-constituted societies" were allowed to "usurp power" and "abridge the rights of others to extend their own." "An aristocracy," Ingersoll concluded, "is not the less detestable, that it moves in a small sphere."[46]

As for the prosecution's views concerning economic growth, Hopkinson made the most extensive argument on this score. First he declared Philadelphia to be "a large, encreasing, manufacturing city. Those best acquainted with our situation," Hopkinson continued, "believe that manufactures will, bye and by [sic], become one of its chief means of support." However, combinations of journeymen were "break[ing] up the manufactories" and destroying Philadelphia's "export trade." If this were allowed to persist, Hopkinson claimed, the journeymen's societies would undermine the economic welfare of the entire "community." These "secret clubs" and dangerous associations must be contained by the courts or there would be no way for Philadelphia to compete successfully with New York and Baltimore in sustaining a healthy pattern of economic growth. It was both "proper" and important, Hopkinson concluded, for the jury to protect both the continuity of the common law and "the flourishing state of our manufactures" by following the English courts and convicting the striking cordwainers of criminal conspiracy.[47]

Thus, economic interest and injury, even from the prosecution's point of view, were considered to be collective rather than individual goods. The dominant language of economic arguments at the *Pullis* trial was not that of market competition, individual interest, and private gain. Instead, eco-

[44] Commonwealth v. Pullis, 222.
[45] Commonwealth v. Pullis, 222.
[46] See Commonwealth v. Pullis, 206–07.
[47] For Hopkinson's economic argument, see Commonwealth v. Pullis, 136–37, 142. For Ingersoll's economic argument, see 208.

nomic growth was considered a public good and an integral component of city welfare. The "good of the community," the "flourishing commerce of the city," and the "public welfare" were the dominant terms of analysis and the health of the city the object to be preserved. To the extent that competition was a factor in the legal debate, the contending forces generally were cities and towns rather than individuals or social classes.[48]

The public dimension of antebellum economic arguments can be seen particularly clearly in the prosecution's conception of economic benefits and harms. For example, Hopkinson carefully pointed out that the master cordwainers were not simply protecting their own economic interests, but were trying to defend the welfare of the community as a whole. "It must be plain to you, that the master employers have no particular interest in the thing . . . if they pay higher wages, you must pay higher for the articles. They, in truth, are protecting the community. . . . They have no interest to serve in the prosecution; they have no vindictive passions to gratify . . . they merely stand as the guardians of the community from imposition and rapacity."[49] Private gain was not yet accepted as a legitimate interest that ought to be protected by the court. Instead, the masters' actions had to be seen as benefiting the community as a whole.

Similarly, Hopkinson characterized the public nature of the economic injury that followed the cordwainers' combination by drawing an analogy with a monopoly boycott in the baking trade. "Suppose the bakers were to combine, and agree not to sell a loaf of bread, only for one week, under a dollar, would not this be an injury to the community? . . . Certainly it would: and few men, unless their pockets were filled with money, could support it for any considerable length of time. All combinations to regulate the price of commodities is against the law. Extend the case to butchers, and all others who deal in articles of prime necessity, and the good policy of

---

[48] The phrases are taken from Commonwealth v. Pullis, 136–37, 142, 208, 214, 229. To be sure, there were some references to liberty, individualism, and legal rights in the *Pullis* trial. For examples, see Commonwealth v. Pullis, 142–43. However, these more familiar terms should not obscure the significant presence of the more collectivist language that also pervaded the early conspiracy trials. For elaboration of eighteenth-century views of economic relations in the secondary literature, see E. P. Thompson, "The Moral Economy of the English Crowd in the Eighteenth Century," *Past and Present* 50 (February 1971): 76–136; Stedman Jones, "Rethinking Chartism"; and Smail, "New Languages for Labour and Capital." In the American context, see J. E. Crowley, *This Sheba Shelf: The Conceptualization of Economic Life in Eighteenth-Century America* (Baltimore: Johns Hopkins University Press, 1974); and Thorelli, *The Federal Antitrust Policy*, chap. 1.

[49] Commonwealth v. Pullis, 137–38. For similar arguments denying masters' personal interests in the outcome of the conspiracy trials, see Commonwealth v. Morrow, 85, where Judge Roberts claimed that masters cannot continuously raise the price of goods because, if they did, these same items would be readily supplied from afar, thus leading to their own business ruin. See also Commonwealth v. Carlisle, 41, where Judge Gibson argued that competition will always break up masters' combinations to depress wages.

the law is then apparent."[50] Prosecution attorneys in the *Melvin, Fisher,* and *Hunt* trials all drew the same analogy between workingmen's combinations and a bakers' boycott.[51] District Attorney Riker elaborated the public hardship argument with particular force in the New York case of *People v. Melvin* in 1809.

> Suppose all the bakers in New-York were to refuse to bake till they received an exorbitant remuneration. . . . What will become of the poor, whose case the counsel takes so feelingly to heart? The rich will, by their money, find supplies; but what will be the sufferings of the poor classes? . . .
>
> There are duties which every man owes to the society of which he enjoys the benefits and protection, which never can be detailed, but must be regulated by acknowledged principles of judicature. A baker, therefore, who lives by the supply of the public, shall not abuse that public by a sudden interested and malicious withholding of his ordinary supplies; . . . if he combines with others to do so, he is guilty of a distinct and well defined offence, that of an unlawful conspiracy, for which he is indictable and punishable.[52]

The bakers' analogy was used repeatedly in the antebellum trials in order to convince the jury that injuries to an individual business or trade quickly became "offenses against the whole community" and as such were "subject to public prosecution."[53]

The defense counsel, Caesar Rodney and Walter Franklin, engaged in a lengthy critique of the prosecution arguments and advocated an alternative interpretation of English conspiracy law. First, as to the boundaries of the doctrine and the related question of judicial authority, Rodney asserted that the prosecution had misunderstood the original basis of the English convictions and as a consequence had misrepresented their authority to the Philadelphia court. Combination itself was not a criminal offense; rather, the conspiracy doctrine was only applicable to combinations engaged in activities that were themselves unlawful. The prosecution's definition of conspiracy was untenable, as it provided no grounds for distinguishing between legal and criminal associations. Unless the action was itself indictable, there was no way of distinguishing unions, church meetings, funerals, and dances: "a country dance would be criminal, a cotillion unlawful, even a minuet a conspiracy; and nothing but a hornpipe or a solo would be stepped with impunity!"[54] Differences between unions and dances could

---

[50] Quoted from Commonwealth v. Pullis, 140.

[51] See People v. Melvin (N.Y. 1809), 313–14, 327, and Sampson's reply at 359; People v. Fisher, 19; and Commonwealth v. Hunt (Mass. 1842), 134. See also Judge Gibson's reference to the bakers' boycott in Commonwealth v. Carlisle, 40.

[52] Quoted from People v. Melvin (N.Y. 1809), 313–14.

[53] People v. Melvin (N.Y. 1809), 314.

[54] Commonwealth v. Pullis, 183.

only be discerned, Rodney argued, by recognizing the statutory origins of many English conspiracy cases and limiting the authority of English precedents accordingly.[55]

The prosecution's mistake, the defense concluded, had been to consider all English conspiracies to be common law crimes, whereas, in fact, a large number of English convictions had rested on violation of existing statute law. As a consequence, several precedents cited by the prosecution were simply irrelevant to the Philadelphia case. *Rex v. Journeymen Tailors*, for example, did not demonstrate that combinations to raise wages were indictable at common law as the prosecution claimed. On the contrary, the Cambridge tailors had been found guilty because their association violated an earlier English statute that explicitly prohibited tailors from raising their wages.[56] Violation of the statute, not the common law, provided the illegality necessary to make the tailors' combination indictable. Without the statute, the tailors' actions would not have been criminal.

Identifying the origins of *labor* conspiracy convictions was especially important, the defense continued, because of the extensive statutory regulation of labor in England. Ever since the Plague, English workers had been subject to innumerable laws so that many English conspiracies were statutory offenses rather than common law crimes. As these statutes had not been adopted by American legislatures, the English cases had no authority in American courts. Rather than considering English conspiracy cases to be controlling precedents, the English convictions must be reevaluated, the defense argued, in light of their statutory origins to determine which, if any, were applicable in the United States.[57]

The defense counsel's attack on English precedents called into question the common law and the autonomy it afforded American courts. All legal doctrine, according to the defense, including common law crimes, ultimately rested on political choices embodied in statute law. The defense's conception of legal doctrine had considerable appeal to a number of antebellum legal reformers who also wanted to limit the discretionary power of the courts. Not surprisingly, then, two of the most noted antebellum codification reformers, William Sampson and Robert Rantoul, Jr., acted as defense counsel in subsequent conspiracy trials.[58] In all the antebellum conspiracy cases, and in the cases argued by Sampson and Rantoul in

[55] Commonwealth v. Pullis, 152–62, 186–87.

[56] Commonwealth v. Pullis, 193–95.

[57] Commonwealth v. Pullis, 152, 156–62, 192, 195–96. But see also People v. Melvin (N.Y. 1809), 256–72; and Commonwealth v. Hunt (Mass. 1840), 623, and (Mass. 1842), 117.

[58] William Sampson advocated for the New York Cordwainers in *People v. Melvin* (N.Y. 1809), and Robert Rantoul, Jr., defended the Boston bootmakers in the historic case of *Commonwealth v. Hunt* in 1840 and 1842.

particular, defense attorneys equated acquittal with a more general attack on the common law and the assertion of statutory law as a more democratic legal system.

As for the prosecution's economic argument, the defense's response was more succinct. They, too, believed that economic prosperity was vital to Philadelphia's future and "must be the sincere wish of us all," but disagreed over how it was to be secured.[59] If Philadelphia was really to rival New York and Baltimore, it had to ensure that skilled workmen were not lured away with higher wages or treated too severely by the Philadelphia courts. Deleterious consequences would surely follow the cordwainers' conviction, as skilled workingmen would leave Philadelphia for more hospitable locations: "New York and Baltimore will gladly receive them, as they take care to profit by every other advantage which our inattention or narrow policy throws into their way. You are not ignorant of the rapid strides they have made to engross your commerce; drive away your artists [sic], and mechanics, and your manufactures will in like manner dwindle."[60] Acquitting the defendants, on the other hand, "will do incalculable benefit to this city, . . . scarcely a breeze will blow, but what will waft to our shores, experienced workmen from those realms, where labour is regulated by statutable provisions."[61] The city's future, Rodney claimed, was inextricably tied to the happiness and well-being of skilled workingmen, who were, after all, the source of the "real wealth of a community."[62]

The Philadelphia Mayor's Court was not persuaded by the defense arguments and convicted the cordwainers of criminal conspiracy. The defendants were fined eight dollars each plus the costs of the suit. The fine was equal to approximately one week's wages for an average cordwainer in the period.[63] Recorder Levy's charge to the jury has often been noted for his hostility to workingmen's combinations.[64] What has been overlooked by previous scholars, however, is Levy's preoccupation with maintaining judicial authority and economic growth in the wake of political independence.

Levy began his charge to the jury by stressing first the importance of maintaining the continuity of common law.

> The moment courts of justice loose [sic] their respectability from that moment the security of persons and of property is gone. The moment courts of justice

[59] Commonwealth v. Pullis, 178–81.

[60] Commonwealth v. Pullis, 179.

[61] Commonwealth v. Pullis, 180.

[62] Commonwealth v. Pullis, 180.

[63] For estimates of cordwainers' wages, see testimony given during the *Pullis* trial (Commonwealth v. Pullis, 83, 106, 118, 123–124, 171).

[64] See Turner, *The Early American Labor Conspiracy Cases*, 39–42; and Holt, "Labour Conspiracy Cases in the United States," 621–25.

have their character contaminated by a well founded suspicion, that they are governed by caprice, fear or favor; from that moment they will cease to be able to administer justice with effect, and redress wrongs of either a public or a private nature. Every consideration, therefore, calls upon us to maintain the character of courts and juries; and that can only be maintained by undeviating integrity, by an adhesion to the rules of law, and by deciding impartially in conformity with them.[65]

Levy went on to raise the problem of reconciling the Revolution and common law more directly as follows: "An attempt has been made to shew [sic] that the spirit of the revolution and the principle of the common law, are opposite in this case. . . . The inquiry on that point, was unnecessary and improper. Nothing more was required than to ascertain what the law is. The law is the permanent rule, it is the will of the whole community. After that is discovered, whatever may be its spirit or tendency, it must be executed, and the most impervious duty demands our submission to it."[66] Whether or not the law indeed was a "permanent rule" that demanded loyal submission, however, was precisely the issue that political independence had called into question. Levy's bold assertion that the common law remained intact despite the Revolution by no means settled the matter. Whether or not English and American law were synonymous remained a subject of political struggle for decades to come.

The difficulty of grounding the common law in the new republic can be seen in Levy's awkward justification for maintaining the conspiracy doctrine in Pennsylvania courts: "If a rule [of law] be clear, we are bound to conform to it even though we do not comprehend the principle upon which it is founded. We are not to reject it because we do not see the reason of it. . . . If it is law, there may be good reasons for it though we cannot find them out. But the rule in this case is pregnant with sound sense and all the authorities are clear upon the subject."[67] Levy's confidence in the rule of law enabled him to claim that the conspiracy cases ought to be decided by the same legal principles as the English precedents. However, his inability to "see the reason" behind the Philadelphia conviction left the American doctrine in a precarious position. Without a clear definition of the offense, it was impossible to distinguish lawful and criminal combinations consistently. Levy's decision thus failed to provide clear boundaries to the conspiracy doctrine and left the courts with little or no defense against charges of judicial arbitrariness.

Levy's remarks were by no means exceptional; several judges referred directly to the Revolution and political independence during the ante-

[65] Commonwealth v. Pullis, 224–25.
[66] Quoted from Commonwealth v. Pullis, 225.
[67] Quoted from Commonwealth v. Pullis, 233.

bellum conspiracy trials.[68] The pervasiveness of questions of judicial authority, however, is not captured by these remarks alone. It is important to recognize that the entire debate over the origins of the English convictions that pervaded the antebellum trials was essentially a struggle over the appropriateness of English precedents for American courts. Whether or not the English conspiracy cases had been statutory or common law crimes would determine, to a considerable extent, the outer limits of English doctrine as the principal legal authority in the new republic. Labor disputes thus provided an important vehicle for establishing the terms on which the common law was to be adopted in the United States.

On the economic questions, Levy again came down firmly on the prosecution side: "In every point of view, this measure is pregnant with public mischief and private injury . . . [it] tends to demoralize the workmen . . . destroy the trade of the city, and leaves the pockets of the whole community to the discretion of the concerned. If these evils were unprovided for by the law now existing, it would be necessary that laws should be made to restrain them."[69] The "public mischief," according to Levy, lay in the "unnatural, artificial means of raising the price of work beyond its standard, and taking undue advantage of the public." Protecting the individual rights and profits of employers was not Levy's primary concern. Rather, the problem with the workingmen's combination lay in the harm it inflicted on the "whole community." "To make an artificial regulation, is not to regard the excellence of the work or the quality of the material, but to fix a positive and arbitrary price, governed by no standard, controuled by no impartial person, but dependant on the will of the few who are interested; this is the unnatural way of raising the price of goods or work." Such conduct, Levy concluded, "exposes" the commerce of the city "to inconveniences, if not to ruin; therefore it is against the public welfare."[70]

The "private injury" involved was twofold. First, Levy summed up the harmful effects of combination on the defendants and their fellow workingmen. By forcing the journeymen shoemakers to refrain from working, Levy claimed, the "idle" and impoverished workers might be tempted to support their wives and children through "the commission of crimes." "A father cannot stand by and see, without agony, his children suffer; if he

---

[68] Explicit reference to the impact of the Revolution on the common law was also made in People v. Melvin (N.Y. 1809), 347; and State v. Buchanan 5 Harris and Jhn. (Md. 1821), 317. But more important is how all the conspiracy cases raised the question of judicial continuity. For additional remarks about the Revolution and political independence, see Commonwealth v. Pullis, 158–59, 222, 225; People v. Melvin (N.Y. 1809), 261, 275–76, 311, 320–21, 377; Commonwealth v. Morrow, 62, 71; State v. Buchanan, 358; and Rantoul's case notes for Commonwealth v. Hunt quoted in Nelles, "Commonwealth v. Hunt," 1145.

[69] Commonwealth v. Pullis, 230–31.

[70] Commonwealth v. Pullis, 228–29.

does, he is an inhuman monster; he will be driven to seek bread for them, either by crime, by beggary, or a removal from the city." Second, the standard of workmanship in the trade would decline as "the botch" who was "incapable of doing justice to his work" would be put on the same level as the "best tradesmen," leaving little incentive for cordwainers to "excel" in their trade.[71] Levy concluded his charge by denouncing the compulsion involved when journeymen forced their fellow workingmen to join their society. Infringing the liberties of the other journeymen aggravated the dangers of collective action and further demonstrated the need to regulate the cordwainers' behavior by convicting them of criminal conspiracy.[72]

Economic factors certainly were important for Levy, but in a rather different way than previous scholars have claimed. The problem with workingmen's combinations, according to Levy, was not that they infringed the rights and profits of employers. Rather, the economic injury generally was cast in terms of community interest and the public welfare. Class conflict had not yet emerged as an important dynamic in the conspiracy trials.

Modifying the Doctrine, 1809–1842

In general, questions of judicial authority and economic growth continued to dominate the conspiracy trials from *Pullis* to *Commonwealth v. Hunt*. However, both the relative weight given to each of these concerns and the particular arguments used by prosecution and defense attorneys to make their claims evolved during the first three decades of the nineteenth century. After the *Pullis* and *Morrow* trials, concerns about the continuity of common law diminished somewhat while arguments concerning incursions of individual liberty and restraint of trade increased. Although arguments over judicial authority played a less prominent role in trials of the 1820s and 1830s, these concerns by no means disappeared altogether. As we will see in the discussion of *Commonwealth v. Hunt* later in the chapter, establishing the continuity of common law remained a significant issue even into the 1840s.[73]

More specifically, the particular arguments advanced in the antebellum trials were modified as both prosecution and defense attorneys struggled to establish a firm footing for the conspiracy doctrine in the United States. The conspiracy doctrine, however, proved to be an awkward mechanism for reasserting the authority of common law and ensuring a healthy pattern of economic growth. The major problem lay in the difficulty of specifying

[71] Commonwealth v. Pullis, 230–31.
[72] Commonwealth v. Pullis, 231, 234–35.
[73] See Commonwealth v. Hunt (Mass. 1840), 636–37, 639, 645; and discussion of *Hunt* in this chapter.

clear boundaries to the offense that would enable professionals and laymen to distinguish lawful and criminal collective action. As long as unions, dances, and business associations could not be easily distinguished, convictions remained open to charges that they were no more than arbitrary English remnants—an inauspicious means of securing an effective judicial policy in the postrevolutionary era. If the common law was to be maintained and growth ensured, the courts must find a set of principles to ground American law.

In the conspiracy cases between 1806 and 1842, prosecution attorneys and judges alike were no longer willing to condemn workers on the basis of combination alone and searched instead for a set of conditions, or rules, to justify the American convictions. Two steps in particular were taken to refine the doctrine by specifying further the common law principles undergirding the convictions. First, prosecution attorneys placed greater emphasis on the illegal means or illegal ends of the combination as the basis of conviction rather than relying on the act of combination itself. Here prosecution arguments relied more heavily on the level of coercion associated with the workingmen's action, which frequently infringed, so the prosecution claimed, the rights and liberties of both their employers and fellow workingmen. Workingmen's associations, prosecution attorneys argued, clearly crossed the line between lawful and criminal collective action when they "compelled" their fellow journeymen to join their associations and tried to force employers to comply with their demands. The courts repeatedly held such action to be unlawful and to fall clearly within the conspiracy doctrine.[74]

As early as 1815, in Commonwealth v. Morrow, even the defense counsel had accepted the modified illegal means-end definition of conspiracy which enabled the courts to distinguish more effectively between unions and civic associations. By focusing on the level of coercion, courts now could exempt church assemblies and dances from conspiracy prosecutions without simultaneously legalizing all forms of collective action.[75] The narrowing of the conspiracy doctrine, however, still did not distinguish labor combinations from other associations sufficiently, as although the workingmen's tactics were abhorrent to many citizens, often they were not,

[74] For discussion of compulsion and infringement of liberty, see People v. Melvin (N.Y. 1809), prosecution arguments by Emmet and Griffin, 329, 378–79, and Mayor Radcliff, 384–85; Commonwealth v. Morrow, 24, 83, 85 (unfortunately Wilkins' argument is not reported, but see defense attorneys' counterarguments at 68, 69); People v. Fisher, 18, 19; People v. Faulkner, 316–17, 318, 331; and Commonwealth v. Hunt, (Mass. 1840) 610, 614, 635, 638, 643, 649.

[75] The means-end definition was first adopted in 1810 in the New York case of People v. Melvin (N.Y. 1809). For defense counsel accepting the revised definition, see Commonwealth v. Morrow, 59.

in and of themselves, unlawful. In order to bring labor combinations within the doctrine while continuing to exempt church meetings, dances, and business associations, prosecution attorneys had to specify additional grounds for unlawfulness.

Prosecution attorneys did so through their second line of argument in which they refined their economic claims. Instead of describing economic injury in general terms as prejudicial to public welfare and city trade, prosecutors tried to specify the economic harms by identifying the workingmen's dangerous monopoly practices and restraint of trade that had long been considered violations of common law.[76] Again, arguments based on restraint of trade enabled New York and Pennsylvania courts to claim that workingmen's associations were in special need of judicial regulation without simultaneously compromising the legal status of other forms of collective action. Under the narrower definition of conspiracy, almost any strike action or "turn out," as they were known, now could be indicted: pickets, boycotts, and closed shops were easily characterized as "subversi[ve] of liberty" or "injurious to trade." American courts now could follow the English precedents with greater ease, and did so by continuing to convict workers of criminal conspiracy throughout the antebellum era.[77]

During the antebellum trials, workingmen and their legal allies attacked the refined doctrine on two fronts. First, the case of *Commonwealth v. Carlisle*, heard in a Philadelphia court in 1821, tried to use the doctrine against employers by charging the master ladies shoemakers with criminal conspiracy.[78] If workingmen's associations were subject to prosecution, then why not charge employers' combinations with the same offense? Judge Gibson readily admitted the "unsettled state of the law of con-

[76] For discussion of monopoly and restraint of trade, see People v. Melvin, (N.Y. 1809) 313, 315, and counterarguments at 336; Commonwealth v. Morrow, 71, 81, 82, 84, 86; People v. Fisher, 12, 15, 18, 19; People v. Faulkner, 315, 318, 322, 327; Commonwealth v. Hunt (Mass. 1840), 613–14, and Kimball and Rantoul countering at 617, 623. For an excellent discussion of eighteenth-century economic arguments about monopoly and restraint of trade, see Thorelli, *The Federal Antitrust Policy*, chap. 1; and Stickney, *State Control of Trade and Commerce*, chaps. 1, 3.

Restraint of trade may well have been discussed with greater frequency in New York courts after 1828 because of the codification of New York case law into the Revised Statutes that year. The definition of conspiracy contained in the Revised Statutes explicitly included combinations to "commit any act injurious to the public health, to public morals, or to trade or commerce; or for the perversion or obstruction of justice or the due administration of the laws." For discussion of the Revised Statutes, see People v. Fisher, 14; and People v. Faulkner, 318, 321, 323.

[77] The quotations are taken from Commonwealth v. Morrow, 82, 84; People v. Faulkner, 318; and People v. Fisher, 19.

[78] Commonwealth v. Carlisle.

spiracy" and tried to clarify the "nature and principles of the offence." Gibson declared "the motive for combining" to be "the discriminative circumstance" that enabled courts to distinguish lawful from criminal association.[79] Gibson illustrated his principle of "criminal intention" by reflecting on different forms of combination and competition: "if a number of persons should combine to establish a ferry, not from motives of public or private utility, but to ruin or injure the owner of a neighboring ferry, the wickedness of the motive would render the association criminal, although it is otherwise where capital is combined, not for the purposes of oppression, but fair competition with others of the same calling."[80] Because combinations of bakers and ferry builders could just as easily create "public mischief" and "private injury" as workingmen's associations, Gibson asserted that the only way to establish an effective definition of conspiracy was by considering the confederates' "wickedness of the motive." Although Gibson's argument had considerable influence before the Civil War, it only went partway in establishing clear boundaries to the conspiracy law. Identifying "wicked" forms of collective action helped to contrast unions and dances, but remained dangerously vague when it came to separating "fair competition" from illegal combination where business associations were concerned. The *Carlisle* case was remanded to the lower court. Unfortunately, no further record of the proceedings has been found. *Carlisle* did not become an important precedent for prosecuting employers for conspiracy. Indeed, only a handful of conspiracy cases involving employers' restraint of trade have been identified in the remainder of the nineteenth century.[81]

The defense counsel's second, and more successful, line of attack was to question the technical construction of indictments. In a number of antebellum cases, defense attorneys moved to quash the indictments altogether, or appealed lower court convictions owing to the indictments' inadequate construction. Adoption of the illegal means-end definition of conspiracy, the defense claimed, meant that confederacy alone was no longer sufficient grounds for conviction, and an adequate indictment had to reflect the

[79] Commonwealth v. Carlisle, 38–39.

[80] Commonwealth v. Carlisle, 40.

[81] For discussion of the influence of Gibson's decision in *Carlisle*, see Tomlins, *Law, Labor, and Ideology*, chap. 5. The two best-known nineteenth-century conspiracy cases against employers' combinations after *Carlisle* were Commonwealth v. Tack, 1 Brewst. 511 (Pa. 1868); and Morris Run Coal Co. v. Barclay, 18 P. F. Smith 186 (Pa. 1871). *Morris Run* was actually a civil action; however, much of the *dicta* in the case have been used to sustain the claim that combinations in restraint of trade were criminal at common law. Interestingly, neither *Tack* nor *Morris Run* sustained the charge of conspiracy in restraint of trade. For useful discussion of employers' conspiracies in restraint of trade, see Thorelli, *The Federal Antitrust Policy*, chaps. 1, 3; and Allen, "Criminal Conspiracies in Restraint of Trade."

doctrinal change and identify the illegal means or ends of the combination. Indictments that failed to specify the charge sufficiently were inadequate and ought to be dismissed.[82]

Prosecutors countered these claims by pointing out that English precedents did not require such detailed identification of conspiracy offenses. As indictments that did not specify the illegal means or ends of the combination had been accepted by English courts in the *Poulterers' Case* and *Rex v. Eccles*, the prosecution argued, similar indictments should be sustained by American courts. However, it was precisely the authority of the English precedents that defense attorneys wished to challenge. Again, defense attorneys claimed that cases such as *Poulterers'* and *Eccles* were not controlling precedents for American courts because these cases, too, had rested on parliamentary statutes that were not in force in the United States.[83]

For the most part, journeymen and their lawyers lost these legal contests and were convicted of conspiracy by the state courts.[84] The inadequate construction of indictments, we will see later in this chapter, was one area in which defense attorneys eventually won out over their prosecution rivals. Otherwise, judges generally followed prosecution arguments when charging the jury and left little doubt as to the criminality of the workingmen's combinations. Penalties, however, were generally quite light in the antebellum cases. As Edwin Witte has pointed out, no American workers were sentenced to jail before the Civil War, and most fines ranged from one dollar to ten dollars, the exception being the heavy penalties assigned to New York tailors in 1836 in *People v. Faulkner*. The *Faulkner* case, however, was definitely an exception; in all other antebellum conspiracy trials identified to date journeymen received surprisingly lenient sentences from state courts.[85]

---

[82] For example, construction of the indictment was questioned in People v. Melvin (N.Y. 1809), 316–17, 334–36; State v. Buchanan, 317; *State v. Rickey*, and Commonwealth v. Hunt (Mass. 1842), 120.

[83] For example, see People v. Melvin, (N.Y. 1809), 316–17, 324, 332–33, 334, 348; and Commonwealth v. Hunt (Mass. 1842), 120, and Shaw at 125–26.

[84] Christopher Tomlins has provided the most complete list of antebellum labor conspiracy convictions and acquittals to date. On his reckoning, of the twenty-three antebellum labor conspiracies identified to date, twelve resulted in conviction, eight were acquitted, and the remaining cases were continued, dismissed, or settled before trial. The above count is a bit confusing, as, departing from Tomlins, I have counted the two appealed cases of *Fisher* and *Hunt* twice—once for each verdict. Tomlins correctly omits *Commonwealth v. Carlisle* and *Thompsonville Carpet Manufacturers v. Taylor* from the count, as *Carlisle* involved prosecution of master shoemakers and *Thompsonville* was a civil suit. For a complete list of individual verdicts, see Tomlins, *Law, Labor, and Ideology*, chap. 5, note 1. See also Turner, *The Early American Labor Conspiracy Cases*, 2–3; and Nelles, "Commonwealth v. Hunt," 1166–69. For verdicts in the New York and Pennsylvania cases see Appendix A.

[85] Witte, "Early American Labor Cases," 828. An exception is *People v. Faulkner*, in which twenty journeymen tailors were convicted of conspiracy and fined heavily by Judge

Even though legal arguments were revised in the early labor trials, it is very important to note that the more communitarian language that dominated the *Pullis* proceedings continued to shape legal arguments throughout the antebellum decades. Even the *Fisher* and *Faulkner* trials, which have been viewed by previous scholars as prime examples of class conflict and judicial bias, on closer inspection continued to emphasize the public dimension of the conflict at hand. Chief Justice Savage, for example, described the New York cordwainers' combination as a "monopoly of the most odious kind" which interfered with trade and commerce by "artificial means" and as such was injurious "not only to the individual particularly oppressed, but to the public at large."[86] Similarly, Judge Edwards is reported to have warned the *Falkner* jury about neglecting the public interest in their deliberations: "Much pains [*sic*] had been taken to show that this prosecution was a spiteful proceeding between the Masters and Journeymen. This, however, was but a narrow and partial view of the subject, and not what the legislature had in view when they established a law for the community at large, and if their law could be now set at nought and rendered inoperative, the bad effects would be felt by every member of society."[87] To be sure, Judge Edwards' adherence to the collectivist vision was more ambivalent than that of his colleagues in earlier trials. Indeed, some of his remarks suggest a growing awareness of the increased class conflict that would eventually tear the communitarian vision apart.[88]

Edwards. The two most prominent defendants, Henry Faulkner, president of the Union Society of Journeymen Tailors, and Howell Vail, "who had made himself particularly conspicuous," were fined $150 and $100 each. The remaining defendants were fined $50 each. The total fines amounted to $1,150—a substantial sum in 1836. See People v. Faulkner, 332.

[86] People v. Fisher, 18–19.

[87] People v. Faulkner, 322–23. At the end of his charge to the jury, Judge Edwards again declared: "The Court would again impress upon the minds of the jury that the present question was not to be considered a mere struggle between the masters and journeymen. It was one upon which the harmony of the whole community depended." See *People v. Faulkner*, 324; see also 325. Interestingly, Judge Roberts also made a similar argument against interpreting the dispute in *Commonwealth v. Morrow* in terms of class. Roberts claimed: "It would be taking a very contracted, and by no means a just view of this case, to consider it as a controversy between the employers and the journeymen. And your time would be very unprofitably employed, in calculating the respective profits of the one or the other." Instead, Roberts went on to argue that it was a community matter in which the public interest would be served by maintaining Pittsburgh as a healthy trading and manufacturing town. See Commonwealth v. Morrow, 81.

[88] For example, in his charge to the jury Edwards is reported as saying: "It would be for the jury to say, whether any body of men could raise their crests in this land of law, and control others by self-organized combination." Later in his charge Edwards remarked: "Judging from what we have witnessed within the last year, we should be led to the conclusion that the trades of the country, which contribute immeasurably to its wealth, and upon which the prosperity of a most valuable portion of the community hinges, is [*sic*] rapidly passing from

However, fear of workers' collective power did not yet dominate the judges' remarks. Instead, these concerns remained a minor refrain in a discourse that continued to evaluate economic conflicts by a set of community standards and moral norms that was quite different from notions of economic interest and harm that came to dominate the conspiracy trials after the Civil War.

ANTEBELLUM COURTS AND THE QUESTION OF CLASS

A skeptical reader still might suspect that questions of judicial authority and economic growth were simply surrogates for class. After all, securing judicial authority might actually have been a means of insulating antebellum elites from the democratic clamoring of the mob. Similarly, couching economic interests in public terms often has been used to mask private interests at work. Communitarian rhetoric, so critics might claim, was simply a means of disguising the class bias of the courts. Additional evidence is needed to show that the language of the antebellum conspiracy trials was more than a guise for controlling the newly emerging working class. Four additional sources of evidence can be marshaled to buttress my claim that these early labor trials were not yet dominated by questions of class.

First, the minimal penalties imposed by the courts bear witness to the relative importance of the legal and class issues in the early conspiracy cases. If the courts had been primarily concerned with working-class organization, then conviction *plus* heavy fines would have been the most effective strategy for deterring subsequent working-class organization. However, conviction alone was sufficient to ensure the continuity of the common law. Whatever the penalty, conviction was sufficient to confirm English precedents as viable authorities within the American legal system and thereby reassert the natural law foundation of American law. Heavy fines were not needed to solve the legal problem raised by the conspiracy trials before the Civil War, and indeed may have provoked greater opposition to the courts' rulings.

Interestingly, Joseph Hopkinson made precisely this point when prosecuting the Philadelphia cordwainers in the *Pullis* trial. Hopkinson called for light penalties as follows:

---

the control of the supreme power of the state into the hands of private societies. A state of things which would be as prejudicial in its consequences to the journeymen as it is to the employers, and all who have occasion for the fruits of their labor." See People v. Faulkner, 323, 330; see also 324, 332. For additional references to increased class conflict, see Commonwealth v. Morrow, 64–65; and especially Judge Thacher's remark in Commonwealth v. Hunt (Mass. 1840), 332, quoted in note 40.

When I use the word punish, I would not be understood that it is intended to do any personal injury to the defendants; nor that they should come under any severe penalty. . . . All I wish is to establish the principle by the decision of the court, and the correspondent verdict of a jury. We have no wish to injure these men, but we trust you will decide as the law decides; and after establishing the illegality of the measures pursued by the defendants, no men will be more ready than the prosecutors to shield the journeymen from any disagreeable consequences from a conviction.[89]

A quite different appeal would have been needed had the prosecutors wanted to persuade the jury that the workingmen's combinations were a dangerous force that had to be contained through judicial regulation. Thus, Hopkinson was well aware that the verdict and penalties could serve rather different purposes in the *Pullis* trial; as long as the legal "principle" was established by convicting the journeymen, Hopkinson was willing to have the defendants treated leniently by the court.[90]

Second, the dominance of legal concerns over questions of class in the antebellum labor conspiracies also can be seen by considering the *non-labor* conspiracy cases alongside the labor trials. What is striking about the nonlabor conspiracies is that exactly the same questions that lay at the heart of the labor trials also were being negotiated in cases that had little to do with the emerging class struggle. Conspiracies to seduce, defame, and cheat and defraud are especially interesting because they, like the labor trials, often were held to be conspiracies at common law. Even though some of the contemplated actions were themselves civil offenses, several antebellum judges clearly asserted that it was the confederacy that provided the gist of the offense, regardless of whether the contemplated actions were

[89] Quoted from Commonwealth v. Pullis, 132.

[90] It should be noted, however, that Judge Edwards presented a more class-based argument for light penalties in *People v. Faulkner*. Edwards claimed, "We have had in this country so little experience of these combinations, that we are at a loss to know what degree of severity may be necessary to rid society of them. From the considerations which I have before stated, and from a hope that the explicit declarations of the law, not only by this, but by the Supreme Court, will have the effect to prevent such practices, we are disposed to impose a very mild punishment, compared to the offence. But if this is not found to answer the purpose, we shall proceed from one degree of severity until the will of the people is obeyed; until the laws are submitted to." Quoted from People v. Faulkner, 332. Edwards concluded his argument by imposing the harshest penalties of any of the antebellum conspiracy trials, with fines totaling $1,150. However, I do not see Edwards' view as typical of the 1820s and 1830s, as no other court followed his argument or practice in imposing heavy fines. Indeed, even though workingmen continued to organize during the antebellum decades, with the exception of *Faulkner*, state courts did not increase the penalties handed down in the antebellum trials. The postwar experience, we will see in the section that follows, was quite different. In the three decades after the Civil War, state courts handed down heavy fines and jail terms in the labor conspiracy trials. For specific postwar penalties, see note 120.

unlawful.[91] In *State v. Burnham*, for example, which involved a conspiracy to cheat and defraud an insurance company, Judge John Gilchrist insisted that conspiracy was a common law crime in the following terms:

> When it is said in the books that the means must be unlawful, it is not to be understood that those means must amount to indictable offenses, in order to make the offence of conspiracy complete. It will be enough if they are corrupt, dishonest, fraudulent, immoral, and in that sense illegal, and it is in the combination to make use of such practices that the dangers of this offence consist. . . . Conspiracies may be indictable where neither the object, if effected, nor the means made use of to accomplish it, would be punishable without the conspiracy.[92]

By including "immoral" actions in his definition, Gilchrist opened the way for otherwise lawful combinations to be subject to criminal prosecution. These dicta in the *Burnham* case often have been used to sustain subsequent convictions for conspiracy at common law.[93] Judge Gibson, who also had presided at the *Carlisle* trial, advanced an equally broad definition of conspiracy in the nonlabor trial of *Commonwealth v. Mifflin*. Gibson denounced the confederacy to assist a minor marrying against her father's wishes, claiming: "The law of conspiracy is certainly in a very unsettled state. . . . It is settled, however, that there are acts which, though innocent when done by an individual, are criminal when done in concert; but they are not very satisfactorily defined."[94] Thus, legal arguments in the nonlabor cases mirrored the labor trials; in most of the antebellum conspiracy cases attorneys and judges struggled to establish coherent boundaries to the conspiracy law and to determine whether or not common law crimes had any authority in American courts.

State v. Buchanan, one of the major antebellum nonlabor conspiracy cases, provides a remarkable parallel to the workingmen's trials.[95] First, attorneys engaged in a lengthy debate over the legitimacy of common law crimes in the new republic. As in the labor trials, Judge Buchanan came down firmly in favor of maintaining conspiracy as a common law offense.[96] The similarity with the labor cases, however, does not stop there; Buchanan, too, was preoccupied with reconciling political independence

[91] For example, see State v. Younger; Hood v. Palm; State v. Buchanan; and State v. Burnham, 15 N.H. 396 (N.H. 1844). See also Sayre, "Criminal Conspiracy," 406–9, 420–21; and Carson, *Criminal Conspiracies*, chap. 3, esp. 140–43.

[92] Quoted from State v. Burnham, 403–4.

[93] See Sayre, "Criminal Conspiracy," 408–9.

[94] The case involved a confederacy to help a minor elope against her father's wishes. See Commonwealth v. Mifflin, 461–62.

[95] State v. Buchanan.

[96] State v. Buchanan, 233–51.

with the continuity of common law. Toward the end of his decision, Buchanan discussed the impact of the Revolution on American law, saying, "If the political connection between this and the mother country had never been dissolved, the expression of a doubt would not now be hazarded on the question, whether the same law was in force here."[97] However, as everyone was well aware, the "political connection" between England and the United States had been broken, thereby raising the difficult question of whether or not the common law was in force in the new republic. The defendants lost the case when the Maryland Court of Appeals reversed the lower court decision and remanded the case to the lower court for further deliberation.[98]

Placing labor cases within the context of the nonlabor conspiracies ameliorates claims of judicial bias and hostility toward labor. When considered in the larger legal context of conspiracy cases as a whole, we see that workingmen's combinations were not singled out for especially severe regulation by the courts. On the contrary, state courts treated labor and nonlabor conspiracies with remarkable consistency when they tried and convicted very different combinations for criminal conspiracy with equal vigor before the Civil War.[99]

Third, attending to questions of judicial authority, in particular, provides a more satisfying account of the landmark case of *Commonwealth v. Hunt* in 1842. Class-based analyses of the antebellum trials have had considerable difficulty accommodating Chief Justice Shaw's acquittal of

[97] Quoted from State v. Buchanan, 358. Buchanan continued with a lengthy discussion of the Bill of Rights in order to show "that it was not the intention of the framers of that instrument to exclude any part of the common law, merely because it had not been introduced and used in the courts here, and strongly implies, that there were portions of that valuable system which had not been actually practised upon." Quoted from State v. Buchanan, 359. The impact of the Revolution on common law doctrine also was discussed explicitly in Commonwealth v. Pullis, 225; and People v. Melvin (N.Y. 1809), 347.

[98] State v. Buchanan, 868.

[99] In addition to comparing labor conspiracy cases with their nonlabor counterparts, it is also instructive to take an individual justice and examine his labor and nonlabor rulings. For example, two of the most visible antebellum labor cases, *People v. Fisher* and *Commonwealth v. Hunt*, take on a different significance when compared to other decisions handed down by Justices Savage and Shaw. In *People v. Lambert* (9 Cowen's Rep. 578 [N.Y. 1827]), Judge Savage treated this conspiracy to cheat and defraud as harshly as the labor conspiracy seven years later in the *Fisher* trial. Given the *Lambert* ruling, Savage's very broad definition of conspiracy cannot be effectively explained exclusively in class terms. Similarly, Shaw's landmark acquittal of the Boston cordwainers in *Hunt* was preceded that same year by his notoriously antilabor decision of *Farwell v. Boston and Worcester Railroad*, (4 Metc. 49 [Mass. 1842]). To be sure, *Farwell* was not a conspiracy case, but rather involved the fellow servant rule. Nevertheless, the *Farwell* decision makes it difficult to explain the *Hunt* acquittal strictly as a product of Shaw's allegiance to the upper class. For an interesting comparison of *Farwell* and *Hunt*, see Levy, *The Law of the Commonwealth and Chief Justice Shaw*, chaps. 10, 11.

the Massachusetts cordwainers. If the courts' object was to contain the working class, then why was Shaw willing to overrule the lower court conviction and establish an important victory for organized labor?[100] Many of the difficulties raised by the *Hunt* decision disappear when we set aside questions of class and consider the ways in which Shaw's decision provided a skillful resolution to the problem of legal authority that had plagued state courts since 1806. Shaw broke with past legal practice and presented a new interpretation of the conspiracy doctrine. By selecting pieces from both prosecution and defense arguments, Shaw constructed a new approach that enabled the court to provide clearer limits to the offense without challenging the authority of the common law in toto. Shaw clarified the conspiracy law by simultaneously affirming two previously contradictory claims. Shaw asserted both that the common law was in force in the Commonwealth of Massachusetts and that combination itself was not a criminal offense.[101] In previous conspiracy cases, judges and attorneys had advocated only one or the other of these propositions, forcing courts to choose between reaffirming common law doctrine and maintaining doctrinal coherence. Shaw, however, established a middle ground that enabled him to embrace both these claims, and as a consequence helped to quell some of the uncertainty associated with the conspiracy law.

There were four steps to Shaw's argument. First and foremost, he affirmed the authority of the common law. The opinion opened with the statement, "We have no doubt that by the operation of the constitution of this Commonwealth, the general rules of the common law, making conspiracy an indictable offence, are in force here."[102] With the rule of law

---

[100] Several scholars who adhere to the class analysis have attempted to explain the *Hunt* anomaly largely by identifying additional class interests that Shaw was trying to serve. For example, see Nelles, "Commonwealth v. Hunt," sec. 3, 1151–66; and Holt, "Labour Conspiracy Cases in the United States," sec. 4, esp. 638–53. According to Nelles, Shaw's primary concern in acquitting the Boston shoemakers was not so much to grant workers the right to organize and strike as to placate labor in order to secure safe passage of tariff legislation in Massachusetts. Similarly, Holt argued that Shaw's primary concern was establishing the courts' legitimacy rather than workers' industrial rights. Thus, for both Nelles and Holt the *Hunt* victory was not what it appeared; the class bias of the courts can be seen just below the surface. However, neither of these interpretations of Hunt is satisfactory. Leonard Levy has uncovered evidence showing that Shaw was in fact an advocate of free trade rather than tariff reform. Similarly, there is little evidence to support Holt's claim of Shaw's "true colors"; indeed, Holt must resort to assertions of "subconscious motives" to make the case for class bias. For elaboration of these criticisms, see Levy, *The Law of the Commonwealth and Chief Justice Shaw*, chap. 11; and Victoria Hattam, "Unions and Politics: The Courts and American Labor, 1806–1896" (Ph.D. diss., Massachusetts Institute of Technology, 1987), chap. 2.

[101] See Commonwealth v. Hunt (Mass. 1842), 121, for claims that the common law was still in force in Massachusetts, and 129–31 for claims that combination itself was not criminal.

[102] Commonwealth v. Hunt (Mass. 1842), 121.

clearly asserted, Shaw turned to the problems of limiting the offense, which had been so ably articulated by defense attorneys in earlier cases.

Shaw narrowed the English doctrine without breaking with the common law completely by allowing "local laws" to limit the authority of English precedents. Thus, Shaw argued that the conspiracy doctrine "may be equally in force as a rule of the common law, in England and in this Commonwealth; and yet it must depend upon the local laws of each country to determine, whether the purpose to be accomplished by the combination, or the concerted means of accomplishing it, be unlawful or criminal in the respective countries."[103] English convictions that had rested on their "local laws" had no authority over American cases. Thus, Shaw explicitly accepted defense counsel arguments from earlier trials concerning the statutory origins of many English convictions. As many of the English statutes, especially in the field of labor regulation, had not been adopted in the Commonwealth, Shaw argued, Massachusetts courts could adhere to the broad features of the common law without being bound by all English precedents.[104] As Shaw put it, "although the common law in regard to conspiracy in this Commonwealth is in force, yet it will not necessarily follow that every indictment at common law for this offence is a precedent for a similar indictment in this state."[105] Thus, Shaw sustained the common law in principle while allowing specific cases to deviate from it in order to meet the particular conditions of a newly independent nation.

Third, Shaw cleverly drew on defense arguments concerning the technical construction of indictments in order to provide a mechanism through which the "local laws" could limit the amorphous common law doctrine. The vagueness of the conspiracy doctrine, Shaw claimed, made it especially important for indictments to specify as clearly as possible the exact sources of unlawfulness. "From this view of the law respecting conspiracy, we think it an offense which especially demands the application of that wise and humane rule of the common law, that an indictment shall state, with as much certainty as the nature of the case will admit, the facts which constitute the crime intended to be charged."[106] Indictments that failed to specify the grounds of unlawfulness were inadequate and could not sustain a conviction. By requiring indictments to specify the grounds of illegality, national differences could be built into the legal doctrine without reducing all legal doctrine to statute law. Shaw, thus, skillfully reaffirmed the common law while allowing particular doctrines to be modified by state legislation.

Now Shaw could conclude his opinion by affirming the two previously

103 Commonwealth v. Hunt (Mass. 1842), 122.
104 Commonwealth v. Hunt (Mass. 1842), 122.
105 Commonwealth v. Hunt (Mass. 1842), 123.
106 Commonwealth v. Hunt (Mass. 1842), 125.

contradictory claims: the common law was in force in the Commonwealth, yet combination per se was not an offense in Massachusetts. The act of combination alone did not distinguish sufficiently between laudable and criminal associations; workingmen's associations could be established either for "useful and honorable purposes, or for dangerous and pernicious ones."[107] The lower court conviction might have been sustained, Shaw concluded, had the indictment specified the illegal means or ends employed by the Boston bootmakers according to the "local laws" of the Commonwealth.[108] However, as the indictment failed to identify the particular grounds of unlawfulness, the court had no choice but to overrule the municipal court decision and acquit the bootmakers. Shaw's carefully crafted decision provided American courts with an intermediary position in which judicial authority could be more effectively limited by "local laws" without automatically severing all ties with the common law heritage.

Viewing *Commonwealth v. Hunt* exclusively from the perspective of class conflict, as previous scholars have done, has obscured the major issues at stake in the case. To be sure, the acquittal was indeed an important victory for American workers, but the central question addressed by the court was not whether workers should be granted the right to organize and strike. Rather, the case is best understood in the context of the postrevolutionary struggle over the power of the judiciary within the American republic. *Hunt* was indeed a landmark case, but not because it was labor's Magna Carta. Rather, the decision was distinguished because it addressed head on the antebellum problem of judicial authority and provided an innovative means of reconciling the previously conflicting pressures that faced state courts in the aftermath of the American Revolution.

The very ingenuity of Shaw's solution, however, was also its greatest weakness. In order to maintain judicial authority, Shaw deliberately eschewed a substantive break with the common law doctrine of criminal conspiracy. Although the *Hunt* decision protected the judiciary from demands to democratize the legal system, the technical grounds for the reversal also limited its power as a precedent in future conspiracy cases.[109] Few labor conspiracies cases have been identified between 1842 and 1862, but *Hunt* did little to prevent a revival of the doctrine after the Civil War. The 1867 New Jersey Supreme Court case *State v. Donaldson* makes a particularly interesting comparison with *Hunt*.[110] The two cases involved remarkably similar disputes, yet the New Jersey defendants were convicted,

[107] Commonwealth v. Hunt (Mass. 1842), 129.

[108] Commonwealth v. Hunt (Mass. 1842), 129.

[109] For an interesting discussion of this aspect of *Hunt*, see Landis and Manoff, *Cases of Labor Law*, chap. 1.

[110] State v. Donaldson, 3 Vroom 151 (N.J. 1867).

despite the earlier *Hunt* ruling. The New Jersey court did not consider *Hunt* a controlling precedent precisely because the indictment in the Donaldson case had been adequately constructed.[111] By clarifying the boundaries and principles behind the doctrine, Marjorie Turner has argued, Shaw not only established clearer guidelines for future defense attorneys, but also simplified the legal issues for prosecution attorneys.[112] Shaw's opinion in *Commonwealth v. Hunt* helped insulate the courts from democratic reform, but did little to protect workers' industrial rights over the long term. In 1842, the struggle for state protection of industrial rights was far from resolved. In fact, the battle had hardly begun.

Finally, perhaps the most compelling evidence of the influence of questions of judicial authority and republican conceptions of economic growth on the early labor trials can be found by contrasting the language and arguments from the antebellum cases with the second wave of conspiracy convictions handed down in the three decades following the Civil War. The increased class conflict of the postwar decades clearly was reflected in the language and penalties of the postwar trials. Moreover, workers' response to the convictions also changed quite dramatically before and after the war. Examining the second wave of conspiracy trials thus helps to highlight the influence of eighteenth-century concerns on judicial behavior before the Civil War.

POSTWAR REVIVAL OF THE DOCTRINE, 1865–1896

Conspiracy prosecutions did not stop with *Commonwealth v. Hunt* in 1842 but were renewed with a vengeance in both New York and Pennsylvania after the Civil War. Most of the cases fell within the years 1865 through 1896, but some conspiracy prosecutions can still be found in the early decades of the twentieth century. Although the legal doctrine remained largely unchanged and most of the postwar cases, like their antebellum counterparts, resulted in conviction, much had changed with the second wave of conspiracy trials.[113]

When first comparing the early- and late-nineteenth-century conspiracy

---

[111] State v. Donaldson, 157.

[112] Turner, *The Early American Labor Conspiracy Cases*, 58–66.

[113] Many American conspiracy cases, especially in the lower courts, went unreported. Thus some cases can be identified only through local newspapers, organization proceedings, and government reports. Nevertheless, the major late-nineteenth-century conspiracy cases in New York and Pennsylvania identified to date can be found in Appendix A.

For examples of twentieth-century conspiracy cases, see People v. McFarlin et al., 43 Misc. Rep. 591, 89 N.Y.S. 527 (Pa. 1904); State v. Stockford, 77 Conn. 227, 58 A 769, 107 Am St. Rep. 28 (Conn. 1904); People v. Makvirka, 224 App. Div. 419, 231 N.Y.S. 279 (N.Y. 1928); and People v. Commerford, 233 App. Div. 2, 251 N.Y.S. 132 (N.Y. 1931).

trials, I was struck by the quite dramatic change in the language and categories used to describe economic and social relations before and after the Civil War. In the postwar cases judges and prosecution attorneys no longer stressed the public dimension of economic benefits and harms. References to the "public good" and to maintaining the city's "flourishing trade" had all but disappeared. Instead, in the second wave of conspiracy trials economic injuries were described in individual terms, as a loss or harm suffered by specific businessmen and their firms.[114] The decreased trade in George Theiss's musical club, Mrs. Landgraff's bakery, and to the Russel & Evans coal company, for example, were accepted by the postbellum courts as legitimate harms that could be appropriately redressed by convicting striking workingmen of conspiracy.[115] The contrast with the arguments in the antebellum trials is clear. Before the Civil War, the economic interests of particular employers were rarely mentioned; if raised at all, they generally were linked, via the bakers' analogy, to the public good and community welfare. After the Civil War, references to the bakers' analogy were gone, as prosecution attorneys no longer needed to demonstrate that the economic injuries at hand were of a public rather than a private nature.

Characterizations of the defendants changed in the postwar trials as well. The increased sense of social disruption and distrust can be seen in several postwar trials. Judge George Barrett's comments in the New York case of *People v. Wilzig* illustrate the changes nicely. Barrett commenced the sentencing with the following remarks:

> The moral guilt attaching to the crime of which you have been convicted is heightened by the fact that you are not American citizens. Such *socialistic crimes* as these are *gross breaches* of national hospitality. What would you think of a man who, having sought an asylum from oppression or poverty in a friend's house, then proceeded to violate his friend's domestic rules, to disregard his customs and to disturb the peace, order and well being of his household! Yet that is just what you and others of your union have been doing with regard to the national household of this country; a country that welcomed you and offered you equal opportunity with its own native-born citizens. Common gratitude should

[114] For example, see Commonwealth v. Curren, 3 Pitts. 143, 146–47 (Pa. 1869); People v. Wilzig, 4 N.Y. Cr. 403, 414–15, 426 (N.Y. 1886); People v. Kostka, 4 N.Y. Cr. 429, 436 (N.Y. 1886); and Newman et al., v. the Commonwealth, 34 Pittsburgh Law Journal 313, 314 (Pa. 1886). To be sure, some communitarian language can be found in the postwar cases. For instance, see reference to "prejudice the public" and "business interests of the community" in Commonwealth v. Curren, 147, 148. However, these remarks were eclipsed by the more extensive discussions of economic damages inflicted on particular individuals and their businesses in these same trials.

[115] These businesses were mentioned in the following conspiracy cases: People v. Wilzig, 415–16; People v. Kostka, 436; and Commonwealth v. Curren, 146–47.

have prevented you from *outraging* public opinion, and using here those methods of a *socialistic character* which you brought with you from abroad.[116]

Although questions of citizenship also had been raised in some antebellum trials, the identification of foreigners with undesirable "socialistic" views was new.[117]

Greater danger and power also was attributed to the postwar defendants and their un-American actions than to defendants in the antebellum trials. Again, Judge Barrett captured the new sense of fear when he continued the sentencing as follows:

> All these things, however, while they may have encouraged your disgraceful proceedings at Theiss' establishment, did not suggest the almost unspeakable excesses which attended the finale of your acts, when, having reduced this man to submission, having compelled him to sign the most degrading document which was ever presented to an American citizen, you completed your outrage by forcing him, still with your boycott pistol at his head, to pay, so to speak, for the powder and ball with which it was loaded, and which had been the threat of his business ruin.[118]

Something indeed had changed since the antebellum trials; the New York and Pennsylvania courts now viewed the labor conspiracies as dangerous conflicts between workers and employers and were willing to go to considerable lengths to contain the heightened class struggle. In place of the communitarian rhetoric, many of the postwar trials focused instead on identifying the respective rights and privileges of workers and employers in the new market economy.[119]

[116] Quoted from People v. Wilzig, 425; emphasis added.

[117] For an even more explicit equation of American citizenship with the smooth functioning of the labor market, see Newman et al. v. the Commonwealth, 315. When charging the jury, Judge Hart declared "prolonged" strikes to be "unrepublican, not American, and treasonable." Hart continued: "The true American idea is,—and it is the law of the land,—that every laboring man shall be allowed the utmost freedom to carry his labor to the market, and get for it what he can, without molestation or hindrance." For reference to citizenship in the antebellum conspiracy trials, see Commonwealth v. Pullis, 135, 139, 140, 209; and People v. Faulkner, 326, 331–32, 333.

[118] Quoted from People v. Wilzig, 426.

[119] In Chapter 4, we will see that the New York and Pennsylvania courts interpreted the postwar anticonspiracy statutes very broadly in order to continue convicting striking workers of criminal conspiracy. Most of the postwar cases revolved around judicial interpretations of the "hindering provisions," which specified that acts of "intimidation" were not covered by the statutes and thus could still be prosecuted for criminal conspiracy. In practice, New York and Pennsylvania courts found almost all collective action by labor to be intimidating. For example, see People v. Wilzig and the D. R. Jones Trial in Westmoreland County, Pennsylvania. These and other postwar cases are discussed in detail in Chapter 4.

For discussion of the rights and privileges of workers and employers, see Commonwealth v. Curren, 144–45. Judge Ryon outlined the economic issues as follows: "Now, Russel, Evans

The language and categories of analysis were not the only things to change between the first and second wave of conspiracy trials. Penalties, too, increased significantly after the Civil War. Where antebellum courts imposed quite small fines of one to ten dollars and did not sentence defendants to jail at all, New York and Pennsylvania courts adopted quite a different strategy after the Civil War. Convictions in the postbellum decades frequently were accompanied by jail terms of up to three years and eight months and bail terms as high as one thousand dollars.[120] The increased penalties imposed by the courts provide a useful marker of shifts in the relative weight accorded to questions of judicial authority and questions of class. The heavier fines and jail terms signaled, I believe, many judges' increased desire to contain working-class protest after the Civil War. The problem of judicial authority largely had been solved in the antebellum trials. The social upheaval associated with the labor conflicts in the 1870s and 1880s, however, required a different response; substantial punishments as well as convictions were needed to deter workers from organizing on a massive scale.

Finally, the changing significance of the conspiracy trials also can be seen in the way workers responded to the second wave of conspiracy trials. Unlike their antebellum counterparts, postwar labor unions paid considerable attention to the second wave of conspiracy convictions and embarked on an extensive campaign to repeal the conspiracy law. Between 1865 and 1891, the New York Workingmen's Assembly, the Pennsylvania miners' unions, and later the Federation of Organized Trades and Labor Unions (FOTLU) all made repeal of the doctrine one of their highest priorities and tried repeatedly to check the courts' power and to limit application of the conspiracy doctrine to American labor. These organizations were no

---

& Co. own this colliery. They have a right to employ whomsoever they please to work for them, and they have a right to discharge those they employ whenever they do not require their services for any reason. No man will put his capital into business without he can control it. This is more essential in the production of coal than in most businesses. It requires good management to make the investment profitable, and unless he can control his business he had better abandon it and this would be the result, from choice or necessity, sooner or later."

[120] The penalties assessed in the postwar conspiracy convictions were as follows: *People v. Van Nostrand* (1867), fines ranged from $25 to $50; *Commonwealth v. Curren* (1869), thirty days in prison plus fines of $100, costs of the suit, and $500 security for one year's good behavior; Xingo Parks and John Siney Trial (1875), jail terms ranged from sixty days to one year, plus fines of $25, and costs of the suit; D. R. Jones Trial (1881), $100 fine, plus costs of the suit, and imprisonment for twenty-four hours; Miles McPadden Trial (1882), bail ranged from $500 to $1,000 (the suit was eventually dropped); *Newman et al. v. the Commonwealth* (1886), jail terms ranged from three to eight months, plus $1 fine, and costs of the suit; *People v. Wilzig* (1886), jail terms ranged from one year and six months to three years and eight months; *People v. Kostka* (1886), jail terms ranged from ten to thirty days; and Knights of Labor Trials (1887), jail terms of four months.

longer willing to accept the conspiracy law as part-and-parcel of a larger program of antimonopoly reform. Instead, the conspiracy convictions became highly politicized and were the object of a sustained campaign for legal change. The outcome of this postwar struggle between labor and the courts, we will see in Chapter 4, had a considerable impact on the future course of labor movement development in the United States.

Conclusion: Courts and the Question of Class

Past accounts of the antebellum conspiracy cases have focused too heavily on the level of judicial hostility toward labor. To be sure, state courts did oppose working-class organization, but this does not distinguish the United States from other advanced industrial societies. Most governments tried to prevent workers from organizing in the late eighteenth and early nineteenth centuries, but only the United States relied heavily on the courts to implement this policy. The dominance of the courts in regulating industrial conflict was distinctively American and indeed had important consequences for workers' conceptions of politics and for labor strategy in the United States.

The impact of the courts on labor movement development did not lie in the class bias of the American legal system. In fact, claims of judicial hostility toward labor must be tempered by a closer examination of the antebellum cases. The light penalties imposed by the courts, the public characterization of economic interests and harms during the antebellum labor trials, state regulation of a wide range of collective action during the antebellum decades, albeit via different channels, and the limited scope of workingmen's protest against the conspiracy trials all suggest that state courts were motivated by issues other than class. Maintaining judicial authority in the wake of the Revolution and promoting a republican pattern of economic growth were the twin concerns, I have argued, that motivated judicial behavior during the antebellum conspiracy trials. After the Civil War, questions of class conflict came to the fore and as a consequence state-labor relations increasingly were politicized around the conspiracy law. Even in the postbellum decades, however, assertions of judicial hostility and class bias should not be overdrawn, as they obscure the more subtle ways in which judicial regulation shaped working-class organization and politics after the Civil War. The remainder of this book reexamines the impact of judicial regulation on organized labor by tracing workers' quite different reaction to the two waves of conspiracy convictions before and after the Civil War. Some of the distinctive features of judicial regulation that were crucial in shaping workers' political strategy can be seen in embryonic form in the conspiracy doctrine and cases discussed here. Thus some of the themes that are developed in subsequent chapters can be anticipated, although the specific ways in which the courts shaped the labor movement can be considered fully only by examining working-class organization and politics itself.

Regulation of labor under the conspiracy doctrine reveals three aspects of judicial policymaking that were especially important for American labor movement development. First, the conspiracy doctrine and cases illustrate the intricate relationship between law and the surrounding political economy. Judges did not resolve the labor cases by simply applying existing legal doctrine to current industrial disputes. The boundary between law and society was not so easily drawn. In regulating industrial conflict, the judiciary was neither a neutral arbitrator nor the handmaiden for capital. Legal doctrine alone was indeterminate. Prosecution and defense attorneys could provide quite different interpretations of the conspiracy doctrine, while still adhering to the very same legal precedents and practices. The competing interpretations of the doctrine, however, entailed radically different conceptions of judicial authority and economic growth, which greatly influenced labor movement development in the United States.

Rather than resolving contemporary industrial conflicts, the courts provided another arena in which the political struggles were continued. Once a particular doctrinal interpretation had been accepted, and had established a hegemonic position within the legal profession, the particular form of judicial intervention that followed was crucial in shaping the process of class formation and politics in the United States. Legal institutions both reflected and shaped the political struggles that accompanied the process of industrialization. The intricate ways in which the courts both were embedded in the larger political context and influenced the pattern of American labor movement development are traced in considerable detail in the chapters that follow.

Second, the difficult task of changing judicial policy that plagued the labor movement after the Civil War was, in many respects, prefigured in *Commonwealth v. Hunt*. The inability of *Hunt* to reorient judicial policy away from conspiracy convictions was symptomatic of the more general difficulty of securing a definitive change in legal doctrine, explored at length in Chapter 4. What we see in *Hunt*, and to an even greater extent in the postwar struggle to repeal the conspiracy doctrine, is the tremendous insulation of the courts from internal and external pressure for reform. American workers faced unusually difficult task of changing government policy toward labor. The problem was not so much a question of overcoming government hostility, as workers in most countries faced some form of opposition from the state. The peculiarly American problem lay in the added difficulties associated with changing the particular form of state regulation in force in the United States, namely, judicial rather than statutory regulation. The mercurial nature of legal doctrine seen in the antebellum conspiracy cases, and the insulation of the courts from political reform, demonstrated the impotence of electoral and party politics for large segments of the organized labor movement.

Finally, judicial regulation of labor had a profound influence on workers' perceptions of politics and the state. Conflicting interpretations of the conspiracy doctrine were not presented as disputes over public policy or as questions for political debate. Instead, whether or not the court should adhere to a broad or narrow definition of conspiracy was considered a legal problem to be resolved by the court through legal rather than political argument. The dominance of the courts in regulating labor tended to depoliticize state intervention in industrial conflict. Judicial decisions often were not experienced as "state intervention," but were more readily seen as the neutral application of common law doctrine to industrial disputes. Workers' perceptions of and response to judicial regulation are explored more fully in the next chapter, which examines workers' organization and politics before the Civil War. Turning away from the state to look more closely at workers' reaction to the conspiracy convictions helps to identify the more indirect, but by no means less powerful, ways in which judicial regulation shaped working-class formation in the United States.

CHAPTER THREE

The Producers' Vision: A Republican Political Economy

METROPOLITAN INDUSTRIALIZATION AND WORKINGMEN'S PROTEST BEFORE THE CIVIL WAR

The antebellum era was by no means a period of stable economic and social relations. On the contrary, recent work by a number of labor historians has documented important changes under way in the early decades of the nineteenth century. Studies of several cities, including New York, Philadelphia, Baltimore, and Lynn, Massachusetts, have shown that metropolitan industrialization did not proceed directly from craft to factory production in a single bound, but rather followed a more uneven course. Production was expanded in the antebellum decades through the reorganization of work and the division of labor rather than through the adoption of new machinery and new methods of production. Despite the varied and incremental nature of economic change, the reorganization of work, nevertheless, had tremendous consequences for social relations in many trades.[1]

For much of the eighteenth century, work had been organized along craft lines such that skilled workers, or artisans, produced high-quality goods for a limited market. This system of craft production presumed mobility within the trade as artisans progressed from apprentice, to journeyman to master craftsman. Workshops generally were small, employing four or five

---

[1] See Howard B. Rock, *Artisans of the New Republic: The Tradesmen of New York City in the Age of Jefferson* (New York: New York University Press, 1979); Wilentz, *Chants Democratic*; Alan Dawley, *Class and Community: The Industrial Revolution in Lynn* (Cambridge, Mass.: Harvard University Press, 1976); Paul Faler, *Mechanics and Manufacturers in the Early Industrial Revolution: Lynn, Massachusetts, 1780–1860* (Albany: State University of New York Press, 1981); Bruce Laurie, *Working People of Philadelphia, 1800–1850* (Philadelphia: Temple University Press, 1980); Sharon V. Salinger, "Artisans, Journeymen, and the Transformation of Labor in Late Eighteenth-Century Philadelphia," *William and Mary Quarterly*, 3d series, 40, 1 (January 1983): 62–84; Charles G. Steffen, "Changes in the Organization of Artisan Production in Baltimore, 1790 to 1820," *William and Mary Quarterly*, 3d series, 36, 1 (January 1979): 101–17; and David Montgomery, "The Working Classes of the Pre-Industrial American City, 1780–1830," *Labor History* 9, 1 (Winter 1968): 3–22.

men, often working alongside their masters. Individual artisans, historians have found, felt tremendous pride in their craft and loyalty to their trade.[2]

Between 1780 and 1820, the craft economy was radically transformed. The major impetus for change came from expanding markets, which made large-scale production a viable option for the first time.[3] Not all trades were affected by more extensive markets, and those that were affected at different rates and times. Butchers, bakers, and the metal trades, for example, remained largely unchanged, with as many as one half to three quarters of their shops continuing traditional craft production as late as 1850. On the other hand, artisans in the consumer finishing trades, such as shoemakers, tailors, cabinetmakers, and weavers, found their worlds changing dramatically as entrepreneurial masters tried to capitalize on the growing markets. In the first decade of the nineteenth century, artisans have been estimated at 50 percent of the New York work force. Moreover, the consumer finishing trades are thought to have employed approximately 40 percent of all New York artisans and 65 percent of journeymen in New York.[4]

Output was increased in most of the consumer finishing trades through production of "ready-made" goods alongside the traditional custom-order items. New markets could be secured, some entrepreneurs believed, by selling lower-quality goods more cheaply in greater volume. Production costs generally were reduced by increasing the division of labor and hiring less skilled men and women for routine tasks. By reorganizing work, fully trained artisans could be kept for custom orders while relegating the "ready-mades" to "half-way journeymen" or "two-thirders" who had completed only a part of their training and therefore worked for lower wages.[5] By 1830 most workshops no longer employed four or five skilled artisans, but hired as many as twenty-five semiskilled workers. In these larger shops, moreover, masters and journeymen no longer worked side by side, or even under the same roof. Instead, lower-quality work was often subcontracted to less skilled workers, to be completed at home for minimal wages. This system of "sweated labor" dominated the consumer finishing

[2] Wilentz, *Chants Democratic*, chaps. 1, 2; Laurie, *Working People of Philadelphia*, chap. 1; Dawley, *Class and Community*, chap. 2; Salinger, "Artisans, Journeymen, and the Transformation of Labor."

[3] Laurie, *Working People of Philadelphia*, chap. 1; Rock, *Artisans of the New Republic*, chap. 9; Wilentz, *Chants Democratic*, chap. 3.

[4] For composition of the Jeffersonian work force, see Rock, *Artisans of the New Republic*, 243–46; and Laurie, *Working People of Philadelphia*, 25.

[5] For a description of "half-ways" and "two-thirders," see George A. Stevens, *New York Typographical Union, No. 6: Study of a Modern Trade Union and Its Predecessors* (Albany, N.Y.: J. B. Lyon, State Printers, 1913), 65–70.

trades until midcentury, and was the source of considerable concern for skilled artisans in these trades.[6]

However, not all artisans, even within the "conflict trades," suffered with the reorganization of work. Some fortunate masters were able to keep pace with the growing markets and accumulated substantial fortunes in this period of economic change.[7] Apprentices, too, often welcomed the breakdown of the craft economy, as it enabled them to escape years of training and move more quickly into the wage-earning world. Of all of the artisans, it was the journeymen who lost out most frequently in this period. After investing several years in their trade, journeymen were confronted with declining wages, limited mobility, and lower social status as craft production was replaced by production of poor-quality goods through sweated labor.[8]

Displaced journeymen were quick to oppose the reorganization of work that both accompanied and fueled industrialization. In Philadelphia, for example, some skilled workers began to organize and protest economic change even before the end of the eighteenth century.[9] By the 1820s, masters and journeymen in a number of cities increasingly conceived of their interests as distinct and conflictual rather than as complementary aspects of a common trade. The growing conflict between masters and journeymen was not confined to the workplace, but pervaded many aspects of workers' lives. Sean Wilentz, for example, has shown how the increased tension within the trades was reflected in artisan festivals before the Civil War. Under the old system of craft production, artisans celebrated together, marching side by side under a single banner. By the early decades of the nineteenth century, this was no longer the case. Instead, masters and journeymen increasingly walked separately in distinct groups, reflecting the emergence of different interests within the trade.[10] A similar shift took place in some workingmen's associations as masters and journeymen in some trades began to organize separate societies in order to protect and promote their diverging concerns.[11]

Indeed, it was precisely the increased conflict within the consumer finish-

[6] See Wilentz, *Chants Democratic*, chap. 3, esp. 119–29.

[7] One of the most renowned entrepreneurial successes was the New York cabinetmaker Duncan Phyfe, who had amassed $500,000 at his death. However, Phyfe was exceptional; the more typical successful artisan would generally accumulate $10,000 to $50,000 in a lifetime. See Rock, *Artisans of the New Republic*, 246–48.

[8] See ibid., 246, 264–83; and Wilentz, *Chants Democratic*, 48–60.

[9] See Salinger, "Artisans, Journeymen, and the Transformation of Labor."

[10] Sean Wilentz, "Artisan Republican Festivals and the Rise of Class Conflict in New York City, 1788–1837," in Daniel J. Walkowitz, ed., *Working-Class America: Essays on Labor, Community, and the American Society* (Urbana: University of Illinois Press, 1983), 37–77.

[11] Montgomery, "Working Classes of the Pre-Industrial City," 6; Salinger, "Artisans, Journeymen, and the Transformation of Labor," 77–78.

ing trades that lay behind the conspiracy convictions before the Civil War. Most of the antebellum cases involved disputes between master craftsmen and their own journeymen. Moreover, almost all of the early conspiracy cases involved shoemakers, tailors, spinners, and weavers: the very same crafts that were being reorganized to capture the ready-made trade. Thus, in many ways, the conspiracy trials provide a useful barometer of the increased social conflict during the early stages of industrialization as one group of workingmen after another was convicted of conspiracy, their strikes broken up, and their associations at least temporarily disbanded.[12] In order to explore further the relationship between working-class formation and the first wave of conspiracy trials, we must first identify the major episodes of working-class protest in the antebellum decades.

The high point of artisan protest, at least in New York and Philadelphia, was reached in the 1820s and 1830s with the formation of three successive workingmen's organizations: the Working Men's political parties of 1827–1831; the city-based General Trades' Unions (GTUs) of 1833–1839; and the Loco-foco party in New York City of 1835–1837. Although none of these organizations lasted more than a few years, they have been viewed by many historians as the first signs of working-class consciousness in the United States. Artisans responded to metropolitan industrialization, so the argument runs, by calling into question existing economic and social relations and constructing in their stead a new, more class-conscious view of the world.[13]

Philadelphia workers were the first to establish a Working Men's party in 1827 when a meeting of the Mechanics' Union of Trade Associations resolved to go into politics. Working Men's parties soon appeared in New York in 1829, in New England in 1831, and in several other states under a variety of names, but with similar platforms and tactics. The principal objective of these parties was to contest and influence electoral politics at the state level in order to secure preferential legislation on a broad range of policy issues. The Working Men's concerns can be seen clearly in the internal debates within the New York Working Men's party. To be sure, the New York party was more divided than its Philadelphia or New England counterparts; the substantive platform changed significantly with two factional disputes that divided the party in its very first year. Nevertheless,

---

[12] Many lower court cases went unreported, especially in the antebellum era. Thus it is difficult to construct a complete list of antebellum conspiracy trials. Nevertheless, a list of the major cases can be found in the following sources: Nelles, "Commonwealth v. Hunt," 1166–69; Turner, *The Early American Labor Conspiracy Cases*, 2–3. For the reorganization of work and the conspiracy trials, see Quimby, "The Cordwainers' Protest." For the limited impact of conspiracy convictions on working-class organization, see Mayer, "People v. Fisher: The Shoemakers' Strike of 1833," 8–9.

[13] See Wilentz, *Chants Democratic*, chaps. 5, 6, esp. p. 214; Laurie, *Working People of Philadelphia*, chaps. 4, 5; and text and notes following.

these disagreements help to highlight the range of issues advocated by workingmen before the Civil War.[14]

The New York journeymen's protest began in the spring of 1829 when workingmen organized in order to resist a rumored increase in the length of the workday. A public meeting was called for April 28 in the Bowery Long Room; it was attended by 5,000 to 6,000 people. The meeting participants agreed on some general principles concerning the equal rights of all citizens, the "guaranty [sic]" of a comfortable living for "reasonable toil," and a commitment to work a "just and reasonable" time of ten hours a day. Employers who demanded more than ten hours were to be struck against and the names of workingmen in their employ published in the local newspaper. Finally, a "Committee of Fifty" was appointed to help achieve these goals. Interestingly, the committee included both small masters and journeymen, but special care was taken to avoid appointing those who "employed a large number of hands."[15]

The Committee of Fifty met during the summer and early fall of 1829 and eventually decided to run its own slate of candidates in the upcoming local elections. On October 19, another meeting was called to select the Working Men's ticket and to present the committee's report. Again the meeting was attended by an estimated 5,000 workingmen and their allies. The committee's report, which supposedly had been drafted by Thomas Skidmore, became the principal manifesto for the New York Working Men's party in the elections that fall. The centerpiece of the Skidmore program was the call for an equal division of the soil and the abolition of the "hereditary transmission of wealth." In addition, the report called for creation of a system of state education, passage of a mechanics' lien law, and abolition of chartered monopolies (especially the banks), reform of the

---

[14] Commons et al., *History of Labor in the United States* 1:285–86; John R. Commons, "Labor Organization and Labor Politics, 1827–37," *Quarterly Journal of Economics* 21 (February 1907): 323–29; Frank T. Carlton, "The Workingmen's Party of New York City: 1829–1831," *Political Science Quarterly* 22, 3 (September 1907): 401–15; Walter Hugins, *Jacksonian Democracy and the Working Class: A Study of the New York Workingmen's Movement, 1829–1837* (Stanford: Stanford University Press, 1960); Seymour Savetsky, "The New York Working Men's Party," (M.A. thesis, Columbia University, 1948); Louis H. Arky, "The Mechanics' Union of Trade Associations and the Formation of the Philadelphia Workingmen's Movement," *Pennsylvania Magazine of History and Biography* 76 (April 1952): 142–76; Leonard Bernstein, "The Working People of Philadelphia from Colonial Times to the General Strike of 1835," *Pennsylvania Magazine of History and Biography* 74 (July 1950): 322–39; and Edward Pessen, "The Working Men's Party Revisited," *Labor History* 4, 3 (Fall 1963): 203–26.

[15] For an excellent contemporary account of the New York Working Men's party, see *The Radical* 2, 1 (January 1842)–2, 4, (April 1843). For the phrases in quotations and a general description of the April 28 meeting, see *The Radical* 2, 1 (January 1842): 7–8.

militia system, and abrogation of imprisonment for debt. The report met with little disagreement and was adopted unanimously at the meeting.[16]

At one of the meetings to prepare for the elections, a resolution was passed requesting all "uninvited persons, not living by useful industry, 'such as bankers, brokers, and rich men,' to withdraw."[17] Thus a new political party was created in order to advance the workingmen's concerns. The party performed remarkably well in the fall elections, especially given their short preparation. The Working Men secured over 6,000 votes out of 21,000 and elected a journeyman carpenter, Ebenezer Ford, to the New York State Assembly. More importantly, support for the Working Men's party cut the previous Tammany vote by a third.[18]

The Skidmorite platform, however, was short-lived. On December 29, a large public meeting was held in Military Hall, which was attended by 3,000. Skidmore and his followers were removed from power by a coalition of Robert Dale Owen, Henry Guyon, and Noah Cook and their supporters. Cook presented a new report that included an address, resolutions, and plan of organization for the party. The new report broke significantly with the earlier Skidmorite platform by declaring that "what-ever may be said to the contrary . . . we have no desire or intention of disturbing the rights of property in individuals, or the public." Property rights and religion were to remain "sacred" and education was put forward as the Working Men's principal demand.[19] After a "brief and somewhat tumultuous discussion" Cook's report was adopted, the Committee of Fifty dissolved, and a new executive council established in its place. Shortly after the meeting, Skidmore and "a few of his most zealous friends" resigned from the party in defeat.[20]

By May 1830, the party had split again, this time over the nature of education reform. The minority faction, led by Robert Dale Owen, believed that a system of "truly republican education" could be ensured only under an extensive program of state education. Specifically, the Owenites advocated a program of "state guardianship" in which children would be taken from their homes and placed in public boarding schools in order to

[16] The Committee of Fifty's report was published in a number of antebellum newspapers. For one of the copies, see *The Radical* 2, 3 (February 1843): 33–43. The report also has been reprinted in Commons et al., *Documentary History* 5:149–54.

[17] Quoted from *The Radical* 2, 3 (February 1843): 43.

[18] Wilentz, *Chants Democratic*, 198; Commons et al., *History of Labor in the United States* 1:240.

[19] Quoted from "Proceedings of a Meeting of Mechanics and other Working Men, held at Military Hall, Wooster-Street, New York, on Tuesday evening, Dec. 29, 1829," reprinted in Commons et al., *Documentary History*, 5:157 (see also 160–64).

[20] See *The Radical*, 2, 4 (April 1843): 55–56.

produce a new generation of "useful, intelligent, virtuous citizens."[21] Their opponents, and victors, led by Noah Cook, proposed a more moderate scheme of state-funded day schools. Education was critical, the Cookites agreed, but removing children from their families and placing them in public boarding schools was an "oppressive and unjust" solution. Most of the benefits of education reform could be achieved through a more moderate scheme of public day schools.[22]

Thus, in each of the factional disputes, whether over property rights or education reform, the more extreme position was defeated and the more moderate faction left in control. By the 1830 election, the New York Working Men's party ran three separate tickets, one for each faction. Not surprisingly, none of the three made a particularly strong showing, leaving the Working Men with little or no influence in New York state politics. By 1831, the party had all but disappeared.[23] Artisan protest, however, did not vanish altogether, but reappeared a few years later with the creation of the city-based unions or GTUs.

In August 1833, New York workers were the first to establish a GTU, which was followed by similar organizations in Philadelphia in November 1833 and New England in 1834. By 1836 there were at least thirteen such unions in the United States.[24] The GTUs were the broadest and most sustained attempts at workers' organization before the Civil War and were generally quite effective at either holding steady or improving hours and wages of their members. The GTUs attracted considerable attention and grew rapidly in membership after their founding. The Philadelphia GTU, for example, was established in November 1833 by the tailors', bookbinders', and cordwainers' societies. By January 1834, more than a dozen unions had joined the central organization, and by March there were seventeen affiliated unions representing about 2,000 members. After two more years, over fifty unions had joined the city central, which now represented over 10,000 workingmen. Similarly, the New York GTU grew from nine trade union affiliates in 1833 to twenty-nine unions in 1834, representing 11,500 members or approximately 20 to 30 percent of the white male work force in New York.[25]

The major purpose of the GTUs was to protest the declining status of

[21] Quoted from the minority report of the subcommittee on education, originally reported in the labor newspaper the *New York Sentinel and Working Man's Advocate*, 19 June 1830, 4. Both the Majority and Minority reports have been reprinted in Commons et al., *Documentary History* 5:165–71.

[22] Commons et al., *Documentary History* 5:171.

[23] Commons et al., *History of Labor in the United States* 1:268–69.

[24] Ibid., 360.

[25] For GTU figures in Philadelphia, see Laurie, *Working People of Philadelphia*, 87; and Commons et al., *Documentary History* 5:325–26. For GTU figures in New York, see Wilentz, *Chants Democratic*, 220.

skilled craftsmen in the antebellum decades. By organizing across trades, artisans hoped to increase their power to oppose the reorganization of their trades. Two issues generally lay at the center of antebellum strikes. First, artisans struggled to maintain a "book of just prices" and to resist the introduction of wage labor. Second, the GTUs wanted to enforce traditional standards of apprenticeship within their trades. The GTUs focused on the workplace rather than on political reform, as both the New York and Philadelphia GTUs explicitly eschewed party politics. However, the new labor historians have shown that strikes to raise or resist reduction of wages, which dominated the 1830s, were not simply motivated by narrow economic concerns. Instead, antebellum strikes over wages and working conditions reflected workingmen's struggle to halt the bastardization of their trades that accompanied industrialization.[26] Although the tactics and arena had changed, the GTUs nevertheless continued to advocate the earlier workingmen's goals of resisting the reorganization of work and securing a place for skilled artisans in the antebellum republic. Toward the end of the 1830s, there were some attempts at national labor organization in both New York and Pennsylvania. However, these schemes never amounted to much and disappeared along with the more successful GTUs in the financial panic and depression of 1837.[27]

The third major instance of antebellum workingmen's protest occurred with the creation of the Loco-foco or Equal Rights party in New York in October 1835. The party began as a splinter group from within Tammany Hall, protesting the policy of government-chartered monopolies.[28] The actual break and party name stem from a ward meeting of the New York Democratic party held in Tammany Hall on 29 October 1935. The meeting was called to approve a Democratic ticket for the upcoming local elections. The Democratic party leaders had preselected candidates, which they announced at the meeting, only to be met with vocal disapproval from

[26] See Wilentz, *Chants Democratic*, chap. 6; and Laurie, *Working People of Philadelphia*, chap. 5.

[27] Commons et al., *History of Labor in the United States*, vol. 1, pt. 3, chap. 6.

[28] My view of the Loco-foco party draws heavily on the contemporary account of the party by Fitzwilliam Byrdsall. See Byrdsall, *History of the Loco-foco or Equal Rights Party*. However, Byrdsall focuses primarily on divisions within the Democratic party and does not cover the role of the journeymen tailors' protest adequately. For the journeymen's protest and the Loco-foco party, see the *New York Evening Post*, 1 June 1836–31 July 1836; and Carl N. Degler, "An Enquiry into the Locofoco Party" (M.A. thesis, Columbia University, 1947). See also Carl N. Degler, "The Loco-focos: Urban 'Agrarians,'" *Journal of Economic History* 16, 3 (1956): 322–53; William Trimble, "Diverging Tendencies in New York Democracy in the Period of the Loco-focos," *American Historical Review* 24, 3 (April 1919): 396–421; William Trimble, "The Social Philosophy of the Loco-foco Democracy," *American Journal of Sociology* 26 (1921): 705–15; Hugins, *Jacksonian Democracy and the Working Class*, chap. 3; and Arthur M. Schlesinger, Jr., *The Age of Jackson* (Boston: Little, Brown, 1953).

the antimonopoly faction within the party. But before any formal objections were lodged, the chairman, Isaac Varian, declared the ticket approved and the meeting closed. To mark the end of the meeting, in typical Tammany Hall fashion, the gaslights were turned off, leaving the protesting antimonopoly men in darkness. But the dissenters had come prepared and immediately took out candles and "Loco-foco" brand matches, creating "living and breathing chandeliers."[29] Antimonopoly Democrats, such as Dr. Stephen Hasbrouck, Fitzwilliam Byrdsall, and Joel Curtis, continued the meeting and adopted their own ticket and resolutions, thereby beginning a two-year break with Tammany Hall.

The dissenting faction met again in January and February 1836 to formalize the separation from Tammany and to pass their Declaration of Principles. Moses Jaques, president of the February Convention, drew up the declaration, which raised three issues of special concern to the new party. First, the Loco-focos declared equal rights of all citizens to be the "true foundation of Republican Government." Second, they stated their "unqualified and uncompromising hostility to bank notes and paper money as a circulating medium"; gold and silver were considered to be "the only safe and constitutional currency." Finally, the Loco-focos strongly opposed "all monopolies by legislation, because they are a violation of the equal rights of The People."[30]

The party received a major boost and slight reorientation when it merged with the movement protesting the *Faulkner* conviction in June 1836.[31] In the spring of 1836, New York tailors struck against a reduction in wages and were arrested, tried, and convicted of criminal conspiracy. When Judge Edwards set the day of sentencing, a placard appeared throughout the city calling for a meeting to protest the conviction. The "Coffin Handbill," as the placard became known, called workingmen to a meeting in the park.

> The Rich against the Poor! Judge Edwards, the tool of the Aristocracy, against the People! Mechanics and workingmen! a deadly blow has been struck at your Liberty! . . . Twenty of your brethren have been found guilty for presuming to resist a reduction of their wages! and Judge Edwards has charged an American jury, and agreeably to that charge, they have established the precedent, that workingmen have no right to regulate the price of labor! or, in other words, the Rich are the only judges of the wants of the Poor Man! . . . On Monday,

[29] Byrdsall, *History of the Loco-foco or Equal Rights Party*, 26; Joseph G. Rayback, *A History of American Labor* (New York: The Free Press, 1959), 85–86.

[30] Byrdsall, *History of the Loco-foco or Equal Rights Party*, 39–40.

[31] Twenty journeymen tailors were convicted of conspiracy in New York in June of 1836 in the case of *People v. Faulkner*. A large protest accompanied their sentencing when Judge Edwards imposed penalties totaling $1,150. The case and protest are discussed at greater length later in the chapter.

the Liberty of the Workingmen will be interred! Judge Edwards is to chant the Requiem! Go! Go! Go! every Freeman, every Workingman, and hear the hollow and the melancholy sound of the earth on the Coffin of Equality! Let the Court-room, the City-hall—yea, the whole Park, be filled with Mourners! But, remember, offer no violence to Judge Edwards! Bend meekly, and receive the chains wherewith you are to be bound! Keep the peace! Above all things keep the peace![32]

Observers estimated that as many as 27,000 to 30,000 attended the meeting in the park to protest the conviction and sentencing of the tailors.[33] After a number of speeches, several resolutions were adopted, proclaiming the equal rights of all citizens and calling for the formation of "a separate and distinct party, around which the laboring classes and their friends, can rally with confidence."[34] Finally, a Correspondence Committee was established to prepare an address to their fellow workingmen outlining their "common grievances" and to plan for a state convention to be held later that year in Utica on September 15.

The committee's address, published later that summer, identified two problems as in need of special attention: currency regulation and the conspiracy laws.[35] The question of finance was placed first in the address and continued many of the earlier Working Men's party concerns. The address outlined the problem in the following terms:

> By the mal legislation of this state, the people are deprived of a most important prerogative of sovereignty—the regulation of the currency. Banks are *combinations* possessing the power to *expand* or *limit* trade and commerce, wages, and prices of all commodities, and therefore in fact, the management of the value of every man's property and labour. They, with other *chartered combinations* are spread over our country like swarms of locusts, preying on the fruits of our industry; and lest these systems of nobility without the name, should not degrade and subject us in vassallage soon enough, the state itself has a workshop to compete with the citizens, and to make the convicted felon the competitor to underwork and undersell, and in many instances to ruin, the honest patriotick [*sic*] artizan.[36]

Second, unlike the Working Men's parties and GTUs, the address explicitly protested the recent "decisions of our Judges, founded on forced construc-

---

[32] Quoted from the *Morning Courier and New York Enquirer*, 8 June 1836, p. 2, col. 1; reprinted in Commons et al., *Documentary History* 5:317–18.

[33] Byrdsall, *History of the Loco-foco or Equal Rights Party*, 109.

[34] *The National Laborer*, 18 June 1836, p. 50, cols. 3, 6; reprinted in Commons et al., *Documentary History* 5:322.

[35] For a complete copy of the Correspondence Committee's address, see *New York Evening Post*, 23 July 1836, p. 2, cols. 4, 5.

[36] Quoted from ibid; emphasis in original.

tions of the statute, and on precedents of British courts of law, which are hung over our heads as grim skeletons to frighten us into the deep vortex of subjection and degredation." The current situation was particularly unjust, the address continued, because "capitalists and employers may combine together, and bind each other under heavy penalties, not authorized by the constitution or the laws. And if the humble operatives dare to oppose, in order to counteract these petty tyrants, they are prosecuted and punished as 'conspirators against the peace and safety of the state.'"[37]

The remedy for both these problems, the address concluded, was the forming of a "united phalanx of enemies to those domestick traitors who would impoverish us with charters and monopolies, and crush us with forced interpretations of our statute law, and the musty precedents of British courts." By combining at the ballot box, workingmen could ensure that laws would be made and administered by men friendly to their cause. Finally, the address recommended that the Utica convention in September should set about establishing a new political party to promote the workingmen's views.[38]

At the Utica convention, the protesting workingmen and the antimonopoly Democrats, who had split from Tammany the previous fall, joined forces and established an independent political party with the official name of the Equal Rights party, but continued to be known informally as the Loco-focos. After the September convention, the Loco-foco party continued to push for antimonopoly legislation and currency reform, but now also focused on the contemporary conspiracy trials and the excessive discretionary power of the courts.[39] By 1837, the party called for legal reform and actually proposed an alternative constitution that attempted to constrain "judicial legislation" by electing judges for a fixed term and by limiting use of English common law precedents in American cases.[40] However, no sooner had these reforms been proposed at the September convention than the party began to disintegrate. By December 1837, the Loco-focos had returned to the Democratic party fold and the independent political party had disappeared.

ARTISAN PROTEST AND WORKING-CLASS CONSCIOUSNESS

Two aspects of the Working Men's parties, GTUs and Loco-focos are seen by the new labor historians as clear manifestations of the increased class consciousness of the antebellum decades. First, both the Working Men's

[37] Quoted from ibid.

[38] See ibid.

[39] *The National Laborer*, 18 June 1836, p. 50, cols. 3–6; reprinted in Commons et al., *Documentary History* 5:319–31.

[40] Byrdsall quotes most of the draft constitution. See Byrdsall, *History of the Loco-foco or Equal Right Party*, 163–65.

parties and GTUs are thought to have displayed a new level of collective identity or solidarity that enabled artisans to unite across the traditional boundaries of their trades. Thus, in the 1820s and 1830s, many historians claim, artisans' loyalties were no longer restricted to their craft, but increasingly were drawn along class lines, as artisans and employers began to organize across trades.[41] Second, labor historians look to particular elements of the substantive agenda of the Working Men's party as further evidence of the artisans' radical potential. Skidmore's attack on existing property relations is thought to be especially significant. Even if only a minority faction, the Skidmorites showed that at least some artisans understood the "present crisis" to be rooted in the underlying economic relations, and began to articulate a program of radical social change. Similarly, the successful general strike for the ten-hour day in Philadelphia in 1835 is thought to signal the "depth of worker unrest" and the extent of union solidarity within the Philadelphia GTU. Finally, the Loco-focos' attack on the unequal treatment of workers and employers by the courts has been identified, by some scholars, as an important recognition by American workers of the inherent class bias of the courts.[42]

Although artisan consciousness changed considerably in the antebellum decades, most labor historians agree that protesting workingmen did not break entirely with the past. Instead, artisans drew on long-standing republican values to critique the new economic order. Even though classic republican theorists paid little attention to economic relations, artisans extended the eighteenth-century assumptions to their own world, the world of work and production, and created their own variation on republican themes. Specifically, displaced artisans, historians have found, drew on republican notions of political rights and civic participation in order to protest the economic inequalities that accompanied industrialization. The major contribution of the republican tradition, from this perspective, was that it provided displaced journeymen with a set of values and precepts with which to challenge the economic changes under way in the early nineteenth century. At times, some scholars seem almost to conflate artisan republicanism and working-class consciousness by focusing primarily on the ways in which republicanism has contributed to the emerging working-class consciousness in the antebellum decades.[43]

[41] See Wilentz, *Chants Democratic*, chaps. 5, 6, esp. 214, 237–48; Wilentz, "Artisan Republican Festivals"; Dawley, *Class and Community*, chap. 2, Conclusion; Faler, *Mechanics and Manufacturers*, chaps. 9–11; Laurie, *Working People of Philadelphia*, chaps. 4, 5.

[42] For discussion of Skidmore's platform, see Wilentz, *Chants Democratic*, chap. 4, esp. pp. 187–89. For discussion of the Philadelphia general strike and the GTU, see Laurie, *Working People of Philadelphia*, 90–91. For discussion of the Loco-focos and the courts, see Degler, "An Enquiry into the Locofoco Party"; and Holt, "Labour Conspiracy Cases in the United States."

[43] See Dawley, *Class and Community*, chaps. 2, 9; Laurie, *Working People of Philadelphia*, chap 4; Wilentz, *Chants Democratic*, chap. 2; and Wilentz, "Artisan Origins of the Amer-

By situating discussions of the Working Men's parties and GTUs in the larger context of metropolitan industrialization and artisan republicanism, the new labor history has gone a long way toward recovering artisan protest of the antebellum era. Historians have shown not only why skilled workers began to organize in the 1820s and 1830s, but, more specifically, they have determined who the protesters were. Antebellum strikes over wages, hours, and working conditions need no longer be viewed as narrow precursors to business unionism, as previous scholars had claimed. Instead, the new labor history has shown that the Working Men's parties and GTUs were the products of a much larger struggle by displaced journeymen over the nature of work and the future place of skilled craftsmen in the changing economy. Status, honor, and pride were as important as more narrowly conceived assumptions of economic interest and material gain.[44]

Despite all that has been gained from the new labor history, prevailing interpretations of the antebellum era remain incomplete. By focusing on the emerging class consciousness, scholars have underestimated the eighteenth-century legacy and as a consequence, I believe, have misinterpreted the nature and significance of artisan protest before the Civil War. The limits of existing accounts can be seen most clearly in three neglected aspects of artisan protest in the antebellum decades. First, the complete substantive agenda pursued by the workingmen needs closer examination. Second, the Working Men's party's and GTUs' rather quiescent response to the antebellum conspiracy trials needs to be explained. Finally, a more satisfying account of the demise of all of these workingmen's associations needs to be given. Exploring each of these issues in turn points the way toward rethinking antebellum social relations and ultimately provides the key to an alternative account of working-class formation in the United States.

First, the new labor history pays insufficient attention to the full range of workingmen's demands before the Civil War. An analysis centered around increased class consciousness cannot explain the particular form of workers' protest in these early decades. Why, for example, were the New York and Philadelphia Working Men's parties preoccupied with education policy and antimonopoly reform rather than questioning more directly the reorganization of work and sweated labor? Why, in short, did workers resist industrialization by advocating a broad range of social reform rather

---

ican Working Class." For the conflation of artisan republicanism with working-class consciousness, see Oestreicher, "Urban Working-Class Political Behavior," 1264–65, where Oestreicher writes of "working-class republicanism" and of "class-conscious artisanal republicanism." See also Wilentz, *Chants Democratic*, 97–101, 188–89, 203.

[44] The enormous gains achieved by the new labor history can be seen by comparing the following accounts of antebellum workers' protest: Wilentz, *Chants Democratic*, chap. 6; Taft, "On the Origins of Business Unionism."

than focusing on more immediate workplace concerns? To be sure, considerable attention has been paid to some elements of the workingmen's program. Thomas Skidmore's platform, for example, has been examined in detail and considered one of the high water marks of artisan radicalism in the antebellum era. Other workingmen's concerns, however, have been largely ignored or, when addressed, have not been integrated sufficiently into workingmen's protest as a whole.[45] Exactly why the chartering of the national bank and education reform captured the workers' imagination has yet to be explained. What is clear is that neither of these concerns can be accommodated easily within existing accounts of the period, which focus too narrowly on the making of the American working class.

Second, given the dominance of the courts for regulating workers' protest in the antebellum era, we might expect workers to have contested the conspiracy convictions and demonstrated a strong interest in legal reform. By repealing the conspiracy doctrine and demanding state protection of the right to organize and strike, workers could have strengthened their hand in the emerging class struggle. Moreover, workingmen did not have to push for legal reform on their own, but could have joined forces quite easily with codification reformers in the antebellum decades who also were trying to limit the power of the courts by codifying the common law.[46] Despite the advantages for working-class organization to be gained from legal reform, apart from the Loco-focos, the New York and Pennsylvania workingmen provided little support for the codification movement in the 1820s and 1830s and generally showed little interest in legal reform. Neither the antebellum Working Men's parties nor the GTUs paid much attention to the conspiracy convictions, and neither made repeal of the doctrine an important plank in their platform.[47] At most, workingmen followed codification at a distance, at times commenting on the need to simplify the

---

[45] For example, Wilentz pays little attention to banks and financial policy in his account of the Working Men's party. Education reform fares somewhat better, but again is considered less significant than Skidmore's platform. See Wilentz, Chants Democratic, chap. 5. Similarly, Laurie pays little attention to questions of education and antimonopoly reform within the Philadelphia workingmen's associations. See Laurie, Working People of Philadelphia, chap. 4.

[46] For an excellent account of the antebellum codification movement, see Cook, The American Codification Movement. See also Maxwell Bloomfield, American Lawyers in a Changing Society, 1776–1876 (Cambridge, Mass.: Harvard University Press, 1976); Levy, The Law of the Commonwealth and Chief Justice Shaw; Roscoe Pound, "The Lay Tradition as to the Lawyer," 12 Michigan Law Review 627 (1914); Gawalt, "Sources of Anti-Lawyer Sentiment in Massachusetts"; and Friedman, "Law Reform in Historical Perspective."

[47] Some evidence of workingmen's interest in codification reform can be seen in The Mechanics' Press, a weekly newspaper published in Utica, N.Y. The first issue appeared on 14 November 1829. For explicit reference to codification, see 3 April 1830, p. 163, col. 1; 22 May 1830, p. 217, col. 1; and 24 July 1830, p. 290, col. 1. In addition, workingmen often complained about the inefficiency and expense of the legal system and called for simplification of the laws. For example, see The Mechanics' Press, 5 June 1830, p. 235, col. 1; The Man, 26

legal system or, more often, attacking lawyers themselves as "parasites" and "pests."[48]

Labor's absence from the legal reform coalition is especially perplexing, as both workers' protest and legal reform were at their height in the 1820s and 1830s, and both movements were strong in New York and Pennsylvania in these same decades. There were, moreover, a number of direct links between workingmen and codification reformers. Two of the leading codificationists, William Sampson and Robert Rantoul, Jr., acted as defense attorneys for shoemakers in two major antebellum conspiracy trials: *People v. Melvin* in 1809 and *Commonwealth v. Hunt* in 1840–1842.[49] In addition, important legal reformers, such as Frederick Robinson, addressed trade union meetings in order to encourage workingmen to join in the fight to check the power of the courts.[50] Despite such connections between the two movements, these links remained strictly an elite phenomenon, with little or no penetration to the rank and file.

To be sure, even in the 1820s and early 1830s, workingmen were by no means oblivious to the conspiracy trials and at times objected to particular convictions. For example, Stephen Simpson of the Philadelphia Working Men's party complained of the unequal treatment of workingmen and capitalists by the courts.[51] Similarly, the Philadelphia GTU also protested the *Faulkner* conviction in 1836 by passing a series of resolutions condemning Judge Edwards' decision and distributing their statement to sev-

---

February 1834, p. 1, col. 1; and Stephen Simpson, *The Working Man's Manual: A New Theory of Political Economy, on the Principle of Production the Source of Wealth* (Philadelphia: Thomas L. Bonsal, 1831), 36–37. These complaints notwithstanding, prior to the emergence of the Loco-foco party in 1835, workingmen did not make legal reform a major plank in their platforms. Nor is there evidence of codification being an important issue of discussion in either the workingmen's newspapers or proceedings of the Working Men's parties and GTUs.

[48] *The Working Man's Advocate*, 14 November 1829, p. 1, cols. 4, 5.

[49] See People v. Melvin (N.Y. 1809); and Commonwealth v. Hunt (Mass. 1840) and (Mass. 1842).

For a discussion of William Sampson's role in the codification movement, see Bloomfield, *American Lawyers in a Changing Society*. For Robert Rantoul, Jr., see Nelles, "Commonwealth v. Hunt"; Merle E. Curti, "Robert Rantoul, Jr.: The Reformer in Politics," *New England Quarterly* 5, 2 (April 1932): 264–80; and Meyers, *The Jacksonian Persuasion*, chap. 10.

[50] For example, see Frederick Robinson, "Reform of Law and the Judiciary," delivered to the Boston Trades' Union on 4 July 1834; reprinted in Joseph L. Blau, ed., *Social Theories of Jacksonian Democracy: Representative Writings of the Period 1825–1850* (New York: Bobbs-Merrill, 1954).

[51] Simpson, *Working Man's Manual*, 86, 138. See also Simpson's complaint against the courts in *The Mechanics' Free Press*, 14 March 1829.

eral local newspapers.[52] John Crossin, a representative from the Saddlers' and Harnessmakers' Union, also proposed that "a committee of five be appointed to prepare a petition to the Legislature, asking for the passage of a definite law in relation to combinations and conspiracies, so far as relates to the operations of Mechanics in regard to their wages or hours of labor." However, when the resolution was discussed at the general meeting, there was insufficient support to sustain Crossin's demand. Instead, "after an animated discussion the whole subject was laid on the table."[53]

Thus, both the Working Men's party and GTU objections to conspiracy convictions remained intermittent, never attracting the same attention as the other demands of the workingmen's associations. Questions of currency and banking reform, education, imprisonment for debt, and abolition of convict labor continued to dominate the discussion and resolutions of both the New York and Pennsylvania Working Men's parties and GTUs.[54]

In 1835 and 1836, however, the workingmen's response to the conspiracy trials began to change. Unlike the earlier trials, the *Fisher* and *Faulkner* trials met with vociferous protest, which, we have seen, played an important part in the founding of the Loco-foco party.[55] Although the Loco-focos clearly objected to judicial regulation of labor more strenuously than earlier workingmen's organizations, the Loco-focos' response, I believe, does not mark an abrupt break with the Working Men's parties and GTUs. In fact, when we examine the situation more closely we will see that there were important continuities across all three waves of antebellum protest. The Loco-focos' hostility to the courts was new, but when forced to choose between competing goals, the Loco-focos ranked the more familiar antimonopoly concerns ahead of their newfound interest in legal reform. Thus, we need to explain why workingmen did not make legal reform a high priority before the Civil War.

Finally, while the new labor history has provided an excellent account of the origins of artisan protest, it has had much less success explaining the movement's demise. If the Working Men's parties and GTUs were protesting the changing relations within the trade, why was it so difficult to sustain these new organizations? The impetus for organization had by no means

[52] Copies of the resolutions can be found in *The National Laborer*, 11 June 1836, p. 47, col. 2; reprinted in Commons et al., *Documentary History* 5:361–68.

[53] For the Crossin resolution, see *The National Laborer*, 23 July 1836, p. 71, col. 2. For discussion of the resolution, see *The National Laborer*, 13 August 1836, p. 83, col. 2. Both articles have been reprinted in Commons et al., *Documentary History* 5:373, 375.

[54] For example, see Simpson, *Working Man's Manual*; "Report of the Committee of Fifty"; "Proceedings of a Meeting of Mechanics and Other Working Men."

[55] See People v. Fisher and People v. Faulkner.

disappeared, yet neither the parties nor the GTUs lasted more than a few years. All too often scholars attribute organizational decline either to the economic depression of 1837 or to the corrupting influence of party politics before the Civil War. Even the very best of these new accounts, Sean Wilentz's *Chants Democratic*, fails to escape the second of these pitfalls, especially in its account of the downfall of the New York Working Men's party. The radical thrust of Skidmore's initial program was quickly derailed, according to Wilentz, as outsiders infiltrated the party, co-opted the membership, and led the party astray. The successive divisions within the party in December and May are viewed by Wilentz as products of external forces "invading" the party and destroying the true class interests of the workingmen.[56]

Wilentz's account of the party's decline ultimately rests on an arbitrary distinction he draws between the movement and the party. The Working Men's "movement," according to Wilentz, included all activity up to Skidmore's defeat and was the authentic component of workers' protest. In contrast, all activity after Skidmore's ousting is arbitrarily designated as "the party," which no longer reflected workers' real interests since it had been captured by professional politicians: "The party seemed to be only an extension of the movement; in fact, it was an invention of the Owenites and Cookites, one that assumed the name of the Working Men in a political coup that stunned and isolated Skidmore and effectively killed off what had been a radical political insurgency."[57] Wilentz is unable to see all three factions of the Working Men's party as equally legitimate, albeit different, responses to metropolitan industrialization. Instead, only the Skidmorites qualify as a genuine "radical political insurgency."

From Wilentz's perspective, the nascent working-class radicalism before the Civil War failed because of external constraints rather than as a result of internal processes. Party politics was the culprit for many of the social historians. More specifically, professional politicians are said to have mysteriously derailed artisan radicalism before it had time to fully take hold. For instance, Wilentz claims: "The Working Men were the first to confront the frustrating power of a professional American party politics just then emerging—the first to learn how, with the many misrepresentations and machinations of American party competition, a popular radical challenge could be turned into its opposite."[58] The political system, not the party membership, was responsible for Skidmore's downfall. Exactly how or

---

[56] See Wilentz, *Chants Democratic*, 211–16.

[57] Quoted from ibid., 212–13. For an excellent review of the literature on the Working Men's parties that clearly illustrates the preoccupation with the authenticity of antebellum workers' protest, see Pessen, "The Working Men's Party Revisited."

[58] Wilentz, *Chants Democratic*, 213. For similar arguments about the debilitating effects of politics on working-class radicalism, see Dawley, *Class and Community*, 70.

why party politics had this "corrupting" or deradicalizing effect is never really explained. One wonders, why were American workers more easily co-opted than English and French artisans? What made the American party system more debilitating than its European counterparts? Unfortunately, these questions have been addressed only fleetingly, leaving us with little or no sense of why this early artisan protest was so easily derailed.

Attending to these neglected aspects of artisan protest raises fundamental questions about the nature and significance of workingmen's protest in the 1820s and 1830s. Only by setting aside our presentist assumptions and rethinking the antebellum concept of class can we begin to make sense of the full range of artisan protest before the Civil War. To be sure, the economic changes and increased conflict were real. But how artisans understood these changes, what meaning they gave to events, must be reconsidered. Labor historians to date have been too quick to presume that an emerging class consciousness informed artisan demands. I believe protesting artisans were engaged in a very different task.

THE PRODUCERS' ALLIANCE: RETHINKING ANTEBELLUM CLASS RELATIONS

Although most contemporary scholars agree that artisan protest was informed by the republican tradition, the influence of republicanism has been too narrowly conceived. For most labor historians, the republican legacy is seen primarily as a different language of class, a different idiom for expressing the grievances of the newly emerging working class.[59] The equation of artisan republicanism and working-class formation that dominates much of the new labor history, I believe, has obscured the more important legacy of eighteenth-century assumptions in the antebellum decades. In fact, the republican legacy was considerably more than a different language of working-class protest. The eighteenth-century concepts and assumptions that infused workingmen's protest were rooted in, and sustained by, a very different set of social relations that prevailed before the Civil War. Put simply, the principal social cleavage in the 1820s and 1830s was not yet between labor and capital, or workers and employers. Instead, skilled artisans considered themselves to be producers, allied with master craftsmen, small manufacturers, and farmers against the nonproducing classes. Bankers, lawyers, merchants, and land speculators were the quintessential nonproducers, who lived by "their wits rather than by useful labor."[60]

[59] See Oestreicher, "Urban Working-Class Political Behavior," 1264–65.

[60] Quoted from The Man, 10 April 1834, 170. Most primary sources identify mechanics, master craftsmen, and small manufacturers as within the producers' ranks. Farmers did not play a significant role in either the New York or Philadelphia workingmen's associations, but

Labor newspapers, political pamphlets, and the platforms and proceedings of the Working Men's parties, the GTUs, and the Loco-foco party were filled with references to the producing and nonproducing classes. In fact, the central rhetorical motif throughout the primary sources generally involved the contrast of "honest industry" and productive labor with the idleness and luxury of the "useless classes." References to labor and capital were infrequent. To be sure, producers made occasional references to "capital," but in these instances they often distinguished between the "natural" and "fictitious" kinds. Unfortunately, the producers complained, much of the new wealth accumulated in the 1820s and 1830s had been secured through speculation and exchange rather than through honest toil. It was this "fictitious capital" that was endangering the republic and became the object of the producers' ire.[61]

Evidence of the producers' alliance, however, is not confined to rhetoric alone. In fact, the division between producers and nonproducers undergirded antebellum social relations and political alliances as well. Skilled workers, master craftsmen, and small manufacturers often were members of the very same organizations: organizations whose task was to mobilize the producing classes. The Working Men's parties, the Loco-focos, and even a number of trade unions generally welcomed masters and small manufacturers into their ranks, and often elected them to positions of considerable influence and power. For example, several of the most influential leaders in both the Working Men's parties and the GTUs, such as Noah Cook, Henry Guyon, Robert Dale Owen, and Thomas Brothers, were not artisans by trade, but rather were "middle-class" reformers who rose to positions of considerable prominence in the New York Working Men's party.[62]

In addition, the producing classes often were anxious to distinguish themselves from other groups in society that lacked the necessary prerequi-

---

were still considered fellow producers by most workingmen. In fact, the New England equivalent of the New York and Philadelphia Working Men's parties was called the Association of Farmers, Mechanics, and Other Workingmen. Even as late as 1842, George Henry Evans, editor of both *The Working Man's Advocate and The Radical*, defined the term *workingmen* as follows: "Whenever I may use the term 'Working Men' in this periodical, I wish to be understood as including not merely the manual laborer, but everyman who earns his bread by *useful* exertion, whether mental or physical." See *The Radical* 2, 1 (January 1842): 1.

[61] For the distinction between "real" and "fictitious" capital, see *The Man*, 24 March 1834, 109; and Simpson, *Working Man's Manual*, 69, 99, 101, 160. See also *The Man*, 22 March 1834, 105.

[62] See Edward Pessen, "Thomas Brothers, Anti-Capitalist Employer," *Pennsylvania History* 24, 4 (October 1957): 321–29; Wilentz, *Chants Democratic*, 178–79; and Edward Pessen, *Most Uncommon Jacksonians: The Radical Leaders of the Early Labor Movement* (Albany: State University of New York Press, 1967), 37–38.

sites for civic participation. Women, blacks, and the very poor were considered, by most producers, to be in positions of dependence and thus ought to be excluded from the producers' alliance. There is some evidence to suggest that the dependent poor and the small number of enfranchised blacks actually allied themselves with the nonproducing classes at the polls.[63] Thus, the division between the producing and nonproducing classes did not sit neatly alongside divisions between workers and employers, poor and rich, or labor and capital. Instead, the producers' alliance brought together the middling ranks of society: skilled workers, small manufacturers, and, where possible, farmers as well. Both the very bottom and the top of the social order were excluded from the producers' ranks and were referred to disparagingly as the "useless classes."

Looking back from the twentieth century, many scholars have lamented the presence of middle-class reformers in the antebellum organizations because they co-opted and betrayed the radical potential of artisan discontent. For participants and contemporary observers, however, the composition of these organizations drew little comment. Skilled workers, master craftsmen, and small manufacturers were natural allies: all three considered themselves to be industrious citizens and legitimate members of the producing classes. To be sure, the producers' alliance was beginning to show signs of strain, especially within the consumer finishing trades. However, the increased conflict between masters and journeymen in the 1820s and 1830s did not lead directly to the transformation of existing social relations. Producers did not simply break with the past and develop a new understanding of economic and social relations based on the struggle between labor and capital. On the contrary, the producers' initial reaction was to hold fast to their existing worldview and interpret their economic distress by drawing on and modifying three classic republican assumptions.

First, producers adhered to republican notions of propertied independence as an important prerequisite for political participation. Liberty would only be preserved, the producers claimed in good Harringtonian fashion, by independent citizens whose political opinions had not been compromised or corrupted through dependent relations.[64] However, producers' claims to propertied independence in the 1820s and 1830s were not at all clear. The reorganization of work and the introduction of wage labor

---

[63] On the exclusion of women and blacks from the producers' ranks, see Simpson, *Working Man's Manual*, 206–10, 219, 235; and Howe, *The Political Culture of the American Whigs*, 17–18. On the exclusion of the unskilled and the poor, see Laurie, *Working People of Philadelphia*, 85–86.

[64] For discussion of propertied independence in the republican tradition, see Pocock, "Civic Humanism," and "Machiavelli," in his *Politics, Language and Time*.

seemed to have placed workers in a dependent relationship with their employers and thus called into question their right to participate in contemporary political struggles.[65]

Displaced artisans were not so willing to concede their claims to civic participation. Instead of accepting their declining status, journeymen began to defend their independence by drawing a firm line between themselves and the unskilled and the dependent poor. Fully trained artisans ought to be considered independent citizens through assertions of property rights in their skill or trade. The labor theory of value justified producers' claims to both propertied independence and the associated right to political participation in the antebellum decades. For example, artisans joined the debate over financial policy in the following terms: "If you really think that we, the working men, have no *real interest* in the present contest, (over the bank) you are very much mistaken; for we think *our labor* is as good as your *real capital*, (the *produce* of labor,) and far better than your *false capital*, (the product of exclusive and therefore unrepublican privileges;)."[66] By declaring skilled labor to be the workingmen's "capital," artisans argued for their status as independent citizens. In so doing, they not only asserted their right to civic participation but also laid claim to their own vision of the antebellum republic.

Second, producers drew on the republican fear of corruption through the concentration and abuse of political power.[67] Again, producers extended republican arguments from the political to the economic realm. The most pressing problem, the producers claimed, lay in the recent accumulation of economic rather than political power, which was making the "rich richer, and the poor poorer," and the "many dependent on the few."[68] The current system of "commercial exchange," in which money rather than labor was used as the measure of value, enabled nonproducers to lay claim to the products of the industrious classes.[69] The deleterious effects of the current system could already be seen in both the political and social realms. Political corruption had increased significantly so that votes were being bought "like cattle in the market."[70] Moreover, society in

---

[65] For discussion of dependent relations in the secondary literature, see Wilentz, *Chants Democratic*, 241, 331–33; and Dawley, *Class and Community*, chap. 2. For a primary source, see *The Mechanics' Free Press*, 14 June 1828, p. 2, cols. 2, 3.

[66] Quoted from *The Man*, 26 April 1834, 231; emphasis in original. For similar equation of skilled labor with poor man's capital, see *The Man*, 1 May 1834, 246.

[67] For discussion of republican fears of concentrated power, corruption, and dependence, see Pocock, "Civic Humanism," 87–88; and "Machiavelli" 123. In the American context, see Bailyn, *Ideological Origins*, chap. 3.

[68] Quoted from *The Man*, 15 March 1834, 81; and 4 April 1834, 149. For similar fears of economic concentration, see also *The Mechanics' Free Press*, 9 August 1828, p. 1, cols. 1, 2.

[69] *The Mechanics' Free Press*, 26 April 1828, p. 2, col. 3; and 21 June 1828, p. 2, col. 5.

[70] See *The Man*, 7 April 1834, 149–50; and 8 April 1834, 161.

general was showing signs of strain as economic concentration, the producers claimed, had brought "ignorance, want, and wretchedness to the majority of mankind."[71] Political decline and social decay indeed seemed to have followed the increased economic dependence of the antebellum decades.

Finally, producers looked to the eighteenth-century belief in the constitutive power of politics. The balanced constitution had long been considered essential to maintaining English liberty. Civic virtue and political participation had been fostered by the appropriate configuration of political institutions.[72] Again, producers extended eighteenth-century assumptions to their antebellum concerns when they argued that the unhealthy accumulations of economic power had been politically created and could be politically reformed. The producers believed that "bad legislation" was responsible for their current economic distress. If only grants of exclusive privilege that had been given "to wealth at the expense of useful labor" could be removed, the economy could be returned to its republican path.[73]

Attending more closely to the influence of these modified eighteenth-century assumptions and social relations in the antebellum era provides the basis for a more complete account of workingmen's protest before the Civil War. Indeed, when considered from the perspective of the producing classes, we can recover several neglected aspects of workingmen's protest and begin to understand what the artisans did and did not protest for.

THE PRODUCERS' VISION: A REPUBLICAN POLITICAL ECONOMY

Producers were well aware that the world of work had changed dramatically in the first three decades of the nineteenth century. After all, they witnessed firsthand the reorganization of work and production. In the 1820s and 1830s, however, producers did not understand these changes in the context of a struggle between capital and labor, but saw them in light of their established worldview. Thus the producers' program is best understood as part-and-parcel of a larger effort to sustain a healthy republic in this era of economic change. Producers were by no means opposed to economic growth. In fact, they often praised the "wonderful discoveries" and "vast improvements in machinery" that enabled the new republic to

[71] Quoted from *The Mechanics' Free Press*, 9 August 1828, p. 1, cols. 1, 2.

[72] For a wonderful discussion of the constitutive power of politics and republican ideology, see Stedman Jones, "Rethinking Chartism."

[73] Quoted from *The Man*, 3 April 1834, 146. For a fascinating discussion of the malleability of society via the manipulation of "laws, institutions, and all species of social arrangements," see *The Mechanics' Free Press*, 9 August 1828, p. 1, cols. 1–2; and 23 August 1828, 1–2.

prosper.[74] Stephen Simpson, one of the leaders of the Philadelphia Working Men's party, claimed that he had no desire "to throw back society to the pastoral state. . . . We may surely profit by an analysis of the present complicated relations of society, without attempting the futile, and preposterous task of throwing it into convulsions, or stripping it of its foliage and fruits, arising from civilization and refinement." Skilled workers, master craftsmen, and small manufacturers had a great deal to gain from increased production if only they could share equally in the benefits.[75]

In the 1820s and 1830s, producers were concerned that the present pattern of economic change was not proceeding along a desirable path. Indeed, there were several indicators suggesting that they had set sail on a dangerous course. Two emerging phenomena were of particular concern: the increased number of monopolies seemed to be fostering unhealthy accumulations of economic and political power, while the new wave of speculation and exchange was disturbing the just distribution of productive labor. These two issues became the central concern of many workingmen's associations before the Civil War.

Producers in general and the Working Men's parties in particular were alarmed at the rapid growth of monopolies in many areas of society. These accumulations of economic and political power signaled that something was indeed "radically wrong" in the republic. Tyranny and oppression would soon follow, producers believed, as long as a few "absorbants" continued to live in luxury and idleness at the expense of the producing classes. Carthage, Sparta, and Rome were held up by producers as the way of the future unless immediate steps were taken to redress the current imbalance of economic and political power.[76] Characteristically, producers considered the origins of monopoly to lie in "bad legislation" and identified state charters of incorporation as the proximate cause of their economic distress. State grants of exclusive privilege had fostered unequal

[74] Quoted from Simpson, *Working Man's Manual*, 59. See also *The Mechanics' Press*, 27 February 1830; and 27 March 1830, p. 154, cols. 1, 2.

[75] Quoted from Simpson, *Working Man's Manual*, 62.

[76] The issue of monopoly can be seen in a number of workingmen's newspapers and in the platforms of the Working Men's and Loco-foco parties. For example, see *The Man*, 18 March 1834 and 19 March 1834; "Address of the City and County Convention to the Working Men of the State," reprinted in Commons et al., *Documentary History* 5:118–19; "Report of the Committee of Fifty," 153; "Proceedings of a Meeting of Mechanics and Other Working Men," 158, 162; and Byrdsall, *History of the Loco-foco or Equal Rights Party*.

For the prevalence of monopoly and the fear of something "radically wrong in the republic," see the prospectus of *The Working Man's Advocate*, 31 October 1829, p. 3, col. 1. For the term "absorbants," see *The Mechanics' Free Press*, 16 August 1828, p. 2, col. 1. For references to Sparta and Rome, see Simpson, *Working Man's Manual*, 60, 199, 220, 231; and "Minority Report on Education," 155, 169. For reference to Carthage, see Byrdsall, *History of the Loco-foco or Equal Rights Party*, 148.

divisions of political and economic power that were undermining the very foundations of the republic.[77]

The monopoly question took on particular intensity for producers over the chartering of the national and state banks. Whenever the National Bank charter was to be renewed, workingmen's newspapers were filled with headlines such as, "The Bank Against the People," or "Banks-Rags-the Issue" as workingmen rallied against "the mamouth" in defense of the republic.[78] A centralized credit system, producers feared, would promote economic concentration and prevent small producers from keeping pace with entrepreneurial masters. A republican political economy would be more likely to succeed if a decentralized banking system were established, providing all producers with ready access to credit.[79] Thus, the National Bank was seen as the ultimate monopoly, and came to symbolize the imminent danger awaiting the American republic. The theme of encroaching monopoly was by no means restricted to legislative charters and banks, but was applied to almost all workingmen's concerns. The absence of a system of state education was said to produce a "monopoly of talent," prison labor was described as a "state monopoly," and even state lotteries and abuses of apprenticeship regulations were presented as "monopoly policies."[80] Framing a policy issue in the language of monopoly immediately established the issue as a legitimate problem in need of government action.

Increased speculation also was a matter of considerable concern. "Stock-jobbers," "merchants," and "lottery brokers" were flourishing in the antebellum decades, even though they had done little or nothing to contribute to the fund of national wealth. Riches achieved through the unproductive activities of speculation and exchange were secured, producers argued, at the expense of the producing classes.[81] The relationship between poverty

77 For discussion of legislation as both the source of and the potential solution to workingmen's problems, see the following: "Address of the City and County Convention to the Working Men of the State," 122; "Report of the Committee of Fifty," 151; Simpson, *Working Man's Manual*, 27, 48, 82; *The Man*, 3 April 1834, 146; *The Mechanics' Free Press*, 21 June 1828, p. 2, cols. 1–3; *The Mechanics' Press*, 9 January 1830, 71; and *The Mechanics' Press*, 5 June 1830, p. 239, col. 1.

78 *The Man*, 18 March 834; and 19 March 1834.

79 See *The Working Man's Advocate*, 1 October 1831, p. 2, col. 5; and Simpson, *Working Man's Manual*, chaps. 21, 23. For discussion of these issues in the secondary literature, see Bray Hammond, "Free Banks and Corporations: The New York Free Banking Act of 1838," *Journal of Political Economy* 44, 2 (April 1936): 184–209.

80 See *The Working Man's Advocate*, 6 March 1830, p. 1, cols. 3–5; and *The Mechanics' Free Press*, 10 July 1830, p. 1, col. 6; p. 2, col. 2. Both articles have been reprinted in Commons et al., *Documentary History* 5:94–107, 114–23.

81 For attacks on merchants as unproductive citizens, see Simpson, *Working Man's Manual*, chap. 5; and *The Man*, 2 April 1834, 141. For complaints about increased speculation and exchange, see *The Mechanics' Free Press*, 26 April 1828, p. 2, col. 3; Stevens, *New York Typographical Union, No. 6*, 158; and George Henry Evans' "Address to the Working Men of

and unproductive speculation was spelled out clearly by Simpson in his *Working Man's Manual:*. "As no country can grow rich, vigorous, powerful, and happy, that does not consume less than it produces—the judicious consumption of labour becomes an essential item in the wealth of nations. Hence the pernicious effects of the *idle* classes of society, who consume, and never produce; hence the virtue of industry, and hence, by parity of reason, the evil tendency of luxury, waste, sensuality, and refinement."[82] Although antebellum producers generally viewed commerce in pejorative terms, they did not shy away from economic issues altogether. On the contrary, in the 1820s and 1830s New York and Pennsylvania workingmen began to distinguish between different patterns of economic growth and to advocate a particular path of economic development that they believed to be compatible with republican precepts.[83]

Those who saved rather than spent their money also were viewed by Simpson and other producers with suspicion and fear. To be sure, parsimonious citizens accumulated wealth, but only by withholding from circulation the equivalent amount of productive labor. Thus, from the producers' perspective, saving was an undesirable act that drained society of productive capacity. Again, Simpson captured the producers' view succinctly:

> Economy is a private virtue, but almost a public negative, in relation to national wealth; except in the unproductive consumption of luxuries. By economy, a man may grow rich, or acquire money; but he will never be able to produce industry by economy. . . . To save, is not to produce. The miser never can be equal to the working man. . . . Poor and miserable, indeed, would be that country, which, under a false system of political economy, would inculcate saving instead of producing, and estimate capital as of superior value to industry.[84]

Productivity and industry were held in the highest esteem and were considered to be the only real sources of wealth. Accumulation by saving and exchange was considered an artificial and dangerous course to follow.

---

the United States," in the inaugural issue of *The Radical* 1, 1 (January 1841): 5. For an excellent discussion of nineteenth-century views on speculation and exchange, see Ann Fabian, *Card Sharps, Dream Books, and Bucket Shops: Gambling in 19th Century America* (Ithaca, N.Y.: Cornell University Press, 1990).

[82] Quoted from Simpson, *Working Man's Manual*, 218.

[83] J.G.A. Pocock has identified the antithetical relationship between virtue and commerce in the eighteenth century. Although I see antebellum producers continuing many of the same fears and criticisms of commerce and exchange that Pocock discusses, I have not found them to be as disinterested in economic issues as Pocock claimed that eighteenth-century adherents of republicanism were. On the contrary, antebellum producers were intimately involved with questions of economic organization and development and tried to extend republican assumptions in order to address these concerns. See Pocock, "Virtue and Commerce in the Eighteenth Century," *Journal of Interdisciplinary History* 3, 1 (Summer 1972): 119–34.

[84] Quoted from Simpson, *Working Man's Manual*, 128–29.

Increased monopoly and speculation were responsible, producers believed, for their economic hardship in this period of economic growth. Instead of all industrious citizens sharing equally in the increased production, only a handful of citizens were reaping a disproportionate share of increased production. Small producers would continue to live in a state of poverty and distress as long as monopolies and speculation were allowed to run wild.[85] In the 1820s and 1830s, the producers did not consider the situation to be hopeless; a healthy pattern of economic development could still be achieved if only workingmen and their legislative allies would mobilize politically to ensure that republican precepts were sustained. If economic and political power could be distributed more evenly throughout the nation and production rewarded over speculation and exchange, then economic growth could continue along republican lines.

The producers' central objective, then, was to halt the current pattern of economic development and establish instead the conditions for a more decentralized pattern of economic growth that would allow all productive citizens to share in the benefits of increased production. Producers placed considerable emphasis on the scale of production. In a healthy republic, producers argued, the political economy was best kept to a small scale: "Small capitals are conducive to happiness and industry . . . large ones become pernicious, by giving to one great capitalist, the profit of the wages of hundreds and thousands of workmen!"[86] In addition, the producers believed that whatever the size of the community and unit of production, a healthy economy could be sustained only if economic expansion reflected real gains in industry and production. Speculative growth was simply a mirage that would soon disappear in the next depression, leaving small producers to suffer the consequences of economic speculation. The workingmen's banner, Simpson claimed, declared "*labour the source of wealth, and industry the arbiter of its distribution.*"[87]

More specifically, both the Working Men's and Loco-focos' political programs were intended to remedy the current problems and to return the nation to its rightful path. The producers' two principal demands, calling for antimonopoly and currency reform, were designed to remedy the problems of economic accumulation and unwanted speculation. Dismantling the National Bank, halting passage of new legislative charters, and distributing public lands to actual settlers would help prevent the concentration of economic power and would make possible a more decentralized pattern of economic growth. The New York Workingmen's newspaper *The Man* summed up the pressing need for antimonopoly legislation in the following terms:

[85] See *The Man*, 4 April 1834, 149; and Simpson, *Working Man's Manual*, chap. 13.
[86] Simpson, *Working Man's Manual*, 66. See also 218, 232–33.
[87] Quoted from Simpson, *Working Man's Manual*, 23.

One of two things must shortly come to pass: either there must be an end of our bad Banking System, or there must be an end of the Republic. We may adhere to the Banking system, and still preserve the name of a republic; but it will be the name alone. Equal rights—the foundation stone of our structure—are already sapped and undermined by the insidious and powerful aristocratic corporations by which we are surrounded. If we go on the same way a little longer—if we go on adding to the power and the number of these chartered companies—our boast of being a country of equal rights, a country of freemen, a country where the people rule, will be an empty boast indeed![88]

In addition to antimonopoly reform, producers pushed repeatedly for a change in the national currency policy. By returning to a hard-money policy producers believed that the worst excesses of speculation and unproductive exchange could be restrained. Again, *The Man* captured the producers' views on the relationship between a soft-money policy and unproductive labor.

We believe that there remains very little doubt among those of the useful classes who have taken the least pains to inform themselves on the subject, that PAPER MONEY is the crying evil of the day in our country; the dead weight upon industry; the clog upon useful labor; the *means* by which the drones obtain the honey; the TOOL which facilitates the operations of the speculator and the gambler to live in luxury on the wealth of the useful laborer, while the latter obtains for his own use but a scanty pittance of the avails of his own labor.[89]

The producers' belief that paper currency was the mechanism by which they were being robbed of their hard-earned labor was no doubt reinforced by payment of wages in rag money. Bank notes, after all, often could only be redeemed at a fraction of their face value, thus leaving the workingman to absorb the costs of a "spurious currency."[90]

The subsidiary planks in the producers' platform, which did not address questions of economic concentration and speculation head-on, nevertheless also were intended to insulate workingmen from the unfortunate consequences of economic development of an undesirable kind. For example, both the New York and Philadelphia Working Men's parties called for passage of mechanics' lien laws to ensure that workingmen had first call on the assets of bankrupt employers. Without these laws, producers often received little reward for their labor because of the precarious financial position of their employers. Similarly, workingmen sought to protect themselves from economic fluctuations by demanding abolition of imprisonment for debt. If small producers were going to participate in the benefits of economic growth, they first had to make sure that they stayed out of jail.

[88] Quoted from *The Man*, 15 May 1834, 293.
[89] Quoted from *The Man*, 7 May 1834, 266.
[90] For the phrase "spurious currency," see *The Man*, 4 April 1834, 149.

This was not an insignificant issue in the 1820s and 1830s for the number of citizens imprisoned for debt was high. Between January 1826 and November 1827, for example, 1,972 debtors were imprisoned in New York state. Similarly, Arthur Schlesinger has estimated that in 1830, five sixths of people in New England and mid-Atlantic jails were debtors owing less than twenty dollars.[91]

The Working Men's program, however, did not focus exclusively on economic concerns. One of their major demands, we have seen, was a system of state-funded education. Rather than dismissing such policies as the product of middle-class infiltration and intrigue, these social reforms are best viewed as an integral component of the producers' republican vision. If workingmen were to remain independent citizens, they had to avoid the dependence and corruption that accompanied wage labor. A good education would enable producers to be well informed and to show themselves "independent at the polls."[92] Although Owenites and Cookites disagreed over the particular content of education policy, both factions defended their schemes by claiming the republican legacy for themselves while denouncing their opponents' plans as aristocratic, monopolistic, and altogether unrepublican.[93]

Finally, when analyzing the producers' platform it is also important to note what the workingmen did *not* demand. Although producers clearly were opposed to economic concentration and the increased economic inequality that followed, with the exception of Skidmore's platform, they did not advocate a program of egalitarian reform. The choice was not so much between monopoly and equality as between monopoly and a more "just balance of power," in which excessive inequities would be removed.[94] The producers' position was expressed succinctly in an editorial for an Albany

[91] For New York figures, see Savetsky, "The New York Working Men's Party," 75. For New England and the mid-Atlantic states, see Schlesinger, *The Age of Jackson*, 134. For an interesting discussion of imprisonment for debt and of economic depression more generally, see Samuel Rezneck, "The Depression of 1819–1822, A Social History," *American Historical Review* 39, 1 (October 1933): 28–47.

[92] Quoted from *The Man*, 25 March 1834, 113. For discussion of the importance of education to civic participation, see *The National Trades' Union*, 13 September 1834, p. 2, col. 6; and p. 3, col. 2; *The Mechanics' Free Press*, 31 May 1828, p. 1, col. 1; and p. 2, col. 1; and *The Mechanics' Press*, 24 July 1830, p. 290, col. 2.

[93] For example, see "Report of the Working Men's Committee from the Philadelphia Working Men's Party," reprinted in Commons et al., *Documentary History*, 5:99, 165–78; and *The Working Man's Advocate*, 28 November 1829, p. 1, col. 5. For an interesting discussion of workingmen and education reform, see Sidney L. Jackson, "Labor, Education, and Politics in the 1830's," *Pennsylvania Magazine of History and Biography* 66, 3 (July 1942): 279–93.

[94] See the preamble of the Mechanics' Union of Trade Associations in *The Mechanics' Free Press*, 25 October 1828, p. 1, cols. 1–3; reprinted in Commons et al., *Documentary History* 5:90. For a similar statement against equality of faculties, see Simpson, *Working Man's Manual*, 28, 83.

labor newspaper in 1830: "We are no *levellers* nor *agrarians*. While the several classes of society move in their respective orbits, and all of them contribute to the comforts and conveniences of life, without disturbing the course of one another, they may be said to resemble a planetary system, which revolving in beautiful harmony sheds luster on the globe it warms, animates and enlightens."[95] This "planetary" image of the good society persisted largely intact throughout the antebellum era. In fact, producers were often careful to emphasize that they had no desire to "invade the rights or sacrifice the welfare of employers," and frequently acknowledged the rights of property even while protesting their own declining status.[96] Aristocrats and "absorbants," rather than masters or employers, were seen as the obstacles to a more just system of production in which small producers would share in the benefits of economic growth.

WORKINGMEN'S PROTEST RECONSIDERED

Rethinking the antebellum social relations in terms of the producers' concept of class provides a more satisfying account of both the producers' demands and the demise of their organization. Neither the factional disputes nor the abrupt decline of the New York Working Men's party needs to be attributed to outside manipulation and betrayal. Instead, we can set aside the long-standing preoccupation with authenticity and see the full range of workingmen's demands as equally legitimate, albeit different, responses to the economic changes under way in the early decades of the nineteenth century. Divisions within the party were not the handiwork of middle-class infiltrators nor the creations of professional politicians, but rather can be recognized as genuine conflicts among producers over exactly what policies to advocate. Indeed, it was precisely these internal divisions that led to the disintegration of the New York party, as members fought bitterly over which program to advance. Party politics is no longer the mysterious nemesis of working-class radicalism; rather, the disintegration of the Working Men's party reflected real divisions within the producers' ranks. The rifts were not created by the American party system, or by professional politicians. They stemmed from differences within the movement itself—differences over what the source of the problem was and over which strategies were most appropriate for securing the republic.

Considering workingmen's protest in light of the eighteenth-century legacy also helps explain workingmen's muted response to the antebellum

[95] Editorial extract from *The Farmers', Mechanics' and Workingmens' Advocate* quoted in *The Mechanics' Press*, 13 March 1830, p. 143, col. 3.

[96] Quoted from Stevens, *New York Typographical Union, No. 6*, 168. For additional sources on the recognition of property rights, see *The Mechanics' Press*, 12 December 1829, 35; and 26 June 1830, 263.

conspiracy convictions before 1835. Neither the Working Men's parties nor the GTUs initiated any fundamental challenge to the courts before the Civil War because they considered the conspiracy doctrine to be a legitimate form of government regulation. As long as the state treated workers and employers equally, forbidding both to organize collectively, the system of government regulation was not contested by producers. Simply put, the conspiracy doctrine was to labor what antimonopoly was to capital; both policies attempted to contain accumulations of wealth and power. The high priority given to antimonopoly legislation by the workingmen went hand in hand, with the acceptance of conspiracy as a reciprocal restraint on their own collective action.[97]

Workingmen's tolerance of the conspiracy doctrine did not extend to all aspects of the law. While accepting the conspiracy doctrine and the authority of the courts, workers nevertheless expressed considerable hostility toward lawyers throughout the first three decades of the nineteenth century. Labor newspapers frequently ran stories denouncing lawyers as "locusts," "pests," and "vultures," who were not to be trusted with the workingmen's concerns.[98] Antilawyer sentiment before the Civil War, however, was not a response to judicial intervention in industrial conflicts. Instead, its roots lay in the republican distinction between productive and unproductive labor. Lawyers, for many workers, were the epitome of useless labor living off the toil of the producing classes. "They have never added anything to the common stock of national honor, or national worth." Instead, lawyers, "possessing nothing of their own, like the drone, extract the substance from the useful and industrious . . . make dark that which ought to be plain and utterly unintelligible that which all should understand."[99] Producers did not attack lawyers for preventing workers from organizing, but rather opposed them as nonproducers living off the backs of the industrious classes. The object of workers' vitriol against the legal profession before the Civil War was not to change judicial doctrine and secure workers' industrial rights. On the contrary, the goal was to rid

[97] Interestingly, some workingmen explicitly denied the inequality of American law. See *The Mechanics' Press*, 12 December 1829, p. 35, cols. 1 and 2; and 10 April 1830, p. 175, col. 2. However, my claim that workingmen accepted the conspiracy doctrine as a reciprocal policy to antimonopoly legislation rests largely on an evaluation of what the producers did and did not demand. I have not found any explicit statements to this effect in the antebellum era. In the postwar period, the Knights of Labor continued in the producers' tradition and did call for a stricter enforcement of the conspiracy laws for combinations of labor and capital. See Chapter 4.

[98] *The Working Man's Advocate*, 14 November 1829, p. 1, cols. 4, 5; *The Mechanics' Press*, 24 April 1830, p. 187, col. 1; and 22 May 1830; *The Mechanics' Free Press*, 19 July 1828, p. 2, cols. 3, 4; 9 August 1828, p. 3, col. 4; and 16 August 1828, p. 2, col. 4; *The National Trades' Union*, 30 August 1834, p. 1, cols. 1–3.

[99] *The National Trades' Union*, 30 August 1834, p. 1, cols. 1–3.

society of "absorbants" and aristocrats so that craftsmen could maintain their rightful position as independent citizens within a healthy republic.

At first glance, the Loco-focos' attacks on the courts seem to be an important exception to the more general pattern of producers' quiescent response to the antebellum conspiracy convictions. Unlike other antebellum parties, the Loco-focos did push for legal reform in their party platforms and meetings in the park. A closer examination of the party's proceedings, however, indicates the limits of the Loco-focos' commitment to legal reform, and underscores important parallels between the Loco-focos and other antebellum workingmen's associations.

Most scholars to date have attributed the party's collapse to the financial panic and depression of 1837.[100] No doubt the severe economic downturn contributed to the party's demise, but if we look more closely at the last meetings of the party in October and November of 1837, we can see other factors at work. In fact, party members did not play so passive a role in determining the party's fate, but rather voted to disband their own organization and return to Tammany in order "to sustain the President in the warfare of the Banks against him."[101] At a general meeting of the party on October 24, a proposal was put forward suggesting that Tammany Hall and the Loco-focos agree to support a united Democratic ticket at the November elections. A Conference Committee was established to investigate the proposal; within a week the Loco-focos had voted in favor of the unity ticket by a substantial margin, with seventy-one in favor and twenty-two opposed. During the next month, the two factions within the Loco-foco party held separate meetings, but by the end of November the pro-unity majority had clearly won the day and the Loco-focos disappeared as an independent voice in New York politics.[102]

Thus, the party was not simply the victim of desperate economic conditions. Rather, the decision to abandon the party was, in large part, a deliberate strategic choice by a majority of party members in order to secure particular policy concerns. When pressed, a majority of Loco-focos clearly placed financial reform above all else—including the existence of their own organization. Moreover, the unity Loco-focos, or "Buffaloes," as they were known, were not disappointed. Although they did not win the local New York elections, Van Buren did succeed in implementing his sub-treasury plan. After an initial defeat in Congress in June 1838, the Independent Treasury Act was passed in July 1840, and sub-treasuries established in a number of cities throughout the nation. Antimonopoly Democrats considered the act a major victory and a significant step toward ensuring a

---

[100] For example, see Trimble, "Diverging Tendencies in New York Democracy"; and Wilentz, *Chants Democratic*, 294–95.

[101] Byrdsall, *A History of the Loco-foco or Equal Rights Party*, 174.

[102] For a detailed account of the demise of the Loco-focos, see ibid., 174–89.

more decentralized pattern of economic growth. The victory turned out to be short-lived; it was repealed by the Whigs later that same year and seems to have had little impact on the general direction of industrialization. These shortcomings, however, were not yet apparent in the antebellum decades, when the producers' vision of a more decentralized pattern of economic development appeared quite feasible and was strongly endorsed by the producing classes and their organizations.

Before the Civil War, then, workers' response to the legal system was very much shaped by modified republican conceptions of politics and society, the essential component of which was the maintenance of a decentralized system of production and authority. Up until the Civil War, the producers' vision of an alternative path of economic development seemed feasible, if only the state would discontinue its despotic policies of granting monopoly privileges to particular groups and adopt a more responsible financial policy. By 1870, workers' optimism about the possibility of sustaining such a decentralized political economy had been considerably shaken. The process of industrialization in the United States shattered the producers' vision of regional economic growth, and as a consequence transformed workers' relationship to the state. These changes are discussed at length in the following chapter. What is important for now is that labor's relatively quiescent response to judicial intervention in industrial disputes before the Civil War be seen as a consequence of workingmen's vision of the just society and not as an indication of the insignificance of judicial regulation of industrial conflict.

Finally, the producers' perspective helps account for the overall pattern of conspiracy cases during the nineteenth century. As we saw in Chapter 2, labor conspiracy cases can be divided into three broad phases: 1806–1842, the early cases; 1842–1865, repeal of the doctrine; and 1865–1895, revival of conspiracy. This unusual decline and resurgence of the doctrine has received little attention from previous scholars. Most discussions of labor conspiracy focus almost exclusively on the first wave of cases and simply assume that the doctrine was indeed overruled in the landmark case of *Commonwealth v. Hunt* in 1842.[103] In the two decades following *Hunt*, there were almost no conspiracy cases against labor; only three have been identified in the entire period.[104] Most scholars attribute this sharp decline to the earlier *Hunt* victory and move on rapidly to discuss the labor injunction, blithely skipping over almost a half-century of judicial regulation.

[103] For example, see Charles O. Gregory and Harold A. Katz, *Labor and the Law* (New York: Norton, 1979); and most labor law casebooks, such as Archibald Cox, Derek C. Bok, and Robert A. Gorman, *Cases and Materials on Labor Law* (Mineola, N.Y.: The Foundation Press, 1981).

[104] Witte, "Early American Labor Cases."

However, if we look more closely at this period between *Hunt* and the adoption of the labor injunction, we see that in fact the conspiracy doctrine was not abandoned altogether but was revived with a vengeance for at least three decades after the Civil War. This postwar revival of the doctrine belies earlier interpretations of the *Hunt* decision and raises larger questions regarding the pattern of conspiracy cases in the nineteenth century and the impact of judicial regulation on American labor. Why were there so few conspiracy cases between 1842 and 1865, and why was the doctrine revived after the war? And finally, why was a new legal remedy—the labor injunction—adopted in the last decades of the century? These questions will be addressed more fully in the following chapter on the postwar period, but some preliminary answers can be developed from the preceding analysis of the antebellum era.

As we have seen, the early conspiracy cases arose out of the increasing conflict between masters and journeymen during the early stages of industrialization. Before 1840, displaced journeymen protested the reorganization of work and were charged with conspiracy by the district attorneys of each state. However, in this first phase, journeymen usually blamed wealthy aristocrats and "absorbants" for their plight, rather than their immediate employers. If anything, workers were quite reluctant to cast their employers in the role of protagonist. Even in the second stage (1842–1865), workers were still reluctant to confront their employers directly and instead looked elsewhere for the sources of their problems. This period is noted for the temperance and nativist movements and for the cooperative and utopian experiments.[105] From the 1840s through the 1860s, journeymen turned to factors outside the workplace to explain and improve their declining status. Not surprisingly, the number of conspiracy cases dropped dramatically in this period as conflict within the trades was displaced from the workplace onto the nativist parties, temperance leagues, and utopian communities, all of which shifted conflict from the workshop into other arenas. For the time being, district attorneys had little reason to bring conspiracy charges against the journeymen.[106]

It was not until after the Civil War that the workplace became the central

[105] In general, see Wilentz, *Chants Democratic*, chaps. 8, 9; Laurie, *Working People of Philadelphia*, chaps. 6, 7; and Norman Ware, *The Industrial Worker, 1840–1860* (Chicago: Quadrangle Books, 1924). For more specific accounts of these movements, see Robert S. Fogarty, "Oneida: A Utopian Search for Religious Security," *Labor History* 14, 2 (Spring 1973): 202–27; John L. Thomas, "Romantic Reform in America, 1815–1865," *American Quarterly* 17 (Winter 1965): 656–81; Kalikst Wolski, "A Visit to the North American Phalanx," *Proceedings of the New Jersey Historical Society* 83, 3 (July 1965): 149–60; and Jayme A. Skokolow, "Culture and Utopia: The Raritan Bay Union," *New Jersey History* 94 (1976): 89–100.

[106] For discussion of artisan support for the nativist movement, see Bridges, *A City in the Republic*, esp. chap. 5; and Gorn, "'Good-Bye Boys, I Die a True American.'"

The Producers' Vision · 109

battleground, and capital and labor the two protagonists. Even before the war had ended, workers embarked on an extensive organization drive and soon initiated some of the most bloody strikes in American labor history. Employers responded with both force and legal action as they tried to contain this wave of working-class unrest with new charges of criminal conspiracy. As we will see in the following chapter, after the war the American Federation of Labor (AFL) and its precursors no longer accepted the convictions, and entered into an extended struggle for legal reform. Chapter 4 explores both the politicization of judicial regulation of labor and the outcome of labor's campaign to check the courts' power. The postwar struggle between labor and the courts helps explain why artisan protest did not develop along European lines, but instead progressed along its peculiar American path.

CONCLUSION: WORKERS AND THE STATE IN THE ANTEBELLUM ERA

Before turning to the postwar era, it is useful to highlight two broad features of state-labor relations before the Civil War. First, we should note that in the antebellum era there was no great division between work and politics. The separation of industrial issues from electoral and party politics that has come to distinguish the United States from other advanced industrial societies in the twentieth century had not yet taken hold. In fact, there is some evidence to suggest that the division between the producing and nonproducing classes was quite directly reflected in antebellum electoral politics, with the producers supporting the Jacksonian Democrats and the nonproducers supporting the Whigs. The mainstays of the Jacksonian coalition, from this perspective, were drawn from the core constituents of the producers' alliance: skilled artisans, master craftsmen, small manufacturers, and yeoman farmers. The very poorest citizens, such as day laborers and the unemployed, generally were excluded from the producers' ranks owing to their dependent and indigent status. As a consequence, we should not expect the poorest and middling wards to have voted for the same candidates in the antebellum decades.[107]

Contemporary accounts of local, state, and national elections often were recounted in terms of victories and defeats for the producers and their

---

[107] For discussion of the producers' relation to antebellum party politics, see Meyers, *The Jacksonian Persuasion*; Ashworth, *'Agrarians' and 'Aristocrats'*; Hahn, *The Roots of Southern Populism*; and Howe, *Political Culture of the American Whigs*.

I by no means want to suggest that there would have been a one-to-one correspondence between social position and political affiliation. Rather, I would expect to find a rough correspondence or central tendency for producers and nonproducers to vote for different parties. We should not be surprised, however, to find a small component of each group deviating from this general pattern.

programs. For example, when analyzing the local election of police officers in Southwark, Pennsylvania, in 1834, *The Man* reported that "honest yeomanry" and "hard working mechanics" had voted for the Democrats, while "brokers, and silk stocking gentry" had supported the "Tory-Whigs."[108] Similarly, the New York mayoral race of 1834 was described as a "triumph" of the "Useful Classes" when they elected "Anti-Bank Candidates" in a majority of wards.[109] Further research is needed to demonstrate fully whether or not producers and nonproducers voted for different political parties. What is clear, however, is that the producers' concerns quite closely paralleled the major political debates of the day. The National Bank controversy, for example, was central to the producers' vision, and brought workers into the heart of antebellum party politics. Moreover, producers were quite successful at securing their demands through political channels. Jackson's bank veto and Van Buren's sub-treasury scheme both were seen as important victories for the producers' antimonopoly platform. In addition, a number of states passed legislation establishing systems of state education and mechanics' lien laws and abolishing imprisonment for debt: all of which had been advocated by the producing classes.[110]

At least initially, then, the American political system did not block workers' political participation, but rather was quite responsive to the producers' demands. The closer links between work and politics in the antebellum era make more puzzling the AFL's turn to business unionism at the end of the century. It becomes even more intriguing to discover what happened in the postwar decades to leave workers so disaffected with political reform. How and why did workplace concerns get removed from the political agenda?

Second, I have argued that workers' relatively quiescent response to the antebellum conspiracy convictions was part of their larger project of maintaining a republican political economy. A skeptic, however, might pose an alternative interpretation of workers' relation to the American state. Although almost all of the antebellum conspiracy cases resulted in convictions, the courts imposed only nominal penalties on striking journeymen. No defendants were sentenced to jail, and with few exceptions, fines generally ranged from one to ten dollars, plus the costs of the suit.[111] Even allowing for legal expenses and adjusting for antebellum wage rates, one might still argue that workers did not contest the conspiracy convictions

---

[108] Quoted from *The Man*, 9 May 1834, p. 1, col. 1. See also the following primary sources for workingmen's analysis of local elections in producers' terms: *The Man*, 9 April 1834, 166; and 12 April 1834, 175.

[109] See *The Man*, 12 April 1834, p. 179, col. 1.

[110] See note 13 to Chapter 1.

[111] See Witte, "Early American Labor Cases," 828. The exception was the New York tailors' case of 1836, in which fines ranged from $50 to $150. See People v. Faulkner, 332.

because they considered judicial regulation to be of little or no importance. Workingmen's absence from the legal reform coalition, from this perspective, was not a product of the producers' republican vision, but was further evidence of the minimal impact of the conspiracy convictions on workers' lives.

Fortunately, the limits of this alternative interpretation can be gauged by contrasting different labor organizations' responses to the conspiracy convictions after the Civil War. In Chapter 4, I show how some postwar organizations that continued in the producers' tradition, such as the National Labor Union (NLU) and the Knights of Labor (KOL), did not contest the conspiracy convictions. On the other hand, organizations such as the New York Workingmen's Assembly and the Federation of Organized Trades and Labor Unions (FOTLU) adopted a very different stance and engaged in an extensive campaign for legal change. These two quite different responses cannot be accounted for by the severity of the legal penalties involved, as all of the postwar organizations were responding to the very same convictions. Thus, the postwar experience confirms the importance of workers' larger social vision for shaping their perceptions of, and responses to, judicial regulation. Only by embedding the conspiracy convictions in the broader social relations can we begin to make sense of workers' changing relationship to the state over the course of the nineteenth century.[112]

[112] Moreover, it is worth noting that workingmen often hired prominent attorneys to represent them at the antebellum conspiracy trials, and no doubt incurred substantial legal expenses. For example, in 1806, the Philadelphia cordwainers hired Caesar Rodney to defend them. Shortly thereafter, Rodney was appointed Attorney General by Jefferson. See Montgomery, "Working Classes of the Pre-Industrial American City," 13. Their willingness to hire such noted attorneys suggests that the workingmen did not treat the conspiracy prosecutions lightly.

CHAPTER FOUR

Disintegration of the Producers' Alliance and Politicization of Judicial Regulation, 1865–1896

AFTER THE Civil War, labor's relation to the state changed significantly when several organizations began to contest the conspiracy convictions and push repeatedly for legal reform. Beginning in 1865 and continuing through the end of the century, the New York Workingmen's Assembly (1865–1897), the Federation of Organized Trades and Labor Unions (FOTLU) (1881–1886), and the American Federation of Labor (AFL) (1886–) all declared judicial regulation of industrial conflict to be oppressive and unjust and embarked on an extensive campaign to check the power of the courts. Understanding how and why conspiracy convictions were politicized after the Civil War holds the key to the distinctive process of working-class formation in the United States. Specifically, we will see that the outcome of labor's postwar struggle with the courts played a decisive role in the AFL's turn to voluntarism at the end of the century.

Not all postwar labor organizations, however, followed this same path. Organizations such as the National Labor Union (NLU) (1866–1872) and the Knights of Labor (KOL) (1869–1902) did not contest the postwar convictions, and, like the antebellum producers, showed little or no interest in legal reform. From the 1870s through the 1890s, then, different organizations had established quite distinct relations with the American state. Only some organizations found themselves locked into a prolonged struggle with the courts, while others had much less difficulty negotiating exactly the same political institutions.

The uneven pattern of state-labor relations cannot be explained by the increased penalties and more frequent convictions in the postbellum decades, as labor organizations responded differently to the very same trials. Instead of focusing on state structure and capacity in isolation, we must look beyond the state to the different visions of economic development that emerged within the labor movement after the Civil War. Simply put, the substantive disagreements that contributed to the breakdown of the producers' alliance had important repercussions for labor's interaction with the surrounding political institutions, especially the courts. Contrasting the different visions and programs of postwar labor organizations both shows the important influence of state structure on labor strategy and highlights the historical contingency of the courts' power for shaping the American working class.

PRODUCERS VERSUS TRADE UNIONISTS: CONFLICTING VISIONS OF ECONOMIC GROWTH

The three decades following the Civil War witnessed some of the most intense protest in American labor history. Workers voiced their discontent in a variety of realms as trade unions, third parties, eight-hour leagues, and a host of other associations sprang up in many cities and towns.[1] During this period of extensive mobilization, no one organization was hegemonic. Instead, there was a proliferation of associations, often advocating quite different programs of labor reform. Several attempts were made to unite these disparate organizations into a single front, but the efforts were largely unsuccessful and usually had difficulty surviving for more than a year. The Junior Sons of '76, the NLU, and the United Labor party, for example, each disbanded when participants failed to agree on a common platform of postwar reform.[2]

Thus, the "industrial question," as issues of economic growth often were referred to, simultaneously mobilized and divided workers in the post-bellum decades.[3] The tremendous proliferation of labor organizations after the war itself was indicative of the enormous uncertainty and diversity of opinion over exactly what labor's project ought to be in the postbellum era. Although dissension within the labor movement was real, not all was chaos and confusion within the postwar decades. On the contrary, two coalitions emerged in which particular delegates and organizations staked

[1] The exact number of participants involved in this new mobilization remains unclear, as membership figures were often unreliable and varied considerably from one source to another. In the late 1860s and early 1870s, for example, contemporary estimates of labor organization varied from 300,000 to 600,000 in the space of a few years. See David Montgomery, *Beyond Equality: Labor and the Radical Republicans, 1862–1872* (1967; Urbana: University of Illinois Press, 1981). For interesting accounts of the postwar mobilization, see Montgomery, *Beyond Equality*; Fink, *Workingmen's Democracy*; Oestreicher, *Solidarity and Fragmentation*; For more precise membership figures for the KOL, FOTLU, and AFL, see note 6 following.

[2] For discussion of the Junior Sons of '76, see Rayback, *A History of American Labor*, 144. For the United Labor party, see David Scobey, "Boycotting the Politics Factory: Labor Radicalism and the New York City Mayoral Election of 1884," *Radical History Review* 28–30 (1984): 280–325; and Steven J. Ross, "The Politicization of the Working Class: Production, Ideology, Culture and Politics in Late Nineteenth-Century Cincinnati," *Social History* 11, 2 (May 1986): 171–95. For the NLU, see Montgomery, *Beyond Equality*.

[3] Terence Powderly, the Grand Master Workman of the KOL, referred to the "industrial question." See Powderly, *Thirty Years of Labor*, 664. See also *Report of the Committee of the Senate* 1:36.

out consistent but different positions on the central issues of the day. The sustaining theme of each of the coalitions was the creation of two different narratives of economic change.

The dominant faction within both the NLU and the KOL remained within the producer tradition. Economic change, for these organizations, continued to be viewed through the republican assumptions of the antebellum decades: the principal social cleavage was still thought to lie between the producing and nonproducing classes; propertied independence and civic participation continued as major goals; concentrations of economic and political power were considered dangerous sources of dependence and corruption; finally, political regeneration was seen as the principal solution to the republic's current problems. The postwar producers, however, did not simply reiterate antebellum arguments. On the contrary, both the NLU and the KOL extended the producers' vision by developing a more detailed and complete analysis of economic growth.[4]

Dissident unionists within the NLU, along with the majority of delegates within the New York Workingmen's Assembly, the FOTLU, and the AFL, began to question producers' assumptions and to construct an alternative vision of economic development. It was no longer possible, the dissenters claimed, to sustain a republican political economy in the postbellum decades. The world had changed in important ways, and workers, too, had to abandon their previous assumptions and adopt a new platform and strategy more suited to a modern industrial economy. These individuals

---

[4] For a fascinating discussion of the producers' alliance within the KOL, see Layton testimony, *Report of the Committee of the Senate* 1:3; and Blair testimony, *Report of the Committee of the Senate*, 2:44. See also the following sources for specific discussion of nineteenth-century class divisions: Sylvis, "What Is Money?" 365, 367. Sylvis's essay was originally published in three parts in the Chicago *Workingman's Advocate* from February to June 1869. The essay was reprinted by Sylvis's brother in 1872; see James C. Sylvis, *The Life, Speeches, Labors and Essays of William H. Sylvis* (Philadelphia: Claxton, Remsem Y. Haffelfinger, 1872). See also Powderly, *Thirty Years of Labor*, 101–2, 150, 162, 503; Industrial Brotherhood platform, plank 12, quoted in Powderly, *Thirty Years of Labor*, 119; Knights of Labor platform, General Assembly Proceedings, 1878, plank 10, p. 6. The platforms and proceedings of the KOL General Assembly are contained in Powderly Papers.

References to civic virtue can be found in a number of postbellum sources. See *The Address of the National Labor Congress to the Workingmen of the United States*, reprinted in Commons et al., *Documentary History* 9:145. (Hereafter cited as *NLU Address*.) The NLU Proceedings were originally published in various labor newspapers. Excerpts have been collected in Commons et al., *Documentary History* 9:126–274. (Hereafter cited as *NLU Proceedings* followed by the year of the congress.) *NLU Proceedings*, 1867, 181; "Majority Report of the Platform Committee," *NLU Proceedings*, 1868, 30, 34.

For fear of concentrated power in the postbellum era, see Sylvis, "What Is Money?" 367. Sylvis writes: "A centralization of wealth is a centralization of power. When the few possess themselves of everything, and the many are reduced to that condition of dependence when it is compulsory to work or starve, then it is that the power of wealth and the rule of the few is absolute."

and organizations no longer considered themselves producers, but rather began to identify as wage earners and members of a distinct working class. The remainder of this chapter, then, explores the internal divisions within the producers' ranks, and traces their consequences for labor's relation to the state.

Before reconstructing the substantive divisions and their ideological foundations, three cautionary notes on the concept of ideology are in order. First, although I restore questions of ideology to the center of the analysis, it is important to distinguish my account at the outset from the "old labor history" in order to avoid some unnecessary confusion. Previous scholars such as Selig Perlman and Gerald Grob also placed considerable emphasis on ideological divisions within the postwar labor movement. These earlier accounts, however, are severely limited by their inaccurate characterization of both participants and issues that distinguished the contending factions. The labor movement was not divided into utopian reformers and business unionists, fighting over whether to pursue unrealistic agrarian reforms or the more pragmatic goal of material gain. Disagreements within the labor movement existed, but did not center around questions of utopian versus pragmatic reform.[5]

Second, the ideological divisions between producers and dissenting unionists did not emerge full-blown in a particular year or single organization, but rather evolved more slowly over several decades and associations. It is a mistake to assume that conflicts appeared only among organizations. As both the NLU and KOL demonstrate, organizations were not monolithic and often contained important factions within them. It is important to attend to *internal* conflicts as well as to differences *between* organizations in order to identify the divisive issues at hand. Finally, the division between producers and trade unionists was by no means exhaustive. Organizations such as the Socialist Labor party, the International Labor Union, and the International Workingmen's Association do not fit easily into my account and would require elaboration of additional ideologies. Exploration of further alternatives would enhance any analysis of the postwar period; however, these other traditions remained minor themes in the United States. The two ideologies presented here represent the major contending factions within the postwar labor movement in terms of both membership and duration of organization. Examining disagreements be-

---

[5] The distinction between the old and new labor history is taken from Brody, "The Old Labor History and the New." For earlier discussions of ideological divisions within the postwar labor movement, see Selig Perlman, "Upheaval and Reorganization," in Commons et al., *History of Labor in the United States*, vol. 2, pt. 4; Perlman, *A Theory of the Labor Movement*; and Gerald N. Grob, *Workers and Utopia: A Study of Ideological Conflict in the American Labor Movement, 1865–1900* (Evanston, Ill.: Northwestern University Press, 1961).

tween producers and their trade union rivals takes us a considerable distance toward understanding the changing conceptions of class in the postbellum decades.[6]

LABOR DIVIDED: DISSENSION WITHIN THE NATIONAL LABOR UNION

Although divisions within the labor movement only came to a head in the 1880s in the conflict between the KOL and the FOTLU/AFL, early signs of dissension already can be seen within the NLU immediately after the Civil War. Recovering these internal disagreements within the NLU not only enables us to return ideological divisions to the center of the analysis, but also lays the groundwork for understanding shifts in state-labor relations and labor strategy after the Civil War. It is important to begin our analysis with the NLU, because prevailing accounts of postwar labor protest have diminished substantive disagreements within the labor movement and have re-created a more unified labor movement than I believe existed in the postwar decades. This more united view of postwar protest originated, in large part, with David Montgomery's classic analysis of the NLU.[7]

[6] Unfortunately, membership figures for the KOL, FOTLU, and AFL prior to 1897 often are unavailable or unreliable. Nevertheless, scholars have reconstructed membership estimates that allow us roughly to gauge both the growth rates and shifting strength of the KOL and the FOTLU/AFL. The KOL remained the dominant labor organization in the 1880s, the KOL and AFL obtained equal membership in 1990, and the AFL became the ascendant labor organization thereafter. The specific membership estimates available are as follows: KOL in 1879 (9,287); 1880 (28,136); 1881 (19,422); 1882 (42,517); 1883 (51,914); 1884 (71,326); 1885 (111,395); 1886 (729,677); 1887 (548,239); 1888 (259,518); 1889 (220,607); 1890 (100,000); 1893 (74,635). AFL in 1881 (40–50,000); 1886 (140,000); 1890 (100,000); 1896 (140,000); 1897 (264,825); 1898 (278,016); 1899 (349,422); 1900 (548,321); 1901 (787,537); 1902 (1,024,399); 1903 (1,465,800); 1904 (1,676,200); 1905 (1,494,300); 1906 (1,454,200); 1907 (1,538,970); 1908 (1,586,885); 1909 (1,482,872); 1910 (1,562,112).

Membership figures were compiled from the following sources: KOL, General Assembly Proceedings 1879–1888, in Powderly Papers; *Report of the Proceedings of the Thirty-First Annual Convention of the American Federation of Labor, Held at Atlanta, Georgia, November 13 to 25, Inclusive, 1911* (Washington, D.C.: Law Reporter Printing Company, 1911), 101–2; Commons et al., *History of Labor in the United States* 2:339–45, 381, 396, 410–23, 482, 494, 522; and Norman J. Ware, *The Labor Movement in the United States, 1860–1895* (Gloucester, Mass.: Peter Smith, 1959), 66–67, 298. I would like to thank Keith Whittington for helping to compile these figures.

[7] See Montgomery, *Beyond Equality*. More generally, see Fink, *Workingmen's Democracy*; Oestreicher, *Solidarity and Fragmentation*; and Ross, *Workers on the Edge*. To be sure, none of these accounts discounts internal divisions entirely, and Oestreicher in particular pays considerable attention to the sources of "fragmentation" within the labor movement. However, all agree that economic concerns provided a potential source of unity and class interest while ethnic and cultural cleavages tended to divide. In contrast, I have found that economic issues and class relations also were divisive as workers disagreed over how to understand the economic changes they were experiencing.

The NLU was established in 1866 by William Sylvis of the Iron Molders' International Union, Jonathan Fincher of the Machinists' Union, and William Harding of the Coachmakers' International Union in an effort to bring together the multitude of postwar labor organizations under a single banner. The organization was quite successful and attracted more than sixty delegates to its initial congress; all but two of the eighteen national unions attended, along with a large contingent of local and city-based unions and some delegates from more general labor reform associations such as the eight-hour leagues. The united front, however, could not be sustained. After six years the organization had all but fallen apart when only seven delegates attended the Cleveland congress in 1872.[8]

The cornerstone of Montgomery's analysis of the NLU rests on his important discovery that a number of key labor leaders were members of supposedly rival organizations simultaneously. Men such as William Jessup, Conrad Kuhn, Henry Lucker, and Jonathan Fincher, Montgomery found, participated in both trade union *and* labor reform organizations between 1862 and 1872. As the participants themselves had little trouble moving between organizations, Montgomery argued, we ought not consider these same institutions to be antagonistic. Instead, organization boundaries were quite permeable, enabling leaders to maintain multiple memberships in a range of associations. Where previous scholars divided the postwar labor movement into competing camps, Montgomery concluded that postwar labor organizations had established an effective division of labor in which each fulfilled a distinct but complementary role in the larger class struggle. Different labor organizations in the postwar decade, Montgomery claimed, were "most meaningfully differentiated not in terms of ideology or membership—in these areas each overlapped significantly with each other—but rather in terms of structure and function. All were constituent parts of the labor-reform movement. All were at least partially represented in the National Labor Union at the epitome of its career, 1869–1870."[9] Montgomery's analysis of overlapping membership understandably has effectively displaced exploration of competing ide-

[8] For the delegate attendance at the 1872 congress, see Commons et al., *Documentary History* 9:273. David Montgomery dates the NLU from 1866 to 1875 because he treats the NLU and the Industrial Congress as a continuous organization. Although there was some continuity of personnel, I think the decline in membership and new name in 1872–1873 mark a more significant break and warrant treating the NLU and Industrial Congress as distinct organizations. From 1866 through 1872 the NLU was dominated by delegates who adhered to the producers' vision. The Industrial Congress, on the other hand, was an attempt by some of the dissenting unions to revive the organization along trade union lines. Montgomery's account of the founding and early workings of the NLU are, nevertheless, very helpful. See Montgomery, *Beyond Equality*, 175–76, 194–95.

[9] For Montgomery's discussion of the division of labor among postwar labor organizations, see Montgomery, *Beyond Equality*, chap. 5. The quotation is taken from p. 135.

ologies and substantive disagreements from the research agenda and fostered instead analyses that emphasize the common thread of workers' discontent. Before divisions within the postwar labor movement can be taken seriously again, the practice of multiple membership must be reexamined and explained.

Despite the tremendously rich account of the immediate postwar decade, Montgomery's argument about overlapping membership cannot be sustained in light of new empirical research. I have found that multiple membership in several different organizations was quite compatible with ideological cleavages within the labor movement. Attending a meeting, or even holding office in an association, by no means guaranteed that a delegate endorsed the organization's substantive program. At times quite the opposite was true. Inferences from behavior to ideology cannot be so easily drawn. Although delegates from a variety of trade unions and labor reform organizations participated in the early NLU congresses, the proceedings were quite "inharmonious" as delegates struggled for control of the early national federation.[10] Moreover, inferences from attendance to ideology are especially problematic for organizations like the NLU, which explicitly sought to unify a diverse array of labor organizations under one roof. Exactly whom the NLU represented, and what its platform would be, was not at all clear in the early years of the organization. Questions of organizational definition and agenda were precisely the issues being negotiated and fought over in each of the NLU congresses, making attendance at any one congress a very poor guide to a delegate's views.

The case of William Jessup is instructive. As Montgomery himself notes, between 1867 and 1872 Jessup was simultaneously president of the New York Workingmen's Assembly, recording secretary of the Workingmen's Union, and vice-president for New York for the NLU.[11] Despite holding office in the NLU, Jessup nevertheless had major reservations about several planks in the NLU platform; participation alone is a poor guide to Jessup's views. In fact, after the 1870 congress in Cincinnati, Jessup spoke out strongly against the direction taken by the NLU since the 1867 congress and specifically identified programmatic issues as the source of his discon-

---

[10] William Jessup was the New York Workingmen's Assembly delegate to the NLU in 1870. His quite detailed and lengthy report was printed in full in the Proceedings of the Seventh Annual Session in 1871. The New York Workingmen's Assembly Proceedings were printed in separate pamphlets after each annual convention. Fortunately, almost all of the pamphlets have been collected together and are available on microfilm at the Martin P. Catherwood Library, Cornell University. (Hereafter cited as *Workingmen's Assembly Proceedings*, followed by the year of the convention.) Jessup described the 1870 NLU congress as "inharmonious" in this report to the Assembly. See *Workingmen's Assembly Proceedings*, 1871, 64.

[11] See Montgomery, *Beyond Equality*, 163–64.

tent. Jessup's reaction to the NLU platform can be found in his account of the Cincinnati congress to his home organization, the New York Working-men's Assembly.

> I could scarcely realize that it was the same organization created a few years since at Baltimore to promote the interests of the workingmen of the United States, and to create a common brotherhood among all trades; at that time the platform went forth composed of resolutions recommending co-operation, improved dwellings for workingmen, the organization of female labor, and the establish-ment of mechanics' institutes, libraries and lectures, and kindred questions of the utmost importance to the working-classes of the country. The last platform adopted speaks of little else than the financial question, of banks, bonds, money and rates of interest. Why the change? Has all that is necessary been accom-plished in the way of co-operation? . . . These reforms have scarce begun. If they are not still worthy a place in the platform of the National Labor Union, I for one cannot recommend a representation from this Assembly to future Congresses.[12]

Jessup's report to the Workingmen's Assembly does not sit easily with Montgomery's claim of little disagreement between the trade unions and NLU. In fact, there appears to have been quite intense conflict over the content of the NLU platform, sufficiently intense for the Workingmen's Assembly to break with the NLU and not send delegates to St. Louis in 1871.[13] Far from there being an effective division of tasks between the NLU and the Workingmen's Assembly, there were instead important substantive disagreements between leaders of these organizations over what con-stituted an appropriate platform for the national organization. From Jessup's perspective, the financial questions that came to dominate the NLU after 1867 were diverting the organization from its rightful path, prompting him to "candidly confess" that he "was not at home in this Convention."[14]

Jessup was not alone in his opposition to the NLU program. A number of local, city, and national trade unions were unhappy with the platform and broke with the NLU after the 1870 congress.[15] Henry J. Walls, secretary of the Cincinnati Trades' Assembly and iron molder by trade, commented on the widespread dissatisfaction with the NLU in a letter to Jessup dated 14

---

[12] See *Workingmen's Assembly Proceedings*, 1871, 64.

[13] The New York Workingmen's Assembly decision not to send delegates to St. Louis was reported in an editorial in the Chicago *Workingman's Advocate*, 18 February 1871.

[14] *Workingmen's Assembly Proceedings*, 1871, 64.

[15] For example, along with the New York Workingmen's Assembly, the Cigar Makers' International Union, the Bricklayers' Union, the Cincinnati Trades' Assembly, and the Inter-national Typographical Union all decided not to send delegates to St. Louis in 1871. See *Workingman's Advocate*, 18 February 1871; and Stevens, *New York Typographical Union, No. 6*, 585.

March 1871: "That the great majority of trades unions and their members do not believe in or indorse the action of the National Labor Union is attested by the fact that every National or State organization of workingmen that has met since the adjournment of the National Labor Union has either declined to elect or withdrawn their delegates to that body."[16] Walls's statement gains credibility when we see that there was indeed a precipitous decline in trade union attendance at the 1871 congress, where the delegate count fell dramatically from ninety-five to twenty-two. Moreover, it was precisely the local, city, and national trade unions that stayed away; the remaining delegates were drawn largely from "labor unions" chartered by the NLU.[17]

Both the small number of delegates and the absence of almost all local, city, and national unions distinguished the 1871 congress from all previous conventions. At no other congress had there been so few trade union representatives.[18] Moreover, the dissenting unions themselves pointed to changes in platform as the basis of their defection from the NLU. Again, Henry Walls captured the trade union dissatisfaction with the particular direction taken by the NLU.

> The question naturally arises now as to whether the object for which the National Labor Union was organized has been accomplished, whether the ideas of its progenitors upon which it was founded have been elucidated by the action of the last congress [1870]. . . . I firmly believe its progenitors never thought of, let alone intended, it should result in what is now the National Labor Union. . . . I claim, however, that the intention of its originators has never been put in practical shape, and consequently has never been tried, and the National Labor Union, as it is today, is not a departure from an original plan adopted, but is, to use a vulgarity, a miscarriage.[19]

There was no easy division of tasks between the unions and the NLU. On the contrary, the NLU was viewed with considerable disdain and was thought to be unworthy of trade union support. Not surprisingly, Walls did not attend the next congress in St. Louis in 1871. Within a year, the national organization had virtually disappeared.

Although disaffection with the NLU was widespread, not all organizations broke with the NLU for the same reasons. No one issue was identified

---

[16] *Workingmen's Assembly Proceedings*, 1871, 82.

[17] Delegate attendance is provided in *NLU Proceedings*. It is important to distinguish between trade and labor unions within the NLU. Trade unions usually were established independently of the NLU and subsequently affiliated with the new national organization. Labor unions, on the other hand, generally were formed under the auspices of the NLU charter and thus were more likely to endorse the NLU platform.

[18] For lists of delegates attending each of the NLU congresses, see *NLU Proceedings* for each year.

[19] See Walls's letter to Jessup in *Workingmen's Assembly Proceedings*, 1871, 82.

by all dissenting unions, but among the criticisms raised, two issues in particular seem to dominate. A number of labor leaders agreed with Jessup and identified the financial and currency questions as the bone of contention. Friederich Sorge, for example, also stressed the divisiveness of financial issues in his accounts of the period, which appeared in the newspaper *Die Neue Zeit* in the early 1890s.[20] Sorge was a music teacher and an active participant in several postwar labor organizations. In January 1869, he helped to revive the Socialist party, which affiliated with the NLU later that same year. In 1870, however, the Socialist party broke with the NLU specifically because of the organization's undue emphasis on financial reform. Differences over currency and credit had emerged much earlier, according to Sorge, when William Sylvis, a longtime financial reformer, was blocked from becoming president of the NLU.[21]

Not all organizations, however, focused on the financial issues when breaking with the NLU. A number of delegates identified party politics as the contentious question within the NLU. At the very first congress in 1866, the NLU had passed a resolution in favor of establishing a National Labor party, but little was done to implement the resolution during the next four years. At the 1870 congress a committee was formed with the authority to call a national convention to establish an independent political party. The resolution favoring party politics, it seemed, finally was to be put into action, thereby prompting the Cigar Makers' International Union, the Cincinnati Trades' Assembly, and the International Typographical Union all to withdraw from the national association.[22] Disagreements were so intense after the 1870 congress that the Chicago *Workingman's*

[20] See Friedrich A. Sorge, "Die Arbeiterbewegung in den Vereinigten Staaten, 1860–1866," *Die Neue Zeit* 9, 2 (1891–1892); and Friedrich A. Sorge, "Die Arbeiterbewegung in den Vereinigten Staaten, 1866–1876," *Die Neue Zeit* 10, 1 (1891–1892).

[21] As well as reviving the Socialist party, Sorge also was active within the International Workingmen's Association in America. He was a delegate to The Hague in 1872 and while there formed a lifelong friendship with Marx and Engels. For Sorge's background, see Commons et al., *History of Labor in the United States* 2:207. For Sorge's views on the NLU, see Charlotte Todes, *William H. Sylvis and the National Labor Union* (New York: International Publishers, 1942), 70–71, 90.

Additional conflict over financial issues also can be seen at the NLU's 1868 congress. The platform committee was divided, with L. A. Hine submitting a minority report that opposed the majority's currency scheme. A lengthy debate over the financial plank ensued, in which Jonathan Fincher joined Hine in critiquing the proposed policy. When the vote was taken the majority report was adopted with strong support from delegates such as Sylvis, Andrew Cameron, and Richard Trevellick. Fortunately, a complete record of the 1868 proceedings is available. See *Proceedings of the Second Session of the National Labor Union, in Convention Assembled at New York City, Sept. 21, 1868* (Philadelphia: W. B. Selheimer, Printer, 1868), 32–38, 40–47 (Hereafter cited as *NLU Proceedings of the Second Session, 1868.*)

[22] See *The Workingman's Advocate*, 18 February 1871, editorial; Walls's letter to Jessup in *Workingmen's Assembly Proceedings*, 1871, 83; and Stevens, *New York Typographical Union, No. 6*, 585.

Advocate ran three consecutive editorials entitled "What Is the National Labor Union?" that attempted to reconcile conflicting views and to prevent the organization from disintegrating. Ultimately, the differences could not be contained, and those who lost out in the struggle to control the NLU agenda withdrew from the organization, leaving only a handful of labor reformers at the 1872 congress.[23]

Whatever the reason for trade union dissent, evidence of antagonism between the unions and the NLU is clear. Far from being functionally distinct organizations, with leaders moving easily back and forth, the NLU is best viewed as an unsuccessful attempt to unify the heterogeneous and fragmented labor movement after the Civil War. Differences between labor organizations, not surprisingly, came to a head within the NLU, as conflicting visions and agenda had to be compromised into a single platform. It was precisely these struggles over how to understand labor's situation, and disputes over which strategy to pursue, that we see played out within the NLU.

Viewing the NLU from this perspective, as an umbrella organization within which conflicting views of the labor question were debated and fought over, enables us to glimpse the very different perspectives that coexisted within the labor movement in the immediate postwar decade. To be sure, in the late 1860s and early 1870s, ideological fault lines were not yet firmly drawn. Instead, differences were just beginning to emerge that would continue to harden over the next two decades. In order to grasp the significance of dissension within the NLU, we need to look beyond the confines of this particular organization to the larger political debate within the labor movement over conflicting visions of economic growth.

RESTORING THE REPUBLIC: THE PRODUCERS' PROJECT

The postwar producers' vision was articulated clearly by both William Sylvis of the NLU and Terence Powderly, Grand Master Workman of the KOL. In trying to mobilize their followers, each of these men spelled out their larger image of both the inner workings and the future path of late-nineteenth-century political economy—always with an eye, of course, to elaborating labor's role in their interpretations of postwar growth. Drawing on Sylvis's and Powderly's more general writings and speeches, and on the platforms and proceedings of the organizations they led, I have reconstructed their particular narrative of labor's plight. Less prominent labor leaders, such as Robert D. Layton and George Blair, both of the KOL, also

---

[23] Andrew Cameron wrote three consecutive editorials that appeared in *The Workingman's Advocate* on 18 February, 25 February, and 4 March 1871. Cameron was a staunch advocate of establishing a national labor organization and was one of the few men to attend all of the NLU congresses and Industrial Brotherhood conventions in the years 1866 to 1875.

adhered to similar views, as can be seen in their testimony before the 1883 Senate Committee on "The Relations between Labor and Capital," which I have used to flesh out the postwar producers' vision of the economic issues at hand.

Postwar producers, such as Sylvis and Powderly, were in no way opposed to economic development per se, and often marveled at the enormous gains to be had from the reorganization of work and the introduction of new machinery. As early as 1867, the NLU declared that "the present is emphatically an age of progress" in which the nature of work had been dramatically transformed.[24] Similarly, at the General Assembly of the KOL in 1880, Powderly praised the "wonderful inventions of improved machinery" that had increased production tenfold over the previous century. In many respects, producers were intrigued by the process of industrialization, and thought that workers, too, could benefit immensely from labor-saving machinery and increased production. If properly administered, the new inventions could reduce the hours of work and allow producers greater opportunity to fulfill their obligations as citizens of the republic.[25]

Neither the NLU nor the KOL contested the importance of economic growth—that much almost all agreed on. The issue at stake for producers was the particular form or path economic development was to take. Both Sylvis's and Powderly's principal mission was to ensure that future growth continued along republican lines. Although the precise contours of the postwar republic remained unclear, the task of applying republican precepts to contemporary economic concerns informed the key components of the producers' platforms.

A truly republican political economy, argued Sylvis, Powderly, and Layton, would allow growth to continue, but in a more *decentralized* way. Smaller firms would maintain control over production, distributing goods to local communities on a more limited scale.[26] If production were sustained on a regional basis, wealth and power also would be distributed more evenly throughout the nation. Current tensions between workers and employers would begin to dissipate as all productive citizens began to reap

[24] The quotation is taken from *NLU Address*, 145.

[25] Quoted in Powderly, *Thirty Years of Labor*, 478. The Grand Master Workman's praise of inventions and machinery was originally contained in a lengthy discussion of these issues at the KOL General Assembly in 1880. Similar acceptance of "improved machinery" can be seen in Layton testimony, *Report of the Committee of the Senate* 1:36; Blair testimony, *Report of the Committee of the Senate* 2:45.

[26] For example, Powderly claimed that railroad pools and farming syndicates had been far from beneficial and, in fact, had decreased healthy competition within these industries. See Powderly, *Thirty Years of Labor*, 455. Powderly also feared the erosion of the "middle ground" as producers were lured into the larger cities. See Powderly, *Thirty Years of Labor*, 387. For similar concerns about the size and scale of production, see Sylvis, "What Is Money?" 358; and Layton testimony, *Report of the Committee of the Senate* 1:5.

the rewards of their hard-earned labor. To be sure, divisions between the producing and nonproducing classes would remain. But the old producers' alliance would no longer be in danger, as both skilled workers and small manufacturers would be able to flourish under a properly republican pattern of economic growth.

Yet not all was well in this "age of progress." Indeed, the postwar economy was not proceeding along republican lines. Under existing conditions of economic development, both the NLU and KOL agreed, few of the advantages of labor-saving machinery and technological improvement had been passed on to workers. Even though producers were responsible for most of the inventions, the NLU claimed, their wages and work hours remained essentially unchanged. The only ones to benefit from the "wonderful inventions" were capitalists and large employers who captured increased production for themselves in the form of higher profits.[27]

The ultimate testimony to the problems of economic development was the uneven pattern of postwar growth. Both the NLU and the KOL, like their antebellum counterparts, pointed repeatedly to the "recent alarming aggression of aggregated wealth."[28] Large corporations and "millionaire manufacturers" were squeezing out the "small traders" and local producers, leaving them with little or no say in the future direction of industrial organization.[29] If this aggregation of wealth in the hands of a few monopolists was allowed to continue, the KOL platform claimed in 1878, it would "invariably lead to the pauperization and hopeless degradation of the toiling masses."[30] For producers to receive their just rewards, the current trend toward increased economic concentration had to be "arrested," and a more republican pattern of economic development resumed.[31]

The dominant faction within both the NLU and the KOL understood the persistence of workers' poverty amidst conditions of economic growth in similar terms: the current pattern of uneven economic development was not inevitable, but was due to the creation of three new monopolies in American society. Monopolization of the transportation and communications systems, of public lands, and of the financial system was distorting current patterns of economic development. The impact of all three monopolies was mutually reinforcing; each in its own way prevented the small producer from securing "the fruits of his toil." The producers' fear of

[27] *NLU Address*, 145. It is important to note that in these early postbellum decades capitalists still were equated with nonproducers. See *NLU Proceedings of the Second Session, 1868*, 32–33.

[28] The KOL preamble described the recent capital accumulation in these terms. The quotation can be found in Powderly, *Thirty Years of Labor*, 116–17, 243.

[29] Quoted in ibid., 454–55.

[30] The phrase "pauperization and hopeless degradation of the toiling masses" appears in the opening paragraph of the preamble to the KOL platform. See General Assembly Proceedings, 1878, 3, Powderly Papers.

[31] Powderly, *Thirty Years of Labor*, 409.

economic concentration was captured vividly by Powderly when he described the growth of corporations as follows: "Fancy a man whose arteries do not belong to him, whose heart-beats are directed by another, by one over whom he has no control, and the reader will form an idea of the condition of this country, with the public highways in the hands of corporations, acting independent of and in some instances in defiance of government." There was no reason, Sylvis and Powderly asserted, for workers to live in a state of poverty and want while a few industrialists amassed all the wealth. A more just economic system would allow all industrious citizens to share more equally in the benefits of increased production. The central task of the producers' program, then, was to remove the new sources of monopoly that had created the current crisis in postwar growth.[32]

Although many aspects of the economy were thought to be in need of immediate reform, the "money problem" was considered by many to be fundamental. An inadequate distribution of currency and credit, to a large extent, made the other forms of monopoly possible. The NLU, for example, declared the money question to be the nation's number one problem in its inaugural platform of 1866: "That this money monopoly is the parent of all monopolies—the very root and essence of slavery—railroad, warehouse and all other monopolies of whatever kind or nature are the outgrowth of and subservient to this power, and the means used by it to rob the enterprising industrial wealth-producing classes of their talents and labor."[33] Reforming the financial system was essential, the NLU argued, because as long as the "money monopoly" remained, small producers and skilled workers would continue to lose out to the large industrialists.

The specific ways in which the financial system was supposed to have promoted economic concentration were spelled out clearly in the late 1860s by Sylvis in a wonderful essay entitled "What Is Money?"[34] Three steps in the argument are clear. First, like many of his contemporaries,

---

[32] The phrase "fruits of his toil" is taken from the preamble of the KOL platform. See KOL General Assembly Proceedings, 1882, 3, Powderly Papers. For the Powderly quote, see Powderly, *Thirty Years of Labor*, 387. For more general attacks on monopolies, see the "Majority Report of the Platform Committee," in *NLU Proceedings of the Second Session, 1868*, 33–34, 40. The NLU and KOL concern that small producers were losing out to the larger industrialists can be seen in the following sources: Sylvis, "What Is Money?" 362–64, 367; Powderly, *Thirty Years of Labor*, 409, 454–55. For arguments about the importance of securing balanced growth, see Sylvis, "What Is Money?" 380, 384; and Powderly, *Thirty Years of Labor*, chap. 9.

[33] *NLU Address*, 178. For a similar claim, see Powderly, *Thirty Years of Labor*, 396–97.

[34] The importance of the financial question has been noted by previous scholars. For example, see Chester McArthur Destler, *American Radicalism 1865–1901: Essays and Documents* (New London, Conn.: Connecticut College Monographs, 1946). David Montgomery also laid out the financial issues in the last chapter of *Beyond Equality*. However, neither of these earlier accounts fully integrates the financial question into its analysis of workers' protest and labor movement development more generally.

Sylvis adhered to the labor theory of value. Labor, not capital, was the source of all wealth. The value produced by man's labor could be represented, but not replaced, by money. Money could be used to measure, represent, accumulate, and exchange value, but in and of itself could not create wealth.[35]

Producers, however, were being robbed of their hard-earned wealth by the current financial policy. The second step in the Sylvis analysis provided a detailed account of contemporary financial policy and of its influence on future patterns of economic growth. The extent and price of credit were the crucial issues, according to Sylvis and the dominant faction within the NLU. Ready access to an abundant and cheap source of money was essential, the NLU argued, for ensuring a more democratic and decentralized pattern of economic development. Producers could reap the benefits of their "labor and talents" only if they had access to the necessary capital for their entrepreneurial ventures. An ample supply of credit thus would promote a "general leveling up" in which all industrious citizens would share in the benefits of economic growth.[36] A democratic monetary policy, according to Sylvis, would not tie the currency to the supply of gold, but rather would provide a cheap, safe, and abundant paper currency for the community at large.[37]

Sylvis considered the nation's actual postwar financial policy to be woefully inadequate on two counts. First, the volume of currency was too low, unduly restricting access to credit. Second, variable interest rates made credit expensive, and had an enormous redistributive effect on the American economy. These two factors taken together, Sylvis claimed, were responsible for the persistence of workers' poverty amidst conditions of economic growth. When interest rates were allowed to climb above real levels of economic growth, usually estimated at between 3 and 4 percent, money, and those who lent it, absorbed more than their fair share of national wealth.[38] "Unnatural" rates of interest effectively "transferred" the products of labor from the hands of the producer "to the pockets of the money lender."[39] Sylvis compared the rate of interest to a tax collector in

[35] Sylvis, "What Is Money?" 355. Sylvis acknowledged his debt to the earlier work of Edward Kellogg, who also believed the financial system to be crucial to labor. See Edward Kellogg, *Labor and Other Capital: The Rights of Each Secured and the Wrongs of Both Eradicated* (New York: Author, 1849). The NLU also recommended Kellogg's book to delegates. See *NLU Proceedings of the Second Session, 1868*, 21.

[36] The phrase "labor and talents" appears in a number of NLU documents and proceedings. For example, see *NLU Proceedings, 1867*, 176; and *NLU Proceedings of the Second Session, 1868*, 32. The phrase "leveling up" can be found in many nineteenth-century labor sources. For example, see Sylvis, "What Is Money?" 369.

[37] The desire to decouple currency from gold and to create a more democratic financial system both can be seen in Sylvis, "What Is Money?" 380.

[38] Ibid., 362–63, 367–68, 384.

[39] Ibid., 364.

order to drive home his point: "Interest acts like the tax-gatherer; it enters into all things, and eats up the profits of labor. . . . Interest produces nothing, but consumes everything; it gathers together the products of labor into large heaps, making a few rich and many poor."[40] The rate of interest, then, was the mechanism by which wealth and value were redistributed between producers and nonproducers. If interest rates were too high, labor was deprived of its appropriate share of production. If interest rates were fixed at or below the rate of economic growth, then workers would be able to share more equally in the benefits of industrialization.

The final step in Sylvis's argument was to claim that small manufacturers and skilled workers lost equally under the current financial system; bankers and moneylenders—the quintessential nonproducers—were the only ones to profit. High rates of interest hurt small manufacturers, farmers, and businessmen almost as much as they did skilled workers.[41] Striking against one's employer, Sylvis argued, was misguided. Employers were not the enemy: bankers and moneylenders were the real oppressors of American producers. The identity of worker and employer interests can be seen clearly in Sylvis's analysis of industrial conflict: "In many instances, the employer, to keep his works going, must borrow money, and must pay more interest for the use of it than his return in profit; to save himself, he reduces wages; the workmen, not being able to see where the true difficulty is, go on a strike—the works are closed, and employer and workmen go to ruin together."[42] If "idleness, poverty, and want" were to be avoided, workers had to maintain the producers' alliance and strive to implement a program of financial reform. Industrial disputes merely aggravated rather than solved the problem, and were to be used only as a last resort. Existing labor strategies, for the most part, dealt with symptoms rather than causes, and failed to address the true source of labor's degradation, namely, an undemocratic monetary system and the associated monopolies. "Industrial emancipation" would only be achieved, the producers argued, once these problems had been solved politically.[43]

The NLU solution to the "money problem," as with all three monopolies, was to advocate an extensive program of legislative reform. From the producers' perspective, the large corporations and accumulations of capi-

[40] Ibid.

[41] Ibid., 365, 367.

[42] Ibid., 367.

[43] The producers' view of industrial conflict as a last resort can be seen in the following: Layton testimony, *Report of the Committee of the Senate*, 1:16; Sylvis, "What Is Money?" 365, 367; Powderly, *Thirty Years of Labor*, 250, 275, 503; *NLU Address*, 155. For discussion of existing labor strategies as dealing with symptoms rather than causes, see Powderly, *Thirty Years of Labor*, 511; and Sylvis, "What Is Money?" 358–59. For use of the phrase "industrial emancipation," see Powderly, *Thirty Years of Labor*, 49; and the Greenback 1876 platform, reprinted in Donald Bruce Johnson and Kirk H. Porter, eds., *National Party Platforms* (Urbana: University of Illinois Press, 1973), 52.

tal that had emerged in the 1850s and 1860s were *not* considered to be inevitable by-products of economic development achieved through economies of scale. "Unwise and corrupt legislation," the producers argued, was responsible for the postwar problems of monopolized growth. A change in government policy would go a long way toward solving the producers' problems by returning the nation to a less dangerous path.[44]

From the 1870s through 1890s producers mobilized politically and established a series of third parties to contest state and national elections. Between 1872 and 1900, for example, every presidential election was contested by a third party advocating similar programs of antimonopoly reform.[45] By organizing politically and electing their own representatives, producers hoped to revolutionize the American system of finance and thereby ensure a more equitable pattern of postwar growth. To be sure, labor's commitment to political action was not uncritical, as partisan loyalties remained a divisive issue for most workers' organizations in the

---

[44] Powderly wrote of "unwise and corrupt legislation." See Powderly, *Thirty Years of Labor*, 83. Similar concerns about poor legislation can be seen in *NLU Address*, 165–66; *NLU Proceedings, 1867*, 177; and *NLU Proceedings of the Second Session, 1868*, 32.

Although very different from standard twentieth century accounts of industrialization, the producers' claim that economic concentration was a political creation had some empirical foundation. A number of state governments indeed had subsidized internal improvements through land grants, tariffs, monopoly charters, and banking privileges before the war. Without such extensive government promotion of national markets, the producers' vision of small-scale, regional economic development may have remained a viable alternative.

For discussion of government promotion of internal improvements, see Robert A. Lively, "The American System, A Review Article," *Business History Review* 29 (March 1955): 81–96; and Carter Goodrich, "Internal Improvements Reconsidered," *Journal of Economic History* 30, 2 (June 1970): 289–311. For work exploring alternative paths of economic development, see Charles F. Sabel and Jonathan Zeitlin, "Historical Alternatives to Mass Production: Politics, Markets and Technology in Nineteenth-Century Industrialization," *Past and Present* 108 (August 1985): 133–76; Charles F. Sabel, *Work and Politics: The Division of Labor in Industry* (New York: Cambridge University Press, 1982); Patrick O'Brien and Caglar Keyder, *Economic Growth in Britain and France, 1780–1914: Two Paths to the Twentieth Century* (London: Allen and Unwin, 1978); Richard Locke, "Local Politics and Industrial Adjustment: The Political Economy of Italy in the 1980s" (Ph.D. diss., Massachusetts Institute of Technology, 1989); and Gary Herrigel, "Industrial Organization in the Politics of Industry: Centralized and Decentralized Production in Germany" (Ph.D. diss., Massachusetts Institute of Technology, 1990). For more specific arguments along these lines for the United States, see Gerald P. Berk, "Corporations and Politics: American Railroads, 1870–1916" (Ph.D. diss., Massachusetts Institute of Technology, 1987); Gerald P. Berk, "Constituting Corporations and Markets: Railroads in Gilded Age Politics," *Studies in American Political Development* 4 (1990): 130–68; Lawrence Goodwyn, *The Populist Moment: A Short History of the Agrarian Revolt in America* (New York: Oxford University Press, 1978); and Philip Scranton, *Proprietary Capitalism: The Textile Manufacture at Philadelphia 1800–1885* (Philadelphia: Temple University Press, 1983).

[45] For programs and platforms of major third parties contesting presidential elections between 1872 and 1900, see Johnson and Porter, *National Party Platforms*.

postbellum decades. Owing to the war, it was difficult for northern producers to continue their antebellum affiliation with the Democratic party. As a consequence, many labor organizations avoided formally endorsing either of the major political parties in the postbellum decades.[46]

Despite these partisan difficulties, the producers by no means shied away from electoral politics altogether. In fact, their antimonopoly reforms were predicated on *more extensive* government intervention in the American economy. At their most extreme, producers called for nationalization of large monopolies such as telegraph, canal, and railroad corporations. More moderate demands included a call for increased government regulation of interstate commerce, the creation of government arbitration of industrial disputes, and, of course, government control of currency and credit.[47]

THE PRODUCERS' REPUBLIC AND COLLECTIVE ACTION

One element of the producers' program was especially important for their relations with the American state, namely, their attitude toward collective

[46] For discussion of producers' affiliation with the Democratic party in the antebellum era, see Meyers, *The Jacksonian Persuasion*. For evidence of labor being divided between the two major parties after the Civil War, see Robert P. Sharkey, *Money, Class, and Party: An Economic Study of Civil War and Reconstruction* (Baltimore: Johns Hopkins University Press, 1959); and Montgomery, *Beyond Equality*, chaps. 7–9. The producers' ambivalent attitude toward political action is captured in the following sources: *NLU Address*, 164–65; Powderly, *Thirty Years of Labor*, chap. 6. See also Fink, *Workingmen's Democracy*, esp. 23–24, for an excellent discussion of the Knights' ambivalence toward political reform. Finally, for the producers' desire to transform the financial system, see the General Master Workman's "secret circular" that called for "a revolution" in the economic system. After denouncing the French Revolution, the circular continued: "Notwithstanding all of this, I wish to see some killing done; I wish to see the systems by which the worker is oppressed killed off; and I long to see a revolution in the working time of those who toil." The circular was distributed on 15 December 1884. See Powderly, *Thirty Years of Labor*, 483. Similar calls for "a radical change in the existing industrial system" were expressed by the KOL in 1884 when the General Assembly declared that the "attitude of our order to the existing industrial system is necessarily one of war." Quoted in Melvyn Dubofsky, *Industrialism and the American Worker, 1865–1920* (New York: Thomas Y. Crowell, 1975), 55.

[47] For nationalization, see the KOL platform adopted in Philadelphia in 1884, plank 18, *Powderly Papers*. See also Powderly, *Thirty Years of Labor*, 388–90; and the Greenback platform of 1884, plank 4, reprinted in Johnson and Porter, *National Party Platforms*. Producers were quite aware of the irony of advocating nationalization as a means of arresting economic concentration. See Powderly, *Thirty Years of Labor*, 409, 414; and Blair testimony, *Report of the Committee of the Senate* 2:61–65. For increased regulation of interstate commerce, and particular support for the Interstate Commerce Bill, see Powderly, *Thirty Years of Labor*, 394; Greenback platform of 1880, plank 6; Anti-monopoly platform of 1884, planks 5 and 7; and the Greenback platform of 1884, plank 4. Party platforms all are reprinted in Johnson and Porter, *National Party Platforms*. For arbitration, see the KOL platform of 1878, plank 10; the Anti-monopoly platform of 1884, plank 6, and the Union Labor platform of

action. Even though producers had begun to organize quite extensively after the Civil War, they considered their actions to be both temporary and reactive. The Knights, for example, placed the following quotation from Edmund Burke at the head of their platform: "When bad men combine, the good must associate, else they will fall, one by one, an unpitied sacrifice in a contemptible struggle."[48] Moreover, for two decades after the Civil War neither the NLU nor the KOL called for government protection of workers' collective action.[49] The incorporation of trade unions and labor assemblies would not be needed, producers argued, once their antimonopoly reforms had taken hold and the nation returned to its republican path. William Sylvis captured the producers' position nicely in a remark that often was quoted by his contemporaries: "When a just monetary system has been established there will no longer exist a necessity for Trades Unions."[50]

Thus, for several decades after the Civil War, producer organizations remained committed to small-scale, regional economic development. If their antimonopoly program succeeded, *neither* capital nor labor would be allowed to organize collectively. Nor would they want to. The interests of small manufacturers and skilled workers were not considered to be mutually exclusive. Members of the producing classes could live in harmony as long as all industrious citizens were allowed to enjoy the benefits of economic growth.[51] The Sylvis and Powderly position was not simply a uto-

---

1888, preamble, Powderly Papers. For government control of currency and credit, see the KOL platform of 1884, planks 14 and 15, Powderly Papers; Powderly, *Thirty Years of Labor*, chap. 9; and NLU platform, reprinted in Sylvis, *The Life, Speeches, Labors and Essays of William Sylvis*, 284–95.

[48] Quoted in KOL General Assembly Proceedings, title page, Powderly Papers. For producers' views of organization as strictly a defensive and temporary strategy, see Layton testimony, *Report of the Committee of the Senate*, 1:14; *NLU Address*, 153; Powderly, *Thirty Years of Labor*, 78; Sylvis, "What Is Money?" 359; and Henry George, *The Labor Question, Being an Abridgement of the Condition of Labor* (1891; Cincinnati: Joseph Fels Fund of America, 1911).

[49] In 1884 the Knights modified their platform and added a new plank calling for the incorporation of workers' associations. This change in policy, however, did not signal a complete abandonment of their antimonopoly assumptions. The Knights continued to preface their calls for organization with qualifying remarks on their temporary and defensive nature. The last plank in the very same platform, for example, continued to stress the importance of bonds between skilled workers and small manufacturers, an alliance that lay at the heart of the producers' vision. Differences between employers and employees must be arbitrated, the plank declared, "in order that the bonds of sympathy between them may be strengthened and that strikes may be rendered unnecessary." See KOL General Assembly Proceedings, 1884, 3, Powderly Papers.

[50] The Sylvis quotation first appeared in the Chicago *Workingman's Advocate* on 12 December 1868 in a letter from Sylvis addressed to the "Working People of the United States." The Sylvis remark can also be found in Sylvis, *The Life, Speeches, Labors and Essays of William H. Sylvis*, title page; and Powderly, *Thirty Years of Labor*, 397.

[51] For the producers' conception of a harmony of interests between employers and employees, see the following: Henry Charles Carey, *The Harmony of Interests, Agricultural, Man-*

pian dream in which all conflict would disappear. On the contrary, both the NLU and the KOL continued to acknowledge divisions between the producing and nonproducing classes. Conflict and disagreement would persist, the producers argued, but would no longer create unwanted divisions *within* the producers' ranks.

Not all postbellum labor organizations, however, adhered to these republican precepts. Indeed, in the immediate postwar decade a number of trade unionists began to question the producers' vision and to advocate a very different program of labor reform.

BREAKDOWN OF THE PRODUCERS' ALLIANCE:
THE TRADE UNION DISSENT

Local, city, and national trade unions, like their producer counterparts, were preoccupied with the massive changes under way in the American economy. The "hydra headed monster" of monopoly concerned the New York Workingmen's Assembly as much as it did the dominant faction within the NLU. Railroads and public lands again were hailed as prime examples of changing economic conditions.[52] Despite these similarities, however, trade unionists such as William Jessup, Henry Walls, and Conrad Kuhn often responded differently than producers to the increased economic concentration of the postwar economy. In the 1860s and 1870s, it is important to remember, the trade union position was not yet fully formed. Nevertheless, the first steps toward the construction of an alternative vision can be seen in the trade unionists' dissent within the NLU. Instead of drawing on their republican heritage, trade unionists such as Jessup, Walls, and Kuhn began to question the central tenets of the producers' analysis, and to articulate a new interpretation of workers' current situation.[53]

First, the dissident unionists called into question the longstanding producers' alliance between skilled workers and small manufacturers. The old

---

ufacturing and Commercial (1852; Philadelphia: H. C. Baird, 1890); Henry Demarest Lloyd, *Wealth Against Commonwealth* (New York: Harper and Brothers, 1894); George, *The Labor Question*; and Edward Atkinson, *Labor and Capital: Allies Not Enemies* (New York: Harper and Brothers, 1879). See also Layton testimony, *Report of the Committee of the Senate* 1:3–5; and Blair testimony, *Report of the Committee of the Senate* 2:44.

[52] The phrase "hydra headed monster" of monopoly is taken from *Workingmen's Assembly Proceedings*, 1871, 80.

For references to the problem of railroads and public lands, see *Workingmen's Assembly Proceedings*, 1869, 7; 1870, 5–6; and 1871, 80–81.

[53] For a general account of dissension within the NLU, see "What Is the National Labor Union-1," in *The Workingman's Advocate*, 18 February 1871. For elaboration of Jessup's views, see his report on the 1870 NLU congress to his home organization, the New York Workingmen's Association. Jessup's report is reprinted in full in *Workingmen's Assembly Proceedings*, 1871, 57–65. See also Henry Walls's letter to Jessup, also reprinted in *Workingmen's Assembly Proceedings*, 1871, 81–84.

alliance was no longer tenable, the dissenters argued, and was limiting the effectiveness of the NLU. It was time for workers to break with their producer allies and to organize as a distinct wage-earning class. Up until the late 1860s, most labor organizations, including the NLU, had welcomed small manufacturers and middle-class reformers into their associations as fellow producers. Both Jessup and Walls, however, called for an end to this practice, and advocated instead the exclusion of all non-wage-earning delegates from their organizations.[54] Although unsuccessful, this attempt to restrict membership in the national organization to "bona fide labor organizations" suggests that a number of unionists had begun to think differently than producers about prevailing social relations.[55]

Second, unionists and producers responded differently to the concentration of capital. Rather than try to restore the propertied independence of small producers by preventing capital from accumulating, the dissenting unionists advocated a more radical break with their republican past. Workers had to accept increased economic concentration as a fact of life and organize collectively as a countervailing power. Where the producers had tried to change employers' behavior by preventing capital from combining, many trade unionists focused instead on changing labor's strategy by establishing unions with equal powers alongside business corporations.[56]

The platform and proceedings of both the New York Workingmen's

---

[54] Debates over membership were held on several occasions, as delegates disagreed over whether to seat middle-class reformers as well as women and blacks. For hostility to middle-class reformers, see Jessup's report, *Workingmen's Assembly Proceedings*, 1871, 64. See also Henry Walls's letter to Jessup, *Workingmen's Assembly Proceedings*, 1871, 83. At the 1874 Industrial Congress, which met after the NLU disintegrated, a number of trade unions proposed that all non–wage earners be excluded from the organization. Interestingly, Henry Walls, then of the Molders' International Union, sent a communication favoring restriction of membership to delegates from "National and International Trade Organizations." See Commons et al., *History of Labor in the United States* 2:162. For debates over seating Elizabeth Cady Stanton and Susan B. Anthony, see *NLU Proceedings*, 1868, 198; 1869, 231. In fact, the Newark House Painters' Union withdrew their delegate from the NLU in 1868 over the Stanton question. See *NLU Proceedings*, 1868, 219. For debates over "negro labor," see *NLU Proceedings*, 1867, 185–88.

[55] Jessup distinguished "bona-fide trade or labor organizations" from other reform associations. See Jessup's report, *Workingmen's Assembly Proceedings*, 1871, 58.

[56] Jessup, Walls, and Sorge all protested the NLU's undue interest in financial reform precisely because they no longer believed that a change in financial policy would restore propertied independence to small producers. See *NLU Proceedings*, 1870, 265; *Workingmen's Assembly Proceedings*, 1871, 64; and Todes, *William H. Sylvis and the National Labor Union*, 90. In addition, some unionists explicitly called for collective action to counter capital's power. For example, in his letter to Jessup in 1871, Walls stressed the importance of establishing a "purely labor organization" through which the "concentration of the power of labor so much desired by its true friends and so much feared by its enemies would then be near a realization." See Walls's letter to Jessup, *Workingmen's Assembly Proceedings*, 1871, 83.

Assembly and the FOTLU enable us to flesh out more fully the collectivist assumptions underlying the trade union vision. In the early 1870s and 1880s, the New York Workingmen's Assembly and the FOTLU displayed an early commitment to collective action by calling repeatedly for state protection of workers' industrial rights, specifically the right to organize and strike. It was only fair, the Workingmen's Assembly argued, that workers be awarded the "same chartered rights and privileges" as had been "granted to associated capital." In short, workers and employers must be treated equally by the state: both must be allowed to organize.[57] In order for the Workingmen's Assembly and the FOTLU to achieve the desired equality between capital and labor, two aspects of government policy had to be changed. First, trade unions had to be allowed to incorporate. Second, the common law doctrine of criminal conspiracy, which had long enabled criminal prosecution of working-class organizations, had to be repealed. In many respects, these two policies were simply different sides of the same coin; each in its own way tried to secure for workers the right to organize and strike.

Between 1865 and 1885, both the New York Workingmen's Assembly and the FOTLU consistently called for these two policy reforms.[58] Although these were not the only issues they lobbied for, obtaining state protection of workers' industrial rights remained central to both their programs. In fact, the incorporation of trade unions was ranked as either the first or second plank in each of the FOTLU platforms. This attention to state protection of working-class organization contrasts sharply with the producers' view of collective action as a temporary and reactive strategy that would be set aside once economic concentration had been successfully opposed.[59] The dissident unionists did not anticipate any such reversal. On

[57] Quoted from *Workingmen's Assembly Proceedings*, 1870, 42.

[58] For New York Workingmen's Assembly demands for the incorporation of trade unions, see *Workingmen's Assembly Proceedings*, 1870, 45, 55; 1871, 42; 1887, 6; and January 1889, 36. Unfortunately, Workingmen's Assembly proceedings for the years 1872 to 1881 are missing, making it impossible to track the Assembly policy in these years. For Workingmen's Assembly efforts to repeal the conspiracy doctrine, see the sources in note 80 below.

The FOTLU called for incorporation of trade unions as the first or second plank in each of their platforms. The FOTLU reports and the AFL proceedings are collected in *Proceedings of the American Federation of Labor* (Bloomington, Ill.: Pantagraph Printing and Stationery Co., 1906). (Hereafter, proceedings from all FOTLU and AFL congresses will be cited as *FOTLU Reports* and *AFL Proceedings*, respectively, followed by year of session.) The FOTLU demanded that the conspiracy doctrine be repealed at almost all of its sessions between 1881 and 1885. See *FOTLU Reports*, 1881–1885.

[59] For producers' views of collective action as temporary and reactive, see the following sources: *NLU Address*, 152–53; *NLU Proceedings*, 1866, 132 (which stated that organization should "not be taken as a menace to employers, knowing as we do that the principle involved is not aggressive but defensive in character"). In 1884, the KOL revised its platform. One of the changes introduced was the inclusion of a plank calling for incorporation of trade

the contrary, union delegates to the NLU such as Jessup, Walls, and Kuhn believed that collective action was the way of the future and that combination had to remain an essential component of any successful labor strategy in a modern industrial economy.[60]

Finally, it is important to recognize that differences within the NLU over questions of strategy ultimately rested on different visions of economic development. Although not fully articulated until the late 1880s by the AFL, dissenting unionists within the NLU already had begun to rethink the question of economic growth in the first decade after the Civil War. Securing state protection for working-class organization was especially important for the dissenting unions because they no longer believed that growth could be achieved along republican lines. Railroads, telegraphs, and large land grants were not just temporary aberrations or unwanted political creations, but were seen as permanent fixtures of the modern industrial economy. Economic growth increasingly was seen as an evolutionary process through which the logic of development would gradually unfold. From the trade union perspective, the producers' vision of a decentralized political economy was simply untenable; concentrated economic development was here to stay. If workers' interests were to be protected under conditions of economic concentration, it was essential to organize collectively and check the enormous increase in capital's power.[61]

Early attempts to construct an alternative narrative of industrialization can be seen in the testimony of Frank Foster, Adolph Strasser, P. J. McGuire, and Samuel Gompers before the Senate Committee on the Relations Between Labor and Capital in 1883. For example, Gompers clearly linked the origins and benefits of trade unions to economic progress when he testified as follows: "Modern industry evolves these organizations out of the existing conditions where there are two classes in society. . . . Trade unions are not barbarous, nor are they the outgrowth of barbarism. On the contrary they are only possible where civilization exists." Economic concentration, for Foster, Strasser, McGuire, and

---

unions. Despite this plank, many members still adhered to the notion of collective action as a defensive strategy. For example, see plank 22 of the 1884 platform, *Powderly Papers*.

[60] For the New York Workingmen's Assembly's and the FOTLU's contrasting commitment to collective action, see their repeated calls for the incorporation of trade unions in note 58. See also Walls's letter to Jessup, *Workingmen's Assembly Proceedings*, 1871, 83. Frank Foster, of the International Typographical Union and later secretary of the AFL, also noted the importance of organization in 1883 when he wrote: "The growing power of associated capital must needs be met by associated labor. Federation is the motto of the future." Quoted in Philip S. Foner, *History of the Labor Movement in the United States* (New York: International Publishers, 1947), 1:524.

[61] For dissenting unionists' views of economic development within the NLU, see Jessup's and Walls's criticisms of the NLU in *Workingmen's Assembly Proceedings*, 1871, 57–65, 81–84. The unionists' economic vision was elaborated in the 1880s and 1890s. See sources in the two notes following.

Gompers, was a necessary consequence of industrialization, and perhaps even the true source of economic growth. The enormous economies of scale achieved through the modern corporation could not be matched by old methods of production.[62]

The economic vision underlying the trade union dissent was made explicit at the turn of the century and was articulated with particular clarity by Gompers at the Chicago Conference on Trusts in October 1907. "We can not, if we would," Gompers argued, "turn back to the primitive conditions of industry which marked the early part of the last century. It is therefore idle chatter to talk of annihilating trusts. . . . The trust is, economically speaking, the *logical and inevitable accompaniment and development* of our modern commercial and industrial system." Unlike the KOL, Gompers, Foster, and other trade union leaders lost faith in the viability of decentralized economic organization and accepted instead a new vision of large-scale industrial development.[63]

Interestingly, some contemporary observers, themselves, characterized divisions within the postwar labor movement in precisely these terms, as the product of distinct conceptions of economic change. In 1991, for example, Ralph Beaumont, a lecturer in the KOL, distinguished the two wings of the labor movement as follows:

> There have existed in this country, since the close of the war, two different schools of labor reformers. One school was in favor of reform by political methods. The other was composed of those who were in favor of gaining the reform upon the line of what is termed the wage question. They accepted the capitalistic idea of economics, which was in substance that labor was a commodity, and that the law of supply and demand regulated the matter of wages. The political school insisted that, under an industrial republic like ours, it was more a question of legislation, and that by special enactments some were getting more of the products of human effort than they were entitled to. Those who adhered to the capitalistic idea proceeded to organize upon what is termed the "trades-union"

---

[62] For the testimony of Frank Foster, Adolph Strasser, P. J. McGuire, and Samuel Gompers, see *Report of the Committee of the Senate* 1:289–95, 366–79, 459–67, 667–68. Gompers' loss of faith in the producers' economic vision also can be seen elsewhere. For example, Gompers began to interpret the land question differently from producers as early as 1882. See *FOTLU Reports*, 1882, 20. Gompers also denied that the financial system was fundamental. See Bernard Mandel, *Samuel Gompers: A Biography* (Yellow Springs, Ohio: Antioch Press, 1963), 160. More generally, differences between the AFL and KOL on questions of economic concentration and progress can be seen in *AFL Proceedings*, 1888, 9–10; and 1890, 16–17.

[63] See Samuel Gompers, "Labor and Its Attitude Toward Trusts," *American Federationist* 14 (November 1907): 880–86. The quotation is taken from p. 881; emphasis in original. See also Samuel Gompers, *Seventy Years of Life and Labor: An Autobiography* (New York: Dutton, 1925), vol. 2, chap. 26, entitled "My Economic Philosophy"; and *AFL Proceedings*, 1899, 15.

principle, and to fight the battle upon that line, and there are a goodly number that adhere to that method to-day.[64]

How labor leaders interpreted the economic changes they were experiencing, how they explained them to their rank and file, varied considerably across postwar labor organizations, with important consequences for their relation to the state.

Having repudiated the past, the AFL and its precursors embarked on a radically different program of labor reform. For workers to survive in the modern economy, they had to abandon their antimonopoly position and develop a new program and strategy for American labor, even though economic concentration could not be halted, nor should capital be left to run wild. Abuses of the new industrial order still had to be prevented by organized labor, but via a very different route than the NLU and KOL had planned.

The Workingmen's Assembly, the FOTLU, and the AFL centered their strategy around establishing the right to organize collectively and act as a countervailing power. Each step toward greater economic concentration should be matched by renewed efforts at labor organization. Only by countering the combinations of capital with their own organizations would workers maintain an effective voice in American industrial development.[65] The AFL outlined the parallel development between labor and capital in 1899 in the following terms:

> In the early days of our modern capitalist system, when the individual employer was the rule under which industry was conducted, the individual workmen deemed themselves sufficiently capable to cope for their rights; when industry developed and employers formed companies, the workingmen formed unions; when industry concentrated into great combinations, the workingmen formed their national and international unions; as employments became trustified, the toilers organized federations of all unions, local, national and international, such as the American Federation of Labor.[66]

From the AFL's perspective, working-class organization was simply the logical counterpart to the accumulation of capital. The same forces of

---

[64] Quoted from Ralph Beaumont, "The Labor Movement," in N. A. Dunning, ed., *The Farmer's Alliance History and Agricultural Digest* (Washington, D.C.: Alliance Publishing, 1891), chap. 18. I am grateful to Carol Horton for bringing this source to my attention.

[65] For the importance of collective action to the AFL, see the following sources: *FOTLU Reports*, 1881, 6; *AFL Proceedings*, 1890, 16–17; and 1899, 15; *American Federationist* 3 (1896): 217 and 14 (1907): 880–86; and Samuel Gompers' discussion of the Sherman Antitrust Law in his "Attitude of Labor Towards Government Regulation of Industry," *Annals of American Academy of Political and Social Science* 32, 1 (July 1908): 75–81.

For the Workingmen's Assembly and FOTLU, their commitment to labor as a countervailing power took the form of a call for state protection of workers' right to collective action.

[66] *AFL Proceedings*, 1899, 15.

economic development prompted both workers and employers to form associations that became integral components of the modern industrial economy.[67]

TRADE UNIONISTS AND WORKING-CLASS CONSCIOUSNESS

The collectivist vision of the dissenting unions within the NLU, and the dominant faction of the Workingmen's Assembly, the FOTLU, and the AFL by no means signaled labor's capitulation to business interests. Nor did it imply any necessary acceptance of "job-conscious" or "business" unionism, as earlier scholars have claimed. On the contrary, the trade unionists' vision was, in many respects, more class-conscious in a Marxian sense than that of the producers.[68] The dissident unionists no longer believed the producers' alliance to be a viable strategy, and instead urged workers to break with the past and come to accept their lot as wage earners in the new industrial economy.

In 1870, for example, the New York Workingmen's Assembly declared strikes to be a "necessary evil in as much as no remedy has yet been found whereby labor may assert its rights in its unequal conflict with capital."[69] The contrast with the producers' perspective is striking. The language of the producing classes was being replaced by new categories of labor and capital, and the old "harmony of interests" by notions of class conflict. In 1887, the New York Workingmen's Assembly defeated a resolution explicitly claiming employers' and employees' interests to be identical.[70]

Again, the working-class consciousness of the trade union dissent was more fully realized within the AFL. When Samuel Gompers outlined labor's mission at the eighteenth annual convention in 1898, we can see clearly the new sense of class that infused the trade union movement: "The trade unions are the legitimate outgrowth of modern societary and industrial conditions. They are not the creation of any man's brain. They are organizations of necessity. They were born of the necessity of the workers to protect and defend themselves from encroachment, injustice and wrong. They are the organizations *of the working class, for the working class, by the working class.*"[71] Gompers' language contrasts sharply with that of Sylvis, Powderly, and other advocates of the producers' alliance. Workers,

[67] Gompers, "Labor and Its Attitude Toward Trusts," 882.

[68] Both the producers and the trade unionists had a sense of class consciousness, albeit of very different kinds. It is a mistake to identify one faction as more class-conscious than the other. It is more useful to distinguish different kinds of workers' consciousness that coexisted in the late nineteenth century.

[69] *Workingmen's Assembly Proceedings*, 1870, 7.

[70] See *Workingmen's Assembly Proceedings*, 1887, 27–28; and Gompers' testimony, *Report of the Committee of the Senate*, 1:281, 288–90, 376.

[71] Quotation is from *AFL Proceedings*, 1898, 5; emphasis added.

according to Gompers, Jessup, and Walls, were no longer members of the producing classes. The world had changed in important ways, and unless workers realized their new position, they would fail to secure their interests in the modern industrial economy.

Thus, at the end of the nineteenth century, Gompers and the AFL, in many respects, had accepted a more Marxian analysis of economic development than had the KOL. As a consequence, a number of socialists initially were attracted to the ranks of the AFL.[72] The critical task for the AFL was to enable erstwhile producers to identify as workers and to organize collectively as members of a distinct working class. Nick Salvatore has presented Gompers in a somewhat similar light, noting that one of Gompers' socialist opponents considered him "the most class conscious man I [have] met."[73]

From this perspective, the AFL of the 1880s and 1890s was not simply a reactionary organization seeking to protect the interests of skilled workers at the expense of unskilled labor. To be sure, craft unions often looked down upon the unskilled and immigrant labor and tried to exclude them from their organizations. But the AFL's demand for exclusivity, at least initially, was directed equally against the producers' middle-class allies: small businessmen and manufacturers, the trade unionists argued, were equally suspect and ought no longer be allowed to join workers' organizations. Thus, when the AFL turned away from the KOL's strategy of organizing mixed assemblies across trades, this was not just an attempt to narrow union activity along craft lines. Instead, AFL leaders believed that workers must abandon their old allies and establish exclusive organizations to represent the emerging working class.[74]

Although the trade union commitment to collective action remained largely unchanged from 1865 through the end of the century, two separate tactics were used to achieve this end. Initially, the Workingmen's Assembly and the FOTLU, much like the producers' associations, pursued their goals through political reform. Electoral and party politics, it seemed, provided workers with access to the very centers of state power. By organizing

---

[72] Adolph Strasser, Peter J. McGuire, J. P. McDonnell, and Joseph Labadie, for example, all were associated with various socialist organizations and participated in the AFL, or its immediate predecessor, the FOTLU.

[73] Nick Salvatore's introduction to Gompers' autobiography raises similar themes to those developed here. See Nick Salvatore, ed., *Seventy Years of Life and Labor: An Autobiography by Samuel Gompers* (New York: ILR Press, 1984), xvii.

[74] The Knights' mixed assemblies are often seen as precursors to the industrial unions of the 1930s, and the AFL exclusivity as a betrayal of this earlier radical potential. See Ware, *The Labor Movement in the United States*. From my perspective the AFL was in many ways more class-conscious in a Marxian sense than the Knights' mixed assemblies, as the AFL tried to organize workers exclusively as wage earners rather than as a coalition of producers. See *AFL Proceedings*, 1898, 5–6.

politically, workers hoped to change government policy and secure the necessary state protection for American unions. At the turn of the century, however, there was a dramatic change in AFL strategy as they turned away from the state to focus instead on collective action in the economic realm.[75]

This change in AFL strategy raises a number of intriguing questions about the collectivist vision of economic development and its impact on the nature of working-class organization and politics in the United States. Why, for example, did the AFL collectivism take this apolitical turn? Why did the earlier strategies of the Workingmen's Assembly and the FOTLU not provide the foundation for the incorporation of labor along more social democratic lines? What happened to the collectivist vision during the 1880s and 1890s to turn the AFL so sharply away from political reform? The answers to such questions can be found by exploring how different visions of economic development brought the two factions of the labor movement into different relations with the American state. Specifically, we can understand *why* the AFL shifted from a political strategy to business unionism when we see how particular state institutions played into the trade unionists' vision of industrial development.

TRADE UNIONISTS AND THE COURTS: POLITICIZING JUDICIAL REGULATION

The trade unionists' collectivist vision of economic development soon brought this wing of the labor movement up against the American legal system. Working-class organization was central to the trade union strategy in which labor was to act as a countervailing power. In order to secure state protection of workers' right to organize and strike, the AFL and its predecessors understood that the prevailing legal doctrine of criminal conspiracy had to be repealed. The courts, then, became the focus of the trade

[75] The change in labor strategy from extensive political action to voluntarism occurred gradually around the turn of the century. However, some early signs of disenchantment with political reform can be seen as early as 1884, when the AFL secretary, Frank Foster, described the struggle for eight-hours legislation as follows: "This much has been determined by the history of the national eight-hour law—it is useless to wait for legislation in this matter. In the world of economic reform the working classes must depend upon themselves for the enforcement of measures as well as for their conception. A united demand for a shorter working day, backed by thorough organization, will prove vastly more effective than the enactment of a thousand laws depending for enforcement upon the pleasure of aspiring politicians [and] of sycophantic department officials." Quoted from *FOTLU Reports*, 1884, 11. Obviously, individuals and organizations varied in the timing of the shift in strategy, but by 1896 the sixteenth annual convention of the AFL bemoaned the perils of political reform and described partisan politics as the "shoals and rocks upon which so many of labor's previous efforts were wrecked." *AFL Proceedings*, 1896, 21–22. See also the fascinating discussion of the limits of state power to regulate trusts in *AFL Proceedings*, 1899, 15.

union activity as they set about a campaign to change judicial policy that had endured for more than half a century.

The New York Workingmen's Assembly, FOTLU, and AFL proceedings spanning the years 1865 through 1900 reveal an increasing preoccupation with judicial regulation. All three organizations identified the courts and judicial regulation as one of the major obstacles to successful working-class organization and set for themselves the task of repealing the prevailing legal doctrine. The outcome of this extended campaign to change judicial policy played a major role in shaping subsequent AFL strategy and politics. For this wing of the American labor movement, the structure of the American state, and particularly the dominance of the courts over other branches of government, was a crucial factor in promoting the AFL's turn to business unionism at the turn of the century.[76]

The underlying dynamics of state-labor relations for the trade union faction can be seen in microcosm in the New York Workingmen's Assembly's very first attempts to repeal the common law doctrine of criminal conspiracy. By examining the Assembly's campaign to check the power of the courts, we can see clearly how the distinctive structure of the American state provided these workers with few rewards, even for successful political mobilization, and ultimately thwarted the adoption of a more politically active strategy by the AFL.

The Workingmen's Assembly and Criminal Conspiracy

By the end of the Civil War, industrial disputes had increased dramatically, at least in the more heavily industrialized states of the Northeast. Even before the war had ended, miners, railway workers, and bricklayers had begun to organize and strike. In the three decades after the war, workers in many states and across a number of trades embarked on some of the most violent industrial conflicts in American labor history.[77] District attorneys

---

[76] The Workingmen's Assembly and the FOTLU both maintained repeal of the conspiracy doctrine as one of their principal objectives in the years 1870 to 1886. In the early 1890s, the AFL switched its focus from conspiracy to the labor injunction. Despite the change in legal remedy, the underlying issue was much the same, namely, how to curb the courts' power in the area of industrial relations. For the Workingmen's Assembly objectives, see the president's report in the proceedings of the annual convention of the Assembly. For the FOTLU's position, see their official platform contained in their annual report. Finally, for the AFL's attacks on the labor injunction, see the president's report in the annual proceedings and the editorials of the *American Federationist*. For an excellent discussion of the AFL's anti-injunction campaign, see Forbath, "The Shaping of the American Labor Movement," 1148–1233.

[77] For accounts of postbellum industrial unrest, see Jeremy Brecher, *Strike!* (Boston: South End Press, 1972); David Montgomery, "Labor and the Republic in Industrial America: 1860–1920," *Le Movement social* 111 (1980): 201–15; Marvin W. Schlegel, "The Working-men's Benevolent Association: First Union of Anthracite Miners," *Pennsylvania History* 10, 4

tried to help contain this surge of industrial unrest by charging striking workers with criminal conspiracy. Most employers were more than willing to aid in the task by testifying against striking workers at the trials. Strikes were broken up and unions disbanded as one workers' association after another was tried and convicted of criminal conspiracy.[78]

Many workers responded to the new wave of conspiracy indictments by initiating the first major challenge to judicial regulation of industrial conflict. In April 1864 between 10,000 and 15,000 workers attended a mass meeting in New York to protest "Folger's Anti-Trades Union Strike Bill," which attempted to strengthen existing conspiracy law. The protest succeeded, and the proposed amendment was dropped. A more permanent organization grew out of the protest when several of the same union leaders established the New York Workingmen's Assembly in 1865. The Workingmen's Assembly brought together unions primarily in the consumer finishing trades, such as printers, painters, carpenters, cabinetmakers, tailors,

---

(October 1943): 243–67; New York Bureau of Statistics of Labor, *Fourth Annual Report of the Bureau of Statistics of Labor of the State of New York for the Year 1886* (Albany, N.Y.: Argus Company, Printers, 1887), and *Fifth Annual Report of the Statistics of Labor of the State of New York for the Year 1887* (Albany, N.Y.: Troy Press, Printers, 1888). (Hereafter cited as *New York Bureau of Statistics of Labor*, followed by the year.) See also Pennsylvania Bureau of Industrial Statistics, *Annual Report of the Secretary of Internal Affairs of the Commonwealth of Pennsylvania, Industrial Statistics. vol. 9 1880–81* (Harrisburg, Pa.: Lane S. Hart, State Printers and Binders, 1882), and *vol. 10 1881–82* (Harrisburg, Pa.: Lane S. Hart, State Printers and Binders, 1882). (Hereafter cited as *Pennsylvania Bureau of Industrial Statistics*, followed by the volume number.)

[78] Many American conspiracy cases, especially in the lower courts, went unreported. Thus some cases can only be identified through local newspapers, organization proceedings, and government reports. The following are the major postbellum conspiracy cases in New York and Pennsylvania identified to date: Master Stevedores' Association v. Walsh, 2 Daly 1 (N.Y. 1867); People v. Van Nostrand, *Workingmen's Assembly Proceedings*, 1869, 19; 1870, 23 (N.Y. 1867) Cigar-makers' Union No. 66, Kingston, New York, *NLU Proceedings of the Second Session, 1868*, 12; *Workingmen's Assembly Proceedings*, 1869, 19; 1870, 23 (N.Y. 1868); Raybold and Frostevant v. Samuel R. Gaul of Bricklayers' Union No. 2, *NLU Proceedings of the Second Session, 1868*, 12 (N.Y. 1868); Iron Moulders' Union No. 22 v. Tuttle and Bailey, Brooklyn, N.Y., *Workingmen's Assembly Proceedings*, 1870, 23 (N.Y. 1869); Iron Moulders' Union No. 203, Harlem, N.Y. v. United States Iron Works, *Workingmen's Assembly Proceedings*, 1870, 23 (N.Y. 1869); Commonwealth v. Curren; Commonwealth v. Berry et al., 1 *Scranton Law Times* 217 (Pa. 1874); Xingo Parks and John Siney Trial, Clearfield County, Pa., *Pennsylvania Bureau of Industrial Statistics* 9 (1880–1881): 313–15 (Pa. 1875); Commonwealth ex rel. E. Vallette et al. v. Sheriff, 15 Phil. 393 (Pa. 1881); D. R. Jones Trial, Westmoreland County, *Pennsylvania Bureau of Industrial Statistics* 9 (1880–1881): 378–83 (Pa. 1881); Miles McPadden and Knights of Labor Trials, Clearfield County, *Pennsylvania Bureau of Industrial Statistics* 10 (1881–1882): 161–63 (Pa. 1882); Newman et al. v. the Commonwealth; People v. Wilzig; People v. Kostka; Knights of Labor Miners' trials, Allegheny County, in Kuritz, "The Pennsylvania State Government and Labor Controls," 154 (Pa. 1887); People ex rel. Gill v. Smith, 10 N.Y. St. Rptr. 730 (N.Y. 1887); and People ex rel. Gill v. Walsh, 110 N.Y. 633 (N.Y. 1888).

machinists, plasterers, and cigar makers. By 1869 the Assembly estimated its membership to be as high as 25,000. The Assembly operated successfully as an independent organization for thirty-two years, after which it joined forces with the New York state branch of the AFL in 1897.[79]

Right from the start, the Workingmen's Assembly declared the conspiracy prosecutions to be intolerable and established the repeal of the doctrine to be one of its highest priorities. The Assembly's primary strategy for changing judicial policy was political action. In the late 1860s, the Workingmen's Assembly initiated an elaborate campaign to pressure the state legislature into repealing the conspiracy law. Through extensive political mobilization and subsequent state legislation, the Assembly hoped to exempt labor unions from prosecution for criminal conspiracy.[80]

The Workingmen's Assembly's efforts to influence legislative policy were impressive. For more than two decades, the Assembly engaged in a remarkable campaign that demonstrated their considerable knowledge of, and commitment to, legislative politics. First, the Assembly established its own committees to draft alternative labor bills to be presented on the floor of the legislature by friendly representatives. At times they even hired lawyers to screen their draft legislation in order to expedite safe passage through the legislature. Once a labor bill had been introduced into the New York legislature, the Workingmen's Assembly followed its progress with great care, securing hearings with the relevant committees and attending House and Senate sessions on a daily basis in order to urge adoption of their reforms. The Assembly also acted as an information service both for their own members and for state representatives, by printing and distributing

[79] For an account of the founding and early work of the New York Workingmen's Assembly, see Stevens, *New York Typographical Union, No. 6*, chap. 37. For 1869 membership estimates, see Stevens, *New York Typographical Union, No. 6*, 586. Unfortunately, there are few good secondary sources available on the New York Workingmen's Assembly. The material presented here is drawn primarily from proceedings of the Assembly's annual conventions. Some information about the Workingmen's Assembly can be obtained from George Gorham Groat, *Trade Unions and the Law in New York: A Study of Some Legal Phases of Labor Organization* (1903; New York: AMS Press, 1978).

[80] Unfortunately, proceedings for the Assembly's first four sessions have been lost. Nevertheless, the organization's initial interest in repealing the conspiracy laws can be seen in Stevens, *New York Typographical Union No. 6*, chap. 37. Conspiracy convictions were identified as a problem and were discussed at almost all sessions for which proceedings exist. For complaints against conspiracy from 1869 on, see the following proceedings: *Workingmen's Assembly Proceedings*, 1869, 19; 1870, 5, 23, 33–36; 1871, 3, 6; 1885, 21; 1886, 3–4, 6, 8, 10–11; 1887, 6, 30, 37; 1888, 15, 16, 47; January 1889, 8, 14, 20–21, 36, 60; December 1889, 18, 31; 1893, 4, 7, 15, 46, 60; 1894, 5, 8, 8–9, 12, 14–17.

Conspiracy was made a preferred issue by the Workingmen's Assembly in 1886, 1889, 1893, and 1894. See the following: *Workingmen's Assembly Proceedings*, 1886, 11; 1889, 60; 1889, 31; 1893, 46, 60; and 1894, 8.

Finally, for the Assembly's efforts to repeal the conspiracy law in 1868 and 1869, see Groat, *Trade Unions and the Law in New York*, 55–57.

relevant material on pending labor legislation. Finally, proceedings of the annual conventions generally contained a "legislative honors" list in which all New York representatives were ranked on the basis of their voting record in the past year. Representatives were grouped into four or five broad categories under such headings as "special mention," "favorable mention," "black list," and "dodgers" so as to make clear which representatives were aiding workers in their political struggle.[81]

Legal reform was not all that the Workingmen's Assembly pushed for. Their early platforms also called for enforcement of New York's newly enacted eight-hour law (passed by the state legislature on 24 June 1868), passage of a general apprentice law in order to ensure a ready supply of "proficient and competent workmen," abolition of the system of convict and contract labor, support for the formation of "female" and "colored" labor organizations, regulation of the hours of child labor, and the end of grants of public land to corporations. In subsequent years, the Assembly added demands for passage of a weekly pay bill and called for increased regulation of the health and safety of the workplace (especially regulation of scaffolding and tenement house manufacturing). Finally, the Assembly called for creation of a bureau of labor statistics, government printing office, and system of compulsory education. The Workingmen's Assembly's extensive legislative agenda and their relentless efforts to ensure safe passage of these bills are testimony to the organization's strong commitment to political reform. Workers' interests, most members of the Assembly believed, could best be served through mobilizing workers as a political force.[82]

For at least two decades after the Civil War, then, many New York unions still believed that workers' lives could be greatly improved through government intervention. As yet, there was no great separation of work and politics, which became the hallmark of AFL voluntarism at the turn of the

[81] *Workingmen's Assembly Proceedings*, January 1889, 13; and December 1889, 7.

Workingmen's Assembly attendance at State Legislature Committee hearings can be seen in the following: *Workingmen's Assembly Proceedings*, 1870, 34, 58; *Proceedings of the Eighteenth Annual Meeting of the State Trades Assembly, State of New York, January 1884* (Rochester, N.Y.: Truth Publishing, 1884), 4; *Workingmen's Assembly Proceedings*, 1885, 16; and 1888, 21.

The Workingmen's Assembly informed its members on labor issues on several occasions. For example, see *Workingmen's Assembly Proceedings*, 1871, 48; and 1889, 14–23.

The Workingmen's Assembly's "legislative honors" list is mentioned or applied in the following: *Workingmen's Assembly Proceedings, Political Branch*, 1886, 1, 10–11; *Workingmen's Assembly Proceedings*, 1888, 18–20; January 1889, 12; December 1889, 11; and 1893, 7–8.

[82] For the early demands of the New York Workingmen's Assembly, see *Workingmen's Assembly Proceedings*, 1869, 5–10; 1870, 3–9; and 1871, 3–9. For subsequent demands, see especially *Workingmen's Assembly Proceedings*, 1887, 4–8; 1888, 6–8; and January 1889, 6–10.

century. Instead, the Workingmen's Assembly's entire strategy was based on the idea that infusing industrial issues into electoral politics would only strengthen labor's hand. The state was still considered a powerful ally that could greatly assist labor in its struggle with capital. To be sure, the Workingmen's Assembly was no socialist party; it never adopted a radical political ideology calling for broad-based social transformation, nor did it question existing property rights of employers. The history of the Workingmen's Assembly is not the story of a lost socialist alternative for American labor. What the Assembly did represent, however, was a more politically active labor movement than the pure and simple unionism advocated by the AFL early in the twentieth century.

The Workingmen's Assembly's campaign to repeal the conspiracy laws was quite successful. Four anticonspiracy statutes were enacted in New York in 1870, 1881, 1882, and 1887.[83] Each of the statutes explicitly limited application of the conspiracy doctrine to workers' protests and provided the first steps toward state protection of working-class organization. To be sure, the New York statutes did not protect workers' right to organize unconditionally. The legislation limited protection to peaceful, as opposed to coercive, collective action. Working-class organization would be protected under the new laws as long as there was no use of "force, threats, or intimidation" during an industrial dispute.[84] Despite these "hindering provisions," as they were known, the New York anticonspiracy statutes marked the first attempts to delineate a legitimate sphere of action for American labor unions by clearly exempting noncoercive industrial action from criminal prosecution. Whether the Workingmen's Assembly actually was responsible for securing passage of the statutes is, of course, unclear. What is certain, however, is that the Assembly campaigned actively for three of the four statutes and claimed credit for these legislative victories.[85]

[83] Four anticonspiracy statutes were passed by the New York State Legislature. See chap. 19, 1870, in *Laws of the State of New York, Passed at the Ninety-third Session of the Legislature* (Albany, N.Y.: Weed, Parsons, & Co., 1970), 1:30; Penal Code, secs. 168–71, 1881, in *Laws of the State of New York, Passed at the One Hundred and Fourth Session of the Legislature* (Albany, N.Y.: Weed, Parsons & Co., 1881), 3:40–41; chap. 384, 1882, in *Laws of the State of New York, Passed at the One Hundred and Fifth Session of the Legislature* (Albany, N.Y.: Weed,Parsons & Co., 1882), 1:540–47; and chap. 688, 1887, in *Laws of the State of New York, Passed at the One Hundred and Tenth Legislature* (Albany, N.Y.: Banks and Brothers, 1887), 1:897.

[84] Section 168 of the New York Penal Code (1881) illustrates nicely the limits placed on state protection of workers' right to organize. It includes the following statement: "If two or more persons conspire . . . [t]o prevent another from exercising a lawful trade or calling, or doing any other lawful act, by force, threats, intimidation, . . . [they are] guilty of a misdemeanor." Quoted from *Laws of the State of New York*, 41.

[85] *Workingmen's Assembly Proceedings*, 1870, 5; and 1871, 6.

Initially, then, the rewards for political mobilization seemed promising. In the 1870s and early 1880s it looked as if workers could indeed protect their interests through concerted political action. Through diligent organization and persistent pressure on the state legislature, the Workingmen's Assembly seemed to have successfully pushed for and obtained a check on judicial intervention in industrial disputes. Implementing the anticonspiracy statutes, however, was not so straightforward. Upholding the newly won right to organize and strike proved to be an elusive task.

THE TRIUMPH OF THE COURTS

Protecting workers' industrial rights was difficult because the distinction between lawful and coercive action that lay behind the anticonspiracy statutes was continually eroded by the New York state courts. After each of the laws was passed, the courts continued to convict workers of conspiracy despite the new legislative protection. By interpreting the statutory provisions against the use of "force, threats, and intimidation" very broadly, the courts forced the legislature to pass new, more specific legislation exempting workers from conspiracy. Thus, the repeated attempts to enact effective anticonspiracy legislation between 1869 and 1887, in large part, reflected the three-cornered struggle among labor, the state legislature, and the state courts over who should determine government policy toward labor. Whether or not workers would be allowed to organize collectively in their negotiations with employers depended on the outcome of this political struggle.

The test of criminality for workers' industrial action became the legal definition of what did or did not constitute intimidation. The principal task for the prosecution attorneys was to establish that strikers had intimidated their fellow workers, employers, or members of the public. The postbellum cases clearly demonstrate that the test of intimidation provided considerable judicial discretion when applying the anticonspiracy statutes to concrete industrial disputes. The sheer size of a picket line or the number of circulars distributed by union members was held to intimidate, and as such provided sufficient grounds for conviction under the prevailing statutes. The common theme among the postwar convictions was the definition of almost all workers' collective action as tantamount to intimidation.[86]

The case of *People v. Wilzig* provides an excellent illustration of the persistence of conspiracy convictions despite passage of the anticonspiracy

---

[86] Collective action was considered grounds for intimidation in the following labor conspiracy cases: Commonwealth v. Curren; Commonwealth v. Berry et. al.; Xingo Parks and John Siney Trial; D. R. Jones Trial; Newman et. al. v. the Commonwealth; People v. Wilzig; and People v. Kostka.

laws.[87] The dispute took place in the spring of 1886 with the boycotting of George Theiss's musical club on East 14th Street in New York City. Early in March, Paul Wilzig and the other defendants came to Theiss's club and demanded that he dismiss his orchestra, bartenders, and waiters and hire instead union workers at union wages. Theiss protested that the musicians were already members of the Musical Union and that his brother-in-law was the head bartender and his son the head waiter and that he did not want to dismiss them. The defendants refused to negotiate and gave Theiss twenty-four hours in which to comply with their demands. Theiss refused, and a boycott was placed on his business.[88]

The boycott lasted fifteen days, during which "a body of men" picketed Theiss's club, distributed a circular condemning Theiss as "a foe to organized labor," and requested customers to stay away from the club. At one point, the defendants "through their agents" entered the premises and plastered circulars on the tables, in the bathrooms, and on the frescoed walls. They also used "an infernal machine" to create such a stench in the club that it had to be closed for several hours in order to ventilate the building. Finally, the defendants were said to have set fire to scenery on the stage of the club. At times, as many as five hundred bystanders gathered to watch the activity.

The dispute came to a head when the defendants threatened to establish a secondary boycott on Theiss's mineral water and beer suppliers. In order to avert the disaster, Theiss called a meeting of his employees, the defendants, and his suppliers. After eight hours of discussion, Theiss acceded to the defendants' demands and agreed to dismiss his current employees. Before the meeting ended, Charles Beddles of the Central Labor Union demanded that Theiss pay the defendants $1,000 to cover the costs of the boycott. Again Theiss protested, but he eventually gave in to this demand as well. The boycott was immediately called off and the dispute ended. Theiss was able to redress his grievance through the courts when the district attorney charged the defendants with extortion under the New York penal code.[89]

The case was heard before Judge George Barrett in the court of oyer and terminer.[90] In his charge to the jury, Judge Barrett summed up the current

[87] See People v. Wilzig. For useful background material for the *Wilzig* dispute and for other conspiracy cases in 1886, see *New York Bureau of Statistics of Labor*, 1886, 744–87.

[88] The account of the dispute is taken from the prosecution arguments in the trial of Hans Holdorf, one of Wilzig's fellow defendants. Each of the defendants requested and was granted a separate trial. The Holdorf prosecution's account is reprinted in the *Wilzig* case report. See People v. Wilzig, 406–11.

[89] The case was formally one of extortion, but as Judge Barrett noted in his charge to the jury, the threat of conspiracy pervaded the case. See People v. Wilzig, 415.

[90] In England, special tribunals of oyer and terminer were established to hear some criminal cases. In the United States, some states followed the English tradition and used this same term to refer to their higher criminal courts.

status of the conspiracy doctrine. First, he acknowledged that the common law doctrine had been "greatly narrowed" by the recent anticonspiracy statutes. However, he continued, the prevailing laws by no means licensed all forms of collective action owing to the intimidation provisions included in the statutes. The task for the jury, then, was to determine whether the defendants' actions fell within these provisions. Barrett explicitly defined intimidation very broadly for the jury in the following terms:

> Let us see what is meant by the word intimidation. The defendant's counsel seem to have the idea that if a body of men, however large, operating in the manner suggested, only avoid acts of physical violence, they are within the law; and that the employer's business may be ruined with impunity, so long as no blow is struck, nor actual threat by word of mouth uttered. This is an error. The men who walk up and down in front of a man's shop may be guilty of intimidation, though they never raise a finger or utter a word. Their attitude may, nevertheless, be that of menace. They may intimidate by their numbers, their methods, their placards, their circulars and their devices.[91]

Judge Barrett made his view of intimidation quite clear when charging the jury:

> It is one thing for a man or men to go about and talk to their friends, but it is quite another thing for fifty or sixty or one hundred men to band together, not for the purpose of individual persuasion, but to bring the power of combination to bear in an unlawful way to injure the employer's business. . . . Not a hand need be raised, not an oath, nor even a violent word be uttered, and yet, in such a case, I should leave it to a jury to say whether the attitude of those men was not, under the pretense of moral suasion, an attitude of real menace; whether the weak and the timid were not, in reality, driven away, and whether the whole object and purpose was not to intimidate the gentle patrons of the establishment and the general public.[92]

The conspiracy, for Judge Barrett, did not lie in workers' overt use of force or violence during the dispute. Rather, their actions were intimidating because of the size of the protest and the workers' attitude of menace, both extremely nebulous attributes for defining criminal action. All five defendants in the *Wilzig* case were convicted and received sentences ranging from one year and six months to three years and eight months of hard labor in a New York state prison.

Judge Barrett elaborated his legal arguments concerning intimidation the very next week when the case of *People v. Kostka* came before the court. This case, as with many of the labor trials, involved payment of low wages and hiring of nonunion workers in Mrs. Landgraff's Bakery in New York

---

[91] People v. Wilzig, 414.
[92] See People v. Wilzig, 413–14.

City. Paul Kostka and sixteen fellow workers boycotted the bakery, and the district attorney charged the striking workers with conspiring "to prevent and hinder one Josephine Landgraff from using and exercising her lawful trade and calling as a baker."[93]

Judge Barrett again provided an extended discussion of intimidation, which he acknowledged to be the critical test behind the conspiracy charge.

> The question here, then, of special importance is, whether these defendants have by their acts rendered themselves amenable to the conspiracy law. As I said before, they may cooperate to improve their condition and to increase their wages, they may refuse to work for less than the price they have jointly fixed, and they may do everything that is lawful and peaceable to secure that price. They may even go to their brethren and beseech them not to work for less than the fixed rate. . . . All this they may lawfully do. Argument, reasoning and entreaty are lawful weapons. But the moment they go beyond these means and threaten to punish him whom they believe to be their erring brother, threaten him with violence should he stand in the way of their success by accepting a lower rate than that fixed by the cooperators, they bring themselves face to face with the law.[94]

Turning to the specific dispute before the court, Barrett asked whether the defendants had "overstep[ped] the just and lawful line." In determining the answer, Barrett suggested that the jury reflect on four aspects of the defendants' behavior. First, they should consider the allegations that the defendants threatened to kill one of the bakers and spat in the face of others. However, the judge noted that these more overt acts of violence had been contested during testimony at the trial. Second, Barrett pointed to the distribution of circulars and suggested that the jury should consider both the repeated nature of the distribution "for three days in succession" along with the language used to determine "whether they contain appeals to passion or are otherwise inflammatory in their character." Third, Barrett again questioned whether the defendants had displayed an attitude of menace. "The mere fact that no violence was actually used in the street is not conclusive. . . . Nor is it necessary that there should have been a direct threat. If you believe that the attitude actually presented by the distributors of those circulars was an attitude of intimidation, either to the passers-by, or to the woman inside . . . then all who participated in it, directly or indirectly, are within the meaning of that word intimidation, as used in the conspiracy act." Finally, Barrett argued that the size of the boycott—the actual number of workers involved—also should be taken into account when considering whether the defendants' actions were intimidating.[95]

---

[93] See People v. Kostka, 430.

[94] Quoted from People v. Kostka, 434–35.

[95] For Barrett's arguments concerning the four aspects of defendants' actions that might be considered intimidating, see People v. Kostka, 436–37.

The court did not require that all four actions be considered intimidating; any one was sufficient to secure conviction. Although we can never determine the jury's exact deliberations, Barrett's remarks during sentencing suggest that the distribution of circulars provided the element of intimidation required for conviction. Barrett commenced the sentencing by saying:

> Your case differs very materially from that of the so-called Theiss boycotters who were here tried last week. They were men of better education than you, and they extorted a large amount of money in a most unrelenting and abominable manner. You did nothing of that kind, but ignorantly distributed offensive circulars, in a manner calculated to intimidate. . . . As many good people did not know that such a distribution of circulars was wrong, you might well have been mistaken about it. This case has now settled the question that the distribution of these circulars in the manner and under the circumstances here disclosed, is a crime.

The defendants were found guilty and were sentenced to jail for between ten and thirty days. Interestingly, each of the sentences had to be translated into "Bohemian," as the defendants did not speak English.[96]

The *Wilzig* and *Kostka* cases were by no means exceptional; New York courts convicted striking workers for acting collectively in almost all of the postbellum labor conspiracy trials.[97] Moreover, the same pattern of judicial obstruction can be seen in Pennsylvania as well, where a similar struggle to repeal the conspiracy doctrine was under way in the three decades following the Civil War. There, too, workers' demands were by and large successful: four anticonspiracy laws were passed in 1869, 1872, 1876, and 1891.[98] If anything, the Pennsylvania statutes were stronger and more comprehensive than the New York laws. The Pennsylvania legislation contained fewer limitations on workers' right to organize and strike, and tried to restrict judicial intervention in industrial disputes more explicitly than the New York statutes. Faced with a similar set of anticonspiracy laws, the

---

[96] People v. Kostka, 441–42.

[97] For particular rulings in the postbellum labor conspiracy trials, see Appendix A.

[98] The postbellum Pennsylvania anticonspiracy statutes were as follows: PL 1242, 1869, in *Laws of the General Assembly of the State of Pennsylvania, Passed at the Session of 1869, in the Ninety-third Year of Independence* (Harrisburg, Pa.: B. Singerly, 1869), 1260–61; PL 1105, 1872, in *Laws of the General Assembly of the State of Pennsylvania, Passed at the Session of 1872, in the Ninety-sixth Year of Independence* (Harrisburg, Pa.: B. Singerly, 1872), 1275–76; PL 33, 1876, in *Laws of the General Assembly of the State of Pennsylvania, passed at the Session of 1876, in the One Hundredth Year of Independence* (Harrisburg, Pa.: B. F. Meyers, 1876), 45; PL 230, 1891, in *Laws of the General Assembly of the Commonwealth of Pennsylvania, Passed at the Session of 1891, in the One Hundred and Fifteenth Year of Independence* (Harrisburg, Pa.: Edwin K. Meyers, 1891), 300–301.

Pennsylvania courts also were extremely reluctant to recognize workers' right to organize and strike under the new statutes.[99]

Perhaps the most notorious interpretation of an anticonspiracy statute was issued by a Pennsylvania county court in 1881.[100] The defendants, D. R. Jones, Hugh Anderson (both officers of the National Miners' Association), and approximately fourteen others, were charged with conspiracy during a coal miners' strike at the Waverly Coal and Coke Company in Westmoreland County, Pennsylvania. This dispute centered around the payment of lower wages by the Waverly Coal and Coke Company compared to other operators in the district. The Waverly miners, however, had signed a contract agreeing not to strike without giving the company sixty days' notice. If they broke this agreement, the miners had to forfeit 10 percent of the year's wages. On November 17, the Waverly miners met with two representatives of the National Miners' Association and agreed to go on strike to secure the "district price" if the Association would compensate them for their 10 percent forfeiture. The meeting was adjourned for a final decision the following evening. On their way to the town schoolhouse the next night, the defendants were arrested and charged with criminal conspiracy. Two counts were specified on the indictment. First, the defendants were charged with inducing workers to break their contract by suggesting that they ignore their sixty-day warning clause. Second, the defendants were charged with threatening to use a brass band to intimidate strikebreakers during the upcoming dispute![101] The Westmoreland County court found the principal defendants guilty on both counts and stated that the presence of a brass band constituted "a hindrance within the meaning of the [anticonspiracy] act of 1876."[102] The defendants were sentenced to pay the costs of prosecution as well as a fine of $100 each and to be imprisoned for twenty-four hours in the county jail. The total cost of the fine amounted to $355.29, which the Miners' Association paid.[103]

---

[99] See Pennsylvania cases in note 78. For useful discussion of some of the postwar Pennsylvania cases, see Kuritz, "Criminal Conspiracy Cases." For discussion of the Siney and Parks trial in 1875, see Edward Charles Killeen, "John Siney: The Pioneer in American Industrial Unionism and Industrial Government" (Ph.D. diss., University of Wisconsin, 1942), chaps. 9, 10.

[100] The Waverly coal miners' case was not reported in the Pennsylvania law reports. Nevertheless, accounts of the trial can be found in *Pennsylvania Bureau of Industrial Statistics* 9 (1880–1881): 378–82. See also Kuritz, "Criminal Conspiracy Cases," 298–99; and Witte, "Early American Labor Cases," 831.

[101] My account of the Waverly strike is based primarily on *Pennsylvania Bureau of Industrial Statistics* 9:379–80. However, for reference to the specific counts on the indictment, see Kuritz, "Criminal Conspiracy Cases," 299.

[102] See Kuritz, "Criminal Conspiracy Cases," 299.

[103] See *Pennsylvania Bureau of Industrial Statistics* 9:380. Jones actually wrote to the noted jurist Jere S. Black for clarification of the conspiracy law. In his reply, Black concluded

By declaring the mere presence of a brass band to be an act of intimidation, the Pennsylvania court effectively rendered legislative protection of workers' collective action meaningless. The defense counsel appealed the lower court conviction to the Pennsylvania Supreme Court precisely on the grounds that the 1876 statute had legalized the miners' actions and that the county court conviction was in error. The defense requested that the Supreme Court provide an "authoritative technical definition" of the state's conspiracy laws, because "no law is as oppressive as an uncertain one."[104] The decision to hear the appeal was discretionary, and the Pennsylvania Supreme Court determined not to take the case. Therefore, no higher court ruling was given on the county court's extraordinary interpretation of the anticonspiracy statute.

Two queries might be raised about the courts' rather extreme interpretations of the New York and Pennsylvania anticonspiracy laws. First, one might wonder whether the harsher postbellum rulings were the product of a change in legal doctrine between the first and second wave of conspiracy trials. Second, some readers might suspect that the postbellum convictions were as much the product of ineffective legislation as they were a reflection of judicial power. The New York and Pennsylvania statutes might well have been purely symbolic victories that were never really intended to exempt workers from criminal prosecution. Legislators could have passed the statutes with the provisions wittingly attached, knowing full well that the judiciary could exploit these loopholes and continue to convict workers of criminal conspiracy.

In fact, the rather extreme postwar decisions were neither the product of a change in legal doctrine nor that of bad legislation. There was no significant shift in conspiracy law between 1842 and 1865. Indeed, the second wave of conspiracy prosecutions rested on the same legal principles as those used to sustain the antebellum trials. To be sure, passage of the Revised Statutes in New York in 1829 and the successive anticonspiracy laws in both New York and Pennsylvania after the Civil War blurred the boundary between common and statute law. However, no new legal principles were introduced with these reforms. On the contrary, the statutes were intended either to codify or narrow the common law. If anything, on the basis of legal principles alone, we would expect to have seen fewer and less controversial decisions in the conspiracy trials after the Civil War.

---

that the miners ought to have been exempt from prosecution for criminal conspiracy. Black's opinion, however, provided no argument for appealing the decision. Interestingly, the *Waverly* dispute did not end with the defendants' conviction in 1881. The Waverly Coal Company initiated a civil suit against Jones and the proprietors of Pittsburgh's *National Labor Tribune*, claiming damages of $70,000. See *The Central Law Journal* 16 (January–June 1883): 39–40.

[104] See *Pennsylvania Bureau of Industrial Statistics* 9:380; and Witte, "Early American Labor Cases," 830–31.

Similarly, the effectiveness of the New York and Pennsylvania conspiracy statutes can be gauged quickly through comparative research. In Chapter 5, I contrast the English struggle for state protection with the New York and Pennsylvania cases. The comparison is particularly instructive because the legislative provisions in both countries were almost identical. The English courts, however, did not subvert their labor statutes, but rather deferred to Parliament and recognized workers' right to organize and strike. Political mobilization was not obstructed in England as it was in the United States. Instead, legislative victories continually reinforced the effectiveness of electoral politics for changing government policy toward labor. Thus, the New York and Pennsylvania statutes were not the source of labor's problem: the English comparison attests to that. Rather, the obstacle lay in the power of the state courts to override legislative directives and establish the judiciary as the ultimate authority of government policy toward American labor.

Finally, it is important to note that the pattern of legislative victory followed by judicial defeat that characterized the struggle to repeal the conspiracy laws was not an isolated phenomenon. Labor's experience with the conspiracy laws was a classic instance of an oft-repeated battle over a wide range of labor legislation in the postbellum decades. Between 1870 and 1895 many of the New York Workingmen's Assembly, FOTLU, and AFL legislative demands were blocked by the courts. Laws limiting hours of work, establishing regular payment of wages in legal currency, and regulating the health and safety of the workplace all were successfully enacted into law only to be subsequently eroded by the courts. In some instances the New York and Pennsylvania courts undermined the labor statutes through judicial interpretation; in others the courts used their judicial power to declare the statutes unconstitutional. Either way, the impact was much the same; New York and Pennsylvania workers frequently witnessed firsthand the difficulty of obtaining effective change through political channels. The New York Workingmen's frustrating experience with repealing the conspiracy laws, then, was reinforced again and again as other items in their legislative platform met with a similar fate in the New York and Pennsylvania courts.[105]

---

[105] Many of the New York Workingmen's Assembly, FOTLU, and AFL legislative demands were eroded by state and federal courts through either judicial interpretation or judicial review. In Pennsylvania, for example, an 1881 law establishing regular payment of wages in legal tender was declared unconstitutional in Goldcharles v. Wigeman, 113 Pa. 431 (1886). New laws were passed in 1887 and 1891, but these too were interpreted so narrowly by the courts in the mid-1890s that they had little or no impact on employers' behavior. See Hamilton v. Jutte, 16 Pa. C.C. 193 (1895); Sally v. Berwind-White Coal Co., 5 Dist. 316 (1896); Commonwealth v. Isenberg and Rowland, 4 Pa. D. 579 (1895); and Showalter v. Ehlan and Rowe, 5 Pa. Super 242 (1897). Pennsylvania legislation regulating health and safety of the workplace was no more successful. For example, legislation requiring provision of fire

LABOR'S RESPONSE: JUDICIAL OBSTRUCTION AND THE TURN TO VOLUNTARISM

New York and Pennsylvania labor leaders were angered by the postbellum conspiracy convictions and vigorously protested the class bias of the courts. As early as 1869, for example, the president of the New York Workingmen's Assembly, William Jessup, objected to the "unjust" application of the conspiracy law:

---

escapes on all buildings three or more stories high and on every tenement house was passed in 1879 and 1883. State courts, however, made it extremely difficult to hold building owners liable. See Moeller v. Harvey, 16 Phil. 66 (1879); Keeley v. O'Conner, 106 Pa. 321 (1884); and Elizabeth Sewell v. James C. Moore, 166 Pa. 570 (1895).

A similar erosion of legislative victories can be seen in New York during the last two decades of the nineteenth century, first over the Tenement House Cigar Law of 1883 and over subsequent New York factory legislation. The Tenement Law was declared unconstitutional in January 1884 owing to a discrepancy between the title and subject matter of the law. The law was amended to correct the technicality and tighten the statute as a whole. This law, too, was declared unconstitutional in January 1885 on the grounds that the law interfered with individual liberty and private property. See *In re* Jacobs, 98 N.Y. 98 (1885). We will see that this case had a considerable impact on Samuel Gompers' views of political reform. New York factory laws met a similar fate. The first New York factory act of 1886 limited the working hours of women and children. The act was amended on several occasions between 1887 and 1903 so as to encompass regulation of factory health and safety. The health and safety provisions of the factory laws were undercut by the common law doctrine of assumption of risk, which was adhered to even where there was defective machinery or noncompliance with the factory law. For example, see White v. Witteman Lithographic Co., 131 N.Y. 631 (1892); Boehm v. Mace, 28 Abbott's New Cases 138 (N.Y. 1892); Diedolt v. U.S. Baking Co., 72 Hun 403 (N.Y. 1893); Kinsley v. Pratt, 148 N.Y. 372 (1897).

To be sure, not all cases brought under the factory laws went against labor. See Simpson v. New York Rubber Co., 80 Hun 415 (N.Y. 1894); Marino v. Lehmaier, 173 N.Y. 530 (1903); Gallenkamp v. The Garvin Machine Co., 91 AD 141 (N.Y. 1904); and New York v. Chelsea Jute Mills, 88 N.Y.S. 1085 (1904). Each of these more pro-labor decisions, except for *Marino*, involved children and minors who were considered to be in need of special protection. Hours legislation for men generally was overruled by the court. See People v. Coler, 166 N.Y. 1 (1901); and the classic case of Lochner v. New York, 198 U.S. 45 (1905).

For discussion of judicial interpretation and review of New York and Pennsylvania labor legislation, see J. Lynn Barnard, *Factory Legislation in Pennsylvania: Its History and Administration* (Philadelphia: John Winston, 1907); Walker Claire Brandler, "A History of Factory Legislation and Inspection in New York State, 1886–1911" (Ph.D. diss., Columbia University, 1969), chap. 7; Fred Rogers Fairchild, *The Factory Legislation of the State of New York* (New York: Macmillan, 1905), chaps. 1–7; and Howard Lawrence Hurwitz, *Theodore Roosevelt and Labor in New York State, 1880–1900* (New York: Columbia University Press, 1943), chaps. 2, 3. More generally, see Forbath, "The Shaping of the American Labor Movement," pt. 11; Arnold M. Paul, *Conservative Crisis and the Rule of Law: Attitudes of Bar and Bench, 1887–1895* (Gloucester, Mass.: Peter Smith, 1976); Roscoe Pound, "Liberty of Contract," 18 *Yale Law Journal* 454 (1909); Benjamin R. Twiss, *Lawyers and the Constitution: How Laissez Faire Came to the Supreme Court* (New York: Russell and Russell, 1962), chaps. 4–6; and George W. Alger, "The Courts and Factory Legislation," in La Follette, *The Making of America* 8:46–55.

The law is most unjust in its workings, as it seems none but those who toil with their hands are amenable to such law. While those who conspire against the toiler who produces every article consumed by him, can go unscathed. . . . It becomes your duty to take such action as will effectually efface from the Statute Books of the State so unjust and obnoxious a law; one more fitted to the Middle Ages of Great Britain than the present enlightened era in free America, where no slavery, either white or black, is supposed to exist.[106]

Jessup renewed his attack on the conspiracy law the following year in a lengthy speech in which he pondered why combinations of men "moving in the first circles of society—men of money, if not honor" were not also prosecuted for conspiracy. "Truely, it must be a crime to be a working-man, as it seems they only are amenable to the laws—they only are conspirators."[107]

The *Wilzig* decision seemed especially unjust and was denounced explicitly by John Franey, chairman of the Workingmen's Assembly's Executive Committee, at the annual convention in September 1886.

This decision was rendered under the direct authority of no statute or legal enactment of any kind: it was made under cover of an artful misconstruction of a clause in the penal code regarding conspiracy. The word conspiracy has long been a facile legal weapon in the hands of capital, and the New York Judge and District Attorney only demonstrate their ability by finding a new definition for it in sending the Theiss boycotters to prison. It was a class decision in the interests of unscrupulous employers, and intended to intimidate and deter organized labor from even peaceably protecting its members.[108]

Similarly, the president of the New York Workingmen's Assembly, Samuel Gompers, protested the postwar conspiracy convictions the following year.

Such trials, convictions and construction of the laws only tend to bring them [the judges] into discredit and contempt. It had been supposed that long ago the laws of conspiracy were in no way applicable to men in labor organizations having for their object the matter of regulating wages and hours of labor. If, as has now been decided, that the law of conspiracy still obtains in this question, the sooner it is repealed the better. Surely if monarchial England can afford to expunge obnoxious laws from her statutes, the Empire State of the Union can.[109]

Pennsylvania labor leaders were equally opposed to the renewed convictions and spoke out strongly against the conspiracy laws. For example, James Wright, of the Garment Cutters' Association and Philadelphia

[106] Quoted from *Workingmen's Assembly Proceedings*, 1869, 7.
[107] Quoted from *Workingmen's Assembly Proceedings*, 1870, 23.
[108] Quoted from *Workingmen's Assembly Proceedings*, 1886, 3.
[109] Quoted from *Workingmen's Assembly Proceedings*, January 1887, 6.

Trades' Assembly, denounced the doctrine in his presidential address to the Industrial Congress in Indianapolis in 1875:

> You should express your hearty disapproval of the species of class legislation now so much resorted to in 'Conspiracy Laws,' 'Intimidation Acts,' and 'Civil Suit Bills,' whereby the laborer is denied the right to dispose of the only commodity of which he is possessed, upon the best terms he can obtain. These are incompatible with the spirit and genius of our free institutions, and should not disgrace our statute books. Surely our workingmen are no less law-abiding than others, that more stringent laws are needed for them than is deemed just to our criminals.[110]

By the mid-1880s, then, Franey, Gompers, Wright, and other New York and Pennsylvania labor leaders clearly considered the conspiracy convictions to be a considerable burden on American labor.[111] They protested the convictions because they prevented workers from increasing their power through collective action, but also because they believed that labor was being treated unfairly by the courts. Why, each of these labor leaders asked, did workers need to be singled out for special regulation? Why weren't labor unions granted the same rights and privileges as capital? The contrast with workers' response to the first wave of conspiracy trials is clear. Workers no longer were willing to assent to the convictions as part-and-parcel of a larger republican vision. Instead, we see that, at least for this wing of the labor movement, the conspiracy convictions had been

[110] Quoted from *Miners' National Record*, May 1875, 115, in Hyman Kuritz, "The Pennsylvania State Government and Labor Controls from 1865 to 1922" (Ph.D. diss., Columbia University, 1953), 58.

[111] For additional complaints about the unequal application of the conspiracy law by New York labor leaders, see *Workingmen's Assembly Proceedings*, 1889, 18, in which conspiracy was said to be "a strictly legal question" and "an injustice to members of labor organizations." Similarly, the New York Bureau of Labor Statistics summed up labor's view of the postwar conspiracy trials in the 1892 annual report, which claimed that the current effort to "revise" the conspiracy laws "backwards" had led to the "feeling among our laboring class that the law is the poor man's enemy." Quoted from Hurwitz, *Theodore Roosevelt and Labor*, 53. The *National Labor Tribune* also denounced the Siney and Parks trial in Pennsylvania, stating: "Again we repeat it, not a shot was fired, not a club raised, not a man hurt, not a house burned, not a dollar's worth of property destroyed and yet thirty men are tried and convicted; four of them sent to prison for a year and forever disgraced. Great Heaven! Where was the riot; where the conspiracy? In the hearts of the legal mob that hounded these poor men to prison and no where else." Quoted from the *National Labor Tribune*, 26 June 1875, in Killeen, "John Siney," 297. See also attacks on conspiracy in the *Miners' National Record*, October 1875, 115, 199, quoted in Kuritz, "The Pennsylvania State Government and Labor Controls," chap. 2.

For complaints about the unequal treatment of labor and capital, see *Workingmen's Assembly Proceedings*, 1870, 23, 42; 1871, 42, 55; 1885, 20; 1887, 6; and 1889, 36. For remarkable corroboration of the New York case and for parallel developments in Colorado and Illinois, see Forbath, "The Shaping of the American Labor Movement."

politicized and were no longer viewed as a legitimate form of government regulation.

The initial remedy proposed by men such as Jessup, Franey, Gompers, and Wright was to return to the legislature for more effective protection. Neither the New York nor the Pennsylvania labor leaders abandoned politics quickly. Instead, they redoubled their political efforts and tried to close the loopholes in the anticonspiracy laws through passage of more carefully drafted legislation. The successive anticonspiracy statutes passed in New York and Pennsylvania between 1870 and 1887 were, in many ways, a testimony to organized labor's commitment to political change in the three decades after the Civil War.[112]

By the turn of the century, however, the AFL had become disillusioned with the prospects of political reform. Their repeated campaigns to secure state protection of the right to organize and to improve the hours, wages, and working conditions of their members were continually undermined by the courts. No matter how carefully the statutes were crafted, they seemed to have little or no capacity to curb the courts' power. The courts' resistance to the trade unions' legislative agenda after the Civil War demonstrated repeatedly the difficulties of changing government policy toward labor through political channels. Not surprisingly, then, by the turn of the century many labor leaders began to articulate a deep-seated mistrust of poli-

---

[112] Securing passage of anticonspiracy laws was not the only strategy pursued by New York workers in order to check the court's power. The New York Workingmen's Assembly also showed some interest in using the elective judiciary as an additional means of changing judicial policy. See *Workingmen's Assembly Proceedings*, 1886, 3–4; 1888, 41–42. This additional strategy was made possible by the introduction of an elective judiciary in most states at midcentury and specifically in New York in 1846 and Pennsylvania in 1850. Despite its considerable logical appeal, this additional strategy clearly remained of minor concern to the Workingmen's Assembly compared to their strenuous efforts to secure passage of the anticonspiracy laws.

Interestingly, research on the impact of the elective judiciary on judicial policy suggests that the Workingmen's limited interest in this course of action may well have been warranted. Even campaigns that successfully changed judicial personnel appear to have had little impact on the pattern of decisions handed down by nineteenth-century state courts. See Evan Haynes, *The Selection and Tenure of Judges* (Newark, N.J.: National Conference of Judicial Councils, 1944); Russell D. Niles, "The Popular Election of Judges in Historical Perspective," *The Record of the Association of the Bar of the City of New York* 21, 8 (November 1966): 523–38; Kermit L. Hall, "The Judiciary on Trial: State Constitutional Reform and the Rise of an Elected Judiciary, 1846–1860," *Historian* 44 (May 1983): 337–54; Kermit L. Hall, "Progressive Reform and the Decline of Democratic Accountability: The Popular Election of State Supreme Court Judges, 1850–1920," *The American Bar Foundation Research Journal* 1984, 2 (Spring 1984): 345–69; and Gerard W. Gawalt, ed., *The New High Priests: Lawyers in Post–Civil War America* (Westport, Conn.: Greenwood Press, 1984). For more general discussion of the power and autonomy of nineteenth-century state courts, see Harry Hirsch, *A Theory of Liberty: The Constitution and Minorities* (New York: Routledge, 1992), 53 and notes therein.

tics and to advocate instead a change in strategy that would enable them to circumvent the unusual power of the American judiciary.

The debate over the "political programme" at the AFL's Denver convention captures nicely labor's increasing frustration with political reform. Delegates Beerman, Lloyd, Pomeroy, and Strasser opposed the ten-point platform precisely because the courts posed a major obstacle to effective political change. Delegates Beerman, Strasser, and Sullivan all suggested that the conspiracy question be added to the program because it was such an important issue for organized labor. Their proposal, however, was rejected on the grounds that delegates had been instructed to vote on the platform as originally proposed and were not in a position to adjudicate completely new amendments.[113] Despite the absence of a conspiracy plank, the debate over the "political programme" nevertheless shows how persistent judicial obstruction undermined labor's faith in the benefits of legislative change. Delegate Pomeroy, for example, objected to plank 4, which called for "[s]anitary inspection of workshop, mine and home," in the following terms:

> Under the kind of government with which we are infested at the present time everything of a legal nature that will permit the invasion of the people's homes is dangerous. This law could be used to destroy the sacredness that is supposed and did once surround the American home. I believe the home can be made sacred again, can be defended from *the violations of a judiciary that stretches laws at the dictation of their bosses, capital.* . . . Leaving it (the plank) there, you leave a danger and a standing menace that has been already and will be used again against the rights of the citizens of this country.[114]

Delegates Beerman, Lloyd, and Strasser were less concerned with judicial interpretation and raised instead the specter of judicial review and the problems it created for political reform. Adolph Strasser summed up the frustration with politics and began to articulate the basic features of voluntarist strategy during the debate over plank 3, calling for a "legal eight-hour workday." Rather than looking to the government as their savior, Strasser argued that workers would be better off if they directed their energy and resources to trade union organizing and protest on the shop floor.

> There is one fact that cannot be overlooked. You cannot pass a general eight hour day without changing the constitution of the United States and the constitution of every State in the Union. . . . I hold we cannot propose to wait with the eight hour movement until we secure it by law. The cigar makers passed a law, without the government, . . . and they have enforced the law without having policemen in

[113] See *A Verbatum* [sic] *Report of the Discussion on the Political Programme*, 15, 17, 62.
[114] Quoted from ibid., 21–22; emphasis added.

every shop to see its enforcement. . . . I am opposed to wasting our time declaring for legislation being enacted for a time possibly, after we are dead. I want to see something we can secure while we are alive.[115]

The only effective "laws," from Strasser's point of view, were those standards created and enforced by workers themselves. Thus, the antistatist features of AFL voluntarism began to emerge in the last decade of the nineteenth century, when it became clear to many labor leaders that legislatures had little or no capacity to curb the courts' power.

At the close of the Denver convention, the "political programme" was left in an ambiguous position. The convention had voted on and accepted all eleven planks, but at the end of the meeting delegate Pomeroy put forward a motion to adopt the platform as a whole, which was defeated by a substantial margin of 735 in favor and 1,173 against. There was considerable dissatisfaction with the final outcome, and many delegates blamed Gompers for manipulating the vote through his authority as chair. When all was said and done, it remained quite unclear whether or not the "programme" actually had been endorsed.[116]

The AFL's difficulties in circumventing the courts and their increasing frustration with legislative change were summed up nicely by the AFL's new president, John McBride, in 1895. Reflecting on whether the "political programme" had been adopted the previous year, McBride characterized the legislative agenda as follows:

> The experience of the last five years has demonstrated that much labor and money have been wasted in efforts to secure desired legislation, because the statutory enactment secured had but a short life and met death at the edge of the constitutional axe.
>
> The constitution of the national and many of the state governments stands today as a monument to the past greatness and grandness of our country. These constitutions were made and adopted for the purpose of protecting men and methods now dead. They are not suited for the changed industrial conditions and improved mental status of the present time, hence if the modern environments of labor are to be ameliorated by legislation, in keeping with the progress of our people along commercial and industrial lines, it might be well to turn our attention to the cutting away of these constitutional barriers which invalidate legislation enacted in the people's interests.[117]

---

[115] Quoted from ibid., 19–20.

[116] For an account of the final debate and vote on the "political programme," see ibid., 63–64. Interestingly, 1894 was the only year between 1886 and 1924 that Gompers was not reelected as president of the AFL. Gompers refers to this period as his "sabbatical year." See Gompers, *Seventy Years of Life and Labor*, 355.

[117] Quoted from McBride's presidential report to the AFL convention in New York in 1885. See *AFL Reports*, 1895, 14.

Interestingly, McBride himself linked increasing judicial obstruction to "the changed industrial conditions" and "modern environments." The constitution, according to McBride, was suited to earlier times, but was out of step with the commercial and industrial developments under way in the last decade of the nineteenth century. Legislatures, it seemed, were incapable of changing judicial policy in the United States and provided little or no government protection of workers' interests. Thus, as workers in England and France were seizing political power and establishing national political parties, many American workers were witnessing the impotence of even successful political action to change government policy. The postwar conspiracy convictions were a constant reminder of the ineffectiveness of political reform as a means of harnessing state power for workers' own ends.

Perhaps the clearest account of the turn to voluntarism can be found in Samuel Gompers' autobiography. Gompers reflected on his "political work" of the 1880s in a chapter entitled "Learning Something of Legislation." Gompers had by no means always been a staunch advocate of business unionism. On the contrary, during the 1870s and 1880s he campaigned actively to improve the workingmen's lot through political channels. Gompers' account of the New York cigar makers' struggle to regulate tenement manufacturing in the city provides an uncanny parallel with the Workingmen's Assembly efforts to pass the anticonspiracy laws.[118]

Between 1878 and 1885, New York Cigar Makers' Local 144, with the support of the Workingmen's Assembly, undertook an intensive campaign to abolish or at least improve the appalling conditions of tenement manufacturing. First, they lobbied for passage of an amendment to a federal revenue bill that would have placed a prohibitive tax on cigars manufactured under tenement conditions. The amendment passed the House of Representatives in 1879 but did not make it out of the Senate. Next, the cigar makers turned to the state level, where they tried to pressure the New York Assembly to prohibit tenement manufacturing by using its police powers to regulate public health. An extensive lobby was maintained in Albany, with union representatives testifying regularly before the relevant committees, pledging representatives to support the bill, and endeavoring to elect their own representatives to the Assembly. After several abortive efforts, a new state law prohibiting tenement manufacturing was passed in 1883.[119]

[118] Generally see Gompers, *Seventy Years of Life and Labor*, vol. 2, chap. 11. For more general discussion of Gompers' political activity, see Stuart Bruce Kaufman, *Samuel Gompers and the Origins of the American Federation of Labor, 1848–1896* (Westport, Conn.: Greenwood Press, 1973); and Harold Livesay, *Samuel Gompers and Organized Labor in America* (Boston: Little, Brown, 1978), chap. 4.

[119] My account of the cigar makers' campaign for tenement reform is compiled from the following sources: Gompers, *Seventy Years of Life and Labor*, 186–98; Fairchild, *Factory*

However, labor's hard-earned political victories for tenement reform, as with the anticonspiracy laws, seemed to have little or no real power. Soon after the tenement bill was passed, employers successfully challenged the constitutionality of the law in the New York courts on the grounds that the act violated the due process clause. As with the anticonspiracy statutes, New York unions were not so easily deterred and renewed their "political work" in order to enact a more effective statute that could withstand the scrutiny of the court. In May 1884, their efforts were again rewarded with a new, more carefully drafted law, only to be overruled again by the New York Supreme Court and Circuit Court of Appeals.[120]

The cigar makers' unsuccessful struggle for tenement reform, according to Gompers, indeed taught him something about legislation, namely, the ineffectiveness of attempts to secure change through political channels. "Securing the enactment of a law does not mean the solution of the problem as I learned in my legislative experience. The power of the courts to pass upon constitutionality of law so complicates reform by legislation as to seriously restrict the effectiveness of that method."[121] When three decades of "political work" were continually eroded by the courts, New York and Pennsylvania workers looked for other "methods" of protecting workers' interests within the confines of the American state.

To overcome the limitation of political reform within the divided American state, labor had to devise new tactics for pursuing its interests in the industrial economy. The cigar makers' response to the failed tenement legislation might well have served as a blueprint for AFL strategy more generally. Gompers described the change of tactics as follows:

> After the Appeal Court declared against the principle of the law, we talked over the possibilities of further legislative action and decided to concentrate on organization work. Through our trade unions we harassed the manufacturers by strikes and agitation until they were convinced that we did not intend to stop until we gained our point and that it would be less costly for them to abandon the tenement manufacturing system and carry on the industry in factories under decent conditions. Thus we accomplished through economic power what we had failed to achieve through legislation.[122]

Thus the AFL adopted a strategy of antistatist voluntarism, according to Gompers, precisely because of the frustration encountered in court for their "political work." The power of the courts to set government policy

Legislation, chap. 2; and Mandel, *Samuel Gompers*, 29–33. For an interesting discussion of these same events from Roosevelt's point of view, see Hurwitz, *Theodore Roosevelt and Labor*, 79–89.

[120] See Fairchild, *Factory Legislation*, chap. 2; and *In re* Jacobs.

[121] Gompers, *Seventy Years of Life and Labor*, 194.

[122] Ibid., 197.

convinced the AFL and its antecedent organizations that it was extremely difficult to secure enduring change through political reform.

FROM CONSPIRACY TO THE LABOR INJUNCTION

Between 1885 and 1895 the labor injunction began to replace the conspiracy law as the principal legal tool for regulating industrial conflict. During the transition, both remedies were used; by 1895 the change was largely complete, after which the injunction remained the dominant remedy until passage of the Norris–La Guardia Act in 1932. Although the legal remedy had changed, the three-cornered struggle between labor, legislatures, and the courts over workers' industrial rights remained largely the same. Now, however, the contest took place at the national rather than the state level as the AFL, Congress, and the federal courts tried to establish the terms of late-nineteenth-century industrial relations.[123]

Many factors contributed to the shift in legal remedy, not the least of which was the coincidence of employers' and judges' interests in the mid-1880s. Both groups, for rather different reasons, found criminal conspiracy to be a cumbersome tool for containing working-class protest. From the employers' perspective, the increased scope and speed of the injunction and the absence of a jury trial made this new legal weapon a considerable improvement over the conspiracy law. Blanket injunctions and *ex parte* restraining orders, in particular, proved to be formidable weapons in employers' hands and enabled them to constrain a wide array of workers' protests in a single action.[124]

---

[123] The classic work on the labor injunction remains Felix Frankfurter and Nathan Greene, *The Labor Injunction* (New York: Macmillan, 1930). For an excellent account of the transition from conspiracy to the injunction, see Mason, *Organized Labor and the Law*, chaps. 6–8. Walter Nelles has inferred that labor injunctions may well have originated in the 1877 railroad strike, especially where railroads were in receivership. See Walter Nelles, "A Strike and Its Legal Consequences: An Examination of the Receivership Precedent for the Labor Injunction," 40 *Yale Law Journal* 507 (1931): 518–22, 553. However, many scholars date the first injunctions to 1883 and 1884. Despite these differences, all agree that the injunction was not used with any regularity until the late 1880s or early 1890s. See Frankfurter and Greene, *The Labor Injunction*, 21–23; Witte, "Early American Labor Cases," 832–36; Forbath, "The Shaping of the American Labor Movement," 1155–60, 1165–74; and Paul, *Conservative Crisis and the Rule of Law*, 107–30.

[124] Blanket or omnibus injunctions enabled a single restraining order to enjoin thousands of workers at a time, or even to restrain all the trade unionists in a particular city or town. *Ex parte* injunctions were issued on the basis of affidavits alone, without giving the defendants notice or an opportunity to respond. See Frankfurter and Greene, *The Labor Injunction*, chaps. 2, 3; Forbath, "The Shaping of the American Labor Movement," 1184; Paul, *Conservative Crisis and the Rule of Law*, chaps. 6, 7; Edwin Emil Witte, *The Government in Labor Disputes* (1932; New York: Arno and The New York Times, 1969), chap. 5; and Hurvitz, "American Labor Law and the Doctrine of Entrepreneurial Property Rights," 333–38.

Courts, too, had a vested interest in the change in remedy as judges and prosecution attorneys found themselves in an awkward position during the second wave of conspiracy trials. Many judges and attorneys were frightened by the recent upsurge of labor protest and wanted to contain working-class unrest.[125] Under the conspiracy law, however, courts had to choose between conviction and acquittal; it was difficult to establish a middle ground in which working-class organization could be both accepted and regulated at the same time. Convictions could be obtained, but only at considerable cost, by stretching statutory provisions beyond recognition. By the 1880s, then, state and federal courts were in a precarious position: working-class organization was being contained by judicial decisions that simultaneously undermined judicial authority. This situation could not be easily sustained without seriously jeopardizing the courts' legitimacy over the long term.

In the mid-1880s, federal courts faced three choices. They could follow state courts and continue the criminal conspiracy prosecutions. In doing so, however, they risked undermining their own authority. Second, they could capitulate to legislative protection of workers' industrial rights, although the previous two decades' conspiracy convictions at the state level attest to the judiciary's reluctance to pursue this option. Finally, they could change the legal remedy and adopt new grounds for regulating industrial disputes. This third option is the one courts and employers pursued after 1885, when they relied increasingly on the labor injunction rather than conspiracy to regulate working-class organization and conflict.

The change in legal remedy from conspiracy to the injunction enabled courts to reconcile two conflicting demands. Rather than being forced to choose between conviction and acquittal, the injunction enabled employers to enjoin strikes and boycotts without calling into question workers' industrial rights in toto. Thus the injunction provided an ingenious solution to the postbellum struggle between the courts and legislatures over working-class organization; courts could recognize workers' rights to collective action without forfeiting their role as the principal regulators of industrial disputes. Ironically, labor's postbellum challenge to the conspiracy laws was partially successful: labor's victories in the state legislatures did force a change in judicial policy, but not along the lines proposed by labor. The conspiracy doctrine was eventually repealed, but was not replaced by legislative protection of workers' industrial rights. Instead, the courts adopted a new legal remedy that preserved their role as primary regulator of industrial relations into the twentieth century.

Injunctions cut to the core of labor activities by enjoining boycotts,

---

[125] See Nelles, "A Strike and Its Legal Consequences," 520–26; Paul, *Conservative Crisis and the Rule of Law*, 128–30, 142–58; and Hurvitz, "American Labor Law and the Doctrine of Entrepreneurial Property Rights," 356–58.

pickets, and any other action that threatened irreparable injury to property. Between 1880 and 1932 there were at least 524 reported labor injunctions and an additional 500 to 1,000 unreported cases in the state and federal courts.[126] The AFL and other union leaders understood all too well the demoralizing impact of the injunction and renewed their efforts to check the courts' power. Beginning with the Pullman strike in 1894 and culminating in the first three decades of the twentieth century, union leaders such as Eugene Debs, Andrew Furuseth, John P. Frey, John Mitchell, and Samuel Gompers challenged the authority of the injunction as a legitimate weapon for regulating labor. In the face of immediate disputes, Debs, Mitchell, Gompers, and other union officials deliberately defied injunction orders so as to discredit this new legal remedy and were charged and convicted of contempt. In addition, the AFL initiated an extensive anti-injunction campaign in 1906 in which they called for legislative relief from Congress. After a series of unsuccessful attempts, labor's efforts were rewarded with passage of the Clayton Act in 1914.[127]

As with the earlier campaign to repeal the conspiracy laws, the Clayton

[126] For estimates of the number of injunctions, see Sylvester Petro, "Injunctions and Labor-Disputes: 1880–1932," 14 *Wake Forest Law Review* 341 (1978): 351–53. Not all disputes were taken through the federal courts. According to Petro, 342 of the 524 reported cases were state cases. Federal injunctions, however, generally were sought in the major strikes and tended to shape rulings in the state courts. Definitions of property were critical for determining whether an injunction could be sustained. Haggai Hurvitz has done a wonderful job of tracing the expansion of conceptions of property in the decade from 1886 to 1895. Initially courts conceived of property as a tangible good, but in this critical decade, federal courts began to recognize "entrepreneurial property rights" of an intangible nature. For an excellent discussion of these issues, see Hurvitz, "American Labor Law and the Doctrine of Entrepreneurial Property Rights," 338–56.

[127] A famous instance of labor leaders defying an injunction was Debs's and other American Railway Union officials' refusal to comply with the Pullman strike injunction in 1894. As a result, they were tried and convicted of contempt. Debs was sentenced to six months in jail and several associates to three months each. See United States v. Debs, 64 Fed. 724 (1894); and Paul, *Conservative Crisis and the Rule of Law*, chap. 7. Gompers, John Mitchell, and Frank Morrison took a similar stand in the Buck's stove dispute of 1906–1908 and also were charged with contempt. The trial court sentenced Gompers to one year in jail, Mitchell to nine months, and Morrison to six months. The defendants appealed the conviction in 1909 and eventually won when the U.S. Supreme Court dismissed the case in 1911. See Buck's Stove and Range Co. v. American Federation of Labor, 36 Wash. L. Rptr. 822 (D.C. 1908); Gompers v. Buck's Stove and Range Co., 221 U.S. 418 (1911); and Helfand, "Labor and the Courts." For AFL opposition to the injunction, see John P. Frey, *The Labor Injunction: An Exposition of Government by Judicial Conscience and Its Menace* (Cincinnati, Ohio: Equity Publishing Co., 1923); the AFL's "Bill of Grievances," *American Federationist* 13, 3 (May 1906): 293–96. For a very interesting discussion of the AFL's anti-injunction campaign, see Forbath, "The Shaping of the American Labor Movement," 1177, 1179–1233. Frankfurter and Greene claim that between 1894 and 1914 the injunction question was raised in every congressional session but one. See Frankfurter and Greene, *The Labor Injunction*, 163. For excellent legislative histories of the Clayton Act, see Frankfurter and Greene, *The Labor Injunction*, 165–98; and Witte, *The Government in Labor Disputes*, 265–73.

Act also was eviscerated by the courts. Between 1916 and 1920, there were thirteen federal court cases applying section 20 of the Clayton Act.[128] In all but three of these cases the statute was not found to prevent an injunction from being issued. At times the judicial interpretations were even contradictory, claiming that section 20 both did and did not create new privileges for labor. Whatever the specific grounds for particular rulings, the outcome was much the same; labor received little or no protection under the new law. The definitive interpretation of section 20 was not established until *Duplex Printing Press Co. v. Deering* came before the Supreme Court in 1921.[129] Injunctive relief had been denied the Duplex Company by both the District Court and the Circuit Court of Appeals. The Supreme Court, however, found otherwise and reversed these lower court rulings, holding that an injunction could be issued notwithstanding section 20 of the Clayton Act. The Supreme Court reaffirmed the *Duplex* precedent later the same year in the case of *American Steel Foundries v. Tri-City Central Trades Council.*[130] Finally, more than twenty lower court rulings followed the *Duplex* ruling in less than a decade, leaving little doubt as to the ineffectiveness of the Clayton Act for curbing the power of the courts. As federal courts continued to construe the Clayton Act very narrowly, the AFL persevered in its efforts to secure effective legislative protection from the injunction. Throughout the late teens and twenties, the AFL called repeatedly for new legislation until the Norris–La Guardia Act was passed in 1932.[131]

Finally, we might ask why the AFL persisted in its demand for anti-injunction legislation when their earlier political campaigns had already demonstrated the pitfalls of political reform. What, in short, was the relationship between the anti-injunction campaign and AFL voluntarism during the first three decades of the twentieth century? Although the frustrations of injunction reform certainly reinforced earlier lessons about the treachery of politics, there was an important difference between labor's anticonspiracy and anti-injunction campaigns. The earlier struggle to repeal the conspiracy law had gone hand in hand with a larger political program in which the Workingmen's Assembly and the FOTLU looked to the state for aid in their struggle with capital. From the 1870s through the early 1890s, labor still considered the state to be an important ally that could marshal resources to protect working-class concerns. By the turn of the century, the AFL began to back away from its larger political agenda in

---

[128] The following account of judicial interpretation of the Clayton Act draws primarily on Frankfurter and Greene, *The Labor Injunction*, 150–98.

[129] See Duplex Printing Press Co. v. Deering, 254 U.S. 443 (1992).

[130] See American Steel Foundries v. Tri-City Central Trades Council, 257 U.S. 184 (1921).

[131] See Witte, *The Government in Labor Disputes*, 273–82; and Forbath, "The Shaping of the American Labor Movement," 1227–33.

favor of direct negotiation with employers and protest on the shop floor. The AFL did not lead the fight for Progressive Era labor legislation, but either opposed or reluctantly joined middle-class reformers who championed labor's cause. The AFL's anti-injunction campaign became a political demand of last resort, a beachhead from which to secure minimal protections from the state. All other political commitments could be abandoned, but state recognition of the right to organize and strike had to be obtained if labor unions were to survive at all. Thus, the AFL continued to demand anti-injunction legislation alongside its flourishing antistatist voluntarism.[132]

From the Workingmen's Assembly, the FOTLU, and the AFL perspective, the structure of the American state had a formidable impact on labor strategy. Indeed, these organizations had, to a considerable extent, molded their strategies to conform to the juridical nature of the American state. The lesson from their "political work" for men like Jessup, Walls, Gompers, McBride, and Strasser had been to recognize the distinctive configuration of political power in the United States and to understand its implications for organized labor. State structure had shaped trade union strategy on two levels, both through what it precluded and through what it allowed. The power of the courts in the sphere of industrial relations provided few rewards for political action, while simultaneously fostering a more legalistic, contract-oriented system of collective bargaining. Both Christopher Tomlins and William Forbath have done a wonderful job of showing how labor leaders were drawn to legal discourse to make their claims.[133] Moreover, real gains were made in wages, working conditions, and benefits as workers "accomplished through economic power" at least some of the goals they "had failed to achieve through legislation."[134] While

[132] For the best account of AFL politics at the turn of the century, see Horowitz, *Political Ideologies of Organized Labor*, chap. 1. For a more extensive and somewhat different account of the AFL's accommodation of the anti-injunction campaign and voluntarism, see Forbath, "The Shaping of the American Labor Movement," 1202–33. With the exception of section 2 of his essay, Forbath seems to consider the injunction and the failed attempts to reform it to have been influential in the AFL's turn to voluntarism. But, as the AFL's anti-injunction campaign took place between 1906 and 1932, it is difficult to sustain the causal argument, because these were the very years in which voluntarism held sway. The anticonspiracy campaign simply cannot be overlooked and provides the critical link in the AFL's change in strategy at the end of the century.

[133] See Tomlins, *The State and the Unions*, chap 5; and Forbath, "The Shaping of the American Labor Movement," 1202–14.

[134] For accounts of the legalistic, contract-oriented system of collective bargaining established in the United States, and the economic benefits it delivered for American workers, see the following sources: Thomas A. Kochan, Harry C. Katz, and Robert B. Mckersie, *The Transformation of American Industrial Relations* (New York: Basic Books, 1986), esp. chap. 2; Nelson Lichtenstein, "From Corporatism to Collective Bargaining: Organized Labor and the Eclipse of Social Democracy in the Postwar Era" (Paper presented at a conference on

legislative victories proved fleeting, collective bargaining and shop floor militance provided ample incentives for trade union mobilization. Thus the distinctive structure of the American state was, it seems, a decisive factor in the AFL's turn away from politics at the end of the century to its newfound strategy of business unionism.

It would be a mistake, however, to generalize from the trade union experience to the American labor movement as a whole. When we look beyond the unions and consider again the producer organizations, we see that a very different set of state-labor relations prevailed.

POSTWAR PRODUCERS AND THE COURTS

One of the most striking contrasts between producers and trade unionists was the producers' minimal interest in judicial regulation and legal reform. Neither the NLU nor the KOL paid much attention to the role of judicial intervention in industrial disputes. The preambles and platforms of the producers' organizations were not devoted to repealing the conspiracy doctrine or to restricting the labor injunction. In fact, the producers showed little interest in the trade union campaign to change judicial policy. To be sure, neither the NLU nor the KOL ignored the courts altogether, but questions of judicial reform never preoccupied either of them as they had the New York Workingmen's Assembly, the FOTLU, and the AFL.[135]

In the case of the NLU, the question of conspiracy was raised at both the 1868 and 1869 congresses and the Committee on Obnoxious Laws was established in 1869 to help repeal the "injurious" laws. On closer examination, however, it is clear that the NLU's attention to the conspiracy doctrine was in no way comparable to the coterminous efforts of the New York Workingmen's Assembly. First, we should note that questions of conspiracy usually were raised by trade union delegates within the NLU.[136] Second, and more importantly, the unionists' legal concerns were

---

"Historical Perspectives on American Labor: An Interdisciplinary Approach," New York State School of Industrial and Labor Relations, Cornell University, 21–24 April 1988); and Stephen Amberg, "The Old Politics of Inequality: The Autoworkers' Union in the Liberal Keynesian State" (Paper presented at the annual meeting of the American Historical Association, 27–30 December 1988, Cincinnati, Ohio).

[135] Interestingly, J.G.A. Pocock points to a similar discontinuity between republican and legal rights discourse. See Pocock, "Virtue, Rights, and Manners: A Model for Historians of Political Thought," in his *Virtue, Commerce, and History: Essays on Political Thought and History, Chiefly in the Eighteenth Century* (New York: Cambridge University Press, 1985), 37–50.

[136] It was usually trade union delegates from New York in particular who raised the question of conspiracy. For example, William Jessup of the New York Workingmen's Assembly and Workingmen's Union, Henry C. Lucker of the Journeyman Tailors' Protective and Benefit Union, and Thomas J. Walsh of Bricklayers' Union No. 2 all raised the topic of conspiracy. See *NLU Proceedings*, 1868, 200–201, 220; and 1869, 232, 238–39.

never accepted as high-priority issues by the majority of delegates and were not included as planks in any of the NLU platforms. Thus, the question of conspiracy reform remained primarily a concern of dissenting unions, with little or no support from the dominant faction within the NLU.

Fortunately, we can glimpse the NLU's internal discussion of conspiracy through Jessup's account of the 1870 congress to the New York Workingmen's Assembly. In recounting the second day's proceedings, Jessup complained that the Committee on Obnoxious Laws had taken credit for efforts at legal reform that were, in fact, carried out by the New York Workingmen's Assembly. Jessup described the NLU proceedings as follows:

> At the afternoon session, J. W. Browning, of New York, of the Committee on Obnoxious Laws, presented a lengthy report of what said Committee had done in New York, and making it appear that much credit was due the Committee for its earnest labors; at the same time Mr. Browning entirely ignored this State Workingmen's Assembly, to which organization much of the credit was due for what had been accomplished and now claimed by this Committee on Obnoxious Laws. At the conclusion of Mr. Browning's report, your delegate took the floor, objecting to the report and claiming that much that was given in the report as the work of the Committee was actually due to this State Workingmen's Assembly.[137]

According to Jessup, the NLU had done little to advance the task of legal reform. What progress had been made was largely the work of trade unions acting under the banner of the Workingmen's Assembly. After the 1869 congress, conspiracy convictions were rarely mentioned in NLU proceedings and never obtained a position of prominence on the NLU agenda.

The KOL paid greater attention to the courts than earlier producers, but they, too, continued to approach the issue of legal reform differently than their trade union counterparts. While the New York Workingmen's Assembly, FOTLU, and AFL had advocated specific policies to curb the power of the courts, the Knights did little more than call for the repeal of unequal laws.[138] Unlike the trade unionists, the Knights' platform and proceedings rarely identified actual doctrine or cases that needed to be changed, nor did they lobby state legislatures or the national congress to pass anticonspiracy legislation.

On one of the few occasions when the Knights did address the question of criminal conspiracy directly and at length, their proposed reform further

---

[137] *Workingmen's Assembly Proceedings*, 1871, 59.

[138] The KOL routinely contained a plank in their platform calling for the "abrogation of all laws that do not bear equally upon capital and labor, the removal of unjust technicalities, delays, and discriminations in the administration of justice, and the adopting of measures providing for the health and safety of those engaged in mining, manufacturing, or building pursuits." See KOL General Assembly Proceedings, 1878, 5, Powderly Papers.

underscored the gulf that existed between producers and unionists after the Civil War. The "Special Committee on Conspiracy Laws" was established by the Knights' General Assembly in 1886.[139] The report was considerably more detailed than any previous discussion of legal doctrine by either the NLU or the KOL and provided a quite sophisticated analysis of both English and American legal history. The committee's recommendations to the General Assembly, however, were strikingly different from the trade union proposals for legal reform.

The committee did not call for repeal of the conspiracy doctrine, as the Workingmen's Assembly had done. Instead, it recommended that the doctrine be "honestly and impartially applied" with equal vigor to "combinations of aggregated wealth" and "organized greed."[140] The current problem of conspiracy convictions could be remedied, the committee argued, through a more impartial application of the doctrine to both capital and labor. Thus producers and trade unionists responded to the postwar convictions in opposite ways. The Knights were willing to accept judicial regulation of working-class organization as long as employers were subject to the same restrictions. Trade unionists, on the other hand, would no longer tolerate any such regulation, and mobilized instead to secure state protection of workers' industrial rights.

Instead of concentrating on legal reform, producers entered the political arena to harness state power for their own ends. The antimonopoly political parties of the 1870s through the 1890s, as we have seen, worked to reverse the current trend toward economic concentration. Financial reform, regulation of interstate commerce, and limited distribution of public lands remained their central demands. Unlike the trade unionists, the success or failure of the producers' program was not determined by the unusual structure of the American state. Although by no means always successful, the producers' platform was not continually obstructed by the wide-ranging power of judicial interpretation and review. Indeed, the dominance of the courts within the divided state initially had much less impact on the fate of producers' reform. The very same configuration of political institutions that proved so decisive in shaping trade union strategy did not block the producers' reforms. On the contrary, in the 1870s and 1880s the producers' antimonopoly program seemed more compatible with the common law heritage than did the AFL's collectivist demands.[141]

[139] The report is printed in the KOL General Assembly Proceedings, 1887, 1653–68, Powderly Papers.

[140] Quoted in KOL General Assembly Proceedings, 1887, 1667, 1662, 1665, Powderly Papers.

[141] For the common law's antimonopoly heritage, see Edward Coke's discussion of antimonopoly and the Magna Carta in his *Institutes of the Laws of England; Containing the Exposition of Many Ancient and Other Statutes* (London: W. Clarke and Sons, 1817), vol. 2, chaps. 29, 30; Sir William Blackstone's discussion of liberty in his *Commentaries on the Laws*

By contrasting the producers' and trade unionists' relationship to the American legal system, we can begin to understand why the same state structure played very different roles for different labor organizations.

Labor law needed to be changed only if workers wanted to secure state protection of the right to organize and strike. But the producers' vision of economic development required no such change in government policy. State power was not needed to protect workers' collective action, but rather was to be used to arrest the increased concentration of capital. Changing legal doctrine was, in many respects, antithetical to the central premise of the producers' vision: working-class organization simply would not be necessary within a truly republican political economy. In fact, the conspiracy doctrine was in many ways quite compatible with the anti-monopoly future—a future in which both capital and labor would be prevented from combining through renewed government regulation of all unhealthy accumulations of power. Producer organizations often were willing to accept judicial regulation of labor as a reciprocal policy for government control of corporate concentration. The producers were able to avoid the Workingmen's Assembly's judicial defeats because their vision of decentralized economic development did not entail a sweeping challenge to established legal doctrine and practice.

The producers' program, however, was not completely exempt from the unusual power of the American courts. Even though the NLU and KOL showed little interest in legal reform, the policies they did push for were nevertheless subject to judicial interpretation and review. Legislation involving financial reform, the regulation of interstate commerce, the eight-hour workday, and child labor laws, for example, all were challenged in the courts.[142] Despite similar structural conditions, the producers' program survived the process of judicial scrutiny with greater ease than its trade union counterparts, at least in the two decades following the Civil War. Where the trade union demands for state protection of working-class organization met with prolonged judicial opposition, producers' legislation was upheld more frequently by the courts.[143] In the 1870s and 1880s, in

---

of England (Philadelphia: George W. Childs, 1866), chap 1; and J. H. Baker, An Introduction to English Legal History (London: Butterworths, 1979), chap. 22.

[142] Although the antimonopoly program did not attempt to change legal doctrine, a number of "producer issues" were challenged in the courts and subject to judicial review. For example, see the following cases: Veazie Bank v. Fenno, 8 Wallace 533 (1869); Hepburn v. Griswold, 8 Wallace 603 (1870); Knox v. Lee, 12 Wallace 457 (1871); Parker v. Davis, 12 Wallace 457 (1871); Munn v. Illinois, 94 U.S. 113 (1877); Julliard v. Greenman, 110 U.S. 421 (1884); Wabash, St. Louis and Pacific Railroad Co. v. Illinois, 118 U.S. 557 (1886); Chicago, Milwaukee and St. Paul Railroad Co. v. Minnesota, 134 U.S. 418 (1890); and United States v. E. C. Knight Co., 156 U.S. 1 (1895).

[143] Decisions that favored the producers' program were handed down in the following cases: Knox v. Lee; Parker v. Davis; Munn v. Illinois; Julliard v. Greenman; Holden Hardy, 169 U.S. 366 (1898); Addyston Pipe and Steel Co. v. United States, 175 U.S. 211 (1899).

particular, several of the producers' key demands were successfully implemented. The Granger laws, the legal tender acts, and the Interstate Commerce Act, for example, were not undermined by the courts. To be sure, not
all cases were decided in the producers' favor; initially the courts resisted
financial reform and the regulation of commerce. Yet the producers' judicial defeats were more easily reversed as the courts gave way to renewed
legislative initiatives at both the state and the federal level.

The contrast with the New York Workingmen's Assembly experience is
clear. Even with renewed political support, the Workingmen's Assembly
was unable to change judicial policy. The courts simply refused to honor
new legislation exempting workers from criminal conspiracy. Thus the
levels of judicial resistance toward working-class political initiatives *varied
considerably* across different organizations and platforms within the labor
movement. While the "political work" of the AFL and its predecessors was
continually overruled by the courts, the producers' program met with less
extensive, and less persistent, opposition from the legal system. Courts
responded differently to the trade union and producer initiatives precisely
because the assumptions behind their two legislative programs intersected
common law doctrine in different ways.

The unionists' long-standing commitment to collective action inadver-
tently set this wing of the labor movement on a collision course with the
American courts. For centuries the common law had feared the consequences of concerted action and had subjected many forms of association
to extensive judicial regulation. One of the tasks the common law often
assumed was the protection of individual rights against unhealthy accumulations of collective power. The trade union program, with its emphasis on
state protection of working-class organization, ran counter to one of the
core values of Anglo-American law. Recognizing labor's right to collective
action required considerably more than minor adjustments to existing
doctrine. Indeed, establishing the right to organize for American workers
would have had widespread ramifications for corporation law and for
other nonlabor conspiracy cases as well. Thus, the Workingmen's Assembly's demand for the repeal of the conspiracy doctrine could not be accommodated easily within the established legal order. By adhering to the collectivist vision of economic development, the trade unionists set for
themselves the extremely difficult task of changing one of the central tenets
of American law.

The producers' program entailed no such sweeping change in legal doctrine, as their vision of decentralized economic development was in essence
opposed to collective action. Neither of the principal producer initiatives—
for financial reform and increased regulation of large corporations—called
into question fundamental precepts of the common law. To be sure, both
initiatives raised important issues of executive power and legislative juris-

diction that were negotiated in the courts. But neither of these policies challenged the individualistic cast of Anglo-American law. The producers' program, thus, could be affirmed more readily by tinkering at the margins of existing legal doctrine. No major recasting of core values was needed for the court to accommodate the principal demands of the producers' alliance.

Thus the power of the courts to block labor initiatives varied considerably from one segment of the labor movement to another. While the trade unionists found their programs frustrated by the distinctive structure of the American state, producers encountered much less opposition from the American judiciary. The variation in state-labor relations was due in large part to different visions of economic development and the demands these placed on the American legal system.

Despite their juridical advantage, however, the producers' organizations were not the victors. Although some producers' organizations existed through the turn of the century, the Knights' decline in the late 1880s signaled a major defeat for this alternative vision of a more decentralized pattern of economic growth. By the end of the century, the unions' collectivist vision had been accepted by most workers' associations and the producers' organizations had all but disappeared. The ultimate failure of the producers' program had little to do with the structure of the American state, but rather was the result of a complex set of forces that came into play in the last decade and a half of the nineteenth century.

THE PRODUCERS' DEMISE

The failure of the producers' program obviously extends well beyond the story told here. Nevertheless, analysis of the Knights' decline helps to map the interplay of forces that left the producers largely defunct at the end of the century. Three central factors at play in the Knights' defeat must be addressed: first, the Haymarket Affair; second, the strategies of employers and corporations; and third, the shift in legal doctrine in the late 1880s and 1890s.

On 4 May 1886, about 3,000 people attended a meeting in Haymarket Square in Chicago to protest the lockout at the McCormick Harvester works. Toward the end of an otherwise peaceful meeting, a bomb exploded; the police fired into the crowd and a bloody battle ensued. At the end of the night, at least ten were dead, including a policeman, and another fifty or more were injured. In an effort to contain the crisis in the days following, eight men were arrested and charged with the murder of the policeman, Officer Mathias J. Degan. Despite flimsy evidence that any of those arrested were, in fact, responsible for throwing the bomb, seven of the defendants were convicted and sentenced to death while the eighth received a term of fifteen years. On 11 November 1887, four of the defendants were hanged. A fifth committed suicide in his cell. The remaining two appealed for clemency, had their sentences commuted to life imprisonment, and eventually were granted unconditional pardons by Governor John Altgeld in 1893.[144]

The Haymarket Affair has been viewed by many historians as critical to the Knights' demise, because it divided and discredited the organization at the height of its powers. In the year preceding the events at Haymarket, membership in the KOL had risen exponentially after a series of successful strikes on Jay Gould's southwestern railroad. Within a year, membership had jumped by almost 600,000, from approximately 104,000 in July 1885 to 703,000 in July 1886. Moreover, the bulk of the increase had occurred in the first half of 1886, in the very months before the bomb exploded.[145]

The KOL, it seemed, was on a roll and for a brief moment was clearly the ascendant organization within the labor movement. Its success, however, was short-lived, as the new mobilization began to evaporate almost as quickly as it had appeared. By July 1887, membership had fallen by more than 100,000 and dissension within the organization seemed to be tearing it apart.[146] Membership continued to drop precipitously and stood at only 260,000 in 1888.[147] The rise and fall of the KOL seemed to break precisely at the events of Haymarket, which became the focus of considerable conflict within the order.

As with many events in the postwar era, workers were divided in their response to the Haymarket Affair. Most labor organizations were quick to condemn the violence but disagreed over whether or not to support the defendants at the notorious trial. The AFL stood behind the defendants with considerable vigor. Samuel Gompers and Peter McGuire, for example, addressed public meetings calling for clemency and petitioned the governor on the defendants' behalf.[148] The question of supporting the defendants was viewed by the AFL as a matter of working-class solidarity. Although violence ought to be condemned, the AFL had an obligation to support fellow workers and to make a public display of worker unity during the unjust trial.[149]

[144] For an excellent account of Haymarket, see Paul Avrich, *The Haymarket Tragedy* (Princeton: Princeton University Press, 1984).

[145] KOL membership figures are taken from Commons et al., *History of Labor in the United States* 2:381.

[146] Dissension within the Knights over Haymarket can be seen in the General Assembly Proceedings for both 1886 and 1887, Powderly Papers.

[147] Commons et al., *History of Labor in the United States* 2:482.

[148] See Avrich, *The Haymarket Tragedy*, 347–48; and Henry David, *History of the Haymarket Affair: A Study in the American Social-Revolutionary and Labor Movements* (New York: Russell and Russell, 1958), 410–12.

[149] See Avrich, *The Haymarket Tragedy*, 347–48; and David, *History of the Haymarket Affair*, 410–12.

For the KOL, however, the Haymarket Affair was a more divisive issue, revealing internal conflicts between theory and practice that had emerged within the order in the mid-1880s. The enormous mobilization before the Haymarket Affair posed a dilemma for the Knights and in many respects stood at odds with much of the organization's ethos and platform. Producer organizations, such as the NLU and KOL, had consistently denounced class conflict, claiming that strikes should be used only as a last resort; collective action should remain a defensive strategy, to be abandoned once their antimonopoly program succeeded. But the daily practice of being a Knight, of organizing and striking against employers, in many ways belied the order's platform. It was precisely the Knights' success that attracted many workers to its local assemblies. After witnessing their newfound power in 1885 and 1886, many delegates found the formal commitments to social harmony and the producers' alliance to be redundant.[150]

Internal conflicts within the Knights came to a head at the General Assembly meetings of 1886 and 1887. Delegates such as Joseph Labadie of Detroit, George Schilling and Charles Seib of Chicago, and James Quinn of New York argued that the Knights must stand behind the defendants and pass a formal resolution declaring their support.[151] The Grand Master Workman, Terence Powderly, took a different position. Powderly and his supporters steadfastly refused to commit the Knights in any official capacity to aid the accused. Moreover, in December 1886 Powderly insisted that all local assemblies cease and desist in the collection of funds to assist in the defendants' legal appeal or else risk expulsion from the order. Some locals simply defied Powderly's ultimatum and withdrew from the order. But most complied with the directive, and the KOL officially abstained from aiding in the clemency appeal.[152] At the General Assembly the following year, a revolt against Powderly was attempted by about thirty delegates. The "Kickers," as they were known, challenged Powderly's position on the "Haymarket martyrs" and proposed a resolution supporting the defendants. A heated debate ensued, but Powderly was able to contain the dissent. When put to a vote, the resolution was defeated by a substantial two-to-one margin.[153]

The Knights' refusal to support the defendants in any official capacity

[150] I would like to thank Cecelia Bucki for pointing out the tension between the formal program and organizing practice within the Knights. For additional discussion of tensions between structure and mobilization within the Knights, see Garlock, "A Structural Analysis of the Knights of Labor," chap. 1; and William C. Birdsall, "The Problem of Structure in the Knights of Labor," *Industrial and Labor Relations Review* 6, 4 (July 1953): 532–46.

[151] For opposition to Powderly, see Avrich, *The Haymarket Tragedy*, 348–50; and David, *History of the Haymarket Affair*, chap. 16.

[152] District Assembly 49 in New York, Local Assembly 1307, and Women's Assembly 1789 in Chicago all withdrew from the order over the Haymarket Affair. See Avrich, *The Haymarket Tragedy*, 348–50; and David, *History of the Haymarket Affair*, chap. 16.

[153] Avrich, *The Haymarket Tragedy*, 350.

often has been attributed to Powderly's inability to lead the organization forward at the height of its powers. Rather than seizing the moment and consolidating the recent wave of mobilization, Powderly insisted that the KOL distinguish itself from the more radical elements in order to avoid capitalist reprisals. If only Powderly had been less cautious, many scholars have argued, the Knights might have fostered a more class-conscious labor movement in those turbulent years. The opportunity was missed, so the argument runs, and American workers turned instead to more immediate economic gains through the AFL.[154]

However, Powderly's refusal to support the defendants was not a product of inept leadership or fear. On the contrary, Powderly understood all too well what was at stake in the internal struggle. Standing by the defendants, from Powderly's perspective, was tantamount to abandoning the core values of the producers' program. It was essential, especially in this time of crisis, Powderly claimed, for the Knights to reassert their commitment to their producer allies by denouncing firmly the current wave of industrial conflict. Workers must not be drawn into false conflicts with their employers, but must direct their hostilities toward the real enemy: the nonproducing classes.[155] The shrillness of Powderly's attack on the "anarchist element" was not merely a consequence of conservative fear. Rather, Powderly was engaged in a frantic effort to control the order, which seemed to be slipping from his grasp. The Grand Master Workman was well aware that the enormous mobilization of the previous year had changed the character of the order considerably. If the KOL was to adhere to its original principles, the anarchists had to be denounced and defeated and the producers' alliance revered.[156]

The stakes were high for both sides within the Knights as the future mission of the entire organization hung in the balance. The defeat of the Haymarket resolution at the 1887 General Assembly showed that a majority of the delegates still adhered to the producers' alliance and to their vision of an alternative path to economic growth. Yet the rapid decline in KOL membership after 1887 suggests that while Powderly may have carried the vote, he was unable to sustain rank-and-file support at its pre-Haymarket level. Where the dissenting trade unionists had composed only a handful of delegates within the NLU, fully a third of the Knights were willing to vote against Powderly in 1887. At the General Assembly in 1893, membership had fallen to 74,600. Powderly could no longer marshal a

[154] For interpretations of Haymarket that focus on Powderly's inadequacies, see David, *History of the Haymarket Affair*, esp. chap. 16; and Foner, *History of the Labor Movement*.

[155] For discussion of Powderly's views, see Avrich, *The Haymarket Tragedy*, 220, 309, 348–50; and David, *History of the Haymarket Affair*, chap. 16.

[156] For Powderly's tirade against the anarchists, see his *Thirty Years of Labor*, chaps. 12, 13.

majority of delegates and was deposed as Grand Master Workman, after serving for more than a decade.[157] Although the Knights continued to exist for almost a decade, the order was clearly past its peak and never again presented a serious challenge to the AFL once the decade was out.

The fate of the producers' alliance and of their alternative vision of economic development was not determined by workers alone. Differences between producers and trade unionists over the nature and source of economic growth and over labor's role in a modern economy were only part of a much larger struggle that accompanied industrialization in the United States. Employers, large industrialists, farmers, politicians, and judges also were engaged in similar conflicts over the appropriate pattern of economic growth. These extended conflicts have been explored more fully by other scholars and will only be alluded to here to highlight the interplay of forces associated with the producers' defeat.[158]

Several scholars in recent years have completed research on the corporate side and have begun to question the inevitability of concentrated and hierarchical economic organization. The legal status and powers of the corporation, these scholars have shown, also were being negotiated and defined in the postwar era, as many employers and large industrialists attempted to shape development along national lines.[159] The outcome of these battles over corporate authority and market structures was inextricably linked to the fate of the producers' program, as they helped establish the success of the winning mass production model. Although large corporations servicing national markets emerged as the dominant form of economic organization in the late nineteenth century, there may well have been viable alternatives to this winning model that would have enabled the economy to develop along regional lines. If one takes this research seriously, the producers' vision was by no means bound to fail, but lost out in a series of political struggles that influenced that overall pattern of industrialization in several spheres. Had some of the producers' allies won in other

---

[157] Commons et al., *History of Labor in the United States*, 2:494.

[158] For accounts of these additional struggles over the nature and pattern of economic growth, see Goodwyn, *The Populist Moment*; Horwitz, *The Transformation of American Law*; Charles McCurdy, "American Law and the Marketing Structure of the Large Corporation, 1875–1890," *Journal of Economic History* 38, 3 (September 1978): 631–49; Berk, "Constituting Corporations and Markets"; and Hurvitz, "American Labor Law and the Doctrine of Entrepreneurial Property Rights."

[159] Discussion of the influence of politics on corporate authority can be found in the following sources: Oscar Handlin and Mary Flug Handlin, *Commonwealth: A Study of the Role of Government in the American Economy: Massachusetts, 1774–1861* (Cambridge, Mass.: Harvard University Press, 1947); Hurst, *The Legitimacy of the Business Corporation*; McCurdy, "American Law and the Marketing Structure of the Large Corporation"; Horwitz, "Santa Clara Revisited"; Barzelay and Smith, "The One Best System?"; Berk, "Corporations and Politics"; and Piore and Sabel, *The Second Industrial Divide*.

arenas, the Knights might have been able to join a winning coalition. However, Populist farmers, small manufacturers, and their political allies did not succeed, and the producers' wing of the labor movement also went down to defeat.

One last piece of the puzzle must be mentioned, namely, the change in legal doctrine at the end of the century. While the courts had upheld most of the producer legislation in the first two decades after the Civil War, many of these decisions were reversed in the last decade and a half of the nineteenth century. Two issues in particular were subject to important interpretations. The first concerned the legal definition of legitimate collective action; the second centered on the question of government regulation of the economy. On both fronts, the rulings handed down after 1885 left the producers in a more difficult position vis-à-vis the courts than they had been in in earlier decades.[160]

In the *Santa Clara*, In re *Debs*, and *E. C. Knight* cases, for example, the court began to treat corporate entities more favorably than before.[161] By protecting the corporation as a person, and exempting manufacturing from the Sherman Antitrust Act, the court legitimated capital's collective action in new and important ways. The producers' antimonopoly vision that initially sat so well with the common law heritage now was of little advantage. Collective action, at least on capital's side, had been reconciled with the common law, which removed an important legal impediment to the collectivist vision of economic development. Judicial policy concerning economic regulation took a similar turn in the late 1880s and 1890s. The *Wabash*, *E. C. Knight*, *ICC*, and notorious *Lochner* decisions called into question state regulation of the economy.[162] Given that the producers' program demanded extensive economic regulation in general, and of cor-

---

[160] For an excellent account of this change in judicial doctrine, see Paul, *Conservative Crisis and the Rule of Law*. For the classic statements of a more general political realignment in 1896, see Walter Dean Burnham, "The Changing Shape of the American Political Universe," *American Political Science Review* 59, 1 (March 1965): 7–28; and "The System of 1896: An Analysis," in Paul Kleppner, Walter Dean Burnham, Ronald P. Formisano, Samuel P. Hayes, Richard Jensen, and William G. Shade, eds., *The Evolution of American Electoral Systems* (Westport, Conn.: Greenwood Press, 1981), chap. 5.

[161] See Santa Clara Co. v. Southern Pacific R.R. Co., 118 U.S. 394 (1886); *In re* Debs, 158 U.S. 564 (1895); and United States v. E. C. Knight Co.

[162] See Wabash, St. Louis and Pacific Railroad Co. v. Illinois; United States v. E. C. Knight Co.; ICC v. Cincinnati, New Orleans and Texas Pacific R.R. Co., 167 U.S. 479 (1897); and Lochner v. New York. This change in legal doctrine helps account for the more antagonistic relationship between the Populists and the courts in the 1890s than experienced by earlier producer organizations. For an excellent account of the Populists' interaction with the legal system, see Alan Furman Westin, "The Supreme Court, the Populist Movement and the Campaign of 1896," *Journal of Politics* 15, 1 (February 1953): 3–41.

porations in particular, their position was again weakened considerably by the late-nineteenth-century rulings.

The point at issue is not so much the interpretation of any particular case, but rather that the court was inextricably involved in the economic and political struggles of the postwar era. The link between judicial doctrine and economic development was by no means a simple mechanistic one in which the court did the corporation's bidding. But nor was the court isolated from the pressing issues of the day. Instead, the court, too, had to take a position and decide which was the most promising model of economic growth. After all, decisions over the boundaries of collective action and economic regulation were intimately connected to the viability of different visions of economic development and necessarily involved the courts in the current economic and political struggles. Where once the court had supported the producers' antimonopoly claims, the court changed sides in the 1890s and began to support the new vision of large-scale economic development. By legitimating collective action and introducing notions of substantive due process, the court helped determine which of the competing models would succeed. In short, the rulings handed down at the end of the century removed any privileged position the producers' program may have had, and strengthened the hand of those advocating a more concentrated pattern of economic development after the war.

Between 1865 and 1895, then, the balance of power between producers and trade unionists was dramatically transformed. Within the space of a few decades, the producers, once the dominant faction within the NLU and the KOL, became the dissenting minority within a labor movement increasingly dominated by the AFL. The producers' alternative did not altogether disappear, but after the 1890s it was clearly a recessive strain within a labor movement that now adhered to more familiar twentieth-century assumptions of economic and social relations.[163]

Conclusion: Labor Visions and State Power

Contrasting the producers' and trade unionists' response to the same conspiracy trials helps identify the significance of ideology and culture in mediating workers' relation to the state. The unusual configuration of political institutions in the United States with the dominance of the courts over other branches of government indeed played a decisive role in the AFL's turn to business unionism. However, the courts' power to shape

---

[163] For the decline of the Knights and the rise of the AFL, see Commons et al., *History of Labor in the United States* 2:472–95.

labor strategy was not universal, but was operative only for those organizations advocating a particular vision of economic development. Labor organizations that did not break with the republican past, such as the NLU and the KOL, did not find their programs blocked by the courts. It was only when the AFL decided it wanted what the courts had jurisdiction over— namely, the right to collective action—that the legal doctrine and powers of judicial interpretation and review began to shape labor strategy. Ironically, then, the courts' power was not determined by state structure and capacity alone, but was largely dependent on the substantive aspirations and goals of the very organizations the courts sought to regulate. By exploring the precise ways in which particular groups and their substantive agendas encountered American institutions, we can begin to unravel the intricate process of working-class formation in the United States.

Some readers will no doubt claim that contrasting elite narratives of industrialization, even in response to common events in the same period, does not eliminate the possibility that competing economic visions were in fact the product of underlying material rather than cultural conditions. Given the uneven pattern of economic change, so the argument might run, the two visions might have been grounded in the diverse conditions that prevailed in different sectors of the postwar economy. Although the prevalence of mixed assemblies makes it difficult to identify with any precision the occupational composition of the KOL, Jonathan Garlock has gone to considerable lengths to determine the principal trades within the KOL. Interestingly, there appears to be little difference in the occupational basis of the two wings of the postwar labor movement. First, different individuals within the same trades can be found in competing organizations. Both coal miners and iron molders, for example, were at the center of Pennsylvania protest against the conspiracy trials, yet members of these same trades also dominated membership lists in the KOL. Workers within these trades often disagreed over questions of labor strategy and industrial change and debated these questions within their organizations. Second, there is little evidence that the KOL flourished in less industrialized or rural communities. On the contrary, the Knights fared equally well in large industrial centers, again indicating that level of economic change does not account for the producers' distinctive response to industrialization. Finally, jurisdictional disputes between the KOL and the AFL over who should organize particular trades, most notably in the cigar manufacturing industry, also suggest that labor leaders within both the KOL and the AFL anticipated a favorable response from workers placed similarly in the labor market.[164]

---

[164] For an excellent discussion of the occupational composition of the KOL and for the importance of coal miners and iron molders within the order, see Garlock, "A Structural

In short, the two economic visions cannot be traced back with any certainty to underlying differences in skill, trade, or sector. Changing material conditions certainly prompted many workers to organize after the Civil War, but did not determine which interpretation of industrialization captured their imagination and mobilized them into competing camps. Instead of continuing to search for some underlying economic foundation to the competing narratives, I believe working-class mobilization is best analyzed in political terms. An individual's commitment to one interpretation of industrialization, from this perspective, was neither economically determined nor an act of free will, but was the product of established institutional, social, and political relations. The labor leader's task, then, was to articulate as coherent and persuasive a narrative of economic change—a narrative that resonated with workers' daily experience, in the hopes of mobilizing them behind him. Economic conditions and the nature of production certainly were incorporated into the story but by no means delimited the central features of a particular interpretation. Documenting the relationship between elite visions and grass roots mobilization lies beyond the bounds of this study. Nevertheless, reconstructing labor leaders' interpretations of industrialization provides an essential first step to rethinking mobilization of the rank and file.

Analysis of the Knights of Labor," pts. 2–3. For discussion of the coal miners' and iron molders' participation in the Pennsylvania anticonspiracy struggles, see Kuritz, "The Pennsylvania State Government and Labor Controls," chaps. 2, 5. For internal union debates over questions of economic growth and labor strategy, see *Iron Molder's International Journal*, 1864–1880. For evidence of the limited variability in KOL strength in urban and rural centers, see Garlock, "A Structural Analysis of the Knights of Labor," pt. 4. Finally, for discussion of jurisdictional disputes between the KOL and the AFL, see Gompers, *Seventy Years of Life and Labor*, vol. 1, chap. 12; and Mandel, *Samuel Gompers*, chap. 4.

CHAPTER FIVE

The United States in Comparative Perspective: English Labor and the Courts

IN CHAPTER 4, I showed how the dominance of the courts undermined the formation of a politically active labor movement in the United States. This chapter compares American labor movement development with the English experience in order to test further the argument developed for American labor. England provides an excellent comparative case because of the pattern of similarity and difference in the two countries. Not only are American and English courts both members of the common law legal system, but the process of working-class formation was remarkably similar in the two countries for almost a century, between 1780 and 1880. Yet, by the outbreak of the First World War, the two labor movements had developed along quite different lines, adopting very different strategies for advocating workers' interests within their respective political economies.

By 1914, the AFL had largely abandoned political action and endorsed instead a voluntarist strategy, in which direct negotiation with employers and the labor contract were the central concerns of organized labor. In contrast, English workers continued to pursue their interests through electoral and party politics during the very same period. To be sure, the exact ideological cast of British labor politics was not yet completely settled, as various factions within the labor movement continued to advocate a range of political alternatives. But despite differences between groups such as the Trades Union Congress's Parliamentary Committee, the Independent Labour party, and the Social Democratic Federation, all of which tried to speak for English workers in the late nineteenth century, at no point did any faction advocate eschewing party politics entirely. Rather, all the competing factions proposed some form of political action, albeit of varying ideological orientations.

The English comparison is especially instructive because it provides a pair of most similar cases. Of all of the advanced industrial societies, the English legal tradition and system of labor regulation most closely resembled that of the United States. In other Western democracies, the power of the courts was even more limited than in Great Britain, thereby providing greater leeway for working-class mobilization than in either England or the

United States. Parliament, after all, although ultimately supreme, nevertheless had to fend off successive judicial encroachments in labor regulation. In other countries, the courts presented even fewer challenges to legislative authority. Thus, if the more limited role of the English courts can be linked to the formation of a more politically active labor movement, then the relationship between state structure and labor strategy should be even clearer in other countries where the contrast with the United States is even more pronounced.

The central question posed by the English and American comparison, then, is how to account for the initial similarity and subsequent divergence of the two labor movements in the late nineteenth century. Why did movements that were initially so similar eventually turn to quite different spheres to further workers' interests? The answer lies, I believe, in the different institutional forms of state regulation of labor in the two countries—specifically, in the more limited role of English courts in regulating working-class organization. Unlike the American courts, the English judiciary *shared* responsibility for regulating labor with Parliament, and, after an extended political struggle, was ultimately less powerful than the House of Commons in setting English industrial relations policy.

Before contrasting the role of the courts in England and the United States, we must first establish the similarities between the two labor movements before 1880. Doing so, however, requires a recasting of traditional interpretations of nineteenth-century English labor history that have obscured important parallels in the initial stages of labor movement development in the two countries.

TRADITIONAL VIEWS OF ENGLISH LABOR HISTORY

Typically, scholars have divided nineteenth-century English labor history into three phases: early radicalism (1830–1850); mid-Victorian accommodation (1850–1880); and, finally, the second awakening (1880–1900).[1] Within this framework, early workers' protest of the 1830s and 1840s has been considered the first sign of working-class consciousness in the United Kingdom. The General Trades' Unions (GTUs), the Chartist

---

[1] For periodization of nineteenth-century English labor history into three phases, see the following sources: Webb and Webb, *History of Trade Unionism*; Cole, *British Working Class Politics*; G.D.H. Cole, *A Short History of the British Working-Class Movement, 1789–1947* (London: Allen and Unwin, 1948). More recent work has maintained the periodization. For example, see Henry Pelling, *A History of British Trade Unionism* (Suffolk, Engl.: Penguin, 1963); Trygve R. Tholfsen, *Working Class Radicalism in Mid-Victorian England* (New York: Columbia University Press, 1977); and John Foster, *Class Struggle and the Industrial Revolution: Early Industrial Capitalism in Three English Towns* (New York: St. Martin's Press, 1974).

movement, and Owenite cooperatives provided important critiques of in-dustrialization and have been hailed by some scholars as "proto-socialist" organizations of the early nineteenth century.[2]

The radical promise of the early period, according to the traditional view, was dissipated during the second phase of working-class organiza-tion, in which labor was integrated into the modern industrial economy. Ever since the Webbs' classic depiction of the large amalgamated unions of engineers, carpenters, iron molders, and bricklayers as "the Junta," the mid-Victorian era has been viewed as a period of labor union acquiescence and accommodation to the existing industrial and political order.[3] Rather than building on the earlier radical heritage, so the argument runs, labor movement leaders in these highly skilled trades set aside demands for large-scale social change in order to secure more immediate benefits for them-selves within the new economic system. The process of accommodation can be seen in both workers' industrial and political action. Industrial accommodation involved the substitution of sliding wage scales and con-ciliation and arbitration policies for more direct forms of industrial un-rest.[4] On the political front, working-class accommodation generally has been associated with labor's support of Gladstonian liberalism and the subsequent Lib-Lab alliance of the late nineteenth century.[5]

Much research has focused on this middle phase of labor movement development in order to explain why the earlier radical potential was derailed. Two general arguments have been proposed to explain the mid-Victorian accommodation. First, the "labor aristocracy" thesis, initially advanced by Eric Hobsbawm, has generated extensive research and debate.[6] Put simply, Hobsbawm argued that British labor movement "re-formism" at midcentury was rooted in the division of labor and accom-panying stratification of the English working class. The amalgamated or

---

[2] Both the Webbs and Tholfsen describe early-nineteenth-century movements as "proto-socialist." See Webb and Webb, *History of Trade Unionism*, 161; and Tholfson, *Working Class Radicalism*, 86.

[3] For discussion of "the Junta," see Webb and Webb, *History of Trade Unionism*, chap. 5.

[4] Industrial accommodation is characterized nicely by Cole, *A Short History of the British Working-Class Movement*, 75. But see also Webb and Webb, *History of Trade Unionism*, chaps. 4, 5; and Eric J. Hobsbawm, *Labouring Men: Studies in the History of Labour* (London: Weidenfeld and Nicholson, 1964), chap. 17, 350.

[5] Political accommodation is outlined in the following works: Cole, *British Working Class Politics*, chap. 8; Richard Price, *Masters, Unions and Men: Work Control in Building and the Rise of Labour, 1830–1914* (London: Cambridge University Press, 1980), Introduction; Cole, *A Short History of the British Working-Class Movement*, chap. 7; Webb and Webb, *History of Trade Unionism*, chap. 5; Robert Gray, *The Aristocracy of Labour in Nineteenth-Century Britain c. 1850–1914* (London: Macmillan, 1981), chap. 6.

[6] See Eric Hobsbawm, "The Labour Aristocracy in Nineteenth-Century Britain," in his *Labouring Men*, 272–315.

"New Model Unions" of the 1860s were not broad-based organizations, but rather represented a much smaller segment of skilled workers, or "labor aristocrats" who benefited from, and were largely responsible for, labor's accommodation to the existing social order.[7]

A second explanation of working-class quiescence has focused on the "cultural" integration of English workers in the middle decades of the nineteenth century. Trygve Tholfson and others have argued that early working-class radicalism was modified by the growing hegemony of middle-class culture and values.[8] After 1850, working-class protest was increasingly expressed within the broader framework of middle-class notions of respect and self-improvement. Tholfson suggests that, although trade unions and friendly societies helped foster a sense of class consciousness, these same organizations simultaneously strengthened the consensual foundations of Victorian society by articulating workers' protest within the language of the middle class.[9]

Despite their many differences, both the "labor aristocracy" and "cultural hegemony" theses rest on shared conceptions of the early period of workers' protest as ideologically radical and industrially militant. For both arguments, the 1830s and 1840s are viewed as decades of radical promise in which a class-conscious labor movement emerged in Britain.[10] In light of this characterization of the early years, working-class organization in the mid-Victorian era appears moderate and reformist, and as such marks a

---

[7] The literature on the "labor aristocracy" is extensive, but the following works are quite representative: Henry Pelling, "The Concept of the Labour Aristocracy," in his *Popular Politics and Society in Late Victorian Britain* (London: Macmillan, 1968); Eric J. Hobsbawm, "Debating the Labour Aristocracy," "The Aristocracy of Labour Reconsidered," and "Artisans and Labour Aristocrats," in his *Workers: Worlds of Labour* (New York: Pantheon, 1984); and Price, *Masters, Unions and Men*.

For an excellent characterization and critique of the labor aristocracy thesis, see Alistair Reid, "The Division of Labour and Politics in Britain, 1850–1920" (Gonville and Caius College, Cambridge).

[8] For discussion of the cultural dimensions of working-class accommodation, see the following works: Tholfsen, *Working Class Radicalism*; Patrick Joyce, *Work, Society, and Politics: The Culture of the Factory in Later Victorian England* (Brighton, Engl.: Harvester, 1980); Trygve R. Tholfsen, "The Transition to Democracy in Victorian England," *International Review of Social History* 6 (1961): 226–48; Geoffrey Crossick, "The Labour Aristocracy and Its Values: A Study of Mid-Victorian Kentish London," *Victorian Studies* 19, 3 (March 1976): 301–28.

[9] Tholfsen, *Working Class Radicalism*, chaps. 7–9, esp. 308. Similar arguments can also be seen in Crossick, "The Labour Aristocracy and Its Values."

[10] The traditional literature generally depicts the era between 1820 and 1840 as a period of early radicalism. For example, although they develop very different arguments, the following authors nevertheless still adhere to the notion of early radicalism: E. P. Thompson, *The Making of the English Working Class* (London: Victor Gollancz, 1963); Tholfsen, *Working Class Radicalism*, chaps. 2, 3; and Foster, *Class Struggle and the Industrial Revolution*.

distinct shift away from the earlier radicalism of the GTUs, Chartists, and Owenite cooperatives.

The third phase of English labor movement development is thought to lie in the resurgence of working-class radicalism in the last decades of the nineteenth and first decade of the twentieth centuries. In particular, the new unionism of 1889–1891, the creation of the Independent Labour party in 1893, and the emergence of the shop stewards' movement in the early twentieth century provided, according to many scholars, the basis for a renewed challenge to the existing political economy. Again, as in the mid-Victorian scholarship, research has focused on the origins of the socialist revival as well as the ultimate failure of this second wave of working-class radicalism.[11]

In sum, traditional conceptions of English labor history generally have stressed the discontinuities in working-class politics during the three phases of nineteenth-century labor movement development. The demarcation of the three eras rests, in large part, on the long-standing characterization of the 1830s and 1840s as the first stage of class-conscious workers' protest in Britain. The early era has been used either implicitly or explicitly as a hallmark of labor radicalism, against which subsequent eras have been measured. The mid-Victorian era, then, has been considered reformist, primarily by contrasting labor strategies in the 1860s and 1870s with the earlier "proto-socialist" radicalism of the 1830s and 1840s, while the third era is seen as a revival of the radical heritage by semiskilled workers and their new organizations.

THE PRODUCERS' ALLIANCE AND CHARTIST REFORM

More recently, however, a number of scholars have begun to question traditional accounts of nineteenth-century English labor history. New research has proceeded on three fronts; ideology, social relations, and economic development all have been reexamined, revealing remarkable parallels between the English and American cases. First, historians have begun to trace the influence of eighteenth-century ideology on workers' protest, especially in the early decades of the nineteenth century.[12] Gareth Stedman

[11] Royden Harrison, *Before the Socialists: Studies in Labour and Politics, 1861–1881* (London: Routledge and Kegan Paul, 1965); James Hinton, *Labour and Socialism: A History of the British Labour Movement, 1867–1974* (Amherst: University of Massachusetts Press, 1983); Price, *Masters, Unions and Men*; James Hinton, *The First Shop Stewards' Movement* (London: Allen and Unwin, 1973); Hobsbawm, *Labouring Men*, chaps. 10, 12; Hobsbawm, *Workers*, chap. 9; and David Howell, *British Workers and the Independent Labour Party, 1888–1906* (Manchester, Engl.: Manchester University Press, 1983).

[12] Prothero, *Artisans and Politics*; Stedman Jones, "Rethinking Chartism"; and Robert Sykes, "Early Chartism and Trade Unionism in South-East Lancashire," in James Epstein and Dorothy Thompson, eds., *The Chartist Experience: Studies in Working-Class Radicalism and Culture, 1830–1860* (London: Macmillan, 1982).

Jones, in particular, has paved the way with his reinterpretation of the Chartist movement. Traditional histories that portray the Chartists as a radical response to the process of industrialization are insufficient, Stedman Jones argues, in that they have largely ignored the *particular form* of workers' protest in this early period.[13] To be sure, the transition from craft to industrial production created considerable economic and social distress, especially among large numbers of displaced artisans. But a satisfactory account of the Chartist movement must not only identify the economic and social changes that prompted workers to rebel; it also must explain why these grievances were expressed in a movement for *political reform*. Why, in short, did workers express their discontent in terms of the suffrage rather than by pressing for more immediate relief from their current economic distress?[14] The particular form of workers' protest can be understood, Stedman Jones claims, by attending more closely to the "linguistic ordering of experience" through which workers understood the economic and social changes under way in the early decades of the nineteenth century.[15]

Situating the Chartist movement within eighteenth-century republican, or Country party, ideology sheds new light on the political dimension of Chartist reform. Chartists, much like their New York and Pennsylvania counterparts, understood their current plight by drawing on republican assumptions about politics and society. Specifically, the Chartist protest was informed by the eighteenth-century republican belief in the constitutive power of politics, in which the balanced constitution had been viewed as an important factor in the preservation of liberty. Chartist reformers, again like the New York and Philadelphia Working Men's parties, extended these assumptions about political power to their own concerns in the early decades of the nineteenth century.

For displaced artisans and their Radical allies, there was nothing natural or inevitable about the process of industrialization. On the contrary, economic distress was thought to be a direct consequence of the particular political arrangement in place in the 1820s and 1830s. A contemporary observer diagnosed the problem as follows: "Knaves will tell you that it is because you have no property, you are unrepresented. I tell you the contrary, it is because you are unrepresented that you have no property . . . your property is the result not the cause of your being unrepresented."[16] Within the Country party ideology, political power was not simply a means of alleviating the symptoms of economic change; rather, access to the political system was an essential precondition for shaping economic and social relations. In short, the process of economic development, for early-

---

[13] Stedman Jones, "Rethinking Chartism," 93, 95.
[14] Ibid., 97.
[15] Ibid., 101.
[16] Quoted from ibid., 109.

nineteenth-century artisans, was thought to be a product of existing institutions and public policies. To alleviate the growing economic distress, one must go to the root cause and transform the system of political representation.

Viewed within the context of eighteenth-century conceptions of politics and society, the Chartists' demand for suffrage reform is no longer so mysterious. The Chartists were not simply struggling to obtain an abstract political right; they were attempting to eliminate the primary obstacle to successful economic and social change. So long as there was a "monopoly of representation," in which some citizens were excluded from the political system, oppression and misery of the working classes would remain.[17] Suffrage reform, then, was the key to successful economic and social reorganization and was thus the cornerstone of workers' protest in these early years.

In addition to the eighteenth-century language of class identified by Stedman Jones, the social alliances of the early nineteenth century also need to be reexamined. In England, as in the United States, the primary social cleavage in the first half of the nineteenth century was not yet between labor and capital, but between the producing and nonproducing classes. Despite the Webbs' claims to the contrary, the "industrious classes" were not manual workers but rather included a wide range of producers in an alliance against the idle or useless classes.[18] Thus, the Chartists embraced both skilled artisans and Radicals that would only later be separated and distinguished as working and middle classes.[19] In the Birmingham Political Union and the early trade unions, for example, artisans and middle-class reformers worked side by side. No formal agreement was needed to sanctify their cooperation, as both groups considered themselves members of the producing classes.[20] From this perspective, it is a mistake to consider the Chartists a class-conscious "proto-socialist" movement that had already begun to organize as a distinct wage-earning class. Instead, the

---

[17] Ibid., 104–10.

[18] Webb and Webb, *History of Trade Unionism*, 168.

[19] Stedman Jones, "Rethinking Chartism," 128, 136, 152; Prothero, *Artisans and Politics*, 334, 336; and Tholfsen, *Working Class Radicalism*, chaps. 2, 3, esp. 50–51, 92, 95. Even though Tholfsen refers to the eighteenth-century legacy as the "archaic elements of radicalism," he nevertheless recognizes their influence in his discussion on p. 51.

[20] Although focusing on the increased tension between middle- and working-class reformers in the 1840s, Clive Behagg documents the early alliance nicely. See Clive Behagg, "An Alliance with the Middle Class: The Birmingham Political Union and Early Chartism," in Epstein and Thompson, *The Chartist Experience*. See also Trygve Tholfsen, "The Chartist Crisis in Birmingham," *International Review of Social History* 3 (1958): 461–80; and Cole, *British Working Class Politics*, chap. 2, esp. 18–19. For an interesting discussion of labor and liberalism in the 1860s to the 1880s, see D. A. Hamer, *Liberal Politics in the Age of Gladstone and Rosebery: A Study in Leadership and Policy* (New York: Oxford University Press, 1972).

Chartist movement, like the New York and Philadelphia Working Men's parties, mobilized the producers against the nonproducing classes.

Finally, a number of scholars have suggested that existing accounts of economic development need to be recast. Industrialization did not proceed directly from craft to factory production. Economic growth was achieved through less dramatic changes in the organization of work, which left traditional methods of production largely intact.[21] Attending to the uneven pattern of economic development helps recover the uncertainty that accompanied the early stages of industrialization. Clearly, old methods of production were changing, but how permanent these changes were, where they were leading, and who would benefit from them was not at all certain. When faced with declining wages and diminishing social status, producers did not abandon their existing social divisions and political alliances quickly. For several decades, producers opposed the reorganization of work by defending the position of producers in the new economic order.

THE MID-VICTORIAN ERA: ACCOMMODATION OR DIFFERENTIATION?

Reconsidering early workers' protest in light of republican ideology has important implications for subsequent eras of English labor history. In particular, the very strategies and organizations that previous scholars have considered central to working-class accommodation in the mid-Victorian era take on a quite different appearance when considered within the producers' notion of class.

If, indeed, early working-class organization and politics were shaped largely by eighteenth-century social relations and ideology, then the defining characteristics of mid-Victorian accommodation also have to be reconsidered. Lib-Lab politics and conciliation and arbitration need not have signaled the continued integration of organized labor into the new industrial economy. Instead, these political alliances and arbitration procedures may well have reflected the fragmentation of existing social relations as producers began to distinguish different classes within their ranks. From this perspective, the mid-Victorian era is best viewed as a period in which workers continued to forge a separate identity for themselves in relation to their middle-class allies. Rather than being assimilated at midcentury, English workers were doing just the opposite—namely, continuing the

---

[21] For discussion of the process of economic development, see Raphael Samuel, "Workshop of the World: Steam Power and Hand Technology in Mid-Victorian Britain," *History Workshop* 3 (Spring 1977): 6–72; Prothero, *Artisans and Politics*, esp. 44–45; and William Lazonick, "Industrial Relations and Technical Change: The Case of the Self-acting Mule," *Cambridge Journal of Economics* 3, 3 (1979): 231–62.

lengthy process of working-class formation that had begun over half a century earlier, in the closing decades of the eighteenth century.

The breakdown of the producers' alliance can be seen in the changing relations between protesting workingmen and middle-class Radicals in the mid-Victorian era. Disputes over the membership policies of the rival workingmen's organizations in the 1860s reveal the increased tension within the producers' ranks. For example, George Potter's London Working Men's Association and the Working Men's Parliamentary Association adopted very different policies on admitting middle-class reformers into their organizations. The manifesto of the more radical London Association, adopted in 1867, explicitly challenged the ability of middle-class Radicals to represent workingmen's interests. In contrast, the more centrist Parliamentary Association continued to welcome middle-class support in their struggle for political reform.[22] The formation of the Labour Representation League in 1869 again quickly raised the question of whether or not middle-class sympathizers should be allowed to join the organization. A compromise was reached in which nonworkers were allowed to join but were subject to a higher membership fee of a guinea a year.[23]

Discussions over the terms of cooperation between workers and middle-class radicals within these midcentury reform organizations did not reflect labor's reformist tendencies. Rather, these cross-class coalitions revealed the rift that was emerging within the previously united producing classes. To be sure, cooperation between workers and Radicals was still possible, but now cooperation between the two had to be formalized into an explicit alliance, whereas in the past no such formal bridging mechanisms had been necessary. Lib-Lab politics, then, in fact may have signified the increased class consciousness of English workers as they began to distance and distinguish themselves from other members of the industrious classes.

Viewed in this way, workers' politics did not oscillate between radicalism and reformism in a discontinuous pattern during the nineteenth century. Instead, we see a gradual transition from producer to worker emerge over the course of the century. A more continuous conception of English labor movement development by no means implies that workers were a fully independent class by 1860. On the contrary, the mid-Victorian era now appears as a period of transition in between the earlier producers' alliance and the formation of an independent working class at the end of the century. In the 1860s, many workers indeed were trying to ally themselves with the Liberal party; only now we can see the Lib-Lab alliance as a

<hr>

[22] Webb and Webb, *History of Trade Unionism*, 393; Cole, *British Working Class Politics*, chap. 4, esp. 44, 50.

[23] Cole, *British Working Class Politics*, chap. 5, esp. 50–51.

reflection of the growing distance between the previously united producing classes.

Nor does the new perspective imply that workers were not concerned with questions of self-respect and independence. These issues clearly permeated many workers' protest movements at mid-century. What is challenged, however, is the interpretation of these concerns as manifestations of workers' assimilation to middle-class culture. Instead, images of self-respect and independence within Victorian reform organizations are seen as an extension of eighteenth-century conceptions of class, in which producers considered themselves to be worthy and industrious citizens who ought to be treated with greater regard. Assertions of self-respect and independence at midcentury reflected producers' efforts to reaffirm their social status and sense of worth, which were being challenged by the changing political economy.

If the mid-Victorian era was not simply a period of working-class accommodation and integration, then what is to be made of workers' acceptance of conciliation and arbitration in the 1870s? Conciliation boards and arbitration procedures frequently were introduced after periods of failed militancy, and thus generally have been viewed as acts of capitulation in the face of defeat.[24] However, adoption of these more formal methods of negotiation and dispute resolution, I believe, also reflect the increased class consciousness of the period. The fact that work relations now were regulated through formal procedures and institutions in many ways signaled the tremendous changes that had taken place in the workplace since the heyday of the craft economy. The bonds of the trade that previously had enabled producers to consider themselves a united class were gone. In their place stood the Arbitration Acts and the conciliation boards, monuments to the steady disintegration of the producers' alliance over the past hundred years.

Finally, reconceptualizing the mid-Victorian era as a period of continued working-class differentiation enables us to understand the prolonged struggle for state protection of industrial rights in the last three decades of the nineteenth century. Rather than considering state protection of workers' industrial rights as simply the final phase of working-class integration, the struggle for the right to organize and strike is best understood as the crucial step in the process of class formation and politics in Britain. It was precisely

---

[24] A useful discussion of conciliation and arbitration can be found in Cole, *A Short History of the British Working-Class Movement*, chap. 7, esp. 228–30. Conciliation and arbitration are most often associated with the mining industry, but conciliation boards also were established in the cotton industry after 1877–1878, in the engineering trades after 1879, and in the boot and shoe industries.

during this struggle for state recognition that English and American labor movements began to diverge. Examining the political struggle for state protection of workers' industrial rights enables us to contrast the role of the courts and the subsequent paths of labor movement politics in the two countries. To be sure, securing protection from the state did not settle the question of the particular form working-class politics was to take in Britain. In fact, in the years following state recognition, between 1875 and 1914, the labor movement split over precisely the question of what kind of politics the British labor movement was to follow.[25] However, it was clear after 1875 that the English labor movement would not have to seek an alternative to electoral and party politics, but could work quite effectively within the existing political system.

THE STRUGGLE FOR STATE PROTECTION OF INDUSTRIAL RIGHTS

As in the United States, the struggle for state protection of workers' right to organize and strike was carried out in two stages. In the first stage, organized labor pressured Parliament for statutory protection of workers' industrial rights in large part by exempting workers from judicial prosecution for criminal conspiracy. Once the legislation had been secured, the second stage of the struggle ensued; Parliament and the courts battled over which institution was to have ultimate authority to interpret the new labor statutes and thereby set government policy in the area of industrial relations. In the first stage of parliamentary lobbying, the English, New York, and Pennsylvania labor movements adopted essentially the same strategies and secured very similar results. Only during the second stage, in the struggle between Parliament and the judiciary, did the two movements for state recognition take quite different paths, in turn creating very different incentives and constraints for subsequent labor movement development. In both England and the United States, the courts and legislatures vied for ultimate authority over government policy toward labor. The outcome of this internal political fight, however, was quite different in the two countries. Put simply, in England the courts eventually deferred to parliamentary authority while in New York and Pennsylvania the courts continually defied their state legislatures. Consequently, quite different institutions were responsible for regulating industrial conflict in England and the United States at the end of the century.

Although English workers lobbied for state protection of workers' in-

---

[25] The labor movement split into "radical" and "reformist" organizations during the 1880s and 1890s. In particular, the Independent Labour party was established in 1893, in part out of dissatisfaction with the more moderate Labour Electoral Association established by the TUC. See Cole, *British Working Class Politics*, chap. 8.

dustrial rights throughout the nineteenth century, the major push for state recognition was carried out in the years from 1867 to 1875.[26] Two successive labor organizations led the fight. In the early years, between 1867 and 1871, the Conference of Amalgamated Trades (CAT) advanced workers' demands, while the Parliamentary Committee of the Trades Union Congress (TUC) took charge between 1871 and 1875.[27]

The CAT was established after the Court of Queen's Bench threatened the legal position of trade unions in the decision of *Hornby v. Close*, in which the court removed union funds from protection under the Friendly Societies Act of 1855.[28] Under the *Hornby* ruling, unions were now liable for damages, and thus were vulnerable to lawsuits from disgruntled employers. After some initial defeats, the CAT was able to claim partial victory with passage of the Trade Union Act in 1871.[29] Unions secured two important checks on judicial power under the act. First, section 2 granted unions immunity from prosecution under the common law doctrine of conspiracy and restraint of trade. Second, section 4 restored protection of union funds by explicitly granting unions the right to register as Friendly Societies, thereby countermanding the courts' ruling in *Hornby v. Close*.[30]

However, the gains established in the Trade Union Act were undermined considerably by passage of the Criminal Law Amendment Act in the same parliamentary session. Initially, both the Trade Union Act and the Criminal Law Amendment Act had been presented as a single bill before the House of Commons. The Parliamentary Committee of the TUC objected strongly to several provisions of the original bill and lobbied extensively

---

[26] Excellent accounts of the 1867–1875 struggle can be found in H. W. McCready, "British Labour's Lobby, 1867–1875," *Canadian Journal of Economics and Political Science* 22, 2 (May 1956): 141–60; H. W. McCready, "British Labour and the Royal Commission on Trade Unions, 1867–1869," *University of Toronto Quarterly* 24, 4 (July 1955): 390–409; H. W. McCready, "The British Election of 1874: Frederic Harrison and the Liberal-Labour Dilemma," *Canadian Journal of Economics and Political Science* 20, 2 (May 1954): 166–75; Cole, *British Working Class Politics*, chap. 5, esp. 55; and Webb and Webb, *History of Trade Unionism*, chap. 5.

For discussions of earlier efforts by labor to secure state protection of workers' industrial rights, see John Victor Orth, "Combination and Conspiracy: The Legal Status of English Trade Unions, 1799–1871" (Ph.D. diss., Harvard University, 1977); John Victor Orth, "The Law of Strikes, 1847–1871," in J. A. Guy and H. G. Beale, eds., *Law and Social Change in British History* (London: Royal Historical Society, 1984); and John Victor Orth, "English Law and Striking Workmen: The Molestation of Workmen Act, 1859," *Journal of Legal History* 2, 3 (December 1981): 238–57.

[27] McCready, "British Labour's Lobby."

[28] Hornby v. Close, 10 Cox C.C. 393 (1867).

[29] Two bills introduced by the CAT in 1867 and 1868 were unsuccessful. See McCready, "British Labour's Lobby," 142, 144. For the union victory, see the Trade Union Act, 35 Vict. c. 31 (1871).

[30] See the Trade Union Act, 35 Vict. c. 31 (1871), secs. 2, 4.

against the dreaded "third clause," which specified a number of actions that remained criminal by codifying existing case law. The committee was unable to kill the third clause, but did manage to split the labor bill in two, thereby isolating the hostile provisions and enabling labor to oppose the third clause without simultaneously jeopardizing the other protections contained in the Trade Union Act. Despite an extensive campaign against the third clause, now the Criminal Law Amendment bill, the bill was passed along with the more favorable Trade Union Act. The Criminal Law Amendment Act, much like the New York and Pennsylvania statutes, specified that the use of "violence, threats, intimidation, molestation or obstruction" during an industrial dispute remained illegal and were still subject to criminal prosecution.[31]

Workers considered passage of the Criminal Law Amendment Act a defeat for the labor movement and immediately set about repealing it through the TUC's Parliamentary Committee.[32] Labor's fears concerning the statute were soon confirmed by a series of court cases in which unionists were convicted of "molestation and obstruction" under the act.[33] The broad provisions of the statute enabled courts to convict workers of conspiracy despite the protection granted unions under the Trade Union Act of the same year. Clearly, further legislation was needed if the right to organize and strike really was to be protected by the state.

In order to repeal the Criminal Law Amendment Act, the Parliamentary Committee embarked on an extensive campaign to lobby sitting members of Parliament. The tactics adopted by the committee were essentially the same as the New York Workingmen's Assembly and included following parliamentary proceedings on a daily basis, sending deputations to the relevant cabinet ministers, endorsing prospective candidates, distributing information on labor issues, and hiring their own legal counsel to draft legislation to be introduced to Parliament by friendly M.P.s.[34] The paral-

[31] Criminal Law Amendment Act, 35 Vict. c. 32 (1871), sec. 1. See also Orth, "Combination and Conspiracy," 243–44.

[32] See Webb and Webb, *History of Trade Unionism*, 280–82; and McCready, "British Labour's Lobby," 146–47.

[33] The major convictions under the Criminal Law Amendment Act were Rex v. Bunn, 12 Cox C.C. 316 (1872); Chipping Norton Cases, 1873, in McCready, "British Labour's Lobby," 152; Rex v. Goodall, 9 Q.B. 557 (1874); and Rex v. Hibbert, 13 Cox C.C. 82 (1875). For a general discussion of the post-1871 legal cases, see R. Y. Hedges and Allan Winterbottom, *The Legal History of Trade Unionism* (London: Longmans, Green, 1930), pt. 2, chap. 4.

[34] Frederic Harrison acted as the committee's legal advisor for a number of years. Henry and Albert Crompten, Professor Beesly, and R. S. Wright also provided the movement with middle-class support and expertise. Inside Parliament, labor usually relied on the assistance of W. V. Hartcourt and Mr. Mundella to introduce their bills. For further discussion of the committee's tactics and allies, see McCready, "British Labour's Lobby," 148–50, 153, 159; and Webb and Webb, *History of Trade Unionism*, 280–91

lels between the English and American strategies are striking; in both countries organized labor tried to secure state protection of workers' industrial rights through legislative politics. As in New York and Pennsylvania, the English campaign was quite successful, and culminated in passage of the Conspiracy and Protection of Property Act in 1875.[35]

The new act repealed the earlier Criminal Law Amendment Act of 1871 and provided workers with more effective immunity from charges of criminal conspiracy. Under the new law, actions committed during trade disputes that were not themselves crimes were exempt from criminal prosecution.[36] However, even the new legislation, which was hailed as a major victory for organized labor, continued to qualify state protection of workers' industrial rights with provisions against the use of violence or intimidation during industrial disputes. Section 7 identified several actions that remained illegal, including the use of violence and intimidation, injury to property, the hiding of tools, and persistently following a person from place to place.[37] Thus, the 1875 statute simultaneously reaffirmed parliamentary protection of workers' rights to organize and strike and further specified the scope of union immunity, while continuing to provide ample grounds for criminal prosecution under section 7. Whether or not the act in fact would establish effective state protection of workers' collective action ultimately depended on subsequent judicial interpretation of section 7.

In 1875, then, the English and American labor movement strategy and legal status were remarkably similar. Workers in both countries had been subject to considerable state opposition for three quarters of a century. Both labor movements had responded to state opposition with the same strategies, in which they pressured state legislatures and Parliament into establishing statutory protection of workers' industrial rights. Moreover, the legislative outcomes of the two labor lobbies were almost identical. Neither country protected workers' industrial rights unconditionally. Both the English and American statutes contained provisions against the use of violence or intimidation in industrial disputes, which were fully exploited by the New York and Pennsylvania courts.[38] The British experience, however, was different. Unlike their American counterparts, English courts did not continue to convict workers of conspiracy after the 1875 statute,

---

[35] Conspiracy and Protection of Property Act 38, 39 Vict. c. 86.

[36] See Conspiracy and Protection of Property Act 38, 39 Vict. c. 86, sec. 3. The gains in the 1875 act can be seen most easily by comparing sec. 3 of the Criminal Law Amendment Act, 1871, with sec. 7 of the 1875 Conspiracy and Protection of Property Act, both of which define the use of violence and intimidation in industrial disputes. The 1871 statute contained many more provisions that made almost any action liable to prosecution. The 1875 act narrowed these provisions considerably, but still left room for future prosecution of striking workers.

[37] See Conspiracy and Protection of Property Act 38, 39 Vict. c. 86, sec. 7.

[38] See Chapter 4 for a discussion of the New York and Pennsylvania cases.

despite the opportunities for convictions provided under section 7. Instead, when English workers were charged with violations of the act, the courts deferred to parliamentary authority and interpreted the provisions against the use of violence and intimidation much more narrowly than their American counterparts.

PARLIAMENTARY STATUTES AND THE COURTS: 1875 TO 1906

Unlike New York and Pennsylvania labor statutes, the Conspiracy and Protection of Property Act was not subjected to judicial interpretation for over a decade. Between 1875 and 1887, no prosecutions were brought under the statute, in large part because unions presented little threat to employers during the "Great Depression."[39] Industrial conflict by no means disappeared, but most strikes in the period ended in major defeats for organized labor. Thus, despite their earlier political gains, unions were generally on the defensive during this particular economic crisis, leaving employers with little reason to test the 1875 statute.[40]

With the emergence of the new unionism in the late 1880s, the balance of power between workers and employers shifted. Union membership in the craft and the new unions increased rapidly, and industrial conflict was soon on the rise as unions adopted a more militant stance by the end of the decade.[41] Employers responded to this new display of union strength by again turning to the courts. Beginning in 1898, a series of conspiracy cases ensued in which workers were charged with violation of the 1875 act.[42]

[39] For the absence of any cases contesting the Conspiracy and Protection of Property Act, see the list of "statutes judicially considered" in the *Law Reports: Digest of Cases* 3: 3572–73. See also Webb and Webb, *History of Trade Unionism*, 596–600; and Pelling, *History of British Trade Unionism*, 110. However, neither the Webbs nor Pelling provide any documentation for their claim.

[40] Cole, *A Short History of the British Working-Class Movement*, pt. 2, chap. 7.

[41] Ibid., chap. 8.

[42] The English cases involving the Conspiracy and Protection of Property Act were as follows: Judge v. Bennett, 52 J.P. 247 (1887); Rex v. McKeevit, Liverpool Assizes (16 December 1890) (unreported), discussed in Hedges and Winterbottom, *Legal History of Trade Unionism*, 122; Gibson v. Lawson, 2 Q.B. 547 (1891); Curran v. Treleaven, 2 Q.B. 553 (1891); Pete v. Apperley, 35 S.J. 792 (1891); Haile v. Lillingstone, 35 S.J. 792 (1891); Rex v. McKenzie, 2 Q.B. 519 (1892); Lyons v. Wilkins, 1 Ch. 255 (1899); Walters v. Green, 2 Ch. 696 (1899); Charnock v. Court, 2 Ch. 35 (1899); Smith v. Moody, Div. Ct., 1 K.B. 56 (1903); Ward, Lock and Co. v. Printers' Assistants Society, 22 T.L.R. 327 (1906).

Interestingly, a number of labor cases involved prosecution of "New Unions" of the 1890s. For example, *Curran v. Treleaven* involved members of three classic, more broadly based New Unions, namely, the National Union of Gas Workers and General Labourers of Great Britain, the Dock Wharf Riverside and General Labourers Union of Great Britain and Ireland, and the Bristol West of England and South Wales Operative Trade and Provident Society. *Haile v. Lillingstone* also involved prosecution of a Shop Assistants' Union, another New Union of the 1880s and 1890s.

Two of the leading cases of this period provide an excellent comparison with the New York and Pennsylvania cases discussed in Chapter 4. Two Queen's Bench cases, decided in 1891, *Curran v. Treleaven* and *Gibson v. Lawson*, like their American counterparts, hinged on the question of how the courts should interpret the provisions against the use of "intimidation" contained in section 7 of the Conspiracy and Protection of Property Act.[43] Thus, late-nineteenth-century labor cases in both England and the United States called into question the earlier political victories of organized labor. Not only were pro-labor statutes litigated in both countries, but the disputes rested on competing interpretations of the very same word, namely, how to define acts of "intimidation" during industrial conflicts.

In *Curran v. Treleaven*, the Court of Queen's Bench was faced with the question of whether or not "injury to trade" qualified as "intimidation" under the Conspiracy and Protection of Property Act.[44] Pete Curran, secretary of the National Union of Gas Workers and General Labourers of Great Britain, had been convicted by the court of petty sessions for "wrongfully and without legal authority intimidating" a Plymouth coal merchant named George Treleaven. The dispute centered on the use of nonunion labor to unload one of Treleaven's coal ships, the *Ocean Queen*. Union workers threatened to strike if Treleaven continued to hire nonunion workers. Treleaven responded by charging the union workers with conspiracy on the grounds that during the dispute he had feared "injury to his business and consequently loss to himself." A strike to benefit workers, the prosecution argued, might have been legal, but a strike to injure the employer's business was an act of intimidation and as such was a criminal offense under section 7 of the 1875 statute.[45]

The court, however, disagreed with the prosecution's interpretation of the statute, and instead adopted a more limited definition of intimidation. Unlike the American courts, the Queen's Bench accepted a much wider range of industrial action as legitimate behavior, exempt from charges of criminal conspiracy. The chief justice delivered the opinion, denying that "injury to trade" was tantamount to intimidation, saying, "Where the object [of a strike] is to benefit oneself, it can seldom, perhaps it can never, be effected without some consequent loss or injury to someone else. In trade, in commerce, even in a profession, what is one man's gain is another's loss: and where the object is not malicious, the mere fact that the

---

[43] Compare these two English acquittals, Curran v. Treleaven, and Gibson v. Lawson, with the following American convictions: People v. Wilzig, Xingo Parks and John Siney Trial, and the D. R. Jones Trial.

[44] Curran v. Treleaven, 563.

[45] Curran v. Treleaven, 554–56.

effect is injurious does not make the agreement either illegal or actionable, and, therefore, is not indictable."[46] The Queen's Bench reversed the lower court conviction and acquitted the workers, thereby reaffirming the earlier statutory protection of workers' industrial rights.

The more restrained approach of the English courts when interpreting the labor statutes can be seen even more clearly in a second case that came before the Queen's Bench in the same term. In *Gibson v. Lawson*, the court again faced the issue of whether or not a particular strike action constituted a violation of section 7 of the Conspiracy and Protection of Property Act.[47] In delivering the opinion, the chief justice explicitly deferred to parliamentary policy on the issue, and advocated a very limited role for judicial interpretation of statute law. The case is worth discussing at length because it contrasts so clearly with the role of the New York and Pennsylvania courts during this period.

The *Lawson* dispute emerged among fitters at the Palmer shipbuilding company in Northumberland. The Amalgamated Society of Engineers protested the company's employment of Gibson, who belonged to a rival union, the National Society of Engineers. Members of the Amalgamated Society threatened to strike unless Gibson joined their union; Gibson refused and was dismissed by the company in order to avoid a strike. Gibson charged Lawson, a "shop delegate" of the Amalgated Society, with violating section 7 of the 1875 statute for having intimidated the company to terminate his employment. After failing to secure a conviction before the Northumberland magistrates, Gibson appealed to the Court of Queen's Bench. The appeal, too, was unsuccessful; the Queen's Bench affirmed the lower court decision and found the defendant not guilty of wrongful intimidation.[48]

The judgment of the court, read by Chief Justice Lord Coleridge, clearly reflected the more limited authority of the English courts. At one point in the opinion, Lord Coleridge noted that denying the appeal might appear to conflict with earlier convictions under the common law, especially the cases of *Rex v. Druitt* and *Rex v. Bunn*. The chief justice dismissed the apparent conflict, saying:

> The cases of *Reg. v. Druitt* and *Reg. v. Bunn* . . . are both said to have held that the statutes on the subject have in no way interfered with or altered the common

---

[46] Curran v. Treleaven, 563. Interestingly, similar arguments about economic competition were not made in the United States until 1896, and even then only as a dissenting opinion in a case decided to the contrary. See Justice Holmes's dissent in Vegelahn v. Guntner, 167 Mass. 92 (Mass. 1896).

[47] Gibson v. Lawson.

[48] Gibson v. Lawson, 547–48.

law, and that strikes and combination expressly legalized by statute may yet be treated as indictable conspiracies at common law, and may be punished by imprisonment with hard labour. . . . We are well aware of the great authority of the judges by whom the above cases were decided, but we are unable to concur in these dicta, and, speaking with all deference, we think they are not law.[49]

Thus, the Queen's Bench rather dramatically repudiated past case law in order to comply with the recent parliamentary statutes. Moreover, Lord Coleridge explicitly acknowledged the supremacy of Parliament in his concluding remarks in the *Lawson* judgment: "It seems to us that the law concerning combinations in reference to trade disputes is contained in 38 and 39 Vict. c 86, and in the statutes referred to in it, and that acts which are not indictable under that statute are not now, if, indeed, they ever were, indictable at common law."[50] The Queen's Bench, then, clearly reaffirmed the supremacy of Parliament for determining what was to be government policy toward labor. At least in *Lawson*, the court was willing to break with past case law in order to comply with new policies established in contemporary labor statutes.

In contrast to the New York and Pennsylvania workers, the English labor movement's struggle for state recognition was a more complete success. Not only did workers secure pro-labor legislation through their intensive lobbying campaign, but these statutes were better able to protect workers from future conspiracy prosecutions. This more effective campaign for state protection, however, was not simply the product of more carefully drafted legislation, as both the American and English statutes contained similar "intimidation" provisions that could have been used by employers and the courts to secure subsequent prosecutions. Nor can the different judicial interpretations be traced to different legal doctrines, as courts in both countries based their decisions on the same common law doctrine of criminal conspiracy and, much of the time, even relied on the very same precedents.

In short, remarkably similar statutes and legal doctrines sustained very different judicial decisions in the American and English courts. The different interpretations cannot be attributed to formal provisions of judicial authority or legal doctrine. Instead, the differences are more readily accounted for as the institutional legacies of past political struggles and social compromises. The more limited role of English courts in regulating industrial conflict was shaped in large part by the effective division of political power between the courts and Parliament negotiated at the end of

[49] Gibson v. Lawson, 560.
[50] Gibson v. Lawson, 560.

the seventeenth century. By deferring to the nineteenth-century labor statutes, the English courts were adhering to a long-standing tradition of parliamentary supremacy of which labor was now the beneficiary.[51]

Whatever the origins of the different judicial behavior, there is no doubt that the English and American courts indeed decided late-nineteenth-century labor cases very differently. In England, the courts were quite willing to interpret the statutory provision against intimidation narrowly, leaving unions much greater latitude during industrial disputes. American courts, on the other hand, paid little or no heed to the statutes and went to considerable lengths to convict workers of conspiracy on the basis of the most innocuous tactics used during industrial disputes.[52]

The contrasting behavior of the courts in the English and American political systems, moreover, provided very different rewards for working-class political action and ultimately was responsible for the divergent development of the two labor movements at the end of the nineteenth century. Put simply, in England, where the courts were less powerful and generally allowed Parliament to establish state policy toward labor, working-class political organization was systematically rewarded. The legislative victories of the English labor movement produced significant changes in government regulation of working-class organization. In contrast, equivalent legislative successes in New York and Pennsylvania provided very little leverage over government policy, which continued to be dominated by the judiciary with little or no regard for statute law. The inability of New York and Pennsylvania legislatures to check the power of the courts left American workers disillusioned with the prospects of even successful political mobilization. The divergent patterns of labor movement development after 1890, then, can be traced to the very different roles played by the courts during workers' struggle for state protection of industrial rights in the closing decades of the nineteenth century. After almost a century of parallel development, the English and American labor movements began to adopt quite different strategies, largely in response to the pattern of frustrations and rewards that flowed from the political systems within which they organized.[53]

---

[51] For a discussion of the seventeenth-century social compromise, see Christopher Hill, *The Century of Revolution, 1603–1714* (New York: Norton, 1961); and Mauro Cappelletti, *Judicial Review in the Contemporary World* (New York: Bobbs-Merrill, 1971), esp. chaps. 1, 2.

[52] For a discussion of the American cases, see the preceding chapter. Especially note People v. Wilzig, People v. Kostka, Xingo Parks and John Siney Trial, and the D. R. Jones Trial.

[53] For an excellent discussion of English labor's successful struggle with the courts and their subsequent commitment to political reform, see William E. Forbath, "Courts, Constitutions, and Labor Politics in England and America: A Study of the Constitutive Power of Law," *Law and Social Inquiry* 16, 1 (Winter 1991): 1–34.

If the supremacy of Parliament indeed was the crucial factor in shaping labor movement strategy in England, then one final issue must be addressed, namely, how to account for the resurgence of judicial hostility toward labor at the turn of the century. Did the revival of judicial hostility undermine past labor victories? Had the balance of power between the courts and Parliament changed? In short, why, after affirming the Conspiracy and Protection of Property Act so firmly in the 1890s, did the courts hand down a series of antilabor decisions in the first decades of the twentieth century?

TAFF VALE AND CIVIL LIABILITIES

Even though the courts had deferred to Parliament when interpreting the Conspiracy and Protection of Property Act, the struggle over state protection of workers' industrial rights was by no means entirely resolved by the turn of the century. In the first two decades of the twentieth century, unions were confronted with new attacks on their legal status, prompting further legislation to protect organized labor from these new legal challenges. In fact, the most infamous antilabor cases were yet to come; *Quinn v. Leathem, Taff Vale,* and the *Osborne* judgment were handed down by the courts in 1901 and 1909, well after the legislative victories of 1871 and 1875.[54] These later cases, however, did not represent a change in judicial interpretation of the existing labor statutes, but rather reflected changes in other areas of common law doctrine that opened up entirely new legal issues that had not been covered by earlier legislation. All of these later convictions were brought as civil rather than criminal prosecutions and thus required additional parliamentary protection. The Conspiracy and Protection of Property Act had succeeded in protecting unions from *criminal* prosecution but had not been designed for and was not capable of protecting workers from claims for *civil* liabilities.

The renewed attack on organized labor in the first two decades of the twentieth century was made possible both by developments in English corporation law during the 1890s and by the particular form of legislative protection provided by the English state. Prior to 1901, labor unions generally had been considered immune from prosecution for damages inflicted during industrial disputes owing to their noncorporate status. Corporate officers had been protected from damage suits through the doctrine of limited liability, which restricted damage claims to company property. Unions, fearing suits against their organization funds, had chosen to re-

---

[54] Quinn v. Leathem, A.C. 495 (1901); Taff Vale Railway Co. v. Amalgamated Society of Railway Servants, A.C. 426 (1901); Osborne v. Amalgamated Society of Railway Servants, A.C. 87 (1910). The *Osborne* judgment was handed down in December of 1909, but it was not published as an official case report until 1910.

main unincorporated, thereby foregoing the "privilege" of limited liability but also protecting unions from civil liability claims.[55]

During the 1890s, however, English company law changed. In a series of nonlabor cases, the courts began to allow "representative actions" to be brought against unincorporated companies. This evolution of legal doctrine enabled the growing number of unincorporated companies to be held legally accountable by allowing individual defendants to be considered representatives of their organizations. In 1893, an enterprising attorney tried to bring a representative action against a number of building trade unions in Hull. The Divisional Court, however, denied the action, and ruled that the defendants could be sued only as individuals and not as representatives of their unions.[56] Although unsuccessful, the *Temperton v. Russell* case in many respects laid the legal groundwork for the historic *Taff Vale* decision of 1901.[57]

The Taff Vale Railway Company successfully sued the Amalgamated Society of Railway Servants precisely because the Law Lords overruled the *Temperton* decision and held that, although not a corporate body, the union itself could be sued just as many *non*labor organizations had been in the previous decade.[58] The court ruled in favor of Taff Vale and ordered the union to pay damages of £23,000 plus expenses, reaching a total of £42,000.[59] The decision was a major defeat for organized labor. The setback, however, was short-lived; within five years Parliament passed the Trades Disputes Act, which established union immunity to civil liabilities as well as criminal conspiracies. Thus, the new vulnerability was quickly foreclosed through further labor lobbying and renewed statutory protection of workers' industrial rights.[60] Again, as in 1875, the Trades Disputes Act was quite effective in protecting union funds from subsequent civil liability suits, thereby reaffirming the benefits of political action.

Changes in corporation law, however, were only partially responsible for the renewed prosecution of English unions. The particular form of legislative protection granted to English labor under the Conspiracy and Protec-

---

[55] Webb and Webb, *History of Trade Unionism*, 595–96.

[56] For discussion of representative actions, see R. Brown, "The Temperton v. Russell Case (1893): The Beginning of the Legal Offensive Against the Unions," *Bulletin of Economic Research* 23, 1 (May 1971): 55–56, 58–59; and Webb and Webb, *History of Trade Unionism*, 601–2, note 1.

[57] Brown, "The Temperton v. Russell Case," 66.

[58] Webb and Webb, *History of Trade Unionism*, 601–2. Law Lords are members of the House of Lords who act as the court of last resort. One may become a Law Lord either by appointment or on the basis of previous legal experience.

[59] Ibid., 601.

[60] Trades Disputes Act, 6 Ed. 7 c. 47, closed the loophole. For a discussion of the act, see Hedges and Winterbottom, *Legal History of Trade Unionism*, pt. 2, chaps. 4, 5.

tion of Property Act also contributed to the pattern of successive waves of statutory protection and judicial prosecution. Although clearly extending state protection to workers in the late nineteenth century, Parliament stopped short of enacting general rights for English workers. Instead, a more limited approach was used in which workers' industrial rights were protected against *specific* kinds of legal prosecution.[61] This form of state recognition has been characterized by Lord Wedderburn and others as a "negative" rather than "positive" definition of workers' rights, in that unions were provided with a series of "immunities" from particular legal doctrines rather than being granted a less qualified right to organize and strike.[62] Thus, the legislative victories of 1871, 1875, and 1905 established distinct exemptions for labor from particular common law doctrines, rather than enacting more wide-ranging industrial rights. Although the Conspiracy and Protection of Property and the Trades Disputes Acts were quite effective in shielding unions from criminal and civil liabilities, the negative definition of workers' rights always left unions vulnerable to new or unanticipated legal actions.[63]

The emergence of representative actions in company law is a perfect example of the way in which the English statutes exposed unions to new prosecution strategies. With each legal innovation, labor had to return to Parliament in order to specify further the precise terms of state protection. Thus, although both English and American labor regulation oscillated between periods of judicial hostility and statutory protection, the origins and impact of the pattern of state regulation was quite different in the two nations. In England, once statutory protection was enacted, the courts deferred to parliamentary authority and honored the particular immunities prescribed by the successive pieces of labor legislation. The alternation between legislative protection and judicial prosecution did not stem from Parliament's inability to check the power of the English courts. Rather, Parliament was quite effective at limiting judicial interpretation, but only on the particular issues covered by the statute. In America, by contrast, state legislatures had little or no success in redirecting judicial regulation of working-class organization and protest. Both the New York and Pennsylvania courts simply overrode the successive statutory protections and continued to convict workers of conspiracy on much the same grounds throughout the nineteenth century. Thus the successive waves of

[61] This argument draws largely on the work of Lord Wedderburn. For example, see Lord Wedderburn, "Industrial Relations and the Courts," *Industrial Law Journal* 9, 2 (June 1980): 65–94.

[62] See ibid.; Roy Lewis, "The Historical Development of Labor Law," *British Journal of Industrial Relations* 14, 1 (1976): 1–17; and Brown, "The Temperton v. Russell Case."

[63] Wedderburn, "Industrial Relations and the Courts," 77.

legislative protection and judicial prosecution in the United States reflected a different balance of power between the courts and legislature than existed in England.

Finally, the *Osborne* judgment of 1909 again underscores the limited protection provided by the English labor statutes, which led to repeated struggles to specify the extent of state protection of workers' collective action. In December 1909, the Law Lords, acting as the ultimate court of appeal, upheld an injunction against the Amalgamated Society of Railway Servants restraining them from using union funds for political purposes. Political contributions were illegal, the Law Lords claimed, precisely because political action had not been specified as a legitimate union activity in the labor legislation of 1875.[64] The *Osborne* judgment thus established that labor statutes not only had to identify particular union immunities, but were expected to specify the range of legitimate union activity as well.

Trade unions and the Labour party immediately set about repealing the judgment through additional parliamentary legislation. Initially, the Liberal party showed little interest in passing a new trade union bill; no doubt they were in no hurry to remedy the Labour party's financial difficulties created by the *Osborne* decision.[65] In 1913, the unions accepted a limited reform bill that nevertheless eliminated the most damaging features of *Osborne*, but also contained a number of restrictions on union activity. The 1913 Trade Union Act restored labor's right to political action under the following conditions: first, unions must conduct a ballot to ensure rank-and-file approval for the union's political activities; second, should a majority approve, the act required that a political fund be established to separate political and regular union finances; third, the act permitted individual union members to "contract out" of the political dues without jeopardizing their union membership.[66]

Organized labor was disappointed with the act and objected to unions' being subject to special requirements not imposed on other organizations. Nevertheless, as with past labor legislation, the act succeeded in protecting unions from further prosecution under the *Osborne* precedent. After 1913, union funds could again be used for political purposes and few workers contracted out of the political levy.[67] If anything, *Osborne* reinforced labor's distrust of the courts and reaffirmed the importance of maintaining an effective voice in national politics.

[64] For discussion of the *Osborne* judgment, see Webb and Webb, *History of Trade Unionism*, chap. 10; and Cole, *A Short History of the British Working-Class Movement*, chap. 3.

[65] Cole, *A Short History of the British Working-Class Movement*, 313–14.

[66] Ibid., 314.

[67] Webb and Webb, *History of Trade Unionism*, 686–87.

Conclusion: The United States in Comparative Perspective

The history of judicial regulation of working-class organization in England provides an excellent counterpoint to the American case. Two key lessons from American labor movement development, in particular, are confirmed by the English comparison. First, the pattern of state regulation, as in the United States, provided a particular set of incentives and constraints that in turn shaped labor strategy. The supremacy of Parliament over the judiciary provided a more favorable environment for working-class political mobilization, in that labor unions and political parties were able to deliver significant benefits to their members through political reform. In the 1860s and 1870s, for example, the CAT and the TUC's Parliamentary Committee were able to secure state protection of workers' industrial rights, and to check the power of the courts in regulating industrial conflict in England. Unlike their New York and Pennsylvania counterparts, then, English workers experienced the rewards of political organization as electoral victories were repeatedly transformed into concrete change in government labor policy.

Second, while reaffirming the importance of the specific institutional form of state regulation of industrial conflict, the English case highlights the importance of considering the courts as institutions, broadly conceived. Differences in judicial behavior in England and the United States cannot be accounted for by the formal provisions of judicial authority alone. Despite legislative and doctrinal similarities, English and American courts played quite different roles in regulating labor in the last quarter of the nineteenth century. The more limited role of English courts in establishing government labor policy was, in large part, a legacy of past historical struggles that created quite different expectations or norms concerning the appropriate division of political power among the different branches of government. As with American workers' changing perceptions of judicial intervention in industrial disputes, explored in Chapters 3 and 4, a satisfactory account of judicial regulation not only must attend to legal doctrine and formal provisions of institutional authority, but also must be sensitive to the broader social and historical context within which legal judgments are made.[68]

---

[68] For a fascinating discussion of the changing role of the courts and legal doctrine in different historical contexts, see Franz Leopold Neumann, "The Change in the Function of Law in Modern Society," in his *The Democratic and the Authoritarian State: Essays in Political and Legal Theory* (New York: The Free Press, 1957).

CHAPTER SIX

Conclusion: Ideas, Interests, and the Concept of Class

VOLUNTARISM, I have argued, was the AFL's strategic response to the unusual configuration of state power in the United States. The separation of powers and the dominance of the courts within the divided state made political action less rewarding for American workers than it was for their counterparts across the Atlantic. When faced repeatedly with an obstructionist court from 1865 through 1895, the AFL eventually devised other means of advancing workers' interests at the turn of the century. However, how the AFL came to this strategic calculation was no simple story. Workers' relation to the state was not invariant, nor did it simply reflect the underlying process of industrialization. Instead, by comparing state-labor relations over time and across organizations, I have shown that workers' relation to the state was mediated by different ideologies and acts of interpretation. Where class boundaries were drawn, which interests were pursued, and ultimately how workers related to the American legal system depended, to a considerable extent, on the different narratives labor leaders constructed of industrialization.

The nature of work and production certainly changed dramatically during the nineteenth century, but how these changes were understood, what implications they had for class relations, was not at all clear. Different labor leaders tried to mobilize the rank and file by constructing distinct narratives of industrialization that provided workers with a framework for understanding the economic changes under way and enabled them to identify their position and interests in the new economic order. Each narrative, moreover, entailed quite different social divisions and political alliances and spawned very different programs of political reform. Only by historicizing the concept of class and attending more closely to these acts of interpretation can we begin to understand the particular pattern of working-class formation in the United States.

Two quite different conceptions of class prevailed in the nineteenth century, distinguished, in large part, by their different visions of economic change. The producers' alliance held sway in the antebellum decades, while the wage earners' concept of class came to dominate in the last two decades of the nineteenth century. The producers' vision was articulated clearly by the Working Men's parties and General Trades' Unions (GTUs) in the 1820s and 1830s and by the National Labor Union (NLU) and Knights of Labor (KOL) from the late 1860s through the early 1880s. Each of these organizations considered the particular path of economic development to have been politically created and to be in need of political reform. If republican precepts were to be secured, the producers argued, the government had to ensure that economic change continued in a decentralized way. By dispersing economic and political power throughout the nation the problems of tyranny and corruption could be averted and independence and civic participation ensured. The long-standing producers' alliance between skilled workers and small manufacturers did not have to be torn apart as long as a series of antimonopoly policies were implemented to prevent large industrialists from compromising the future pattern of economic growth.

After the Civil War, many labor leaders began to question the producers' assumptions and to construct an alternative interpretation of industrialization. The dissenting unionists within the NLU and a majority of delegates in the New York Workingmen's Assembly, the Federation of Organized Trades and Labor Unions (FOTLU), and the American Federation of Labor (AFL) claimed that the old-line producers did not understand the economic changes under way and as a result were not protecting workers' interests with their calls for antimonopoly reform. Instead, leaders of these organizations argued that workers had to accept their lot as wage earners and break with the producers' alliance. Middle-class reformers had to be excluded from labor associations and class boundaries redrawn. Securing state protection of the right to organize and strike became the battle cry of these organizations as they tried to establish labor unions on an equal footing with the business corporation. In addition, dissenting unions looked to the government to improve their hours, wages, and working conditions through passage of a wide range of labor laws. In many ways, the twin commitments of the New York Workingmen's Assembly, the FOTLU, and the early AFL to collective action and political reform had all of the hallmarks of a social democratic alternative in the United States. State intervention was viewed by each of these organizations as the best means of strengthening labor's hand in the class struggle. Had their commitment to political reform paid off, they might well have increased the amount of energy and resources they devoted to political action. As yet the voluntarist mistrust of politics had not set in; voluntarism would not become the AFL's principal strategy until the early decades of the twentieth century.

Although two distinct conceptions of class can be identified in the nineteenth century, the boundaries between the two were not always sharply drawn. During the transition decades, from the late 1830s through the late 1880s, both conceptions of class can be found within the labor movement, and at times even within the same organization, as labor leaders vied for the hearts and minds of the rank and file. Even in these middle decades, however, specific markers can be identified to trace the rise and fall of different conceptions of class. Membership figures, platform debates, leadership battles, and organization maintenance all can be used to identify the dominant and dissenting positions at any one time.

Changing conceptions of class, we have seen, had important consequences for workers' relation to the state. The collectivist assumptions that undergirded the wage earners' narrative of industrialization soon brought this wing of the labor movement into a head-on struggle with the courts. Collective action had long been considered a dangerous activity that required special regulation by the state, which in labor's case was handled through the courts. After a thirty-year campaign to secure state protection of the right to organize and strike, workers found that they had made very little headway in changing government labor policy or in checking the courts' power. Having tried and failed to use political channels for their own ends, the AFL set about developing an alternative strategy for protecting and promoting the interests of their members beyond the bounds of the state. Voluntarism was a carefully crafted strategy that enabled the AFL to avoid the pitfalls of political reform largely by avoiding the state and negotiating and protesting directly with their employers.

Viewing the process of working-class formation as a product of the intersection of changing conceptions of class and the surrounding political institutions raises questions about the causal status of these ideological and cultural factors. Why did different conceptions of class prevail at any one time? How and why did the concepts of class change? To what extent were these factors themselves the product of changing economic conditions? Put bluntly, we need to identify the causal relations at work.

If one restricts the field of analysis to comparisons over time, it is difficult to untangle the causal sequencing, as changes in the conception of class occurred in parallel with industrialization. Fortunately, contrasting the response of different labor organizations to the same conspiracy trials brings the role of ideology and culture into sharper relief. When faced with the same levels of judicial obstruction and heavy penalties, the KOL and New York Workingmen's Assembly responded quite differently to the postbellum trials. The Workingmen's Assembly set about repealing the conspiracy law, while the KOL called for more effective implementation of conspiracy to business combinations. Economic changes alone cannot account easily for this variation, as both organizations were responding to the same economic conditions and judicial regulation. Instead, we have seen that how workers responded to judicial obstruction, what meaning they assigned to the postbellum conspiracy trials, was shaped by the pre-vailing assumptions and ideology within each of the organizations.[1]

Finally, historicizing the concept of class by attending to the transition from producer to worker underscores the importance of dispensing with hard-and-fast divisions between subjective and objective definitions of class. These categories of analysis, I have found, cannot be sustained and frequently have distorted promising lines of research.[2] A more fruitful approach accepts that different conceptions of class were at once a product of both the changing economic conditions and the interpretative frames individuals and organizations brought to these changes. As a consequence, we have seen that no one set of social divisions and political alliances followed naturally or unambiguously from the changes in production. Rather, there was considerable disagreement and political struggle over what these changes meant for American workers, over how workers' inter-ests could best be served, and even over what their interests were in these times of change. Ideas and interests simply cannot be cleanly untangled in order to provide a comforting bedrock on which to ground the analysis. Each was necessarily implicated in the construction of the other. The actual experience of industrialization and working-class formation was inevitably mediated by language, ideology, and culture. Acknowledging the mutually constitutive role of ideas and interests does not require that questions of causation and explanation be set aside. All that is implied is that a non-foundational view of language, ideology, and interests be used. How these factors are configured at any particular historical moment is of great conse-quence, but how these particular linguistic categories and cultural tradi-tions were established cannot be deduced from a priori principles. They were themselves the product of an ongoing political struggle that needs to be researched and explained.[3]

[1] For comparison of the New York Workingmen's Assembly and KOL response to the postbellum conspiracy trials, see Chapter 4.

[2] For a classic example of a narrow definition of class distorting the analysis, see Montgomery, *Beyond Equality*. At one point in chap. 5, Montgomery asks, "Did labor leaders who tasted of political success 'desert their class'?" He notes that the answer is complicated by the role of middle-class reformers in the labor movement of the period. He then goes on to assert that these middle-class reformers have been "excluded from the present sample, despite the prominent role they played in the community of workers' leaders, solely because they did not belong economically to the working classes" (216). Montgomery's presumption that the relevant social cleavages will mirror economic relations, I believe, leads him to misinterpret class relations in the 1860s and 1870s. Montgomery overdraws the sense of working-class cohesion and minimizes the producers' alliance precisely because he ar-bitrarily excludes half of the relevant actors from the field of research. If we construct our categories of analysis from the language and practices of the participants themselves, we can avoid many of these difficulties.

[3] For similar arguments along these lines, see two very interesting articles: Sewell, "Re-thinking Labor History," which convincingly deconstructs the division between the ideal and

Looking back from the twentieth century, it is easy to dismiss those who lost the political struggle as utopian reformers who were doomed to fail. However, if we can recover the uncertainty of the moment, and the sense of confusion that prevailed, we will be able to take seriously the alternative narratives of industrialization. Whether or not we, too, believe that alternative paths of economic development actually were possible in the nineteenth century is not the issue. There is little doubt that many participants considered this to be so and acted on the basis of their convictions. If we dismiss these alternative views as illegitimate or unfounded, we will have considerable trouble understanding the social divisions and political alliances that prevailed. If, on the other hand, we accept a range of interpretations of industrialization as equally valid, we can recapture the changing conceptions of class. Doing so, in turn, provides the key to the varied, but nevertheless decisive, role of the state in shaping working-class formation in the United States.

Toward a New Political History

In the last two decades, both the new labor and new social history have reinvigorated studies of American politics. Where the old labor and traditional political history defined their subjects narrowly, focusing on elites and formal institutions, the new research expanded the "political" to include a much wider range of behavior. First, new labor and social historians no longer restricted their studies to those in positions of power, but began to explore history from the "bottom up." By examining the social practices of ordinary men and women these scholars have been able to reshape our view of the past. Second, the new research also looked beyond the boundaries of formal institutions to consider the social practices of everyday life. Politics, from this perspective, is not limited to official organizations, platforms, and proceedings, but is seen to pervade all realms of experience. By uncovering the power relations embedded in dime novels, picnics, and parks, these scholars have shown that the personal was indeed political and that almost any social experience could be fruitfully analyzed to reveal the underlying class relations and social norms of a particular place and time.[4]

---

the material and argues that labor history would profit from a "post-materialist rhetoric"; and Joan Scott, "The Evidence of Experience," *Critical Inquiry* 17, 4 (Summer 1991): 773–97, in which Scott disavows experience as a means of grounding historical analysis and argues instead for the need to "historicize experience." Thus, according to Scott, the categories through which we construct experience and the identities that it produces need to be explained rather than assumed. A "genuinely non-foundational history," Scott concludes, "retains its explanatory power and its interest in change but does not stand on or reproduce naturalized categories" (12).

[4] For examples of the new labor and social history, see the following: Dawley, *Class and Community*; Laurie, *Working People of Philadelphia*; Faler, *Mechanics and Manufacturers*;

These studies of picnics, parks, and popular culture have convincingly challenged much of the conventional wisdom from the old labor and political history. We can no longer assume that American workers complacently accepted or actively embraced industrialization, as the new research has identified an indigenous radical tradition in the United States in which the dispossessed tried to maintain their dignity and social status by resisting those in power. This resistance was not restricted to politics, narrowly construed, but has been found in all areas of men and women's lives, including their social clubs and recreational activities as well as the popular culture they created and consumed.

Although much has been gained from this expansion of politics, something also has been lost. While most of these studies have self-consciously chosen to ignore traditional forms of political power and state action, this turn away from formal politics, not surprisingly, has led many scholars to underestimate the influence of the state. The story of working-class formation told here, while by no means simply determined by state structure and policy, could not have been told without attending to the legislative protection of working-class organization and the judicial interpretation of these industrial rights. What was possible politically was to a considerable extent set by traditional political institutions, namely, state legislatures and the courts. When these factors are overlooked, it is difficult to discern the underlying logic to the particular form of working-class protest in the United States. I am not the first to lament the absence of formal politics in the new labor and social history; several scholars have made similar criticisms in recent years.[5] These issues, however, show few signs of abating;

Mary Ryan, *Cradle of the Middle Class: The Family in Oneida County, New York, 1790–1865* (New York: Cambridge University Press, 1981); Christine Stansell, *City of Women: Sex and Class in New York, 1789–1860* (Urbana: University of Illinois Press, 1982); Salvatore, *Eugene V. Debs*; Roy Rosenzweig, *Eight Hours for What We Will: Workers and Leisure in an Industrial City, 1870–1920* (New York: Cambridge University Press, 1983); Mari Jo Buhle, *Women and American Socialism, 1870–1920* (Urbana: University of Illinois Press, 1983); Michael H. Frisch and Daniel J. Walkowitz, eds., *Working Class America: Essays on Labor, Community, and American Society* (Urbana: University of Illinois Press, 1983); Fink, *Workingmen's Democracy*; Hahn, *The Roots of Southern Populism*; Wilentz, *Chants Democratic*; Francis G. Couvares, *The Remaking of Pittsburgh: Class and Culture in an Industrializing City, 1877–1919* (Albany: State University of New York Press, 1984); Carroll Smith-Rosenberg, *Disorderly Conduct: Visions of Gender in Victorian America* (New York: Knopf, 1985); Ross, *Workers on the Edge*; Brian Greenberg, *Worker and Community: Response to Industrialization in a Nineteenth-Century American City, Albany, New York, 1850–1884* (Albany: State University of New York Press, 1985); Oestreicher, *Solidarity and Fragmentation*; Kathy Peiss, *Cheap Amusements: Working Women and Leisure in Turn-of-the-Century New York* (Philadelphia: Temple University Press, 1986); Michael Denning, *Mechanic Accents: Dime Novels and Working-Class Culture in America* (New York: Verso, 1987).

[5] For criticisms of the absence of the conception of politics in social history, see Elizabeth Fox-Genovese and Eugene D. Genovese, "The Political Crisis of Social History: A Marxian Perspective," *Journal of Social History* 10, 2 (Winter 1976): 205–20; Tony Judt, "A Clown in

one of the new frontiers of historical research in the area of cultural history raises all the same questions with even more force. While the expansion of substance and method continue apace, this new work pays even less attention to questions of politics narrowly conceived than did labor and social historians before them.[6]

It is time to move beyond these criticisms and formulate a new research agenda that draws on the insights and methods of the new labor, social, and cultural history for studies of more traditional areas of political research. Political elites and institutions can no longer be considered the only, or even the primary, domain of politics. Instead, a conscious effort must be made to resituate studies of formal politics in their larger social and cultural context so as to attend to the multiple dimensions of political power. Reintegrating different levels of political analysis is no easy task and cannot be achieved simply by adding more variables to our studies. Instead, we need to attend to the constitutive role of ideology, language, and culture if we are to incorporate a broader sense of politics into our work. Finally, competing interpretations within a single cultural tradition also must be examined and can often be captured through the different narratives that individuals and organizations constructed of their world. Placing questions of interpretation at the center of the analysis will inevitably bring a host of epistemological issues to the fore. However, making the interpretative turn and engaging this debate will, I believe, provide a new and exciting framework for political research.

Electoral and Party Politics Reconsidered

Although by no means the only fruitful line of research, rethinking nineteenth-century electoral and party politics provides a useful example of how conventional political institutions might be reexamined in light of

---

Regal Purple: Social History and the Historians," *History Workshop* 7 (Spring 1979): 66–94; James A. Henretta, "Social History as Lived and Written," *American Historical Review* 84, 5 (December 1979): 1293–1322; Geoff Eley and Keith Nield, "Why Does Social History Ignore Politics?" *Social History* 5, 2 (May 1980): 249–71. There are, of course, some important exceptions to the general aversion to formal politics, most notably Foner, *Free Soil, Free Labor, Free Men*; Hahn, *The Roots of Southern Populism*; and Salvatore, *Eugene V. Debs*.

[6] For a useful introduction to the new cultural history, see Lynn Hunt, ed., *The New Cultural History* (Berkeley: University of California Press, 1989). I should add that there is nothing in the methods of these cultural historians that precludes examination of formal politics; rather, this simply does not seem to be where the field is heading. For two important exceptions that do examine politics directly, see Lynn Hunt, *Politics, Culture, and Class in the French Revolution* (Berkeley: University of California Press, 1984); and William H. Sewell, Jr., "A Rhetoric of Amnesia, or How the French Revolution Came to Abolish Privilege and Establish Legal Equality" (Macrosociology Area Program, UCLA).

the linguistic categories and cultural narratives within which they operate. For almost eighty years, scholars have debated the relationship between social class and electoral politics in the United States.[7] While two sides of the debate have reached very different conclusions, they nevertheless share many assumptions and generally have operationalized the concept of class in much the same way. Wealth, income, and occupation usually have been taken as surrogate indicators of class and have been examined to see if affluence correlated with support for the Whig or Republican parties while the poorer constituents supported the Democratic party. The results of this research have been mixed. Many careful studies have found repeatedly that there was little or no correlation between class and party politics during the nineteenth century. Partisan affiliation, these scholars claim, is more effectively distinguished by ethnocultural factors than by socioeconomic characteristics.[8] Yet class-based interpretations of particular periods and administrations persist and seem to capture something that the ethnocultural accounts miss.[9] But these analyses have not stood up well to closer scrutiny; economic status and voter preferences simply have not lined up as neatly as a class analysis would predict. Thus, the debate has continued between proponents of class-based interpretations and their critics for almost eighty years.[10]

Documenting fully the social basis of partisanship in light of the producers' alliance is beyond the bounds of this project. Nevertheless, the

[7] The debate over class and American politics was raised in 1913 by Charles Beard in his famous interpretation of the Constitution. See Charles Beard, *An Economic Interpretation of the Constitution of the United States* (New York: The Free Press, 1913).

[8] For the classic ethnocultural interpretation of antebellum politics, see Benson, *The Concept of Jacksonian Democracy*. These arguments have been refined and extended by several scholars. For example, see Michael F. Holt, *Forging a Majority: The Formation of the Republican Party in Pittsburgh, 1848–1860* (New Haven: Yale University Press, 1969); Ronald P. Formisano, *The Birth of Mass Political Parties: Michigan, 1827–1861* (Princeton: Princeton University Press, 1971); Kleppner, *The Cross of Culture*; and Richard Jensen, *The Winning of the Midwest: Social and Political Conflict, 1888–1896* (Chicago: University of Chicago Press, 1971). For an excellent critique of the ethnocultural approach, see Richard L. McCormick, "Ethno-Cultural Interpretations of Nineteenth-Century American Voting Behavior," *Political Science Quarterly* 89, 2 (June 1974): 351–77.

[9] For example, see Schlesinger, *The Age of Jackson*; Burnham, "The System of 1896: An Analysis"; and Thomas Ferguson, "Party Realignment and American Industrial Structure: The Investment Theory of Political Parties in Historical Perspective," *Research in Political Economy* 6 (1983): 1–82.

[10] For criticisms of Schlesinger, see William A. Sullivan, "Did Labor Support Andrew Jackson?" *Political Science Quarterly* 62, 4 (December 1947): 569–80; Joseph Dorfman, "The Jackson Wage-Earner Thesis," *American Historical Review* 54, 2 (January 1949): 296–306; Richard B. Morris, "Andrew Jackson: Strikebreaker," *American Historical Review* 55 (October 1949): 54–68; Edward Pessen, "Did Labor Support Jackson?: The Boston Story," *Political Science Quarterly* 64, 2 (June 1949): 262–74; Milton J. Nadworny, "New Jersey Workingmen and the Jacksonians," *Proceedings of the New Jersey Historical Society* 67, 3

transformation of social relations from producer to worker traced in the preceding chapters suggests new ways of thinking about class and party in the United States. Put simply, I believe that, contrary to prevailing interpretations, there was no major disjunction between class and party in the United States. In fact, the division between the producing and nonproducing classes was reflected quite directly in antebellum electoral politics, with the producers supporting the Jacksonian Democrats and the nonproducers supporting the Whigs. The mainstays of the Jacksonian coalition, from this perspective, were drawn from the core constituents of the producers' alliance: skilled artisans, small manufacturers, and yeoman farmers. The very poorest citizens, such as day laborers and the unemployed, generally were excluded from the producers' ranks owing to their indigent and dependent status. As a consequence, we should not expect the poorest and middling wards to have voted for the same candidates in the antebellum decades.

Recovering the producers' concept of class helps explain why the ethnocultural historians have failed to find any class cleavages in the antebellum electoral returns. By ranking wards according to wealth, income, and occupation and presuming the principal social division to fall between the richer and poorer wards, these studies precluded the discovery of alternative social cleavages along producer lines. A more appropriate research strategy would have left open the definition of class boundaries, allowing the social divisions to emerge from the research itself. Demonstrating that the producers and nonproducers indeed voted for different parties would require additional research; nevertheless, preliminary evidence suggests that there was quite a close correspondence between class position and partisan identification throughout the nineteenth century.

In the antebellum decades, contemporary accounts of local, state, and national elections, we have seen in Chapter 3, often were recounted in terms of victories and defeats for the producers and their programs. Moreover, several scholars have begun to reexamine antebellum party politics in ways that are remarkably compatible with the producers' concept of class. Programmatic differences between the Democrats and Whigs need not be viewed as an indirect means of signaling ethnoreligious difference via the

---

(July 1949): 185–98; and Robert T. Bower, "Note on 'Did Labor Support Jackson?: The Boston Story,' " *Political Science Quarterly* 65, 3 (September 1950): 441–44. For criticisms of realignment arguments, see Philip E. Converse, "Change in the American Electorate," in Angus Campbell and Philip E. Converse, *The Human Meaning of Social Change* (New York: Russell Sage, 1972), chap. 8; Jerrod G. Rusk, "Comment: The American Electoral Universe, Speculation and Evidence," *American Political Science Review* 68, 3 (1974): 1038–49; and Alan Lichtman, "Critical Election Theory and the Reality of American Presidential Politics, 1916–1940," *American Historical Review* 81, 2 (April 1976): 317–51.

state. Rather, all of the substantive disagreements, whether over the National Bank, internal improvements, education, public lands, or the tariff, were rooted in their different interpretations of industrialization. Leaders of the producers' alliance and most of their followers, I have found, understood quite well what was at stake in these partisan choices and mobilized politically to preserve the republican pattern of economic growth. To be sure, not all producers voted the same way, even in the 1820s and 1830s, let alone after the Civil War. The more entrepreneurially inclined, who were willing to gamble that they might be able to benefit from the extension of the market, were willing to vote against their class position and support the Whigs. However, the central tendency within the producers' ranks was to adhere to their antimonopoly vision and vote for the Democrats or Working Men's parties when the opportunity arose.[11]

Interestingly, preliminary evidence also suggests that the very poor and the small number of blacks who could vote in the antebellum decades actually supported the Whigs.[12] While such evidence confounds a traditional class analysis, it further reinforces the notion that partisan identification followed divisions between the producing and nonproducing classes. After all, producers had always excluded the dependent poor from their alliance, while nonproducers embraced them in a paternalistic fashion. The dependent poor were accepted and provided for by the nonproducing classes as long as they remained respectful of the hierarchy that prevailed.[13]

More importantly, the producers' concept of class sheds new light on the transformation of party politics in the middle decades of the nineteenth century. The decline of the Whigs and rise of the Republican party was intimately connected with the breakdown of the producers' alliance and the construction of more familiar social divisions between labor and capital. The Working Men's parties and the GTUs of the late 1820s and 1830s signaled the first signs of strain within the producers' alliance. However, as we have seen in Chapters 3 and 4, the transition from producer to worker was not completed in a single decade, but rather took place more slowly over the remainder of the century. Initially, most skilled artisans were reluctant to abandon their producer allies and fought instead to maintain a republican political economy in which all industrious citizens could benefit from the fruits of economic growth. In the decades following the Civil

[11] Several scholars have begun to rethink antebellum party politics. For example, see Meyers, *The Jacksonian Persuasion*; Foner, *Free Soil, Free Labor, Free Men*; Howe, *Political Culture of the American Whigs*; Bridges, *A City in the Republic*, chap. 4; and Ashworth, *'Agrarians' and 'Aristocrats.'*

[12] See Howe, *Political Culture of the American Whigs*, 13–22.

[13] See ibid., chaps. 1, 2, 4.

War, however, the producers' alliance could no longer be sustained. By the late 1880s and early 1890s, the producers' vision of a decentralized political economy, so central to their program, no longer seemed a viable option, and left the alliance in disarray. Skilled workers ceased to think of themselves as producers and identified instead as wage earners and members of a distinct working class.

The rise and consolidation of the Republican party from its founding in 1854 through Lincoln's election in 1860 rested, I believe, on the shifting political allegiances that accompanied the breakdown of the producers' alliance. Not only did workers begin to cohere as a class, but small manufacturers also began to rethink their political identity from producer to businessman in the middle decades of the nineteenth century. The Republican party both reflected and fostered a new political alliance between small manufacturers and the old nonproducing classes. For this new alliance to be sustained, long-standing definitions of productive and unproductive labor had to be recast.[14]

In the early nineteenth century, for example, producers considered speculation and exchange to be undesirable activities that were endangering the republic. The role of the middleman, so essential to an extended market economy, was not yet considered a worthy occupation but rather was derided as a parasitic and unproductive task by many citizens in the antebellum decades.[15] By the 1870s and 1880s, social definitions of productive labor had been completely redrawn. Managers and middlemen were no longer cast as the idle and useless classes, but were now considered members of legitimate and productive occupations within a modern industrial economy. The recasting of social divisions and political alliances did not follow automatically from the logic of industrialization. Instead, questions of how work was to be organized, what role the government should play in

[14] Some of the most interesting work on social construction of the categories of productive and unproductive labor has been done by feminist scholars exploring divisions between male and female work in advanced industrial societies. For example, see Heidi I. Hartman, "The Family as the Locus of Gender, Class, and Political Struggle: The Example of Housework," *Signs* 6, 3 (1981): 366–94; Lewellyn Hendrix and Zakir Hossain, "Women's Status and the Mode of Production: A Cross-Cultural Test," *Signs* 13, 3 (1988): 437–53; Gayle Rubin, "The Traffic in Women: Notes on the 'Political Economy' of Sex," in Rayna R. Reiter, ed., *Toward an Anthropology of Women* (New York: Monthly Review Press, 1975); and Nancy Folbre, "Exploitation Comes Home: A Critique of the Marxian Theory of Family Labour," *Cambridge Journal of Economics* 6 (1982): 317–29. For more general discussions of language, gender, and identity, see Scott, *Gender and the Politics of History*; and Anne Norton, *Reflections on Political Identity* (Baltimore: Johns Hopkins University Press, 1988). Many of the feminist theorists' analytic insights and research strategies can be extended to the nongender-based changes in conceptions of productivity in the antebellum decades.

[15] For interesting discussions of speculation and exchange during the nineteenth century, see Meyers, *The Jacksonian Persuasion*, chaps. 5, 6; Howe, *Political Culture of the American Whigs*, chap. 5; and Fabian, *Card Sharps, Dream Books, and Bucket Shops*.

the economy, and who would be allies and who foes were highly politicized issues for many decades. The Republican party, I suspect, played an important role in constructing the new conceptions of productive labor and forging the political alliance between small manufacturers and larger industrialists in the second half of the nineteenth century.

Tracing the changing political identity of small manufacturers and exploring the role of the Republican party in reshaping nineteenth-century social relations are tasks for another project. What is clear from the current research is that historicizing the concept of class not only helps to explain the particular path of working-class formation in the United States, but also sheds new light on electoral and party politics. We can finally understand why claims of exceptionalism both persist in studies of American labor and yet remain inadequate as accounts of working-class formation as a whole.[16] From the producers' perspective, American labor strategy no longer seems so exceptional; American workers clearly resisted their declining status during industrialization and initially looked to politics as first line of defense. There was no great gulf between work and politics for most of the nineteenth century. Yet the emergence of AFL voluntarism at the turn of the century still must be explained. It was only after a prolonged campaign to check judicial power that organized labor turned away from politics and developed an alternative strategy of antistatist voluntarism. Examining the transition from producer to worker within the divided American state allows us to recapture a range of labor strategies as equally authentic voices of workers' protest while simultaneously explaining the origins of business unionism in the United States.

[16] Many labor historians have provided trenchant criticisms of American exceptionalism. See especially Foner, "Why Is There No Socialism in the United States?"; and Wilentz, "Against Exceptionalism." Despite their persuasive arguments, notions of exceptionalism continue precisely because they capture an important element of AFL strategy in the twentieth century. A satisfying account of working-class formation in the United States must accommodate both the early labor radicalism and the subsequent turn to voluntarism at the end of the century.

American Labor Conspiracy Cases

ANTEBELLUM CASES

(*Note:* "Doc. Hist." is an abbreviation for John R. Commons, Elrich B. Philips, Eugene A. Gilmore, Helen L. Sumner, and John B. Andrews, eds. *A Documentary History of American Industrial Society.* Vols. 1–10. Cleveland, Ohio: Arthur H. Clark, 1910. See Bibliography for full details of other sources.)

Buffalo Tailors, 4 Doc. Hist. 93 (N.Y. 1824) (conviction)

Chambersburg Shoemakers, 4 Doc. Hist. 273 (Pa. 1829) (conviction)

Commonwealth *ex rel.* Chew v. Carlisle, Brightly Nisi Prius 36 (Pa. 1821) (remanded)

Commonwealth *ex rel.* Felix Campbell v. O'Daniel, 4 Doc. Hist. 264 (Pa. 1829) (continued)

Commonwealth *ex rel.* Kennedy v. Marshall and Treillou, 4 Doc. Hist. 265 (Pa. 1829) (continued)

Commonwealth v. Grinder, 4 Doc. Hist. 335 (Pa. 1836) (acquittal)

Commonwealth v. Hunt, 4 Metc. 111 (Mass. 1842) (reversed on appeal)

Commonwealth v. Hunt, Thacher's Crim. Cases 609 (Mass. 1840) (conviction-appealed)

Commonwealth v. Morrow, 4 Doc. Hist. 15 (Pa. 1815) (conviction)

Commonwealth v. Pullis, 3 Doc. Hist. 59 (Pa. 1806) (conviction)

People v. Cooper, 4 Doc. Hist. 277 (N.Y. 1836) (acquittal)

People v. Faulkner, 4 Doc. Hist. 315 (N.Y. 1836) (conviction)

People v. Fisher, 14 Wendell 9 (N.Y. 1835) (conviction)

People v. Henry Trequier et al., 1 Wheeler C.C. 142 (N.Y. 1823) (conviction)

People v. Melvin, 3 Doc. Hist. 251 (N.Y. 1809) (conviction)

People v. Melvin, in Wilentz, "Conspiracy, Power and the Early Labor Movement" (N.Y. 1811) (acquittal)

State v. Pomeroy et al., 4 Doc. Hist. 269 (Md. 1829) (acquittal)

State v. Powley, 3 Doc. Hist. 249 (Md. 1809) (conviction, judgment suspended)

Thompsonville Carpet Manufacturers v. Taylor, 4 Doc. Hist. 314 and Supp. (Conn. 1834–1836) (acquittal)

POSTBELLUM LABOR CONSPIRACY CASES: NEW YORK AND PENNSYLVANIA

Cigar-makers' Union No. 66, Kingston, New York, *NLU Proceedings of the Second Session, 1868,* 12; *Workingmen's Assembly Proceedings,* 1869, 19; 1870, 23 (N.Y. 1868) (conviction)

Commonwealth *ex rel.* E. Vallette et al. v. Sheriff, 15 Phil. 393 (Pa. 1881) (dismissed)

Commonwealth v. Berry et al., 1 *Scranton Law Times* 217 (Pa. 1874) (conviction)

Commonwealth v. Curren, 3 Pitts. 143 (Pa. 1869) (conviction)

D. R. Jones Trial, Westmoreland County, *Pennsylvania Bureau of Industrial Statistics* 9 (1880–1881): 378–83 (Pa. 1881) (conviction)

Iron Moulders' Union No. 22 v. Tuttle and Bailey, Brooklyn, N.Y., *Workingmen's Assembly Proceedings*, 1870, 23 (N.Y. 1869) (no record of ruling)

Iron Moulders' Union No. 203, Harlem, N.Y. v. United States Iron Works, *Workingmen's Assembly Proceedings*, 1870, 23 (N.Y. 1869) (no record of ruling)

Knights of Labor Miners' Trials, Allegheny County, in Kuritz, "The Pennsylvania State Government and Labor Controls," 154 (Pa. 1887) (conviction)

Master Stevedores' Association v. Walsh, 2 Daly 1 (N.Y. 1867) (demurrer, overruled)

Miles McPadden and Knights of Labor Trials, Clearfield County, *Pennsylvania Bureau of Industrial Statistics* 10 (1881–1882): 161–63 (Pa. 1882) (charges dropped)

Newman et al. v. the Commonwealth, 34 *Pittsburgh Law Journal* 313 (Pa. 1886) (conviction-affirmed)

People *ex rel.* Gill v. Smith, 10 N.Y. St. Rptr. 730 (N.Y. 1887) (remanded)

People *ex rel.* Gill v. Walsh, 110 N.Y. 633 (N.Y. 1888) (conviction-affirmed)

People v. Commerford, 233 App. Div. 2, 251 N.Y.S. 132 (N.Y. 1931) (remanded)

People v. Kostka, 4 N.Y. Cr. 429 (N.Y. 1886) (conviction)

People v. Makvirka, 224 App. Div. 419, 231 N.Y.S. 279 (N.Y. 1928) (conviction-affirmed)

People v. McFarlin et al., 43 Misc. Rep. 591, 89 N.Y.S. 527 (N.Y. 1904) (remanded)

People v. Radt et al., 71 N.Y.S. 846 (N.Y. 1900) (acquittal)

People v. Van Nostrand, *Workingmen's Assembly Proceedings*, 1869, 19; 1870, 23 (N.Y. 1867) (conviction)

People v. Wilzig, 4 N.Y. Cr. 403 (N.Y. 1886) (conviction)

Raybold and Frostevant v. Samuel R. Gaul of Bricklayers' Union No. 2, *NLU Proceedings of the Second Session, 1868*, 12 (N.Y. 1868) (dropped)

Xingo Parks and John Siney Trial, Clearfield County, Pa., *Pennsylvania Bureau of Industrial Statistics* 9 (1880–1881): 313–15 (Pa. 1875) (conviction for Parks and 36 other defendants, acquittal for Siney)

Additional Cases

AMERICAN CASES

Addyston Pipe and Steel Co. v. United States, 175 U.S. 211 (1899)

Boehm v. Mace, 28 Abbott's New Cases 138 (N.Y. 1892)

Buck's Stove and Range Co. v. American Federation of Labor, 36 Wash. L. Rptr. 822 (D.C. 1908)

Chicago, Milwaukee and St. Paul Railroad Co. v. Minnesota, 134 U.S. 418 (1890)

Commonwealth v. Eastman, 1 Cush. 189 (Mass. 1848)

Commonwealth v. Isenberg and Rowland, 4 Pa. D. 579 (Pa. 1895)

Commonwealth v. Mifflin, 5 Watts and Serg. 461 (Pa. 1843)

Commonwealth v. Shedd, 7 Cush. 514 (Mass. 1851)

Commonwealth v. Tack, 1 Brewst. 511 (Pa. 1868)

Diedolt v. U.S. Baking Co., 72 Hun 403 (N.Y. 1893)

Duplex Printing Press Co. v. Deering, 254 U.S. 443 (1992)

Elizabeth Sewell v. James C. Moore, 166 Pa. 570 (Pa. 1895)

Farwell v. Boston and Worcester Railroad, 4 Metc. 49 (Mass. 1842)

Gallenkamp v. The Garvin Machine Co., 91 A.D. 141 (N.Y. 1904)

Goldcharles v. Wigeman, 113 Pa. 431 (Pa. 1886)

Gompers v. Buck's Stove and Range Co., 221 U.S. 418 (1911)

Hamilton v. Jutte, 16 Pa. C.C. 193 (Pa. 1895)

Hepburn v. Griswold, 8 Wallace 603 (1870)

Holden v. Hardy, 169 U.S. 366 (1898)

Hood v. Palm, 8 Pa. St. 237 (Pa. 1848)

ICC v. Cincinnati, New Orleans and Texas Pacific R.R. Co., 167 U.S. 479 (1897)

In re Jacobs, 98 N.Y. 98 (1885)

Julliard v. Greenman, 110 U.S. 421 (1884)

Keeley v. O'Conner, 106 Pa. 321 (Pa. 1884)

Kinsley v. Pratt, 148 N.Y. 372 (1897)

Knox v. Lee, 12 Wallace 457 (1871)

Lochner v. New York, 198 U.S. 45 (1905)

Marino v. Lehmaier, 173 N.Y. 530 (N.Y. 1903)

Moeller v. Harvey, 16 Phil. 66 (Pa. 1879)

Morris Run Coal Co. v. Barclay, 18 P. F. Smith 186 (Pa. 1871)

Munn v. Illinois, 94 U.S. 113 (1877)

New York v. Chelsea Jute Mills, 88 N.Y.S. 1085 (N.Y. 1904)

NLRB v. Jones and Laughlin Steel Corp., 301 U.S. 1 (1937)

Parker v. Davis, 12 Wallace 457 (1871)

People v. Coler, 166 N.Y. 1 (N.Y. 1901)

People v. Lambert, 9 Cowen's Rep. 578 (N.Y. 1827)

Sally v. Berwind-White Coal Co., 5 Dist. 316 (1896)

Santa Clara Co. v. Southern Pacific R.R. Co., 118 U.S. 394 (1886)

Schechter Poultry Corporation v. United States, 295 U.S. 495 (1935)

Showalter v. Ehlan and Rowe, 5 Pa. Super 242 (Pa. 1897)

Simpson v. New York Rubber Co., 80 Hun 415 (N.Y. 1894)

Smith v. The People, 25 Ill. 9 (Ill. 1860)

State v. Buchanan, 5 Harris and Jhn. 317 (Md. 1821)

State v. Burnham, 15 N.H. 396 (N.H. 1844)

State v. Donaldson, 3 Vroom 151 (N.J. 1867)

State v. Norton, 3 Zabriskie 33 (N.J. 1850)

State v. Rickey, 4 Halsted 364 (N.J. 1827)

State v. Stockford, 77 Conn. 227, 58 A 769, 107 Am. St. Rep. 28 (Conn. 1904)

State v. Younger, 1 Devereux 357 (N.C. 1827)

United States v. Butler, 297 US 1 (1936)

United States v. Debs, 64 Fed. 724 (1894)

United States v. E. C. Knight Co., 156 U.S. 1 (1895)

Vaca v. Sipes, 386 U.S. 171 (1967)

Veazie Bank v. Fenno, 8 Wallace 533 (1869)

Vegelahn v. Guntner, 167 Mass. 92 (Mass. 1896)

Wabash, St. Louis and Pacific Railroad Co. v. Illinois, 118 U.S. 557 (1886)

White v. Witteman Lithographic Co., 131 N.Y. 631 (N.Y. 1892)

English Cases

Charnock v. Court, 2 Ch. 35 (1899)

Curran v. Treleaven, 2 Q.B. 553 (1891)

Gibson v. Lawson, 2 Q.B. 547 (1891)

Gregory v. Duke of Brunswick, 134 Eng. Rep. 866, 1178 (1843–1844)

Haile v. Lillingstone, 35 S.J. 792 (1891)

Hornby v. Close, 10 Cox C.C. 393 (1867)

Judge v. Bennett, 52 J.P. 247 (1887)

Lyons v. Wilkins, 1 Ch. 255 (1899)

Osborne v. Amalgamated Society of Railway Servants, 1 Ch. 163 (1901), A.C. 87 (1910)

Pete v. Apperley, 35 S.J. 792 (1891)

Poulterers' Case, 9 Coke 55 (1611)

Quinn v. Leathem, A.C. 495 (1901)

Rex v. Bunn, 12 Cox C.C. 316 (1872)

Rex v. Druitt et al., 10 Cox C.C. 592 (1867)

Rex v. Eccles, 1 Leach C.C. 274 (1783)

Rex v. Goodall, 9 Q.B. 557 (1874)

Rex v. Hibbert, 13 Cox C.C. 82 (1875)

Rex v. Journeymen Tailors of Cambridge, 8 Mod. 10 (1721)

Rex v. Mawbey, 6 T.R. 619 (1796)

Rex v. McKeevit, Liverpool Assizes (16 December 1890)

Rex v. McKenzie, 2 Q.B. 519 (1892)

Rex v. Turner, 13 East 227 (1811)

Smith v. Moody, Div. Ct., 1 K.B. 56 (1903)

Taff Vale Railway Co. v. Amalgamated Society of Railway Servants, A.C. 426 (1901)

Walters v. Green, 2 Ch. 696 (1899)

Ward, Lock and Co. v. Printers' Assistants Society, 22 T.L.R. 327 (1906)

Bibliography

EDITED COLLECTIONS OF PRIMARY SOURCES

Blau, Joseph L., ed. *Social Theories of Jacksonian Democracy: Representative Writings of the Period 1825–1850.* New York: Bobbs-Merrill, 1954.
Commons, John R., Elrich B. Philips, Eugene A. Gilmore, Helen L. Sumner, and John B. Andrews, eds. *A Documentary History of American Industrial Society.* 10 vols. Cleveland, Ohio: Arthur H. Clark, 1910.
Howe, Mark DeWolfe. *Readings in American Legal History.* New York: Da Capo Press, 1971.
Johnson, Donald Bruce, and Kirk H. Porter, eds. *National Party Platforms, 1848–1972.* Urbana: University of Illinois Press, 1973.
Stein, Leon, and Philip Taft, eds. *Religion, Reform, and Revolution: Labor Panaceas in the Nineteenth Century.* New York: Arno and The New York Times, 1969.
Sylvis, James C., ed. *The Life, Speeches, Labors and Essays of William H. Sylvis.* Philadelphia: Claxton, Remsem Y. Haffelfinger, 1872.

NEWSPAPERS

The Man. 18 February 1834–16 May 1834.
The Mechanics' Free Press. 12 April 1828–23 April 1831. Also odd issues, 1833, 1834, 1835.
The Mechanics' Press. 14 November 1829–31 July 1830.
The National Trades' Union. Extracts from July 1834 through April 1836 compiled by the State Historical Society of Wisconsin.
New York Evening Post. 1 June 1836–31 July 1836.
New York Sentinel and Working Man's Advocate. 9 June 1830–3 July 1830.
The Radical. January 1842–April 1843.
Workingman's Advocate (Chicago). 18 February 1871–4 March 1871.
The Working Man's Advocate (New York). 31 October 1829–5 June 1830. (Became *New York Sentinel and Working Man's Advocate.*)

PRIMARY SOURCES

American Federationist. Vols. 1–27 (1894–1920).
American Federation of Labor. "Bill of Grievances." *American Federationist* 13, 3 (May 1906): 293–96.
———. *Proceedings of the American Federation of Labor, 1881, 1882, 1883, 1884, 1885, 1886, 1887, 1888.* Bloomington, Ill.: Pantagraph Printing and Stationery Co., 1906.
———. *Proceedings of the American Federation of Labor, 1889, 1890, 1891, 1892.* Bloomington, Ill.: Pantagraph Printing and Stationery Co., 1906.

_____. *Proceedings of the American Federaton of Labor, 1893, 1894, 1895, 1896.* Bloomington, Ill.: Pantagraph Printing and Stationery Co., 1905.

_____. *Report of Proceedings of the 17th Annual Convention of the American Federation of Labor Held at Nashville, Tennessee, December 13th to 21st Inclusive, 1897.* Published by Direction of the A. F. of L.

_____. *Report of Proceedings of the 18th Annual Convention of the American Federation of Labor Held at Kansas City, Missouri, December 12th to 20th Inclusive, 1898.* Published by Direction of the A. F. of L.

_____. *Report of Proceedings of the 19th Annual Convention of the American Federation of Labor Held at Detroit, Michigan, December 11th to 20th Inclusive, 1899.* Published by Direction of the A. F. of L.: James H. Stone & Co., 1899.

_____. *Report of the Proceedings of the Thirty-First Annual Convention of the American Federation of Labor, Held at Atlanta, Georgia, November 13 to 25, Inclusive, 1911.* Washington D.C.: Law Reporter Printing Company, 1911.

American Federation of Labor, New York State Branch, *Official Book.* New York: American Federation of Labor, 1897.

Atkinson, Edward. *Labor and Capital: Allies Not Enemies.* New York: Harper and Brothers, 1879.

Beaumont, Ralph. "The Labor Movement." In N. A. Dunning, ed., *The Farmers' Alliance History and Agricultural Digest.* Washington, D.C.: Alliance Publishing, 1891.

Bishop, Joel Prentiss. *Bishop on Criminal Trial.* Chicago: T. H. Flood and Co., 1923.

Blackstone, Sir William. *Commentaries on the Laws of England.* Philadelphia: George W. Childs, 1866.

Bricklayers' National Union. *Proceedings of the Sixth Annual Session of the Bricklayers' National Union, Convened in Turner Hall, Pittsburg, PA., Monday, January 9, 1871.* New York: Journeymen Printers' Co-Operative Association, 1871.

_____. *Proceedings of the Seventh Annual Session of the Bricklayers' National Union, Convened in Supervisors' Room, City Hall, Albany, N.Y., Monday, January 8, 1872.* New York: Journeymen Printers' Co-Operative Association, 1872.

Byrdsall, F. *The History of the Loco-Foco or Equal Rights Party, its Movements, Conventions and Proceedings, with Short Characteristic Sketches of Its Prominent Men.* New York: Clement and Packard, 1842.

Carey, Henry Charles. *The Harmony of Interests, Agricultural, Manufacturing and Commercial.* 1852. Philadelphia: H. C. Baird, 1890.

Chitty, Joseph. *A Practical Treatise on the Criminal Law.* Philadelphia: Edward Earle, 1819.

Cigar Makers' Official Journal. 15 November 1882–October 1884.

Coke, Edward. *Institutes of the Laws of England; Containing the Exposition of Many Ancient and Other Statutes.* London: W. Clarke and Sons, 1817.

Federation of Organized Trades and Labor Unions Proceedings 1881–1886. These have been incorporated into and reprinted in the American Federation of Labor Proceedings for 1881–1888, listed above.

George, Henry. *The Labor Question, Being an Abridgement of the Condition of Labor.* 1891. Cincinnati: Joseph Fels Fund of America, 1911.

Gompers, Samuel. "Attitude of Labor Towards Government Regulation of Industry." *Annals of American Academy of Political and Social Science* 32, 1 (July 1908): 75–81.

———. "Labor and Its Attitudes Toward Trusts." *American Federationist* 14 (November 1907): 880–86.

———. *Seventy Years of Life and Labor: An Autobiography.* 2 vols. New York: Dutton, 1925.

Hawkins, Serjeant William. *A Treatise of the Pleas of the Crown; or, a System of the Principal Matters Relating to That Subject, Digested Under Proper Heads.* Vol. 2. 1716. London: His Majesty's Law-Printers, 1787.

International Typographical Union. *Report of Proceedings of the Fifteenth Annual Session of the National Typographical Union, Held in the City of Memphis, Tenn., June 3, 4, 5, 6 and 7, 1867.* New York: Journeymen Printers' Co-Operative Association, 1867.

———. *Report of Proceedings of the Eighteenth Annual Session of the International Typographical Union, Held in Cincinnati, Ohio, June 6, 7, 8, 9 and 10, 1870.* Philadelphia: Cooperative Printing Co., 1870.

———. *Report of Proceedings of the Nineteenth Annual Session of the International Typographical Union, Held in Baltimore, MD., June 5, [sic] 7, 8 and 9, 1871.* Philadelphia: Cooperative Printing Co., 1871.

———. *Report of Proceedings of the Twentieth Annual Session of the International Typographical Union, Held in Richmond, VA., June 3d, 4th, 5th, and 7th, [sic] 1872.* Cincinnati: Wilstach, Baldwin and Co., 1872.

———. *Report of Proceedings of the Twenty-Third Annual Session of the International Typographical Union, Held in Boston, Massachusetts, June, 1875.* Chicago: Evening Journal, Book, Job, and Show Printing House, 1875.

———. *Report of Proceedings of the Twenty-Sixth Annual Session of the International Typographical Union, Held in Detroit, Michigan, June, 1878.* New York: Smith and Schember, Printers, 1878.

———. *Report of Proceedings of the Thirty-Third Annual Session of the International Typographical Union, Held in New York City, June, 1885.* Philadelphia: McCalla and Stavely, 1885.

———. *Report of Proceedings of the Thirty-Fifth Annual Session of the International Typographical Union, Held in Buffalo, New York, June, 1887.* Chicago: Press of the Inland Printer, 1887.

Iron Molders' International Journal. 1864–1880.

Kellogg, Edward. *Labor and Other Capital: The Rights of Each Secured and the Wrongs of Both Eradicated.* New York: Author, 1849.

The Law Reports. The Public General Statutes, Passed in the Thirty-Fourth and Thirty-Fifth Years of the Reign of Her Majesty Queen Victoria, 1871. London: George Edward Eyre and William Spottiswoode, 1871.

Law Reports. The Public General Statutes Passed in the Thirty-Eighth and Thirty-Ninth Years of the Reign of Her Majesty Queen Victoria, 1875. London: George Edward Eyre and William Spottiswoode, 1875.

Laws of the General Assembly of the State of Pennsylvania, Passed at the Session of 1869, in the Ninety-third Year of Independence. Harrisburg, Pa.: B. Singerly, 1869.

Laws of the General Assembly of the State of Pennsylvania, Passed at the Session of 1872, in the Ninety-sixth Year of Independence. Harrisburg, Pa.: B. Singerly, 1872.

Laws of the General Assembly of the State of Pennsylvania, Passed at the Session of 1876, in the One Hundredth Year of Independence. Harisburg, Pa.: B. F. Meyers, 1876.

Laws of the General Assembly of the Comonwealth of Pennsylvania, Passed at the Session of 1891, in the One Hundred and Fifteenth Year of Independence. Harrisburg, Pa.: Edwin K. Meyers, 1891.

Laws of the State of New York, Passed at the Ninety-third Session of the Legislature. Albany, N.Y.: Weed, Parsons & Co., 1970.

Laws of the State of New York, Passed at the One Hundred and Fourth Session of the Legislature. Albany, N.Y.: Weed, Parsons & Co., 1881.

Laws of the State of New York, Passed at the One Hundred and Fifth Session of the Legislature. Vol. 1. Albany, N.Y.: Weed, Parsons & Co., 1882.

Laws of the State of New York, Passed at the One Hundred and Tenth Legislature. Vol. 1. Albany, N.Y.: Banks and Brothers, 1887.

Lloyd, Henry Demarest. *Wealth Against Commonwealth.* New York: Harper and Brothers, 1894.

New York Bureau of Statistics of Labor. *Fourth Annual Report of the Bureau of Statistics of Labor of the State of New York for the Year 1886.* Albany, N.Y.: Argus Company, Printers, 1887.

————. *Fifth Annual Report of the Statistics of Labor of the State of New York for the Year 1887.* Albany, N.Y.: Troy Press, Printers, 1888.

New York State Workingmen's Assembly Proceedings 1869–1894. Martin P. Catherwood Library, Cornell University.

Papers of Terence Vincent Powderly, 1864–1924, and John William Hayes, 1880–1921. Catholic University Archives, Washington, D.C.

Pennsylvania Bureau of Industrial Statistics. *Annual Report of the Secretary of Internal Affairs of the Commonwealth of Pennsylvania, Industrial Statistics. vol. 9 1880-81.* Harrisburg, Pa.: Lane S. Hart, State Printers and Binders, 1882.

————. *Annual Report of the Secretary of Internal Affairs of the Commonwealth of Pennsylvania, Industrial Statistics. vol. 10 1881–82.* Harrisburg, Pa.: Lane S. Hart, State Printers and Binders, 1883.

Powderly, Terence Vincent. *Thirty Years of Labor, 1859–1889.* Columbus, Ohio: Excelsior, 1889.

Proceedings of the Eighteenth Annual Meeting of the State Trades Assembly, State of New York, January 1884. Rochester, N.Y.: Truth Publishing Co., 1884.

Proceedings of the Second Session of the National Labor Union, in Convention Assembled, at New York City, Sept. 21, 1868. Philadelphia: W. B. Selheimer, Printer, 1868.

Report of the Committee of the Senate upon the Relations between Labor and Capital. 5 vols. Washington, D.C.: Government Printing Office, 1885.

Report on the Chicago Strike of June-July, 1894, by the United States Strike Commission. Washington, D.C.: Government Printing Office, 1895.

Simpson, Stephen. *The Working Man's Manual: A New Theory of Political Econ-*

omy, on the Principle of Production the Source of Wealth. Philadelphia: Thomas L. Bonsal, 1831.

Sorge, Friedrich A. "Die Arbeiterbewegung in den Vereinigten Staaten, 1860–1866." *Die Neue Zeit* 9, 2 (1891–1892).

_____. "Die Arbeiterbewegung in den Vereinigten Staaten, 1866–1876." *Die Neue Zeit* 10, 1 (1891–1892).

The Statutes of the United Kingdom of Great Britain and Ireland, 22 Victoria, 1859. London: George E. Eyre and William Spottiswoode, 1859.

Stevens, George A. *New York Typographical Union, No. 6: Study of a Modern Trade Union and Its Predecessors*. Albany, N.Y.: J. B. Lyon, State Printers, 1913.

Stickney, Albert. *State Control of Trade and Commerce by the National or State Authority*. New York: Baker, Voorhis and Co., 1897.

Sylvis, William H. "What Is Money?" In James C. Sylvis, ed., *The Life, Speeches, Labors, and Essays of William H. Sylvis*. Philadelphia: Claxton, Remsem Y. Haffelfinger, 1872.

U.S. Bureau of the Census. *Historical Statistics of the United States, Colonial Times to 1957*. Washington, D.C.: Government Printing Office, 1960.

A Verbatum [sic] Report of the Discussion on the Political Programme at the Denver Convention of the American Federation of Labor, December 14, 15, 1894. New York: The Freytag Press, 1895.

Workingmen's Federation of the State of New York. *Report of Proceedings of the First Annual Convention of the Workingmen's Federation of the State of New York, Held at Albany, NY, January 11–15, 1898*. Wolford Print.

SECONDARY SOURCES

Alger, George W. "The Courts and Factory Legislation." In Robert M. LaFollette, ed., *The Making of America*. Chicago: The Making of America Co., 1906.

Allen, Arthur M. "Criminal Conspiracies in Restraint of Trade at Common Law." 23 *Harvard Law Review* 531 (1910).

Almond, Gabriel. "Corporatism, Pluralism, and Professional Memory." *World Politics* 35, 2 (January 1983): 245–60.

_____. "The Return to the State." *American Political Science Review* 82, 3 (September 1988): 853–74.

Amberg, Stephen. "The Old Politics of Inequality: The Autoworkers' Union in the Liberal Keynesian State." Paper presented at the annual meeting of the American Historical Association, 27–30 December 1988, Cincinnati, Ohio.

_____. "Democratic Producerism: Enlisting American Politics for Workplace Flexibility." *Economy and Society* 20, 1 (1991): 57–78.

Appleby, Joyce. *Capitalism and a New Social Order: The Republican Vision of the 1790's*. New York: New York University Press, 1984.

_____. "Liberalism and the American Revolution." *New England Quarterly* 49 (March 1976): 3–26.

_____. "The New Republican Synthesis and the Changing Political Ideas of John Adams." *American Quarterly* 25, 5 (December 1973): 578–95.

_____. "Republicanism in Old and New Contexts." *William and Mary Quarterly*, 3d series, 43, 1 (January 1986): 20–34.

_____. "The Social Origins of American Revolutionary Ideology." *Journal of American History* 64, 4 (March 1978): 935–58.

Arky, Louis H. "The Mechanics' Union of Trade Associations and the Formation of the Philadelphia Workingmen's Movement." *Pennsylvania Magazine of History and Biography* 76 (April 1952): 142–76.

Armstrong, Gary W. "Utopians in Clayton County, Iowa." *Annals of Iowa* 61 (1972): 923–38.

Arndt, Karl J. R. "George Rapp's Harmonists and the Beginnings of Norwegian Migration to America." *Western Pennsylvania Historical Magazine* 60 (July 1977): 241–63.

Asher, Robert. "Union Nativism and the Immigrant Response." *Labor History* 23, 3 (Summer 1982): 325–48.

Ashworth, John. *'Agrarians' and 'Aristocrats': Party Political Ideology in the United States, 1837–1846*. New York: Cambridge University Press, 1987.

Aumann, Francis R. *The Changing American Legal System: Some Selected Phases*. Columbus: Ohio State University Press, 1940.

Avrich, Paul. *The Haymarket Tragedy*. Princeton: Princeton University Press, 1984.

Bailyn, Bernard. *The Ideological Origins of the American Revolution*. Cambridge, Mass.: Harvard University Press, 1967.

Bain, George S., ed. *Industrial Relations in Britain*. Oxford: Basil Blackwell, 1983.

Baker, J. H. *An Introduction to English Legal History*. London: Butterworths, 1979.

Banning, Lance. "Jeffersonian Ideology Revisited: Liberal and Classical Ideas in the New American Republic." *William and Mary Quarterly*, 3d series, 43, 1 (January 1986): 3–19.

Barnard, J. Lynn. *Factory Legislation in Pennsylvania: Its History and Administration*. Philadelphia: John Winston, 1907.

Barzelay, Michael, and Rogers M. Smith. "The One Best System? A Political Analysis of Neoclassical Institutionalist Perspectives on the Modern Corporation." In Warren J. Samuels and Arthur S. Miller, eds., *Corporations and Society: Power and Responsibility*. New York: Greenwood Press, 1987.

Bassett, T. D. Seymour. "The Secular Utopian Socialists." In Donald D. Egbert and Stow Persons, eds., *Socialism and American Life*, vol. 1, chap. 5. Princeton: Princeton University Press, 1952.

Beard, Charles. *An Economic Interpretation of the Constitution of the United States*. New York: The Free Press, 1913.

Beer, Samuel H. *British Politics in the Collectivist Age*. New York: Vintage Books, 1969.

Behagg, Clive. "An Alliance with the Middle Class: The Birmingham Political Union and Early Chartism." In James Epstein and Dorothy Thompson, eds., *The Chartist Experience: Studies in Working-Class Radicalism and Culture, 1830–60*. London: Macmillan, 1982.

Bendix, Reinhart, and Stein Rokkan. "The Extension of Citizenship to the Lower Classes." In Mattei Dogan and Richard Rose, eds., *European Politics: A Reader*. Boston: Little, Brown, 1971.

Bensel, Richard Franklin. *Yankee Leviathan: The Origins of Central State Authority in America, 1859–1877*. New York: Cambridge University Press, 1990.

Benson, Lee. *The Concept of Jacksonian Democracy: New York as a Test Case*. Princeton: Princeton University Press, 1961.

Bentley, Arthur. *The Process of Government: A Study of Social Pressures*. Bloomington, Ind.: Principia Press, 1949.

Berger, Suzanne, and Michael Piore. *Dualism and Discontinuity in Industrial Societies*. New York: Cambridge University Press, 1980.

Berger, Suzanne, ed. *Organizing Interests in Western Europe: Pluralism, Corporatism and the Transformation of Politics*. New York: Cambridge University Press, 1981.

Berk, Gerald P. "Constituting Corporations and Markets: Railroads in Gilded Age Politics." *Studies in American Political Development*, 4 (1990): 130–68.

———. "Corporations and Politics: American Railroads, 1870–1916." Ph.D. diss., Massachusetts Institute of Technology, 1987.

Bernstein, Irving. *The New Deal Collective Bargaining Policy*. Berkeley: University of California Press, 1950.

———. *Turbulent Years: A History of the American Worker, 1933–1941*. Boston: Houghton Mifflin, 1970.

Bernstein, Leonard. "The Working People of Philadelphia from Colonial Times to the General Strike of 1835." *Pennsylvania Magazine of History and Biography* 74 (July 1950): 322–39.

Berta, Giuseppe. "La formazione del movimento operaio regionale: il caso dei tessili (1860–1900)." In Aldo Agosti and Gian Maria Bravo, eds., *Storia del movimento operaio, del socialismo, e delle lotte in Piedmonte*, vol. 1. Bari: De Donato, 1979.

Birdsall, William C. "The Problem of Structure in the Knights of Labor." *Industrial and Labor Relations Review* 6, 4 (July 1953):532–46.

Birnbaum, Pierre. "The State Versus Corporatism." *Politics and Society* 11, 4 (1982): 477–501.

Blackard, W. Raymond. "The Demoralization of the Legal Profession in Nineteenth Century America." 16 *Tennessee Law Review* 314 (1940).

Block, Fred. "The Ruling Class Does Not Rule: Notes on the Marxist Theory of the State." *Social Revolution* 7, 3 (1977): 6–28.

Bloomfield, Maxwell. *American Lawyers in a Changing Society, 1776–1876*. Cambridge, Mass.: Harvard University Press, 1976.

———. "Law vs. Politics: The Self-Image of the American Bar, 1830–1860." *American Journal of Legal History* 12, 4 (October 1968): 306–23.

———. "Lawyers and Public Criticism: Challenge and Response in Nineteenth-Century America." *American Journal of Legal History* 15, 4 (October 1971): 269–77.

Bodner, John. *The Transplanted: A History of Immigrants in Urban America*. Bloomington: Indiana University Press, 1987.

Bok, Derek C., and John T. Dunlop. *Labor and the American Community*. New York: Simon and Schuster, 1970.

———. "Reflections on the Distinctive Character of American Labor Laws." 84 *Harvard Law Review* 1394 (1971).

Bower, Robert T. "Note on 'Did Labor Support Jackson?: The Boston Story.'"
Political Science Quarterly 65, 3 (September 1950): 441–44.

Bowsma, William. "Intellectual History in the 1980's: From History of Ideas to History of Meaning." *Journal of Interdisciplinary History* 12 (Autumn 1981): 279–91.

Brandler, Walker Claire. "A History of Factory Legislation and Inspection in New York State, 1886–1911." Ph.D. diss., Columbia University, 1969.

Braverman, Harry. *Labor and Monopoly Capital: The Degradation of Work in the Twentieth Century.* New York: Monthly Review Press, 1974.

Brecher, Jeremy. *Strike!* Boston: South End Press, 1972.

Bridges, Amy Beth. "Another Look at Plutocracy and Politics in Antebellum New York City." *Political Science Quarterly* 97, 1 (Spring 1982): 57–71.

————. "Becoming American: The Working Classes in the United States Before the Civil War." In Ira Katznelson and Aristide Zolberg, eds., *Working Class Formation: Nineteenth Century Patterns in Western Europe and the United States.* Princeton: Princeton University Press, 1986.

————. *A City in the Republic: Antebellum New York and the Origins of Machine Politics.* Ithaca, N.Y.: Cornell University Press, 1987.

————. "Nicos Poulantzas and the Marxist Theory of the State." *Politics and Society* 4, 2 (Winter 1974): 161–90.

Briggs, Asa. *The Collected Essays of Asa Briggs.* Vol. 1. Kent, Engl.: The Harvester Press, 1985.

Brigham, Clifford. "Strikes and Boycotts as Indictable Conspiracies at Common Law." 22 *American Law Review* 41 (1887).

Brody, David. "The Old Labor History and the New: In Search of an American Working Class." *Labor History* 20, 1 (Winter 1979): 111–26.

————. *Workers in Industrial America: Essays on the 20th Century Struggle.* New York: Oxford University Press, 1980.

Brown, M. Craig, and Charles N. Halaby. "Bosses, Reform, and the Socioeconomic Bases of Urban Expenditure, 1890–1940." In Terrence J. McDonald and Sally K. Ward, eds., *The Politics of Urban Fiscal Policy.* Beverly Hills: Sage Publications, 1984.

Brown, Martin, and Peter Philips. "Competition and Racism in Hiring Practices Among California Manufacturers, 1860–1882." *Industrial and Labor Relations Review* 40, 1 (October 1986): 61–74.

Brown, R. "The Temperton v. Russell Case (1893): The Beginning of the Legal Offensive Against the Unions." *Bulletin of Economic Research* 23, 1 (May 1971): 50–66.

Bruce, Peter. "Political Parties and the Evolution of Labor Law in Canada and the United States." Ph.D. diss., Massachusetts Institute of Technology, 1988.

Buhle, Mari Jo. *Women and American Socialism, 1870–1920.* Urbana: University of Illinois Press, 1983.

Buhle, Paul. "The Knights of Labor in Rhode Island." *Radical History Review* 17 (Spring 1978): 39–73.

Burdick, Francis M. "Conspiracy as a Crime, and as a Tort." 7 *Columbia Law Review* 229 (1907).

Burki, Mary Ann Mason. "The California Progressives: Labor's Point of View." *Labor History* 17, 1 (Winter 1976): 28–29.

Burnham, Walter Dean. "The Appearance and Disappearance of the American Voter." In Richard Rose, ed., *Electoral Participation: A Comparative Analysis.* Beverly Hills: Sage Publications, 1980.

———. "The Changing Shape of the American Political Universe." *American Political Science Review* 59, 1 (March 1965): 7–28.

———. *Critical Elections and the Mainsprings of American Politics.* New York: Norton, 1970.

———. *The Current Crisis in American Politics.* New York: Oxford University Press, 1982.

———. "The System of 1896: An Analysis." In Paul Kleppner, Walter Dean Burnham, Ronald P. Formisano, Samuel P. Hayes, Richard Jensen, and William G. Shade, eds., *The Evolution of American Electoral Systems.* Westport, Conn.: Greenwood Press, 1981.

Cappelletti, Mauro. *Judicial Review in the Contemporary World.* New York: Bobbs-Merrill, 1971.

Cappelletti, Mauro, and John Clarke Adams. "Judicial Review of Legislation: European Antecedents and Adaptations." 79 *Harvard Law Review* 1207 (1966).

Carlton, Frank T. "An American Utopia." *Quarterly Journal of Economics* 19 (1910): 428–33.

———. "The Workingmen's Party of New York City: 1829–1831." *Political Science Quarterly* 22, 3 (September 1907): 401–15.

Carson, Hampton L. *The Law of Criminal Conspiracies and Agreements: As Found in the American Cases.* Philadelphia: Blackstone, 1887.

Cary, Lorin Lee. "Institutionalized Conservatism in the Early C.I.O.: Alfred Germer, A Case Study." *Labor History* 13 (Fall 1972): 475–504.

Cassity, Michael J. "Modernization and Social Crisis: The Knights of Labor and a Midwest Community, 1885–1886." *Journal of American History* 66, 1 (June 1979): 41–61.

Chambers, William Nisbet, and Walter Dean Burnham, eds. *The American Party Systems: Stages of Political Development.* New York: Oxford University Press, 1975.

Cheyney, Edward P. "The Anti-Rent Movement and the Constitution of 1846." In Alexander C. Flick, ed., *History of the State of New York*, vol. 6. New York: Columbia University Press, 1934.

———. "Decisions of the Courts in Conspiracy and Boycott Cases." *Political Science Quarterly* 4, 1 (1889): 261–78.

Clegg, H. A. "Pluralism in Industrial Relations." *British Journal of Industrial Relations* 13, 3 (1975): 309–16.

Cohen, Joshua. "Review of G. A. Cohen, *Karl Marx's Theory of History: A Defence.*" *Journal of Philosophy* 79 (1982): 253–73.

Cohen, Joshua, and Joel Rogers. *On Democracy: Toward a Transformation of American Society.* New York: Penguin, 1983.

Cole, G.D.H. *British Working Class Politics, 1832–1914.* London: Routledge and Kegan Paul, 1941.

———. *A Short History of the British Working-Class Movement, 1789–1947.* London: Allen and Unwin, 1948.

Commons, John R. "American Shoemakers, 1648–1895: A Sketch of Industrial Evolution." *Quarterly Journal of Economics* 24 (November 1909): 39–84.

──────. "Immigration and Labor Problems." In Robert M. La Follette, ed., *The Making of America*, vol. 8. Chicago: The Making of America Co., 1906.

──────. "Labor Organization and Labor Politics, 1827–37." *Quarterly Journal of Economics* 21 (February 1907): 323–29.

Commons, John R., and John B. Andrews. *Principles of Labor Legislation*. New York: Harper and Brothers, 1916.

Commons, John R., David J. Saposs, Helen L. Sumner, E. B. Mittleman, H. E. Hoagland, John B. Andrews, and Selig Perlman, eds. *History of Labor in the United States*. 4 vols. New York: Macmillan, 1936.

Converse, Philip E. "Change in the American Electorate." In Angus Cambell and Philip E. Converse, *The Human Meaning of Social Change*. New York: Russell Sage, 1972.

Cook, Charles M. *The American Codification Movement: A Study of Antebellum Legal Reform*. Westport, Conn.: Greenwood Press, 1981.

Cooke, Frederick H. *The Law of Combinations, Monopolies and Labor Unions* Chicago: Callaghan & Co., 1909.

Corwin, Edward S. *The 'Higher Law' Background of American Constitutional Law*. Ithaca, N.Y.: Cornell University Press, 1959.

Couvares, Francis G. *The Remaking of Pittsburgh: Class and Culture in an Industrializing City, 1877–1919*. Albany: State University of New York Press, 1984.

Cox, Archibald, Derek C. Bok, and Robert A. Gorman. *Cases and Materials on Labor Law*. Mineola, N.Y.: The Foundation Press, 1981.

Crossick, Geoffrey. "The Labour Aristocracy and Its Values: A Study of Mid-Victorian Kentish London." *Victorian Studies* 19, 3 (March 1976): 301–28.

Crowley, J. E. *This Sheba Shelf: The Conceptualization of Economic Life in Eighteenth-Century America*. Baltimore: Johns Hopkins University Press, 1974.

Cumbler, John T. "Labor, Capital, and Community: The Struggle for Power." *Labor History* 15, 13 (Summer 1974): 395–415.

Curti, Merle E. "Robert Rantoul, Jr.: The Reformer in Politics." *New England Quarterly* 5, 2 (April 1932): 264–80.

Darling, Arthur B. "Workingmen's Party in Massachusetts." *American Historical Review* 29, 1 (October 1923): 81–86.

David, Henry. *History of the Haymarket Affair: A Study in the American Social-Revolutionary and Labor Movements*. New York: Russell and Russell, 1958.

Davis, Mike. "The Barren Marriage of American Labour and the Democratic Party." *New Left Review* 124 (November–December 1980): 43–84.

──────. "Why the U.S. Working Class Is Different." *New Left Review* 123 (September-October 1980): 3–47.

Dawley, Alan. *Class and Community: The Industrial Revolution in Lynn*. Cambridge, Mass.: Harvard University Press, 1976.

Dawley, Alan, and Paul Faler. "Working-Class Culture and Politics in the Industrial Revolution: Sources of Loyalism and Rebellion." *Journal of Social History* 9, 4 (June 1976): 466–80.

Deener, David. "Judicial Review in Modern Constitutional Systems." *American Political Science Review* 46, 4 (December 1952): 1079–99.

Degler, Carl N. "The Loco-focos: Urban 'Agrarians.'" *Journal of Economic History* 16, 3 (1956): 322–53.

_____. "An Enquiry into the Locofoco Party." M.A. thesis, Columbia University, 1947.

Denning, Michael. *Mechanic Accents: Dime Novels and Working-Class Culture in America*. New York: Verso, 1987.

Derber, Milton. "Collective Bargaining in Great Britain and the United States." *Quarterly Review of Economics and Business* 8, 4 (1968): 55–66.

Destler, Chester McArthur. *American Radicalism, 1865–1901: Essays and Documents*. New London, Conn.: Connecticut College Monographs, 1946.

Dietz, Gottfried. "Judicial Review in Europe." *55 Michigan Law Review* 539 (1957).

Dobson, C. R. *Masters and Journeymen: A Pre-history of Industrial Relations*. Totowa, N.J.: Rowman and Littlefield, 1980.

Dorfman, Joseph. "The Jackson Wage-Earner Thesis." *American Historical Review* 54, 2 (January 1949): 296–306.

Douglas, Dorothy. "Ira Steward on Consumption and Unemployment." *Journal of Political Economy* 40, 4 (August 1932): 532–43.

Dubofsky, Melvyn. *Industrialism and the American Worker, 1865–1920*. New York: Thomas Y. Crowell, 1975.

_____. "Legal Theory and Workers' Rights: A Historian's Critique." *Industrial Relations Law Journal* 4, 3 (1981): 496–502.

_____. *We Shall Be All: A History of the I.W.W.* Chicago: Quadrangle Books, 1969.

Dunlavy, Colleen A. "Mirror Images: Political Structure and Early Railroad Policy in the United States and Prussia." *Studies in American Political Development* 5, 1 (1991): 1–35.

_____. *Political Structure and Industrial Change: Early Railroads in the United States and Prussia*. Princeton: Princeton University Press, 1993.

Duverger, Maurice. *Political Parties: Their Organization and Activity in the Modern State*. New York: John Wiley and Sons, 1959.

Eddy, Arthur J. *The Law of Combinations: Embracing Monopolies, Trusts, and Combinations of Labor and Capital; Conspiracy, and Contracts in Restraint of Trade, Together with Federal and State Anti-Trust Legislation*. Chicago: Callagham and Co., 1901.

Edwards, P. K. *Strikes in the United States, 1881–1974*. Oxford: Basil Blackwell, 1981.

Egbert, Donald Drew, and Stow Persons, eds. *Socialism and American Life*. Vol. 1. Princeton: Princeton University Press, 1952.

Eley, Geoff, and Keith Nield. "Why Does Social History Ignore Politics?" *Social History* 5, 2 (May 1980): 249–71.

Ellis, Richard E. *The Jeffersonian Crisis: Courts and Politics in the Young Republic*. New York: Norton, 1971.

Emmons, David. *The Butte Irish: Class and Ethnicity in an American Mining Town, 1875–1925*. Urbana: University of Illinois Press, 1989.

Epstein, James, and Dorothy Thompson. *The Chartist Experience: Studies in Working-Class Radicalism and Culture, 1830–60*. London: Macmillan, 1982.

Erie, Steven P. *Rainbow's End: Irish America and the Dilemmas of Urban Machine Politics, 1840–1895*. Berkeley: University of California Press, 1988.

Erle, Sir William. *On the Law Relating to Trade Unions.* London: Macmillan, 1869.

Ernst, Daniel R. "The Danbury Hatters' Case." In Christopher L. Tomlins and Andrew J. King, eds., *Labor Law in America: Historical and Critical Essays.* Baltimore: Johns Hopkins University Press, 1992.

Evans, Chris. *History of United Mine Workers of America from the Years 1860–1890.* Indianapolis: United Mine Workers of America, 1918.

Evans, Frank. *Pennsylvania Politics, 1872–1877: A Study in Political Leadership.* Harrisburg, Pa.: The Pennsylvania Historical and Museum Commission, 1966.

Fabian, Ann. *Card Sharps, Dream Books, and Bucket Shops: Gambling in 19th Century America.* Ithaca, N.Y.: Cornell University Press, 1990.

Fairchild, Fred Rogers. *The Factory Legislation of the State of New York.* New York: Macmillan, 1905.

Faler, Paul. "Cultural Aspects of the Industrial Revolution: Lynn, Massachusetts Shoemakers and Industrial Morality, 1826–1860." *Labor History* 19, 3 (Summer 1974): 367–94.

_____. *Mechanics and Manufacturers in the Early Industrial Revolution: Lynn, Massachusetts, 1780–1860.* Albany: State University of New York Press, 1981.

Feller, David E. "Arbitration: The Days of Its Glory Are Numbered." *Industrial Relations Law Journal* 2, 1 (Spring 1977): 97–130.

_____. "A General Theory of the Collective Bargaining Agreement." 61 *California Law Review* 663 (1973).

Ferguson, Thomas. "Party Realignment and American Industrial Structure: The Investment Theory of Political Parties in Historical Perspective." *Research in Political Economy* 6 (1983): 1–82.

Ferguson, Thomas, and Joel Rogers, eds. *The Hidden Election: Politics and Economics in the 1980 Presidential Campaign.* New York: Pantheon, 1981.

Fine, Nathan. *Labor and Farmer Parties in the United States, 1828–1928.* New York: Rand School of Social Science, 1928.

Finegold, Kenneth, and Theda Skocpol. "State Party and Industry: From Business Recovery to the Wagner Act in America's New Deal." In Charles Bright and Susan Harding, eds., *State Making and Social Movements: Essays in History and Theory.* Ann Arbor: University of Michigan Press, 1984.

Fink, Gary M. "The Rejection of Voluntarism." *Industrial and Labor Relations Review* 26, 2 (January 1973): 805–19.

_____, ed. *State Labor Proceedings: A Bibliography of the AFL, CIO, and AFL-CIO Proceedings, 1885–1974, Held in the AFL-CIO Library.* Westport, Conn.: Greenwood Press, 1975.

Fink, Leon. "Labor, Liberty, and the Law: Trade Unionism and the Problem of the American Constitutional Order." *Journal of American History* 74, 3 (December 1987): 904–25.

_____. "The New Labor History and the Powers of Historical Pessimism: Consensus, Hegemony, and the Case of the Knights of Labor." *Journal of American History* 75, 1 (June 1988): 115–36.

_____. "The Uses of Political Power: Toward a Theory of the Labor Movement in the Era of the Knights of Labor." In Michael H. Frisch and Daniel J. Walkowitz, eds.,*Working-Class America: Essays on Labor, Community, and American Society*. Urbana: University of Illinois Press, 1983.

_____. *Workingmen's Democracy: The Knights of Labor and American Politics.* Urbana: University of Illinois Press, 1983.

Finkin, Matthew W. "Revisionism in Labor Law." 43 *Maryland Law Review* 23 (1984).

Finn, J. F. "AF of L Leaders and the Question of Politics in the Early 1890s." *Journal of American Studies* 7, 3 (December 1973): 243–65.

Fleming, R. W. "The Significance of the Wagner Act." In Milton Derber and Edwin Young, eds., *Labor and the New Deal*. Madison: University of Wisconsin Press, 1957.

Flora, Peter, Franz Kraus, and Winfried Pfenning. *State, Economy and Society in Western Europe, 1815–1975: A Data Handbook in Two Volumes*. Chicago: St. James Press, 1987.

Fogarty, Robert S. "Oneida: A Utopian Search for Religious Security." *Labor History* 14, 2 (Spring 1973): 202–27.

Folbre, Nancy. "Exploitation Comes Home: A Critique of the Marxian Theory of Family Labour." *Cambridge Journal of Economics* 6 (1982): 317–29.

Foner, Eric. *Free Soil, Free Labor, Free Men: The Ideology of the Republican Party Before the Civil War*. New York: Oxford University Press, 1970.

_____. *Politics and Ideology in the Age of the Civil War*. New York: Oxford University Press, 1980.

_____. "Tom Paine's Republic: Radical Ideology and Social Change." In Alfred F. Young, ed.,*The American Revolution: Explorations in the History of American Radicalism*. DeKalb: Northern Illinois University Press, 1976.

_____. "Why Is There No Socialism in the United States?" *History Workshop* 17 (Spring 1984): 57–80.

Foner, Philip S. *History of the Labor Movement in the United States*. Vol. 1. New York: International Publishers, 1947.

Fones-Wolf, Elizabeth, and Kenneth Fones-Wolf. "Knights versus the Trade Unionists: The Case of the Washington, D.C. Carpenters, 1881–1896." *Labor History* 22, 2 (Spring 1981): 192–212.

Forbath, William E. "Courts, Constitutions, and Labor Politics in England and America: A Study of the Constitutive Power of Law." *Law and Social Inquiry* 16, 1 (Winter 1991): 1-34.

_____. "Rethinking Law's Role in Labor History: The Labor Injunction, the Anti-Injunction Campaigns, and the Transformation of 'Rights Consciousness.'" Paper presented at a conference on "Historical Perspectives on American Labor: An Interdisciplinary Approach." New York State School of Industrial and Labor Relations, Cornell University, 21–24 April 1988.

_____. "The Shaping of the American Labor Movement." 102 *Harvard Law Review* 1109 (1989).

Forkosch, Morris D. "The Doctrine of Criminal Conspiracy and Its Modern Application to Labor." Pts. 1 and 2. 40 *Texas Law Review* 303 (1962).

Formisano, Ronald P. *The Birth of Mass Political Parties: Michigan, 1827–1861*. Princeton: Princeton University Press, 1971.

——. "Deferential-Participant Politics: The Early Republic's Political Culture, 1789–1840." *American Political Science Review* 68 (1974): 473–87.

——. "Toward a Reorientation of Jacksonian Politics: A Review of the Literature, 1959–1975." *Journal of American History* 63, 1 (June 1976): 42–65.

Foster, James Caldwell. *The Union Politic: The CIO Political Action Committee.* Columbia: University of Missouri Press, 1975.

Foster, John. *Class Struggle and the Industrial Revolution: Early Industrial Capitalism in Three English Towns.* New York: St. Martin's Press, 1974.

Fox, Alan. *History and Heritage: The Social Origins of the British Industrial Relations System.* London: Allen and Unwin, 1986.

Fox, Alan, and Allan Flanders. "The Reform of Collective Bargaining: From Donovan to Durkheim." *British Journal of Industrial Relations* 7, 2 (July 1969): 151–80.

Fox, Dixon Ryan. "New York Becomes a Democracy." In Alexander C. Flick, ed., *History of the State of New York*, vol. 6. New York: Columbia University Press, 1934.

Fox-Genovese, Elizabeth, and Eugene D. Genovese. "The Political Crisis of Social History: A Marxian Perspective." *Journal of Social History* 10, 2 (Winter 1976): 205–20.

Frankfurter, Felix, and Nathan Greene. *The Labor Injunction.* New York: Macmillan, 1930.

Frey, John P. *The Labor Injunction: An Exposition of Government by Judicial Conscience and Its Menace.* Cincinnati, Ohio: Equity Publishing, 1923.

Friedman, Lawrence M. *A History of American Law.* New York: Simon and Schuster, 1973.

——. "Law Reform in Historical Perspective." 13 *St. Louis University Law Journal* 351 (1969).

Friedman, Lawrence M., and Harry N. Scheiber, eds. *American Law and the Constitutional Order.* Cambridge, Mass.: Harvard University Press, 1978.

Frisch, Michael H., and Daniel J. Walkowitz, eds. *Working Class America: Essays on Labor, Community, and American Society.* Urbana: University of Illinois Press, 1983.

Frug, Gerald E. "The City as a Legal Concept." 93 *Harvard Law Review* 1057 (1980).

Funston, Richard. "The Supreme Court and Critical Elections." *American Political Science Review* 69, 3 (September 1975): 795–811.

Fusfeld, Daniel R. *The Rise and Repression of Radical Labor: USA—1877–1918.* Chicago: Charles H. Kerr, 1980.

Galambos, Louis. "The Agrarian Image of the Large Corporation, 1879–1920: A Study in Social Accommodation." *Journal of Economic History* 28, 3 (September 1968): 341–62.

Galenson, Walter, ed. *Comparative Labor Movements.* New York: Russell and Russell, 1968.

——. "Why the American Labor Movement Is Not Socialist." *American Review* 1, 2 (Winter 1961): 31–53.

Garlock, Jonathan Ezra. "A Structural Analysis of the Knights of Labor: A Prolegomenon to the History of the Producing Classes." Ph.D. diss., University of Rochester, 1974.

Gash, Norman. *Politics in the Age of Peel: A Study in the Techniques of Parliamentary Representation, 1830–1850*. New York: Norton, 1953.

Gawalt, Gerard W. "Sources of Anti-Lawyer Sentiment in Massachusetts, 1740–1840." *American Journal of Legal History* 14, 4 (October 1970): 283–307.

_____, ed. *The New High Priests: Lawyers in Post–Civil War America*. Westport, Conn.: Greenwood Press, 1984.

Geertz, Clifford. *The Interpretation of Cultures*. New York: Basic Books, 1973.

_____. *Local Knowledge: Further Essays in Interpretive Anthropology*. New York: Basic Books, 1983.

Geldart, W. M. "The Status of Trade Unions in England." 25 *Harvard Law Review* 579 (1912).

George, M. Dorothy. "The Combination Laws." *Economic History Review* 6, 2 (April 1936): 172–78.

_____. "The Combination Laws Reconsidered." *Economic History* 1 (1927): 214–28.

Getman, Julius G., and Thomas C. Kohler. "The Common Law, Labor Law, and Reality: A Response to Professor Epstein." 92 *Yale Law Journal* 1415 (1983).

Gitelman, H. M. "The Labor Force at Waltham Watch During the Civil War Era." *Journal of Economic History* 25, 2 (June 1965): 214–43.

Gold, D., C. Lo, and E. O. Wright. "Recent Developments in Marxist Theories of the State." Pts. 1 and 2. *Monthly Review* 26, 5 and 6 (1975): 29–43, 36–51.

Goldfield, Michael. "Class, Race, and Politics in the United States: White Supremacy as the Main Explanation for the Peculiarities of American Politics from Colonial Times to the Present." *Research in Political Economy* 12 (1990): 83–127.

Goldman, Alvin L. *The Supreme Court and Labor-Management Relations Law*. Lexington, Mass.: Lexington Books, 1976.

Goldthorpe, John H. "Industrial Relations in Great Britain: A Critique of Reformism." In Tom Clarke and Laurie Clements, eds., *Trade Unions under Capitalism*. Atlantic Highlands, N.J.: Humanities Press, 1978.

_____, ed. *Order and Conflict in Contemporary Capitalism: Studies in the Political Economy of Western European Nations*. Oxford: Clarendon Press, 1984.

Goodrich, Carter. "Internal Improvements Reconsidered." *Journal of Economic History* 30, 2 (June 1970): 289–311.

Goodwyn, Lawrence. *The Populist Moment: A Short History of the Agrarian Revolt in America*. New York: Oxford University Press, 1978.

Gordon, Michael. "The Labor Boycott in New York City, 1880–1886." *Labor History* 16, 2 (Spring 1975): 184–229.

Gordon, Robert W. "Critical Legal Histories." 36 *Stanford Law Review* 57 (1984).

Gorn, Elliot J. " 'Good-Bye Boys, I Die a True American': Homicide, Nativism, and Working-Class Culture in Antebellum New York City." *Journal of American History* 74, 2 (September 1987): 388–410.

Grant, J.A.C. "Judicial Control of Legislation: A Comparative Study." *American Journal of Comparative Law* 3, 2 (1954): 186–98.

Gray, Robert. *The Aristocracy of Labour in Nineteenth-Century Britain c. 1850–1914*. London: Macmillan, 1981.

Green, James. "Working Class Militancy in the Depression." *Radical America* 6, 6 (November–December 1972): 1–35.

Greenbaum, Fred. "The Social Ideas of Samuel Gompers," *Labor History* 7, 1 (Winter 1966): 35–61.

Greenberg, Brian. *Worker and Community: Response to Industrialization in a Nineteenth-Century American City, Albany, New York, 1850–1884*. Albany: State University of New York Press, 1985.

Greene, Julia. " 'The Strike at the Ballot Box': The American Federation of Labor's Entrance into Electoral Politics, 1906–1909." *Labor History* 32, 2 (Spring 1991): 165–92.

Greenstone, J. David. *Labor in American Politics*. New York: Knopf, 1969.

————. "Political Culture and American Political Development: Liberty, Union, and the Liberal Bipolarity." *Studies in American Political Development* 1 (1986): 1–49.

Gregory, Charles O., and Harold A. Katz. *Labor and the Law*. New York: Norton, 1979.

Grimsted, David. "Ante-bellum Labor: Violence, Strike, and Commercial Arbitration." *Journal of Social History* 19, 1 (Fall 1985): 5–28.

Griswold, Erwin N. *Law and Lawyers in the United States: The Common Law Under Stress*. London: Hamlyn Trust, 1964.

Groat, George Gorham. *Trade Unions and the Law in New York: A Study of Some Legal Phases of Labor Organization*. 1903. New York: AMS Press, 1978.

Grobb, Gerald N. "The Knights of Labor, Politics, and Populism." *Mid-America* 40, 1 (January 1958): 3–21.

————. "Reform Unionism: The National Labor Union." *Journal of Economic History* 14, 2 (Spring 1954): 126–42.

————. "Terence V. Powderly and the Knights of Labor." *Mid-America* 39, 1 (January 1957): 39–55.

————. *Workers and Utopia: A Study of Ideological Conflict in the American Labor Movement, 1865–1900*. Evanston, Ill.: Northwestern University Press, 1961.

Gross, James A. "Conflicting Statutory Purposes: Another Look at Fifty Years of NLRB Law Making." *Industrial Labor Relations Review* 39, 1 (October 1985): 7–18.

Gutman, Herbert G. *Work, Culture and Society in Industrializing America*. New York: Vintage Books, 1977.

Gutman, Herbert G., and Donald H. Bell, eds. *The New England Working Class and the New Labor History*. Urbana: University of Illinois Press, 1987.

Hahn, Stephen. *The Roots of Southern Populism: Yeoman Farmers and the Transformation of the Georgia Upcountry, 1850–1890*. New York: Oxford University Press, 1983.

Haines, Charles Grove. "Some Phases of the Theory and Practice of Judicial Review of Legislation in Foreign Countries." *American Political Science Review* 24, 3 (August 1930): 583–605.

Hall, Kermit L. "The Judiciary on Trial: State Constitutional Reform and the Rise of an Elected Judiciary, 1846–1860." *Historian* 44 (May 1983): 337–54.

————. "Progressive Reform and the Decline of Democratic Accountability: The

Popular Election of State Supreme Court Judges, 1850–1920." *The American Bar Foundation Research Journal* 1984, 2 (Spring 1984): 345–69.

Hall, Peter A. *Governing the Economy: The Politics of State Intervention in Britain and France.* New York: Cambridge University Press, 1986.

Hamer, D. A. *Liberal Politics in the Age of Gladstone and Rosebery: A Study in Leadership and Policy.* New York: Oxford University Press, 1972.

Hammond, Bray. "Free Banks and Corporations: The New York Free Banking Act of 1838." *Journal of Political Economy* 44, 2 (April 1936): 184–209.

———. "Jackson, Biddle, and the Bank of the United States." *Journal of Economic History* 7, 1 (May 1947): 1–23.

Hammond, Jabez D. *The History of Political Parties in the State of New York, from the Ratification of the Federal Constitution to December 1840.* Vols. 1 and 2. Albany, N.Y.: C. Van Benthuysen, 1842.

Handlin, Oscar, and Mary Flug Handlin. *Commonwealth: A Study of the Role of Government in the American Economy: Massachusetts, 1774–1861.* Cambridge, Mass.: Harvard University Press, 1947.

Hanson, C. G. *Trade Unions: A Century of Privilege? An Historical Explanation of the 1971 Industrial Relations Act and the Perennial Issues of Trade Union Power and Law.* Westminster, Engl.: Institute of Economic Affairs, 1973.

Harrison, John F. C. "The Owenite Socialist Movement in Britain and the United States: A Comparative Study." *Labor History* 9, 3 (Fall 1968): 323–37.

Harrison, Royden. *Before the Socialists: Studies in Labour and Politics, 1861–1881.* London: Routledge and Kegan Paul, 1965.

Harrison, Royden, and Jonathan Zeitlin, eds. *Divisions of Labour: Skilled Workers and Technological Change in Nineteenth Century England.* Urbana: University of Illinois Press, 1985.

Hartman, Heidi I. "The Family as the Locus of Gender, Class, and Political Struggle: The Example of Housework." *Signs* 6, 3 (1981): 366–94.

Hartz, Louis. *The Founding of New Societies: Studies in the History of the United States, Latin America, South Africa, Canada, and Australia.* New York: Harcourt, Brace, and World, 1964.

———. *The Liberal Tradition in America: An Interpretation of American Political Thought Since the Revolution.* New York: Harcourt Brace Jovanovich, 1955.

———. "Seth Luther: The Story of a Working-Class Rebel." *New England Quarterly* 13, 3 (September 1940): 401–18.

Hattam, Victoria. "Economic Visions and Political Strategies: American Labor and the State, 1865–1896." *Studies in American Political Development* 4 (1990): 82–129.

———. "Institutions and Political Change: Working-Class Formation in England and the United States, 1820–1896." *Politics and Society* 20, 2 (June 1992): 133–66.

———. "Unions and Politics: The Courts and American Labor, 1806–1896." Ph.D. diss., Massachusetts Institute of Technology, 1987.

———. "The Courts, Labor, and the Question of Class: Criminal Conspiracy Cases, 1806–1896." In Christopher Tomlins and Andrew King, eds., *Labor Law in America: Historical and Critical Essays.* Baltimore: Johns Hopkins University Press, 1992.

Haynes, Evan. *The Selection and Tenure of Judges.* Newark, N.J.: National Conference of Judicial Councils, 1944.

Heath, Frederick M. "Labor and the Progressive Movement in Connecticut." *Labor History* 12, 1 (Winter 1971): 61–62.

Hedges, R. Y., and Allan Winterbottom. *The Legal History of Trade Unionism.* London: Longmans, Green, 1930.

Helfand, Barry F. "Labor and the Courts: The Common-Law Doctrine of Criminal Conspiracy and Its Application in the Buck's Stove Case." *Labor History* 18, 1 (Winter 1977): 91–114.

Henderson, Elizabeth K. "The Attack on the Judiciary in Pennsylvania, 1800–1810." *Pennsylvania Magazine of History and Biography* 61, 2 (April 1937): 113–36.

Hendrix, Lewellyn, and Zakir Hossain. "Women's Status and the Mode of Production: A Cross-Cultural Test." *Signs* 13, 3 (1988): 437–55.

Henretta, James A. "Social History as Lived and Written." *American Historical Review* 84, 5 (December 1979): 1293–1322.

Herrigel, Gary. "Industrial Organization in the Politics of Industry: Centralized and Decentralized Production in Germany." Ph.D. diss., Massachusetts Institute of Technology, 1990.

Higginson, Thomas W. "The Sunny Side of the Transcendental Period." *Atlantic Monthly* 93 (January 1904): 6–14.

Hill, Christopher. *The Century of Revolution, 1603–1714.* New York: Norton, 1961.

Hinton, James. *The First Shop Stewards' Movement.* London: Allen and Unwin, 1973.

———. *Labour and Socialism: A History of the British Labour Movement, 1867–1974.* Amherst: University of Massachusetts Press, 1983.

Hirsch, Fred, and John H. Goldthorpe. *The Political Economy of Inflation.* Cambridge, Mass.: Harvard University Press, 1978.

Hirsch, Harry. *A Theory of Liberty: The Constitution and Minorities.* New York: Routledge, 1992.

Hobsbawm, Eric J. *Labouring Men: Studies in the History of Labour.* London: Weidenfeld and Nicholson, 1964.

———. *Workers: Worlds of Labor.* New York: Pantheon, 1984.

Hobsbawm, Eric J., and George Rudé. *Captain Swing: A Social History of the Great English Agricultural Uprising of 1830.* New York: Norton, 1975.

Hobsbawm, Eric J., and Joan Scott. "Political Shoemakers." *Past and Present* 89 (November 1980): 86–114.

Hochschild, Jennifer L. *What's Fair? American Beliefs about Distributive Justice.* Cambridge, Mass.: Harvard University Press, 1981.

Hofstadter, Richard. *The American Political Tradition and the Men Who Made It.* New York: Random House, 1974.

———. "William Leggett, Spokesman of Jacksonian Democracy." *Political Science Quarterly* 58, 4 (December 1943): 581–94.

Holt, Michael F. *Forging a Majority: The Formation of the Republican Party in Pittsburgh, 1848–1860.* New Haven: Yale University Press, 1969.

———. *The Political Crisis of the 1850s.* New York: Norton, 1978.

Holt, Wythe. "Labour Conspiracy Cases in the United States, 1805–1842: Bias and Legitimation in Common Law Adjudication." 22 *Osgoode Hall Law Journal* 591 (1984).

Hornblower, William B. "A Century of 'Judge-made' Law." 7 *Columbia Law Review* 452 (1907).

Horowitz, Ruth L. *Political Ideologies of Organized Labor.* New Brunswick, N.J.: Transaction Books, 1978.

Horwitz, Morton J. "The Changing Common Law." 9 *Dalhousie Law Journal* 55 (1984).

———. *The Transformation of American Law, 1870–1960: The Crisis of Legal Orthodoxy.* New York: Oxford University Press, 1992.

———. "The History of the Public/Private Distinction." 130 *University of Pennsylvania Law Review* 1423 (1982).

———. "Progressive Legal Historiography." 63 *Oregon Law Review* 679 (1984).

———. "Santa Clara Revisited: The Development of Corporate Theory." 88 *West Virginia Law Review* 173 (1985–1986).

———. *The Transformation of American Law, 1780–1860.* Cambridge, Mass.: Harvard University Press, 1977.

Hovenkamp, Herbert. "The Classical Corporation in American Legal Thought." 76 *Georgetown Law Journal* 1593 (1988).

———. "Labor Conspiracies in American Law, 1880–1930." 66 *Texas Law Review* 919 (1988).

Howe, Daniel Walker. *The Political Culture of the American Whigs.* Chicago: University of Chicago Press, 1979.

Howe, Mark DeWolfe. "The Creative Period in the Law of Massachusetts." *Proceedings of the Massachusetts Historical Society* 69 (1949): 234–51.

———, ed. *Readings in American Legal History.* Cambridge, Mass.: Harvard University Press, 1949.

Howell, Chris. *Regulating Labor: The State and Industrial Relations Reform in Postwar France.* Princeton: Princeton University Press, 1992.

Howell, David. *British Workers and the Independent Labour Party, 1888–1906.* Manchester, Engl.: Manchester University Press, 1983.

Howell, George. *Labour Legislation, Labour Movements, and Labour Leaders.* London: T. Fisher Unwin, 1902.

Hugins, Walter. *Jacksonian Democracy and the Working Class: A Study of the New York Workingmen's Movement, 1829–1837.* Stanford: Stanford University Press, 1960.

Hunt, Lynn. *Politics, Culture, and Class in the French Revolution.* Berkeley: University of California Press, 1984.

———, ed. *The New Cultural History.* Berkeley: University of California Press, 1989.

Huntington, Samuel P. "American Ideas Versus American Institutions." *Political Science Quarterly* 97, 1 (Spring 1982): 1–37.

———. *American Politics: The Promise of Disharmony.* Cambridge, Mass.: Harvard University Press, 1981.

———. *Political Order in Changing Societies.* New Haven: Yale University Press, 1968.

Hurst, Willard. *The Legitimacy of the Business Corporation in the Law of the United States, 1780–1970*. Charlottesville: University Press of Virginia, 1970.

Hurvitz, Haggai. "American Labor Law and the Doctrine of Entrepreneurial Property Rights: Boycotts, Courts, and the Juridical Reorientation of 1886–1895." *Industrial Relations Law Journal* 8, 3 (1986): 307–61.

Hurwitz, Howard Lawrence. *Theodore Roosevelt and Labor in New York State, 1880–1900*. New York: Columbia University Press, 1943.

Hutchinson, Allan C., ed. *Critical Legal Studies*. Totowa, N.J.: Rowman and Littlefield, 1989.

Hyman, Richard. *Industrial Relations: A Marxist Introduction*. London: Macmillan, 1975.

———. "Inequality, Ideology and Industrial Relations. *British Journal of Industrial Relations* 12, 2 (July 1974): 171–90.

Irons, Peter H. *The New Deal Lawyers*. Princeton: Princeton University Press, 1982.

Jackson, Sidney L. "Labor, Education, and Politics in the 1830's." *Pennsylvania Magazine of History and Biography* 66, 3 (July 1942): 279–93.

Jaffin, George H. "Theorems in Anglo-American Labor Law." 31 *Columbia Law Review* 1104 (1931).

Jensen, Richard. *The Winning of the Midwest: Social and Political Conflict, 1888–1896*. Chicago: University of Chicago Press, 1971.

Jones, Gareth Stedman. *Languages of Class: Studies in English Working Class History, 1832–1982*. London: Cambridge University Press, 1983.

———. *Outcast London: A Study in the Relationship Between Classes in Victorian Society*. New York: Pantheon, 1971.

Joyce, Patrick. "The Factory Politics of Lancashire in the Later Nineteenth Century." *The Historical Journal* 18, 3 (1975): 525–53.

———. *Work, Society, and Politics: The Culture of the Factory in Later Victorian England*. Brighton, Engl.: Harvester, 1980.

Judt, Tony. "A Clown in Regal Purple: Social History and the Historians." *History Workshop* 7 (Spring 1979): 66–94.

Kairys, David, ed. *The Politics of Law: A Progressive Critique*. New York: Pantheon, 1982.

Kassalow, Everett M. *Trade Unions and Industrial Relations: An International Comparison*. New York: Random House, 1969.

Katznelson, Ira. *City Trenches: Urban Politics and the Patterning of Class in the United States*. Chicago: University of Chicago Press, 1981.

———. "Considerations on Social Democracy in the United States." *Comparative Politics* 11 (October 1978): 77–99.

Katznelson, Ira, and Aristide R. Zolberg, eds. *Working-Class Formation: Nineteenth-Century Patterns in Western Europe and the United States*. Princeton: Princeton University Press, 1986.

Kaufman, Stuart Bruce. *Samuel Gompers and the Origins of the American Federation of Labor, 1848–1896*. Westport, Conn.: Greenwood Press, 1973.

Kelman, Ellen M. "American Labor Law and Legal Formalism: How 'Legal Logic' Shaped and Vitiated the Rights of American Workers." 58 *St. John's Law Review* 1 (1983).

Kennedy, Duncan. "Critical Labor Law Theory: A Comment." *Industrial Relations Law Journal* 4, 3 (1981): 503–6.

_____. "The Structure of Blackstone's Commentaries." 28 *Buffalo Law Review* 205 (1979).

Kerr, Thomas J. "The New York Factory Investigating Commission and the Minimum Wage Movement." *Labor History* 11, 3 (Summer 1971): 373–91.

Killeen, Edward Charles. "John Siney: The Pioneer in American Industrial Unionism and Industrial Government." Ph.D. diss., University of Wisconsin, 1942.

Klare, Karl E. "Critical Theory and Labor Relations Law." In David Kairys, ed., *The Politics of Law: A Progressive Critique*. New York: Pantheon, 1982.

_____. "Judicial Deradicalization of the Wagner Act and the Origins of Modern Legal Consciousness, 1937–1941." 62 *Minnesota Law Review* 265 (1977–1978).

_____. "Labor Law as Ideology: Toward a New Historiography of Collective Bargaining Law." *Industrial Relations Journal* 4, 3 (1981): 450–82.

Kleppner, Paul. *The Cross of Culture: A Social Analysis of Midwestern Politics, 1850–1900*. New York: The Free Press, 1970.

_____. "Partisanship and Ethnoreligious Conflict: The Third Electoral System, 1853–1892." In Paul Kleppner, Walter Dean Burnham, Ronald P. Formisano, Samuel P. Hayes, Richard Jensen, and William G. Shade, eds., *The Evolution of American Electoral Systems*. Westport, Conn.: Greenwood Press, 1981.

Kochan, Thomas A. *Collective Bargaining and Industrial Relations: From Theory to Policy and Practice*. Homewood, Ill.: Irwin-Dorsey, 1980.

Kochan, Thomas A., Harry C. Katz, and Robert B. Mckersie. *The Transformation of American Industrial Relations*. New York: Basic Books, 1986.

Kramnick, Isaac. "The 'Great National Discussion': The Discourse of Politics in 1787." *William and Mary Quarterly* 45, 1 (January 1988): 3–32.

_____. "Republican Revisionism Revisited." *American Historical Review* 87, 3 (June 1982): 629–64.

Krasner, Stephen. "Approaches to the State: Alternative Conceptions and Historical Dynamics." *Comparative Politics* 16, 2 (January 1984): 223–46.

Kuritz, Hyman. "Criminal Conspiracy Cases in Post-bellum Pennsylvania." *Pennsylvania History* 18 (October 1950): 292–301.

_____. "The Pennsylvania State Government and Labor Controls from 1865 to 1922." Ph.D. diss., Columbia University, 1953.

Landes, David S. *The Unbound Prometheus: Technological Change and Industrial Development in Western Europe from 1750 to the Present*. New York: Cambridge University Press, 1969.

Landis, James McCauley, and Marcus Manoff. *Cases on Labor Law*. Chicago: The Foundation Press, 1942.

LaPalombara, Joseph, and Myron Weiner, eds. *Political Parties and Political Development*. Princeton: Princeton University Press, 1966.

Laslett, John H. M., and Seymour Martin Lipset, eds. *Failure of a Dream? Essays in the History of American Socialism*. New York: Doubleday, 1974.

Laurie, Bruce. "Nothing on Compulsion: Life Styles of Philadelphia Artisans, 1820–1850." *Labor History* 15, 3 (Summer 1974): 337–66.

_____. *Working People of Philadelphia, 1800–1850*. Philadelphia: Temple University Press, 1980.

Lazerow, Jama. " 'The Workingmen's Hour': The 1886 Labor Uprising in Boston." *Labor History* 21, 2 (Spring 1980): 200–220.

Lazonick, William. "Industrial Relations and Technical Change: The Case of the Self-acting Mule." *Cambridge Journal of Economics* 3, 3 (1979): 231–62.

Lenhoff, Arthur. "A Century of American Unionism." 22 *Boston University Law Review* 357 (1942).

Levine, Susan. "Labor's True Woman: Domesticity and Equal Rights in the Knights of Labor." *Journal of American History* 70, 2 (September 1983): 323–39.

Levy, Leonard W. *The Law of the Commonwealth and Chief Justice Shaw.* Cambridge, Mass.: Harvard University Press, 1957.

Lewis, Roy. "The Historical Development of Labour Law." *British Journal of Industrial Relations* 14, 1 (1976): 1–17.

Lichtenstein, Nelson. "Ambiguous Legacy: The Union Security Problem During World War II." *Labor History* 18, 2 (Spring 1977): 214–38.

——. "Auto Worker Militancy and the Structure of Factory Life, 1937–1955." *Journal of American History* 67, 2 (September 1980): 335–53.

——. "From Corporatism to Collective Bargaining: Organized Labor and the Eclipse of Social Democracy in the Postwar Era." Paper presented at a conference on "Historical Perspectives on American Labor: An Interdisciplinary Approach." New York State School of Industrial and Labor Relations, Cornell University, 21–24 April 1988.

——. *Labor's War at Home: The CIO in World War II.* New York: Cambridge University Press, 1982.

Lichtman, Alan. "Critical Election Theory and the Reality of American Presidential Politics, 1916–1940." *American Historical Review* 81, 2 (April 1976): 317–51.

Liebow, Elliot. *Tally's Corner: A Study of Negro Streetcorner Men.* Boston: Little, Brown, 1967.

Lincoln, Charles Z. *The Constitutional History of the State of New York from the Beginning of the Colonial Period to the Year 1905.* 5 vols. Rochester, N.Y.: Lawyers Co-operative Publishing Company, 1906.

Lipset, Seymour Martin. "The Changing Class Structure and Contemporary European Politics." *Daedalus* 93, 1 (Winter 1964): 271–303.

——. *The First New Nation: The United States in Historical and Comparative Perspective.* New York: Doubleday, 1963.

——. "Radicalism or Reformism: The Sources of Working-Class Politics." *American Political Science Review* 77, 1 (March 1983): 1–19.

——. "Trade Unions and Social Structure: I." *Industrial Relations* 1, 1 (October 1961): 75–89.

——. "Trade Unions and Social Structure: II." *Industrial Relations* 1, 2 (February 1962): 89–110.

Lipset, Seymour Martin, and Stein Rokkan. *Party Systems and Voter Alignments: Cross-National Perspectives.* New York: The Free Press, 1967.

Lively, Robert A. "The American System, A Review Article." *Business History Review* 29 (March 1955): 81–96.

Livesay, Harold. *Samuel Gompers and Organized Labor in America.* Boston: Little, Brown, 1978.

Locke, Richard. "Local Politics and Industrial Adjustment: The Political Economy of Italy in the 1980s." Ph.D. diss., Massachusetts Institute of Technology, 1989.

Lorwin, Val R. "Working-Class Politics and Economic Development in Western Europe." In Mattei Dogan and Richard Rose, eds., *European Politics: A Reader.* Boston: Little, Brown, 1971.

Lothian, Tamara. "The Political Consequences of Labor Law Regimes: The Corporatist and Contractualist Models Compared." 7 *Cardozo Law Review* 1001 (1986).

Lynd, Staughton. "Government Without Rights: The Labor Law Vision of Archibald Cox." *Industrial Relations Law Journal* 4, 3 (1981): 483–95.

———. "The Possibility of Radicalism in the Early 1930s: The Case of Steel." *Radical America* 6, 6 (November–December 1972): 36–64.

Macpherson, C. B. *The Political Theory of Possessive Individualism: Hobbes to Locke.* Oxford: Oxford University Press, 1962.

Maier, Pauline. *From Resistance to Revolution: Colonial Radicals and the Development of American Opposition to Britain, 1765–1776.* New York: Vintage Books, 1972.

Mandel, Bernard. *Samuel Gompers: A Biography.* Yellow Springs, Ohio: Antioch Press, 1963.

March, James G., and Johan P. Olsen. "The New Institutionalism: Organizational Factors in Political Life." *American Political Science Review* 78, 3 (September 1984): 734–49.

Marks, Gary. *Unions in Politics: Britain, Germany, and the United States in the Nineteenth and Early Twentieth Centuries.* Princeton: Princeton University Press, 1989.

Mason, Alpheus T. *Organized Labor and the Law: With Special Reference to the Sherman and Clayton Acts.* Durham: Duke University Press, 1925.

Matlack, Samuel Dreher. "John Bannister Gibson, 1780–1853." In William Draper Lewis, ed., *Great American Lawyers: A History of the Legal Profession in America*, vol. 3. Philadelphia: John C. Winston, 1908.

Mayer, Stephen. "People v. Fisher: The Shoemakers' Strike of 1833." *New York Historical Society Quarterly* 62 (1978): 6–21.

Mayhew, Anne. "A Reappraisal of the Causes of Farm Protest in the U.S., 1870–1900." *Journal of Economic History* 32, 2 (June 1972): 464–75.

Mayhew, David R. *Placing Parties in American Politics: Organization, Electoral Settings, and Government Activity in the Twentieth Century.* Princeton: Princeton University Press, 1986.

McCloskey, Robert G. *The American Supreme Court.* Chicago: University of Chicago Press, 1960.

McCormick, Richard L. "Ethno-Cultural Interpretations of Nineteenth-Century American Voting Behavior." *Political Science Quarterly* 89, 2 (June 1974): 351–77.

McCormick, Richard P. "New Perspectives on Jacksonian Politics." *American Historical Review* 65 (January 1960): 288–301.

McCoy, Drew R. "Benjamin Franklin's Vision of a Republican Political Economy for America." *William and Mary Quarterly*, 3d series, 35, 4 (October 1978): 605–28.

———. *The Elusive Republic: Political Economy in Jeffersonian America*. New York: Norton, 1980.

McCready, H. W. "The British Election of 1874: Frederic Harrison and the Liberal-Labour Dilemma." *Canadian Journal of Economics and Political Science* 20, 2 (May 1954): 166–75.

———. "British Labour and the Royal Commission on Trade Unions, 1867–1869." *University of Toronto Quarterly* 24, 4 (July 1955): 390–409.

———. "British Labour's Lobby, 1867–1875." *Canadian Journal of Economics and Political Science* 22, 2 (May 1956): 141–60.

McCurdy, Charles. "American Law and the Marketing Structure of the Large Corporation, 1875–1890." *Journal of Economic History* 38, 3 (September 1978): 631–49.

McDonald, Terrence J. "The Burdens of Urban History: The Theory of the State in Recent American Social History." *Studies in American Political Development* 3 (1989): 3–29.

———. "The Problem of the Political in Recent American Urban History: Liberal Pluralism and the Rise of Functionalism." *Social History* 10, 3 (October 1985): 323–45.

Meyers, Marvin. "The Jacksonian Persuasion." *American Quarterly* 5, 1 (Spring 1953): 3–15.

———. *The Jacksonian Persuasion: Politics and Belief*. Stanford: Stanford University Press, 1957.

Miller, Ernest C. "Utopian Communities in Warren County, Pennsylvania." *Western Pennsylvania Historical Magazine* 49 (1966): 301–17.

Mink, Gwendolyn. *Old Labor and New Immigrants in American Political Development: Union, Party, and State, 1875-1920*. Ithaca, N.Y.: Cornell University Press, 1986.

Mitchell, J.D.B. "Sovereignty of Parliament—Yet Again." *79 Law Quarterly Review* 196 (1963).

Montgomery, David. *Beyond Equality: Labor and the Radical Republicans, 1862–1872*. Urbana: University of Illinois Press, 1981.

———. *The Fall of the House of Labor: The Workplace, the State, and American Labor Activism, 1865–1925*. New York: Cambridge University Press, 1987.

———. "Labor and the Republic in Industrial America: 1860–1920. *Le Movement social* 111 (1980): 201–15.

———. "Radical Republicanism in Pennsylvania, 1866–1873." *Pennsylvania Magazine of History and Biography* 85 (October 1961): 439–57.

———. "The Shuttle and the Cross: Weavers and Artisans in the Kensington Riots of 1844." *Journal of Social History* 5, 4 (Summer 1972): 411–46.

———. "To Study the People: The American Working Class." *Labor History* 21, 4 (Fall 1980): 485–513.

———. "William H. Sylvis and the Search for Working-Class Citizenship." In Melvyn Dubofsky and Warren Van Tine, eds., *Labor Leaders in America*. Urbana: University of Illinois Press, 1987.

———. *Workers' Control in America: Studies in the History of Work, Technology, and Labor Struggles*. New York: Cambridge University Press, 1980.

_____. "The Working Classes of the Pre-Industrial American City, 1780–1830." *Labor History* 9, 1 (Winter 1968): 3–22.

Moore, Barrington, Jr. *Social Origins of Dictatorship and Democracy: Lord and Peasant in the Making of a Modern World.* Boston: Beacon Press, 1966.

Morgan, Edmund S. "The Puritan Ethic and the American Revolution." *William and Mary Quarterly*, 3d series, 24, 4 (October 1967): 3–43.

Morris, Richard B. "Andrew Jackson: Strikebreaker." *American Historical Review* 55 (October 1949): 54–68.

_____. "Criminal Conspiracy and Early Labor Combinations in New York." *Political Science Quarterly* 52, 1 (March 1937): 51–85.

_____. *Government and Labor in Early America.* New York: Octagon Books, 1965.

_____, ed. *A History of the American Worker.* Princeton: Princeton University Press, 1983.

Myers, Howard A. *Labor Law and Legislation.* Cincinnati, Ohio: South-Western, 1968.

Nadel, Stanley. *Little Germany: Ethnicity, Religion, and Class in New York City, 1845–80.* Urbana: University of Illinois Press, 1990.

Nadworny, Milton J. "New Jersey Workingmen and the Jacksonians." *Proceedings of the New Jersey Historical Society* 67, 3 (July 1949): 185–98.

Nash, Gary B. "Social Change and the Growth of Pre-revolutionary Urban Radicalism." In Alfred F. Young, ed., *The American Revolution: Exploration in the History of American Radicalism.* DeKalb: Northern Illinois University Press, 1976.

Nelles, Walter. "Commonwealth v. Hunt." 32 *Columbia Law Review* 1128 (1932).

_____. "The First American Labor Case." 41 *Yale Law Journal* 165 (1931).

_____. "A Strike and Its Legal Consequences: An Examination of the Receivership Precedent for the Labor Injunction." 40 *Yale Law Journal* 507 (1931).

Nelson, Daniel. "Origins of the Sit-Down Era: Worker Militancy and Innovation in the Rubber Industry, 1934–1938." *Labor History* 43, 2 (Spring 1982): 198–225.

Nelson, William E. *Americanization of the Common Law: The Impact of Legal Change on Massachusetts Society, 1760–1830.* Cambridge, Mass.: Harvard University Press, 1975.

Nettl, J. P. "The State as a Conceptual Variable." *World Politics* 20, 4 (July 1968): 559–92.

Neufield, Maurice F. "The Persistence of Ideas in the American Labor Movement: The Heritage of the 1830s." *Industrial and Labor Relations Review* 35, 2 (January 1982): 207–20.

Neumann, Franz Leopold. *The Democratic and the Authoritarian State: Essays in Political and Legal Theory.* New York: The Free Press, 1957.

Niles, Russell D. "The Popular Election of Judges in Historical Perspective." *The Record of the Association of the Bar of the City of New York* 21, 8 (November 1966): 523–38.

Nolan, Mary. "Economic Crisis, State Policy, and Working-Class Formation in Germany, 1870–1900." In Ira Katznelson and Aristide Zolberg, eds., *Working-*

Class Formation: Nineteenth-Century Patterns in Western Europe and the United States. Princeton: Princeton University Press, 1986.

Norton, Anne. *Alternative Americas: A Reading of Antebellum Political Culture*. Chicago: University of Chicago Press, 1986.

―――. *Reflections on Political Identity*. Baltimore: Johns Hopkins University Press, 1988.

O'Brien, Patrick, and Caglar Keyder. *Economic Growth in Britain and France, 1780–1914: Two Paths to the Twentieth Century*. London: Allen and Unwin, 1978.

O'Connor, James. *The Fiscal Crisis of the State*. New York: St. Martin's Press, 1973.

Oestreicher, Richard. "Socialism and the Knights of Labor in Detroit, 1877–1886." *Labor History* 22, 1 (Winter 1981): 5–30.

―――. *Solidarity and Fragmentation: Working People and Class Consciousness in Detroit, 1875–1900*. Urbana: University of Illinois Press, 1986.

―――. "Terence V. Powderly, the Knights of Labor, and Artisanal Republicanism." In Melvyn Dubofsky and Warren Van Tine, eds., *Labor Leaders in America*. Urbana: University of Illinois Press, 1987.

―――. "Urban Working-Class Political Behavior and Theories of American Electoral Politics, 1870–1940." *Journal of American History* 74, 4 (March 1988): 1257–86.

Offe, Claus. *Disorganized Capitalism*. Cambridge, Mass.: MIT Press, 1985.

O'Higgins, Paul, and Martin Partington. "Industrial Conflict: Judicial Attitudes." 32 *Modern Law Review* 53 (1969).

Orloff, Ann Shola, and Theda Skocpol. "Why Not Equal Protection? Explaining the Politics of Public Social Spending in Britain, 1900–1911, and the United States, 1880s–1920." *American Sociological Review* 49 (December 1984): 726–50.

Orren, Karen. *Belated Feudalism: Labor, the Law, and Liberal Development in the United States*. New York: Cambridge University Press, 1991.

―――. "Metaphysics and Reality in Late Nineteenth Century Labor Adjudication." In Christopher L. Tomlins and Andrew J. King, eds., *Labor Law in America: Historical and Critical Essays*. Baltimore: Johns Hopkins University Press, 1992.

―――. "Organized Labor and the Invention of Modern Liberalism in the United States." *Studies in American Political Development* 2 (1987): 317–36.

Orren, Karen, and Stephen Skowronek. "Beyond the Iconography of Order: Notes for a 'New' Institutionalism." Paper presented at the annual meeting of the American Political Science Association, Washington D.C., 30 August 1991.

Orth, John Victor. "Combination and Conspiracy: The Legal Status of English Trade Unions, 1799–1871." Ph.D. diss., Harvard University, 1977.

―――. "English Law and Striking Workmen: The Molestation of Workmen Act, 1859." *Journal of Legal History* 2, 3 (December 1981): 238–57.

―――. "The Law of Strikes, 1847–1871." In J. A. Guy and H. G. Beale, eds., *Law and Social Change in British History*. London: Royal Historical Society, 1984.

Panitch, Leo. "The Development of Corporatism in Liberal Democracies." *Comparative Studies* 10, 1 (April 1977): 61–90.

Paul, Arnold M. *Conservative Crisis and the Rule of Law: Attitudes of Bar and Bench, 1887–1895*. Gloucester, Mass.: Peter Smith, 1976.

Peck, Gunther. "Crisis in the Family: Padrones and Radicals in Utah, 1908–1912." In Dan Georgakas and Charles C. Moskos, eds., *New Directions in Greek-American Studies*. New York: Pella Press, 1991.

Peiss, Kathy. *Cheap Amusements: Working Women and Leisure in Turn-of-the-Century New York*. Philadelphia: Temple University Press, 1986.

Pelling, Henry. *A History of British Trade Unionism*. Suffolk, Engl.: Penguin, 1963.

_____. *Popular Politics and Society in Late Victorian Britain*. London: Macmillan, 1968.

_____. *A Short History of the Labour Party*. New York: Macmillan, 1965.

Perlman, Selig. *A Theory of the Labor Movement*. Philadelphia: Porcupine Press, 1928.

_____. "Upheaval and Reorganization." In John R. Commons, David J. Saposs, Helen L. Sumner, E. B. Mittleman, H. E. Hoagland, John B. Andrews, and Selig Perlman, eds., *History of Labor in the United States*. New York: Macmillan, 1936.

Persons, Stow. "Christian Communitarianism in America." In Donald Drew Egbert and Stow Persons, ed., *Socialism and American Life*. Princeton: Princeton University Press, 1952.

Pessen, Edward. "Did Labor Support Jackson?: The Boston Story." *Political Science Quarterly* 64, 2 (June 1949): 262–74.

_____. *Jacksonian America: Society, Personality, and Politics*. Homewood, Ill.: Dorsey Press, 1978.

_____. *Most Uncommon Jacksonians: The Radical Leaders of the Early Labor Movement*. Albany: State University of New York Press, 1967.

_____. "Should Labor Have Supported Jackson?; Or, Questions the Quantitative Studies Do Not Answer." *Labor History* 13, 3 (Summer 1972): 227–37.

_____. "Thomas Brothers, Anti-Capitalist Employer," *Pennsylvania History* 24, 4 (October 1957): 321–29.

_____. "The Workingmen's Movement of the Jacksonian Era." *Mississippi Valley Historical Review* 43, 3 (December 1956): 428–43.

_____. "The Working Men's Party Revisited." *Labor History* 4, 3 (Fall 1963): 203–26.

Peterson, Florence. *Strikes in the United States, 1880–1936*. Bureau of Labor Statistics, Bulletin 651, August 1937.

Petro, Sylvester. "Injunctions and Labor-Disputes: 1880–1932." 14 *Wake Forest Law Review* 341 (1978).

_____. "Unions and the Southern Courts: Part III—The Conspiracy and Tort Foundations of the Labor Injunction." 60 *North Carolina Law Review* 544 (1982).

Phelps, Orme, and John E. Jeuck. "Criticisms of the National Labor Relations Act." *Journal of Business* 12 (1939): 30–50.

Piore, Michael J. "Convergence in Industrial Relations? The Case of France and the

United States." Working Paper no. 286, Department of Economics, Massachusetts Institute of Technology, July 1981.

———. "Unions and Politics." Conference on the future of unionism in manufacturing in the 1980's. Lake Bluff, Ill., 21–23 June 1978.

Piore, Michael J., and Charles F. Sabel. *The Second Industrial Divide: Possibilities for Prosperity*. New York: Basic Books, 1984.

Pizzorno, Alessandra. "On the Rationality of Democratic Choice." *Telos* 63 (Spring 1985): 41–69.

Plucknett, Theodore F. T. "Bonham's Case and Judicial Review." 40 *Harvard Law Review* 30 (1926).

Pocock, J.G.A. "The Classical Theory of Deference." *American Historical Review* 81 (1976): 516–23.

———. *The Machiavellian Moment: Florentine Political Thought and the Atlantic Republican Tradition*. Princeton: Princeton University Press, 1975.

———. *Politics, Language and Time: Essays on Political Thought and History*. New York: Atheneum, 1973.

———. "Virtue and Commerce in the Eighteenth Century." *Journal of Interdisciplinary History* 3, 1 (Summer 1972): 119–34.

———. *Virtue, Commerce, and History: Essays on Political Thought and History, Chiefly in the Eighteenth Century*. New York: Cambridge University Press, 1985.

Poggi, Gianfranco. *The Development of the Modern State: A Sociological Introduction*. Stanford: Stanford University Press, 1978.

Polanyi, Karl. *The Great Transformation: The Political and Economic Origins of Our Time*. Boston: Beacon Press, 1957.

Pole, J. R. "Historians and the Problem of Early American Democracy." *American Historical Review* 67, 3 (April 1962): 626–46.

Porter, Kirk H. *A History of Suffrage in the United States*. New York: Greenwood Press, 1969.

Pound, Roscoe. "Common Law and Legislation." 21 *Harvard Law Review* 383 (1908).

———. "A Comparison of Systems of Law." 10 *University of Pittsburgh Law Review* 271 (1948).

———. "The Development of American Law and Its Deviation from English Law." 67 *Law Quarterly Review* 49 (1955).

———. *The Formative Era of American Law*. Boston: Little, Brown, 1938.

———. "The Lay Tradition as to the Lawyer." 12 *Michigan Law Review* 627 (1914).

———. "Liberty of Contract." 18 *Yale Law Journal* 454 (1909).

Price, Richard. *Masters, Unions and Men: Work Control in Building and the Rise of Labour, 1830–1914*. London: Cambridge University Press, 1980.

Prothero, Iorwerth J. *Artisans and Politics in Early Nineteenth Century London: John Gast and His Times*. Folkestone, Kent, Engl.: William Dawson and Son, 1979.

———. "Chartism in London." *Past and Present* 44 (August 1969): 76–105.

———. "London Chartism and the Trades." *Economic History Review* 24, 2 (May 1971): 202–19.

Przeworski, Adam. "Material Basis of Consent: Economics and Politics in a Hegemonic System." *Political Power and Social Theory* 1 (1980): 21–66.

———. "Material Interests, Class Compromise, and the Transition to Socialism." *Politics and Society* 10, 2 (1980): 125–53.

———. "Proletariat into a Class: The Process of Class Formation from Karl Kautsky's 'The Class Struggle' to Recent Controversies." *Politics and Society* 7, 4 (1977): 343–401.

———. "Social Democracy as an Historical Phenomenon." *New Left Review* 122 (July–August 1980): 27–58.

Purrington, William A. "The Tubwomen v. the Brewers of London." 3 *Columbia Law Review* 447 (1903).

Quimby, Ian M. G. "The Cordwainers' Protest: A Crisis in Labor Relations." *Winterthur Portfolio* 3 (1967): 83–101.

Rachleff, Peter. *Black Labor in Richmond, 1865–1890*. Urbana: University of Illinois Press, 1989.

Radosh, Ronald. "The Corporate Ideology of American Labor Leaders from Gompers to Hillman." In James Weinstein and David W. Eakins, eds., *For a New America: Essays in History and Politics from Studies on the Left, 1959–1967*. New York: Random House, 1970.

Rae, Douglas W. *The Political Consequences of Electoral Laws*. New Haven: Yale University Press, 1967.

Rancière, Jacques. "The Myth of the Artisan: Critical Reflections on a Category of Social History." *International Labor and Working Class History* 24 (Fall 1983): 1–16.

Rayback, Joseph G. *A History of American Labor*. New York: The Free Press, 1959.

Reid, Alistair. "The Division of Labour and Politics in Britain, 1850–1920." Gonville and Caius College, Cambridge.

Rezneck, Samuel. "The Depression of 1819–1822, A Social History." *American Historical Review* 39, 1 (October 1933): 28–47.

Ricciadi, Joseph. "Rereading Marx on the Role of Money and Finance in Economic Development: Political Perspectives on Credit from the 1840s and 1850s." *Research in Political Economy* 10 (1987): 61–81.

Richards, Paul. "The State and Early Industrial Capitalism: The Case of the Handloom Weavers." *Past and Present* 83 (May 1979): 91–115.

Ricker, Ralph R. "The Greenback-Labor Movement in Pennsylvania." Ph.D. diss., Pennsylvania State University, 1955.

Ritter, Gretchen. "The People Versus the Money Power: Anti-Monopolism and the Politics of Finance, 1865–1896." Ph.D. diss., Massachusetts Institute of Technology, 1992.

Rock, Howard B. *Artisans of the New Republic: The Tradesmen of New York City in the Age of Jefferson*. New York: New York University Press, 1979.

Roediger, David. "'Labor in White Skin': Race and Working-Class History." In Mike Davis and Michael Sprinker, eds., *Reshaping the US Left: Popular Struggles in the 1980s*. New York: Verso, 1988.

Rogers, Joel. "Divide and Conquer: The Legal Foundations of Postwar U.S. Labor Policy." Ph.D. diss., Princeton University, 1984.

Rogin, Michael. "Progressivism and the California Electorate." *Journal of American History* 55 (September 1968): 305–34.

―――. "Voluntarism: The Political Functions of an Anti-political Doctrine." *Industrial and Labor Relations Review* 15, 4 (July 1962): 521–35.

Rosenblum, Gerald. *Immigrant Workers: Their Impact on Labor Radicalism.* New York: Basic Books, 1973.

Rosenzweig, Roy. *Eight Hours for What We Will: Workers and Leisure in an Industrial City, 1870–1920.* New York: Cambridge University Press, 1983.

Ross, Steven J. "The Politicization of the Working Class: Production, Ideology, Culture and Politics in Late Nineteenth-Century Cincinnati." *Social History* 11, 2 (May 1986): 171–95.

―――. *Workers on the Edge: Work, Leisure, and Politics in Industrializing Cincinnati, 1788–1890.* New York: Columbia University Press, 1985.

Rubin, Gayle. "The Traffic in Women: Notes on the 'Political Economy' of Sex." In Rayna R. Reiter, ed., *Toward an Anthropology of Women.* New York: Monthly Review Press, 1975.

Rusk, Jerrod G. "Comment: The American Electoral Universe, Speculation and Evidence." *American Political Science Review* 68, 3 (1974): 1028–49.

Ryan, Mary. *Cradle of the Middle Class: The Family in Oneida County, New York, 1790–1865.* New York: Cambridge University Press, 1981.

Sabel, Charles F. *Work and Politics: The Division of Labor in Industry.* New York: Cambridge University Press, 1982.

Sabel, Charles F., and Jonathan Zeitlin. "Historical Alternatives to Mass Production: Politics, Markets and Technology in Nineteenth-Century Industrialization." *Past and Present* 108 (August 1985): 133–76.

Sahlins, Marshall. *Culture and Practical Reason.* Chicago: University of Chicago Press, 1976.

Salinger, Sharon V. "Artisans, Journeymen, and the Transformation of Labor in Late Eighteenth-Century Philadelphia." *William and Mary Quarterly*, 3d series, 40, 1 (January 1983): 62–84.

Salvatore, Nick. *Eugene V. Debs: Citizen and Socialist.* Urbana: University of Illinois Press, 1982.

―――. "Railroad Workers and the Great Strike of 1877: A View from a Small Midwest City." *Labor History* 21, 4 (Fall 1980): 522–45.

―――, ed. *Seventy Years of Life and Labor: An Autobiography by Samuel Gompers.* New York: ILR Press, 1984.

Samuel, Raphael. "Workshop of the World: Steam Power and Hand Technology in Mid-Victorian Britain." *History Workshop* 3 (Spring 1977): 6–72.

Sapelli, Giulio. "La cultura della produzione: 'autorita tecnica' e 'autonomia morale.'" In Bruno Bottiglieri and Paolo Ceri, eds., *Le Culture de lavoro: L'esperienza di Torino nel guardo europeo.* Bologna: Il Mulino, 1987.

Savetsky, Seymour. "The New York Working Men's Party" M.A. thesis, Columbia University, 1948.

Saxton, Alexander. *The Indispensable Enemy: Labor and the Anti-Chinese Movement in California.* Berkeley: University of California Press, 1971.

Sayre, Francis B. "Criminal Conspiracy." 35 *Harvard Law Review* 393 (1922).

―――. "Labor and the Courts." 39 *Yale Law Journal* 682 (1929–1930).

Schattschneider, E. E. *The Semi-Sovereign People: A Realist's View of Democracy in America.* Hinsdale, Ill.: Dryden Press, 1960.

Scheiber, Harry N. "Federalism and the American Economic Order, 1789–1910." *Law and Society Review* 10, 1 (Fall 1975): 57–118.

Schlegel, Marvin W. "The Workingmen's Benevolent Association: First Union of Anthracite Miners." *Pennsylvania History* 10, 4 (October 1943): 243–67.

Schlesinger, Arthur M., Jr. *The Age of Jackson.* Boston: Little, Brown, 1953.

Schneider, Linda. "The Citizen Striker: Workers' Ideology in the Homestead Strike of 1892." *Labor History* 23, 1 (Winter 1981): 47–66.

Scobey, David. "Boycotting the Politics Factory: Labor Radicalism and the New York City Mayoral Election of 1884." *Radical History Review* 28–30 (1984): 280–325.

Scott, Joan Wallach. *Gender and the Politics of History.* New York: Columbia University Press, 1988.

———. "The Evidence of Experience." *Critical Inquiry* 17, 4 (Summer 1991): 773–97.

Scranton, Philip. *Proprietary Capitalism: The Textile Manufacture at Philadelphia 1800–1885.* Philadelphia: Temple University Press, 1983.

Selfridge, Arthur James. "American Law of Strikes and Boycotts as Crimes." 22 *American Law Review* 233 (1888).

Sellers, Charles Grier, Jr. "Andrew Jackson Versus the Historians." *Mississippi Valley Historical Review* 44, 4 (March 1958): 615–34.

Sewell, William H., Jr. "Ideologies and Social Revolutions: Reflections on the French Case." *Journal of Modern History* 57, 1 (March 1985): 57–85.

———. "A Post-Materialist Rhetoric for Labor History." In Lenard Berlanstein, ed., *Rethinking Labor History.* Urbana: University of Illinois Press, in press.

———. "A Rhetoric of Amnesia, or How the French Revolution Came to Abolish Privilege and Establish Legal Equity." Macrosociology Area Program, UCLA.

———. *Work and Revolution in France: The Language of Labor from the Old Regime to 1848.* New York: Cambridge University Press, 1980.

Shalhope, Robert E. "Republicanism and Early American Historiography." *William and Mary Quarterly*, 3d series, 39, 2 (April 1982): 334–456.

———. "Towards a Republican Synthesis: The Emergence of an Understanding of Republicanism in American Historiography." *William and Mary Quarterly*, 3rd Series, 29, 1 (January 1972): 49–80.

Sharkey, Robert P. *Money, Class, and Party: An Economic Study of Civil War and Reconstruction.* Baltimore: Johns Hopkins University Press, 1959.

Shefter, Martin. "The Electoral Foundations of the Political Machine: New York City, 1884–1897." In Joel H. Silbey, Allan G. Bogue, and William H. Flanigan, eds., *The History of American Electoral Behavior.* Princeton: Princeton University Press, 1978.

———. "Trade Unions and Political Machines: The Organization and Disorganization of the American Working Class in the Late Nineteenth Century." In Ira Katznelson and Aristide Zolberg, eds., *Working Class Formation: Nineteenth Century Patterns in Western Europe and the United States.* Princeton: Princeton University Press, 1986.

Skeels, Joyce Goldy. "The Early American Federation of Labor and Monetary Reform." *Labor History* 12, 4 (Fall 1971): 530–50.

Skocpol, Theda. "Bringing the State Back In: Strategies of Analysis in Current Research." In Peter Evens, Dietrich Rueschemeyer, and Theda Skocpol, eds., *Bringing the State Back In*. New York: Cambridge University Press, 1985.

————. "Cultural Idioms and Political Ideologies in the Revolutionary Reconstructon of State Power: A Rejoinder to Sewell." *Journal of Modern History* 57, 1 (March 1985): 86–96.

————. *Protecting Soldiers and Mothers: The Political Origins of Social Policy in the United States*. Cambridge, Mass.: Harvard University Press, 1992.

————. "Political Response to Capitalist Crisis: Neo-Marxist Theories of the State and the Case of the New Deal." *Politics and Society* 10, 2 (1980): 155–201.

————. *States and Social Revolutions: A Comparative Analysis of France, Russia and China*. New York: Cambridge University Press, 1979.

Skocpol, Theda, and Kenneth Finegold. "State Capacity and Economic Intervention in the Early New Deal." *Political Science Quarterly* 97, 2 (1982): 255–78.

Skokolow, Jayme A. "Culture and Utopia: The Raritan Bay Union." *New Jersey History* 94 (1976): 89–100.

Skowronek, Stephen. *Building a New American State: The Expansion of National Administrative Capacities, 1877–1920*. New York: Cambridge University Press, 1982.

————. "National Railroad Regulation and the Problem of State-Building: Interests and Institutions in Late Nineteenth Century America." *Politics and Society* 10, 3 (1981): 225–50.

————. "Presidential Leadership in Political Time." In Michael Nelson, ed., *The Presidency and the Political System*. Washington, D.C.: Congressional Quarterly Press, 1984.

Slotkin, Richard. *The Fatal Environment: The Myth of the Frontier in the Age of Industrialization*. New York: Atheneum, 1985.

Smail, John. "New Languages for Labour and Capital: The Transformation of Discourse in the Early Years of the Industrial Revolution." *Social History* 12, 1 (January 1987): 49–71.

Smith, Carolyn, ed. *The 1984 Vote*. New York: ABC News, 1985.

Smith, Rogers M. "After Criticism: An Analysis of the Critical Legal Studies Movement." In Michael McCann and Gerald Houseman, eds., *Judging the Constitution: Critical Perspectives on the Constitution*. Boston: Little, Brown, 1989.

————. "The New Non-Science of Politics: On Turns to History in Political Science." Working Paper 59, Comparative Studies of Social Transformation, Ann Arbor, Mich., 1990.

Smith-Rosenberg, Carroll. *Disorderly Conduct: Visions of Gender in Victorian America*. New York: Knopf, 1985.

Sokolow, Jayme A. "Culture and Utopia: The Raritan Bay Union." *New Jersey History* 94 (1976): 89–100.

Sombart, Werner. *Why Is There No Socialism in the United States?* 1906. New York: M. E. Sharpe, 1976.

Stansell, Christine. *City of Women: Sex and Class in New York, 1789–1860.* Urbana: University of Illinois Press, 1982.

Steffen, Charles G. "Changes in the Organization of Artisan Production in Baltimore, 1790 to 1820." *William and Mary Quarterly,* 3d series, 36, 1 (January 1979): 101–17.

Steinfeld, Robert J. "The Philadelphia Cordwainers' Case of 1806: The Struggle over Alternative Legal Constructions of a Free Market in Labor." In Christopher L. Tomlins and Andrew J. King, eds., *Labor Law in America: Historical and Critical Essays.* Baltimore: Johns Hopkins University Press, 1992.

Steinmo, Sven, Kathleen Thelen, and Frank Longstreth. *Structuring Politics: Historical Institutionalism in Comparative Analysis.* New York: Cambridge University Press, 1992.

Stephan, Alfred. *The State and Society: Peru in Comparative Perspective.* Princeton: Princeton University Press, 1978.

Stock, James H. "Real Estate Mortgages, Foreclosures, and Midwestern Agrarian Unrest, 1865–1920." *Journal of Economic History* 44, 1 (March 1983): 89–105.

Stone, Katherine Van Wezel. "Labor and the Corporate Structure: Changing Conceptions and Emerging Possibilities." 55 *University of Chicago Law Review* 73 (1988).

———. "Labor Relations on the Airlines: The Railway Labor Act in the Era of Deregulation." 42 *Stanford Law Review* 1485 (1990).

———. "The Legacy of Industrial Pluralism: The Tension Between Individual Employment Rights and the New Deal Collective Bargaining System." 59 *University of Chicago Law Review* 575 (1992).

———. "The Post War Paradigm in American Labor Law." 90 *Yale Law Journal* 7 (1981).

Stone, Lawrence. *The Causes of the English Revolution, 1529–1642.* New York: Harper and Row, 1972.

Sullivan, William A. "Did Labor Support Andrew Jackson?" *Political Science Quarterly* 62, 4 (December 1947): 569–80.

Sykes, Robert. "Early Chartism and Trade Unionism in South-East Lancashire." In James Epstein and Dorothy Thompson, eds., *The Chartist Experience: Studies in Working-Class Radicalism and Culture, 1830–1860.* London: Macmillan, 1982.

Taft, Philip. "On the Origins of Business Unionism." *Industrial and Labor Relations Review* 17, 1 (October 1963): 20–38.

———. *Organized Labor in American History.* New York: Harper and Row, 1964.

Tarrow, Sidney G. "Lochner versus New York: A Political Analysis." *Labor History* 5, 3 (Fall 1964): 277–312.

Tholfsen, Trygve. "The Chartist Crisis in Birmingham." *International Review of Social History* 3 (1958): 461–80.

———. "The Transition to Democracy in Victorian England." *International Review of Social History* 6 (1961): 226–48.

———. *Working Class Radicalism in Mid-Victorian England.* New York: Columbia University Press, 1977.

Thomas, John L. "Romantic Reform in America, 1815–1865." *American Quarterly* 17 (Winter 1965): 656–81.

Thompson, Dorothy. *The Chartists: Popular Politics in the Industrial Revolution.* New York: Pantheon, 1984.

Thompson, E. P. *The Making of the English Working Class.* London: Victor Gollancz, 1963.

———. "The Moral Economy of the English Crowd in the Eighteenth Century." *Past and Present* 50 (February 1971): 76–136.

———. *Whigs and Hunters: The Origin of the Black Act.* New York: Pantheon, 1975.

Thorelli, Hans B. *The Federal Antitrust Policy: Origination of an American Tradition.* London: Allen and Unwin, 1954.

Tocqueville, Alexis de. *Democracy in America.* New York: Doubleday, 1969.

Todes, Charlotte. *William H. Sylvis and the National Labor Union.* New York: International Publishers, 1942.

Toews, John E. "Intellectual History after the Linguistic Turn: The Automony of Meaning and the Irreducibility of Experience." *American Historical Review* 92, 4 (October 1987): 879–907.

Tolliday, Steven, and Jonathan Zeitlin, eds. *Shop Floor Bargaining and the State: Historical and Comparative Perspectives.* Cambridge: Cambridge University Press, 1985.

Tomlins, Christopher L. "AFL Unions in the 1930s: Their Performance in Historical Perspective." *Journal of American History* 65, 4 (March 1979): 1021–42.

———. "Criminal Conspiracy and Early Labor Combinations: Massachusetts, 1824–1840." *Labor History* 28, 3 (Summer 1987): 370–85.

———. "The New Deal, Collective Bargaining, and the Triumph of Industrial Pluralism." *Industrial and Labor Relations Review* 39, 1 (October 1985): 19–34.

———. *Law, Labor, and Ideology in the Early American Republic.* New York: Cambridge University Press, 1993.

———. *The State and the Unions: Labor Relations, Law, and the Organized Labor Movement in America, 1880–1960.* New York: Cambridge University Press, 1985.

"Tortious Interference with Contractual Relations in the 19th Century: The Transformation of Property, Contract, and Tort." 93 *Harvard Law Review* 1510 (1980).

Trimble, William. "Diverging Tendencies in New York Democracy in the Period of the Loco-focos." *American Historical Review* 24, 3 (April 1919): 396–421.

———. "The Social Philosophy of the Loco-foco Democracy." *American Journal of Sociology* 26 (1921): 705–15.

Turner, Marjorie S. *The Early American Labor Conspiracy Cases: Their Place in Labor Law.* San Diego: San Diego State College Press, 1967.

Twiss, Benjamin R. *Lawyers and the Constitution: How Laissez Faire Came to the Supreme Court.* New York: Russell and Russell, 1962.

Ulman, Lloyd. *The Rise of the National Trade Union.* Cambridge, Mass.: Harvard University Press, 1968.

Unger, Irwin. *The Greenback Era: A Social and Political History of American Finance, 1865–1879*. Princeton: Princeton University Press, 1964.

Unger, Roberto Mangabeira. *The Criticial Legal Studies Movement*. Cambridge, Mass.: Harvard University Press, 1986.

_____. *Law in Modern Society: Toward a Criticism of Social Theory*. 3 vols. New York: The Free Press, 1976.

_____. *Politics, A Work in Constructive Social Theory*. New York: Cambridge University Press, 1987.

Valenzuela, Julio Samuel. "Labor Movement Formation and Politics: The Chilean and French Cases in Comparative Perspective, 1850–1950." Ph.D. diss., Columbia University, 1979.

Van Deusen, Glyndon G. "Some Aspects of Whig Thought and Theory in the Jacksonian Period." *The American Historical Review* 63, 2 (January 1958): 305–37.

Walker, Samuel. "Terence V. Powderly, Machinist: 1866–1877." *Labor History* 19, 2 (Spring 1978): 165–84.

Ware, Norman. *The Industrial Worker: 1840–1860*. Chicago: Quadrangle Books, 1924.

_____. *The Labor Movement in the United States, 1860–1895*. Gloucester, Mass.: Peter Smith, 1959.

Warner, Sam Bass, Jr. *The Private City: Philadelphia in Three Stages of Its Growth*. Philadelphia: University of Pennsylvania Press, 1968.

Warren, Charles. *A History of the American Bar*. Boston: Little, Brown, 1911.

_____. *The Supreme Court in United States History*. Vol. 2. Boston: Little, Brown, 1924.

Webb, Sidney, and Beatrice Webb. *The History of Trade Unionism*. New York: Augustus M. Kelley, 1965.

Wedderburn, Lord. "Industrial Relations and the Courts." *Industrial Law Journal* 9, 2 (June 1980): 65–94.

Weir, Margaret. "Ideas and Politics: The Diffusion of Keynesianism in Britain and the United States." Paper presented at conference sponsored by the Committee on States and Social Structures of the Social Science Research Council, September 1981.

Wesser, Robert F. "Conflict and Compromise: The Workmen's Compensation Movement in New York, 1890s–1913." *Labor History* 11, 3 (Summer 1971): 346–51.

Westin, Alan Furman. "The Supreme Court, the Populist Movement and the Campaign of 1896." *Journal of Politics* 15, 1 (February 1953): 3–41.

Wiebe, Robert H. *The Opening of American Society*. New York: Knopf, 1984.

_____. *The Search for Order, 1877–1920*. New York: Hill and Wang, 1967.

Wieck, Edward A. *The American Miners' Association: A Record of the Origin of Coal Miners' Unions in the U.S.* New York: Russell Sage Foundation, 1940.

Wilentz, Sean. "Against Exceptionalism: Class Consciousness and the American Labor Movement." *International Labor and Working Class History* 26 (Fall 1984): 1–24.

_____. "Artisan Origins of the American Working Class." *International Labor and Working Class History* 19 (Spring 1981): 1–22.

_____. "Artisan Republican Festivals and the Rise of Class Conflict in New York City, 1788–1837." In Daniel J. Walkowitz, ed., *Working-Class America: Essays on Labor, Community, and the American Society*. Urbana: University of Illinois Press, 1983.

_____. *Chants Democratic: New York City and the Rise of the American Working Class, 1788–1850*. New York: Oxford University Press, 1984.

_____. "Conspiracy, Power and the Early Labor Movement: The People v. James Melvin et al., 1811." *Labor History* 24, 4 (Fall 1983): 572–79.

_____. "On Class and Politics in Jacksonian America." In Stanley I. Cutler and Stanley N. Katz, eds.,*The Promise of American History, Progress and Prospects*. Baltimore: Johns Hopkins University Press, 1982.

Williams, Jerre S. *Labor Relations and the Law*. Boston: Little, Brown, 1965.

Williamson, Chilton. *American Suffrage: From Property to Democracy, 1760–1860*. Princeton: Princeton University Press, 1960.

Witte, Edwin Emil. *The Development of Labor Legislation and Its Effect Upon the Welfare of the American Workman*. Urbana, Ill.: Institute of Labor and Industrial Relations, 1954.

_____. "Early American Labor Cases." 35 *Yale Law Journal* 825 (1926).

_____. *The Government in Labor Disputes*. 1932. New York: Arno and The New York Times, 1969.

Wollen, Evans. "Labor Troubles Between 1834–1837." 1 *Yale Law Review*, o.s. 87 (1892).

Wolski, Kalikst. "A Visit to the North American Phalanx." *Proceedings of the New Jersey Historical Society* 83, 3 (July 1965): 149–60.

Wood, Gordon S. *The Creation of the American Republic, 1776–1787*. Chapel Hill: University of North Carolina Press, 1969.

_____. "Rhetoric and Reality in the American Revolution." *William and Mary Quarterly*, 3d series, 23, 1 (January 1966): 3–32.

Woodiwiss, Anthony. *Rights v. Conspiracy: A Sociological Essay on the History of Labour Law in the United States*. New York: Berg, 1990.

Wright, R. S. *The Law of Criminal Conspiracies and Agreements*. Philadelphia: Blackstone, 1887.

Yellowitz, Irwin. *Labor and the Progressive Movement in New York State, 1897–1916*. Ithaca, N.Y.: Cornell University Press, 1965.

Young, Alfred F. *The American Revolution: Explorations in the History of American Radicalism*. DeKalb: Northern Illinois University Press, 1976.

Zysman, John. *Political Strategies for Industrial Order: State, Market, and Industry in France*. Berkeley: University of California Press, 1977.

Index

act of incorporation, historical background on, 41n.30

Altgeld, John, 172

Amalgamated Society of Railway Servants, 200–202

American Federation of Labor (AFL): business unionism and voluntarism advocated by, 3–10, 157–61, 180, 204, 206; courts' abrogation of reforms of, 152; disillusionment over political reform, 156–61; economic visions of, 9–10, 114–15, 205; electoral and party politics and, 214–15; judicial regulation reforms and, 112; labor injunctions resisted by, 163–66, 165n.132; labor reform program of, 136–37; membership figures of, 116n.6; politicization of judicial regulation, 140–45; support of Haymarket Affair defendants, 172; working-class consciousness in, 137–39

American Railway Union, 163n.127

American Revolution: antebellum conspiracy trials and, 44–47; common law interpretations and, 53–55; impact on nonlabor conspiracy trials, 65

American Steel Foundries v. Tri-City Central Trades Council, 164

Anderson, Hugh, 150

antebellum conspiracy trials: class issues in, 46–47, 60–62; and common law crimes, 33–38; and criminal offense, 30–33; light penalties in, 60–62; metropolitan industrialization and, 76–86; modification of conspiracy doctrine in, 49–62; and unlawful crimes, 33–34; workingmen's quiescence regarding, 88–93, 104–9. *See also* conspiracy doctrine

anticonspiracy statutes: English-U.S. comparisons of, 152; judicial erosion of, 145–52; New York statutes, 145–49; passage of, 144–45; Pennsylvania statutes, 149–51; return to voluntarism and, 156; Revised Statutes in New York, 151–52

antimonopoly reform: antebellum industrialization and, 84–86; collective action and, 130–31; conspiracy doctrine and, 105n.97; postwar producers' concern over, 168–71; producers' economic vision and, 98–104, 106–7, 124–29; Working Men's parties' concern with, 88–89. *See also* producers

arbitration, English labor movement's use of, 188–90

Arbitration Acts, 189

artisans: antebellum conspiracy trials and, 108–9; and antebellum industrialization, 8–10, 76–86; Chartist movement and, 185–87; electoral and party politics of, 212–15; emergence of GTUs and, 82–84; producers' alliance and, 95–97; working-class consciousness and, 86–93. *See also* producers; Working Men's parties

Association of Farmers, Mechanics, and Other Workingmen, 94n.60

bakers' analogy, use of, in antebellum conspiracy trials, 51

bankers: labor movement's view of, 127–29; producers' concern over, 99–100

Barrett, George (Judge), 70. See also *People v. Kostka*; *People v. Wilzig*

Beaumont, Ralph, 135

Beddles, Charles, 146

Beerman, 157

Beesley, Professor, 192n.34

Birmingham Political Union, 186

blacks: disintegration of producers' alliance and, 132n.54; electoral and party politics of, 213; exclusion from producers' alliance of, 95; labor reforms for, 143

Blair, George, 122–23

boycotts: as intimidative action, 146–47; labor injunctions against, 162–63

Brothers, Thomas, 94

Buchanan, John (Justice), 34

business unionism: advocated over political reform, 3–10; AFL's turn to, 177–78; alternative explanations of, 21–27; American party system and, 24–25; antebellum conspiracy trials and, 110; ide-